David J. Dent

TOUCHSTONE
Rockefeller Center
1230 Avenue of the Americas
New York, NY 10020

First Touchstone Edition 2001
TOUCHSTONE and colophon are registered trademarks
of Simon & Schuster, Inc.
Designed by Karolina Harris
Manufactured in the United States of America
10 9 8 7 6 5 4 3 2 1
The Library of Congress has cataloged the Simon & Schuster edition
as follows:
Dent, David J.
   In search of Black America: discovering the African-American
dream / David J. Dent.
      p. cm.
   1. Afro-Americans—Social conditions—1975–   2. Afro-
Americans—Social life and customs.   3. Middle class—United
States.   4. Afro-Americans—Interviews.   I. Title.

E185.86 .D468 2000
305.896'073—dc21   99-059843
ISBN 0-684-81072-7
    0-7432-0305-4 (Pbk)

AUTHOR'S NOTE

The people's stories that appear in In Search of Black America are
real. There are not any fictional characters. A few names have
been changed or withheld at the request of those interviewed, or
when someone mentioned in a quotation could not be reached for
the verification of facts. When pseudonyms appear, they are noted
in the text.

   The details of the lives of those presented—ages, residences, careers, and professions and views—all reflect the time of the interview, which is indicated in all of the stories. Nearly all of the
comments are on tape. In a few instances, for readability, I have
altered the sequence, in which remarks were made.

In Search of

BLACK AMERICA

Discovering the African-American Dream

A Touchstone Book
Published by Simon & Schuster
New York London Toronto Sydney Singapore

Acknowledgments

My family was a central part of this project. Thanks, Valerie, for eagerly reading every draft, offering valuable criticism, and traveling with me across the country. I thank my children, Lynnette and David Jr., who were also good troopers and traveled with us. I must also thank my parents, Thelma Gumbs Dent and George Calvin Dent; my sisters, Georgette and Sharon; and my niece, Dara. I especially thank my mother, from whom I inherited a love of literature, for her avid support and for being such a great conversationalist. Our talks helped to crystallize some of the ideas in this book. I also thank my cousins, Henry and Artis Crews, for opening their home in Chicago at short notice; Wilbur and Elsie Blount and Jacqueline and Elizabeth Blount in Columbus, Ohio; Anirl Lewis Morton in Henderson, NC, and Ulysses Horne in Panama City, FL.

I am extremely fortunate to have friends who believed in this project from the beginning and never shied away from offering their support in so many ways. Chief among them are Terry and Rita Woodard, Christopher David King, and Kevin M. Sweeney. I am also grateful to Mervyn Keizer, Professor Bart Landry, and Ahmad Wright for reading the manuscript and offering thoughtful and comprehensive criticism that strengthened the final draft. Thanks, Merv, for also lending your brilliance and expertise as a researcher and fact checker.

There are other friends and colleagues who read and critiqued sections. There were also research assistants who worked on the project over the past five years. I am also appreciative of the people who suggested places that would be interesting to explore and the names of people to interview. Sometimes a seemingly innocuous conversation helped to direct me to pivotal points of this journey. Thanks to all: Jules Allen, John Alleyne, Professor Regina Austin, Claude Bailey, Todd Barbee, Adler Bernard, Zelmer Bothic, Lisa Brown, Regine Bruny, Gerald "Cisco" Brown, Meredith Carey, Candace Chambers, Glenn Cherry, Warren and Cynthia Colter, Howlie Davis, St. Clair and Kim Davis, Duane and Carol Davis, Leslie Davis, Leonard and Norma Davis, Harold Doley Jr., Harold Doley III, Kemba Durham, Audrey Edwards, Hosea Givan, Miriam Gladden, Camille Goodison, Racquel Goodison, Nathaniel and Joyce Grant, Roger Headon, Fred and Kim Humphries, Marianne Ilaw, Wesley and Lisa King, Carlos Little, Tebogo Mahlen, Craig Marberry, Herman and Elizabeth Martin, Marlon Milner, Asim Mustafa, Evan J. Narcisse, Jonathan Phillips, Marcus Reeves, Henry Rice, Mary Rice, Delbert Rigsby, Damien Scott, Neal Sokol, Mark Smith, Clarence Still, Olufemi D. Terry, Moji Terry, Lisa Varlack, Linda Waller, Chuck and Janis Watts, David M. White and Rakisha R. Kearnes-White, and Larry Zabriskie. A big thanks also goes to Jacqueline Goldman and Marlene Ross, the "gals" at Mystic Word, and Angela Kinamore for such a splendid job transcribing tapes. I also thank my good friends from Omega Diversified Investment Corporation for years of encouragement and friendship.

I thank professors Pamela Newkirk, Jane Stone, and the rest of my colleagues in the Department of Journalism and Mass Communication at New York University and Manthia Diawara, chairman of the NYU Program in Africana Studies.

I am extremely grateful to the great team of pros at Simon & Schuster. Thank you, Dominick Anfuso, my editor, for your rigor and commitment to the right word. Thanks also go to Cherise Grant and Ana DeBevoise.

And finally, thanks to the Faith Childs Literary Agency and its impressive team—Debbie Goodison, Arlene Stoltz, Vanessa Manko, Lori Pope, and, of course, Faith Childs herself. Thank you, Faith, for embracing this book with an infectious enthusiasm when it was just an idea. I am forever grateful for your patience, support, friendship, and brilliance, which helped nurture an idea into a book.

For my family: my supportive wife and best friend, Valerie,
whose enthusiasm over this book was unyielding; my daughter,
Lynnette Amantha, who was born just as I was beginning this
journey and quickly became a great traveler; and my son, David
Jonathan Jr., who was born in the middle-stretch of it and also learned
to love the road during his first months of life.

Contents

Four: Soul and Cold Country   237

Five: Leisure   309

Six: Home   393

The ache for home lives in all of us, the safe place where we can go as we are and not be questioned. It impels mighty ambitions and dangerous capers. We amass great fortunes at the cost of our souls, or risk our lives in drug dens from London's Soho to San Francisco's Haight-Ashbury. We shout in Baptist churches, wear yarmulkes and wigs and argue even the tiniest points in the Torah, or worship the sun and refuse to kill cows for the starving. Hoping that by doing these things, home will find us acceptable, or failing that, that we will forget our awful yearning for it.

—MAYA ANGELOU, *All God's Children Need Traveling Shoes*

Introduction

YOU never quite know where the good road will lead you. Even when tires curl over familiar asphalt, something new or surprising looms ahead in your lane—sometimes waiting for you to unmask its invisibility. American roads, especially, bustle with so much life. Much of it is distant, elusive, and only seen or felt through a car window—unless you take an exit. And the exits aren't always the end. They are often extensions of the life of a highway and can become journeys unto themselves.

Take exit 312 off Interstate 57 south in northeast Illinois. Follow a series of left and right turns and cross over a set of railroad tracks. The two-lane roads, along with a dusty one of gravel, will take you to the Latting family ranch. The Lattings are a family of cowboys and cowgirls. The rodeos they produce are considered among the best in the country, attracting competitive bull riders like Danell Tipton, who will drive all the way from Oklahoma to compete in a Latting rodeo. All the fourth-generation cowboy has to do is take off the earring and the gold chain and throw on the cowboy attire, and he's ready to wrestle with the bulls. Or sometimes he leaves on the chain, which is covered anyway by his cowboy shirt. With or without it, he's always ready for the bulls.

Take exit 129 off Interstate 95 south. You are just inside Florida and on Route 200E. That takes you to Fernandina Beach. Follow A1A south to Amelia Island and then follow the signs to American Beach. The unofficial mayor of the beach is MaVynee, formerly MarVynee. You won't speed by her like you might pass a tree on the highway. How could you miss her fingernails? They are covered with long plastic bags and are as long as her arm. And her hair is even longer. It is styled into a shape of the continent of her ancestors.

She's so much of a naturalist and environmentalist that she struck the *r* from her birth name because it figures prominently in the name of an American president with whom she prefers to share nothing because of his record on the environment. The Oberlin grad and former opera singer spends most of her time trying to preserve the culture of American Beach, founded in 1935 by her millionaire great-grandfather and his business partners.

Take any exit in Washington, D.C. But if you end up at a certain Sheraton on the night before New Year's Eve, don't enter the Cotillion Room unless you are on the approved guest list of "the Ball." According to the Tuxedo Ball's founders, many of those on the list can trace success in their family roots to "before the Civil War" and are the sons and daughters of an American aristocracy that may be foreign to the Daughters of the American Revolution.

Over the past five years, I took those exits and many more. The people I found residing in those corners of American life became this book. This is not a book about my encounters on the roads to those corners, nor is it a book about my own personal experiences inside those cultural spheres. Rather, it is the story of the exits and the people who call them home.

This idea to find and travel into corners of Americana was conceived on an actual corner—a street corner in the Crown Heights section of Brooklyn. In September 1991, the community was just exiting the national media spotlight, after rebelling youths had turned their rage to the streets in August. I was commissioned to do a story on the community in the wake of the riots. A community activist suggested that I come to the corner if I wanted to hear truth from the voices of youth. The corner was a popular gathering spot for a group of young men, roughly ages twenty to twenty-five, who grew up in the neighborhood.

When I arrived, there were four men on the corner, which was a few feet away from a makeshift basketball hoop—a milk crate that was nailed to a tree. The crate was used by a younger crowd that congregated there earlier in the day. Some of the young men, who come to the corner as the day approaches night, remember playing on a similar makeshift goal years ago.

Initially, their eyes looked at my pen and pad with apprehension. However, their reserve withered with the early-evening sunlight; soon they talked and talked freely. The presence of an outsider—even one recording their comments—was not enough to quell the spontaneity, comfort, and freedom that they carry to the corner.

As I listened, I became captivated by pieces of the conversation that would never fit into the story that I was contracted to do. I was assigned to look at the source of "black rage" in Crown Heights and how it crossed class lines. Yet I was becoming more transfixed by the street corner and its role in the lives of residents who seemed to consider it another home. Through the world they created on the corner, I could see their lives beyond a conflict that helped to superficially define them as young, black, and angry.

I was on the corner for hours, listening and watching its hangers. They came in basketball jerseys, dress pants, T-shirts, designer jeans, and tennis shoes without laces. They were a diverse group: a navy man just home for a break, a college student who was soon returning to Hampton University, a messenger, a community-college student, and others. I would later learn that one had served time for burglary and was trying to become law abiding.

Sometimes they would speak with the values of *The Cosby Show*'s Cliff Huxtable, or *Father Knows Best*. Often their language carried the street wit of *Menace II Society* and *Boyz N the Hood*. Never did their view of the world possess the despair of Bigger Thomas or Claude Brown in *Manchild in the Promised Land*. They were not victims waiting for Jesse Jackson, Louis Farrakhan, or any "leader" to rescue them. Nor did they possess a blind optimism and belief in the purity of American meritocracy in the vein of Shelby Steele or Thomas Sowell. Their views of the world were harsh, masculine, and real. Still, that world encompassed a vitality that they created and controlled on this corner.

What struck me most about the corner was the absence of racism as a topic of discussion, so soon after a major racial disturbance. Only my questions would turn the men's focus to the riots and issues of race. On this corner, race seemed to rarely take center stage. And when it did, it was merely another element fitting comfortably among others in conversation or debate. It could be easily shoved to the sidelines or thrown beyond the borders of the corner when attention spontaneously moved to something more interesting for the moment: sports, women, family, careers, money, celebrities, music, goals, travel, or any number of other subjects.

On the corner, I heard and saw pieces of the political and cultural diversity in African-American cultures that I knew existed through what I've seen all my life in social and professional encounters, but had rarely been seen in a substantial way in media and scholarly portraits of black America. This is not to ignore the valuable work of scholars like Elijah Anderson, whose *A Place on the Corner* looks closely and thoughtfully at the lives and inner worlds of a group of black men who congregate on a street corner. But I was more interested in how a space of their own seemed to free these African Americans of some of the baggage of race and thus helped to crystallize their true humanity. I was not interested in celebrating their virtues or apologizing for their vices, nor would I want to hide either. I was not interested in denigrating them or searching for traces of moral failure and decadence that would suit some inherently racist political ideology under the pretense of scholarship or journalism.

I made the decision that night to one day travel into corners of African-Americana—it was one of those things that I would get around to someday. Not all of these corners would be spatial or literal, but they would all be cultural spaces created by black people, places where individuality—independent of the baggage of race—may thrive. They are worlds of black diversity or worlds whose very existence are testimonials to such diversity. Inside these spaces, people may find the room to be an American. They are the spaces in which untold stories of black America are aching to be discovered.

As I developed the idea, I decided to look beyond spaces as public as street corners. I would look for the many exits created or rejuvenated in the post–civil rights era, though all still would be places where people were likely to feel free enough to look honestly, exhaustively, critically, comfortably, and, sometimes, painfully at themselves, their community, their exit, their country, and the world. I would look for spaces fertile enough to explore the many contradictions that beset us all. How easily, or not, do we live with them, including the obvious contradiction inherent in our latest label—"African Americans"? Is that really a contradiction at all?

Many African Americans constantly enter and exit these worlds. Some come for a moment each day, week, year, or decade. Some choose to reside in these worlds for most of their lives. Others may choose to avoid them all together.

I made a list of places. I brainstormed. I opened up old reporter pads and pulled out names. I called friends and sources. Some of the spaces on the list were places where writers and reporters (including, sometimes, myself) had traveled only when there was a race-related story. In those cases, the views of blacks were needed to balance a story. Some of the spaces on the list were virtually unknown to many blacks or whites. Some had seen friendly press, portrayed as the exceptional black institution, school, neighborhood, street, vacation community, or some such, when, in fact, they were not so exceptional or unique at all. Their praise in the press and scholarly journals was sometimes a tribute to the subtleties of a latent form of contemporary racism that tags everything that is good and black as new, rare, and worthy of enormous applause.

I decided to avoid the nationally famous, such as celebrities and the underclass. Like the lives of black celebrities, the portraits of those living below the poverty line had been explored more exhaustively in the media during the seventies and the eighties than the lives of the black majority had. By excluding these groups, I would restrict the list to spaces inhabited mostly by members of the black majority—working-, middle-, and upper-class people.

I made a decision to concentrate on this majority months after my trip to the Crown Heights corner, while I was working on a magazine piece on the increasing number of middle- and upper-middle-income African Americans moving to Prince Georges County, Maryland. As I traveled throughout the county, I found many parents who moved to predominantly black middle- and upper-middle-class communities because they feared that their children would see success as anathema to the black experience if they were isolated from other black middle-class children. Most were not segregationists—but nor were they integrationists, for that matter. Often, through the street or neighborhood they chose, a club to which they belonged, or recreational activity they pursued, they were attempting to carve a corner for themselves and their families that was free of the limitations imposed by American racial attitudes.

Like the men on the street corner in Crown Heights, many of the Prince Georges families sought temporary havens in social, political, and cultural worlds they controlled. And like the men on the street in Crown Heights, and like virtually every other grouping in America, they were diverse in many ways. Some were conservative, some liberal, and some a mixture of both or just plain centrists. There were the Afrocentric conservatives, multicultural liberals, and those who hadn't given much conscious thought to whether they were either. Some grew up in middle-class families, while others were the first in a family to go to college. Many were entrepreneurs; others were wedded to careers in government or *Fortune* 500 America. Some hated the rap their children could not live without, but others couldn't resist the urge to snap to the beat of the same music. Some parents, and even some children, preferred Kathleen Battle to the latest musical fad, while some had never heard of either.

Such diversity is not unusual, but it still seems to elicit surprise in parts of the country. Why? There are 2.2 million African-American families with incomes above $50,000 per year—that's 25.9 percent of all black families, according to U.S. Census Bureau 1997 data. And the majority of African

Americans—76 percent, in fact—have incomes above what is considered poor or low-income. Nevertheless, the existence of this black majority seems to carry an air of abnormality in the American conscience. Nowhere was this more evident than in the questioning of whether Bill Cosby's Huxtable family was "authentic." Witness too the shock of many white television commentators and reporters at the number of black professionals appearing at the Clarence Thomas–Anita Hill hearings. Then there was the flash of surprise evident in the proliferation of stories on the black middle-class market that made Terry McMillan a millionaire and the movie based on her novel *Waiting to Exhale* such a success. Yet another surprise was the polling data on the Million Man March that showed a large share of the men there were middle income. Why would they want to march?

The black middle class—vastly diverse and complex—is one of the most frequently "discovered" groups in the nation's history, yet one of the most misunderstood, too, and it often remains all but invisible between its periodic rediscoveries. If you travel back through the pages of American journalism since Reconstruction, few years go by without at least one publication focusing an article on the "new" group of elite or middle-class coloreds or Negroes or blacks or, most recently, African Americans.

An 1895 *New York Times* article on wealthy blacks in New York, for example, revealed that

> Those who imagine that the negro population of this city is composed of pedlars, whitewashers and bootblacks would be considerably enlightened if they could observe the real progress which the race has made in New York, as indicated by the prosperity of its representative men and women. It will be news to many white persons to learn that many negro men own and occupy brownstone dwellings in fashionable neighborhoods, employ white servants, and ride their own carriages behind horses driven by liveried coachmen. Some not only own the houses they live in but also houses tenanted by rich white families.

One unnamed black woman quoted in the article stated, "There are various grades of colored people just as there are various grades of white people. The lowest grades of whites and blacks are about on a par. No respectable negro would want to associate with either. We are not to be judged by the street loungers and drunkards of our race."

Eighty-three years later, the black middle class was still "new" in the mainstream media, and even in some black-owned publications. A cover story in the *New York Times Magazine* in 1978, "The Black Middle Class

Making It," explored the lives of blacks torn between the two worlds of their ghetto past and middle-class present. Writer William Brashler reported:

> [A]n American black middle/professional class is flourishing and swelling. . . . [F]or the new black middle class, led by a segment of up-wardly mobile young professionals, has opened a double door exit from the ghetto. . . . Now they glide through society. They have evolved and as-similated, and have retained only one common characteristic, besides their blackness: that of having made it and being confident they can keep it.

The Brashler piece provides one half of a "two nations" portrait of black America: there is one nation underclass that dwells in the ghetto and an-other nation newly middle class and painfully estranged from its roots but still rising in mainstream America. Such a portrait is riddled in fallacy. To frame any culture in such bipolar terms defies the complexity and variety of the culture. And there are many black middle-class cultures, not to mention many black upper-class cultures. The two-nations portrait, however, does not so much as acknowledge an upper class and leaves little room for any-thing even between the underclass and middle class. Yet in reality, there was once a vast world spanning the two, composed of the black working class. Although this sector of society has decreased in recent decades due largely to changes in the economy, it was once large and vital. Many African-American professionals did not exit from a ghetto—though some did. Many of today's black professionals are in fact products of black work-ing-class households. Some of those families possessed mainstream, mid-dle-class values, but not middle-class incomes, but others enjoyed the abundance of postwar blue-collar jobs providing middle- and sometimes even upper-middle-class incomes—jobs that would shrink with the coming information age and corporate America's exploitation of the overseas job market. Then there were also the black professionals in the preintegration days—roughly 6 percent of the black adult working population in 1950. (By August 1999, the number had grown to 21 percent of the black working population, compared to 31 percent of the white employed population.)

In the 1970s and early '80s, the press was hot on articles about a "new class" of blacks living in a culture quite foreign to their past and distant from the world of other blacks. In most cases, the articles reported that members of the so-called new class had detached black culture from their new middle-class lifestyle. Their success was often described as personal tragedy; they were sometimes portrayed as guilty blacks in conflict over leaving their less-fortunate brethren behind. In such portraits, success always seemed to revolve around the ability to transcend race, but the real story of black achievement in America is the story of transcending societal expectations, not race. And if a reader looked closely, too, somewhere in many of the stories there was a body of people pulling together in a space they created or one created for them by the previous generation: a church, a fraternal organization, or, of course, a school.

At one time, the most common of black secluded worlds centered on education. The uncompromising desire for a quality education is as African American as Frederick Douglass, Martin Delany, *Brown vs. Board of Education,* and the Little Rock Nine. As W. E. B. Du Bois notes in *The Souls of Black Folk,* "The opposition to Negro education was at first bitter and showed itself in ashes, insult, and blood; for the South was not wholly wrong; for education among all kinds of men has had, and always will have, an element of danger and revolution, of dissatisfaction and discontent."

Still, Du Bois and many of his contemporaries dared to be dangerous through education, carrying on a tradition rooted in the era of slavery, when underground schools thrived even as the threat of severe punishment loomed large with the possibility of discovery by slave masters. While attending Fisk University, Du Bois and his peers traveled to rural farms of Tennessee to teach sharecroppers and their children. This was often done behind the backs of landowners, who preferred Negroes uneducated.

In her collection of short stories *Some Soul to Keep,* J. California Cooper's characters demonstrate how their lives are influenced by secluded corners of black life. In one story, a young girl named Superior is about to make her first exit from the segregated world of the South. Superior's teacher in the segregated school found her a job and gives the girl instructions before her first day of work:

> Superior, do you understand me . . . these are white people. They are not like you or me or us. They have the power to hurt you and sometimes it's fun to them when they do. Their power is not because they are smart. It's because something happened sometime, started somewhere and they got on top of the world. They got the power. The only power you got is to learn to live with them, learn to read their minds until you can do better.

Today, decades after the passage of civil-rights laws, legally segregated schools for children like Superior do not exist. Those schools and many other segregated spaces died with integration. But today, many similar worlds are reestablished—often voluntarily and consciously—to suit the new millennium. The number of black private, independent schools, for example, has dramatically increased, with more than four hundred schools founded across the country since 1985. This also coincides with the renewed popularity of black vacation communities, the growth of black professional and networking organizations, and calls for black self-sufficiency from liberals and conservatives alike. In his autobiography, *No Free Ride: From the Mean Streets to the Mainstream,* Kweisi Mfume, president and CEO of the National Association for the Advancement of Colored People (NAACP) and former congressman, comments on this phenomenon:

> One of the major shortcomings of integration was that it destroyed our powerful sense of social and economic self-sufficiency. Working together to create a new attitude of self-reliance might allow us to shed our anger and bitterness and low self-esteem. Too many of us have been succumbing to defeatism—blaming everyone and everything for our woes rather than taking the future into our own hands and doing something about it ourselves.

While diversity and multiculturalism within the African-American community are rich, there are still some common threads running throughout it. I would argue that Mfume's call for preintegration-style black self-reliance is shared by a majority of the black middle class. I'd heard it from elders and older baby boomers before my journey, I heard it from Detroit to Stone Mountain during the journey, and I still hear it and have read it from scholars and writers including Nobel laureate Toni Morrison, who once wrote in a *New York Times Magazine* article, "There was a time when soul food was called supper, when black men laughed at pimps as failed men, when violence was the White Man's Thing."

Why do so many blacks hold such fondness for those segregated days and places? Is it akin to the Italian American or Greek American who may speak of the "old country" with a gleam in the eye? Why does the romanticism come from many younger blacks who were not even alive in that era? What does that romanticism say about the prospects for African Americans to find a comfortable space in the broader and integrated society? Have they found that comfort by creating new, secluded spaces or by resurrecting old ones while still participating in the larger American mainstream? Is it only natural, perhaps, that African Americans would seek the comforts of two worlds—to literally embody the famous words of W. E. B. Du Bois in *The Souls of Black Folk:* "One ever feels his twoness, an American, a Negro; two souls, two thoughts, two unreconciled strivings; two warring ideals in one dark body whose dogged strength alone keeps it from being torn asunder."

I would find that beyond its role in providing the circumstances or perceived need for the creation of the corner, race often fades as an issue and loses much of its influence on life in many secluded black spaces. In some ways, residents of a space had constructed a world based on their reality. Often, it was a reality that ran counter to many of the stereotypes of African Americans that sometimes pervade nonblack and, yes, black American thought too. In some cases, African Americans had come together to create a space so that they could escape or resist the limitations that other blacks had imposed on the meaning of being African American. In *Conversations: Straight Talk with America's Sister President,* anthropologist and former Spelman College president Johnnetta B. Cole explains how and why many African-American women often fail to relish the diversity among their numbers. Her observations could apply to blacks of both genders:

> Yes, there are ties that bind us one to another, but they do not and should not restrain us from being ourselves. On one level we are aware of our diversity; so evident is it in our outer selves . . . but when it comes to the real fabric of our lives—political views, sexual preference, talents, interest—often we cannot imagine its existence. If confronted with the evidence we sometimes pretend it isn't there. Or, worse, we ridicule and censure it.
>
> Far too many of us assume that African Americans have only one party: Democratic. When we discover a Republican, a Communist, or a Libertarian we are dumbstruck. Many presume that every African American woman is a Christian or at least believes in God. Then up speaks an agnostic or an atheist, and we fall silent and wary. Upon encountering an African American woman who is studying Russian, Chinese, or Sanskrit for that matter, some of us no less than White folk, react as if that woman were an aberration, or, worse, "trying to be White." And is it actually the strangest thing in the world for an African American woman to have a passion for Vivaldi, Liszt, or Gershwin? Must she only love Duke Ellington and Ella Fitzgerald, Anita Baker and Stevie Wonder?
>
> Indeed, this inability to recognize how very different we are in our tastes, interests, and perspectives is in part a consequence of stereotypes perpetuated about us. But it is also a by-product of that sense of solidarity so vital to our survival and which to varying degrees has at times called for and practically demanded uniformity.

Yet, despite black stereotyping of blacks, is it still easier and more common for one to be a black Republican or something else that speaks to black diversity when one lives in an all-black town? When African Americans enter social, cultural, and physical spaces that they have created and dominated, are they more likely to assume partisan roles or other positions that they would never pursue in integrated environments that impose racially based expectations on them? Would many conservative African Americans want to exist publicly as a conservative in a sphere where their ideology is associated with race baiting or racism? Those too are more questions I carried on this journey to places like Lawnside, New Jersey, a town that traces its roots to the Underground Railroad.

I encountered many people in these corners who lack high levels of rage, hostility, or bitterness toward the world. They wouldn't be good characters in a story on the raging and angry black man or woman who is beaten down and feels like an American orphan. Some lived in ways that inadvertently underscored the words of writer Zora Neale Hurston in her 1928 essay "How It Feels to Be Colored Me":

I AM COLORED but I offer nothing in the way of extenuating circumstances except the fact that I am the only Negro in the United States whose grandfather on the mother's side was not an Indian chief. . . .

BUT I AM NOT tragically colored. There is no great sorrow dammed up in my soul, nor lurking behind my eyes . . . I do not belong to the sobbing school of Negrohood who hold that nature somehow has given them a lowdown dirty deal and whose feelings are all hurt about it. Even in the helter-skelter skirmish that is my life, I have seen that the world is to the strong regardless of a little pigmentation more or less. No, I do not weep at the world—I am too busy sharpening my oyster knife.

While I didn't find people weeping, I did run across people who were realistic about how race matters, such as Clarence Thomas—not the Supreme Court justice, but a dentist in Yellow Springs, Ohio. "We have not had the luxury to be that liberal," he told me.

"Money has a tendency to liberate people. . . . A lot of our white counterparts, their kids are just free spirits. We're much more conservative than that. . . . We know our kids don't have a lot of options. . . . And whereas the white counterparts or their peers can go in many different directions at any time in their lives, we know we have to direct our children. . . . Let's look at a student who comes to Antioch [in Yellow Springs]. He's from New York. His dad owns a manufacturing company. He comes in. He spends four years. He doesn't wash. He doesn't brush his teeth. He doesn't comb his hair. He never changes his clothes, and he lives this experience for four years. Then, upon graduation, he puts on a three-piece suit and he goes to work for his dad's company. My kids don't have that option. . . . There's a whole set of rules that we have to live by. This is something you pick up at a very early age, and you just have to learn to live that way. Also as you come up in an integrated society, you learn the rules for the other side of the fence too. And if you're smart, you learn those rules well and use them in your best interest.

Like anywhere else in America, of course, the corners I explored were not utopian. Many people who've retreated to them have also fled them—sometimes finding the spaces too suffocating, too conservative, too nationalist, too classist. Some found them little more than a black analogue of an old white world.

I was not surprised to discover that many African Americans consider the Reagan years to be the beginning of an era resembling post-Reconstruction America, when the racist impulses in society were free to go public. It is an era marked by the image of black welfare queens—and then came Willie Horton, which helped launch yet another day in which almost everything wrong with America was given a black face. It is an America where an African American may get called a separatist for wanting to occasionally retreat from it all into a space where one won't be mistaken for a criminal. Or where one won't have to simplistically defend or attack rap lyrics, Louis Farrakhan, or the O.J. Simpson jury. Or where one won't have to exert emotional energy wondering if a slight was really just a slight or another form of racism.

In *Waking from the Dream: My Life in the Black Middle Class,* journalist Sam Fulwood III notes, "I can't escape the thought that white America, which stopped short of embracing middle-class blacks at the moment we wanted inclusion, may have already lost its opportunity." Before my journey, I would have agreed strongly with Fulwood's comment. Now I temper such endorsement. I would not say that the exits I visited wholly owe their existences to black perceptions of the persistence of racism. I would discover that some African Americans have turned to these corners out of a desire to build upon the connections with their families or their cultural traditions and values. Some of the spaces are even rooted in the era of segregation and maintain that period's conservative values that still resonate profoundly with many African Americans. For many, retreating to cultural havens has nothing to do with running from racism or whites. In fact, some people who retreat to the spaces I visited told me that they don't want to make room for African Americans who will pollute the atmosphere with a preoccupation of how racism or white people impair black progress. Many also say racism is no longer a crippling problem in America and profess little patience for black people who seem obsessed otherwise.

In May 1993, I was loaded with questions and places to visit. I began what would become a five-year, intermittent journey. Still, I traveled into only a fraction of the secluded spaces of black culture in America—yet the trip produced more than 350 hours of taped interviews. I often arrived at a space with an expectation that was shattered quickly upon my entry. Inevitably, one space would lead to another and another.

Ultimately, my exploration indirectly and inadvertently responded to a call eloquently made by Zora Neale Hurston in *Negro Digest* in 1950. In her essay, "What the White Publishers Won't Print," Hurston wrote:

> The realistic story around a Negro insurance official, dentist, general practitioner, undertaker and the like would be most revealing. . . . To grasp the penetration of Western civilization in a minority, it is necessary to know how the average behaves and lives. . . . For various reasons, the average, struggling, non-morbid Negro is the best-kept secret in America. His revelation to the public is the thing needed to do away with that feeling of difference which inspires fear and which ever expresses itself in dislike.
>
> It is inevitable that this knowledge will destroy many illusions and romantic traditions which America probably likes to have around. But then, we have no record of anybody sinking into a lingering death on finding out that there was no Santa Claus.

One

TRADITIONS

The Emancipation: Day One

THE habit formed with Nigger Hair Tobacco. Nearly twenty years ago, Elaine Armstrong, now forty-eight, saw a tin can bearing that name. The words seemed to shout at Armstrong, who lives in rural Gallia County, Ohio.

She ran across the brown can for sale at a flea market. It was empty; the grain either chewed or inhaled decades ago—spat on some ground or blown into the air and lost into the earth.

The value today is in the clarity of the brand name on the can—"Nigger Hair Tobacco"—and an advertising tease on its back: "Chew or Smoke Nigger Hair."

At first sight, the can angered Armstrong. It outraged and insulted her. But eventually, after several stares, it captivated her. She became so fixated on it that she soon found herself searching her wallet for the $75 to buy it. Armstrong didn't have the cash on her at the time. But she was prepared with money on subsequent trips to flea markets, antique shops, garage sales, and other places in search of authentic—not recreated—remnants of a racist past. At another flea market four years later, she would find the same tin can. "I bought it right here at the fairgrounds," Armstrong says. "An antique dealer had it."

That dealer didn't openly display the can or any other racist collectibles from the days of Jim Crow. Armstrong, however, by then an experienced collector, had an intuitive hunch. She suspected that the dealer might own something racist and worthy. So she posed the question, and the dealer answered, "Well, I have a can."

"Nigger Hair?" Armstrong pressed.

Armstrong recalls her body bouncing in excitement when the dealer's smile obviated the need to say yes. "She was a white lady. They are primarily the people that have this."

Armstrong picks up the can and places its opening in my face. "The stamp is still on it—1910. It was sold around that time. The dealer wanted $550 for it. I bargained it down."

She paid $450.

Armstrong's collection is spread over two tables at the Gallia County Fairgrounds, in the heart of the Ohio Valley on this September weekend in 1994. She displays it at one of her favorite events: the Emancipation. It's perhaps the nation's longest-running celebration of the Emancipation Proclamation, an annual Appalachian Ohio event only a year younger than the announcement of the proclamation itself.

At age eleven, Armstrong moved to Gallia County from San Diego with her father and stepmother, who was originally from the county. She attended her first Emancipation that same year and has been coming ever since. Only recently, though, has she displayed her collection, which also includes a Darkie Toothpaste box—with a portrait of a minstrel-looking black man shining his white teeth above the product's promise of full fluoride protection—and an old sign from Texas that once hung in the window or door of a restaurant and says "Open but No Dogs, Negroes and Mexicans."

Her collection is in the exhibition barn for vendors, most of whom sell Afrocentric items. Unlike Armstrong, the vendors are dressed in African-inspired clothing. Armstrong's apron-wearing black woman, molded in porcelain, faces the other vendors' products—T-shirts that brazenly proclaim African pride, black greatness, and O.J.'s heroism and innocence (three months after The Chase), along with some oil and incense and other products that claim an African connection.

Many who stop at Armstrong's table are stunned to learn that she paid money for such offensive items. "A lot of people, especially blacks, will say 'You paid somebody money for that. Why?'

"I do it for history's sake. Black history just fascinates me. The things that we've been through as a people, I don't understand how we haven't been wiped off the face of the earth."

The images at Armstong's table reflect a force in American life that many African Americans live to defy—sometimes consciously through self-realized versions of the Afrocentric items across from Armstrong's table, and sometimes inadvertently by living a life that bears little or no resemblance to her collectibles. Occasionally, the defiance even rivals the showmanship of the degrading brand of tobacco and toothpaste: there is the raised fist of a body shrouded in African-style clothing, the crisp English of the old-fashioned school teacher, the professional precision of a corporate operator, or even the lavish gowns and tuxedos of a Jack and Jill or debutante ball. Many African Americans live as far beyond and above Armstrong's collectibles as they can, and force the ideas inherent in those objects into a space beneath them. Yet that space can sometimes be opened in an instant, by a flashing blue light or a passing cab driver or a rude store clerk. So why would a black woman display offensive items before those who would justifiably be outraged at the sight of such on a white neighbor's lawn or in a storekeeper's front window? Why are a small yet increasing number of African Americans collecting such items? And why do they appear here, at the Emancipation, in a safe space—at an event that, in some ways, celebrates African-American resistance to the ideas that those very objects represent?

Armstrong feels compelled to directly confront the past and the stain of racism on the present. Perhaps like other blacks who pay for racist collectibles, she seeks more control over the interpretation of her history. She wants to possess all parts of it, not just the heroic elements that one easily finds all over the fairgrounds today. "I hate them [the collectibles] too, but at the same time, they fascinate me. They really do," Armstrong explains. "It tells a lot about what we've had to go through to get us where we are now. Generally when I get them I go through a cycle. I look at it and I'm either shocked, like 'Oh my gosh,' or I bust out laughing, or get angry. But I always end up the same way: How much do you want for it? Even though they make me angry, I end up the same way. For example, this bank, this iron bank."

There is a black face on the front of the bank. On the back, it says, "Young Nigger Bank." Armstrong paid $400 for it.

"I came through a period of time, in the fifties and sixties, when I did not want to be black," says Armstrong, who now directs a program at the University of Rio Grande that helps guide public-assistance recipients through school. "I don't know whether anybody else will own up to it, but I was embarrassed or ashamed to be who I was. I did not want to be black, and now I know why I felt that way about me. A lot of it came through these objects and things that you would see in the store."

Armstrong picks up a postcard with a picture of five young African-American boys under the heading "A possum and a lucky nigger."

"This was probably in any five-and-ten-cents store," she says

The imprint on the bottom of the card says, "Published expressly for F. W. Woolworth Co."

"This went through the mail," she continues. "This was 1915. The collectibles with real people fascinate me the most, more so than the cartoon characters. Someone probably just asked these boys to sit down, and somebody took a picture and produced this."

Not everyone can look to these items and find a reason why they were ever uncomfortable with the color of their skin. Of course, not everyone of African descent has shared the discomfort that Armstrong isn't hesitant to claim. Yet, historically and collectively, African Americans have confronted views that grow out of the collectibles. It is not always a direct confrontation, but the impact is still there. Take Lois Solomon, a middle-aged woman who stops to look at the display. She is a social worker in Columbus who grew up on the other end of Ohio in the state's big city—Cleveland. She had never even heard of this annual event until a friend recently told her about it. This is her first Emancipation, and her eyes are stuck on a porcelain black woman who is standing on a base that carries the caption, "Every Kitchen Needs a Mammy." Perhaps her parents indirectly were driven by the images of black women spotlighted in Armstrong's exhibit as they steeped themselves and her in Victorian values.

Solomon's parents were determined to raise a Negro "lady" with manners and class who would look and act nothing like the white expectation. Her father owned a construction company and her mother was an interior designer; both were products of a historically black college in Mississippi. They believed that girls should grow up to be cultured and refined ladies and wives, with a minimum of two years of college. They sent their daughter to Nashville's Fisk University, a bastion of black middle-class values. "I am from the old school," she says. "I got my two years of college before I got married. I started off at Fisk because we needed to have a black experience. That's what they thought."

After two years of Fisk, Solomon found a husband and took an academic hiatus. She followed her husband to Dayton, where she eventually finished college. Then he landed a job in Columbus, and she was the diligent wife who always followed her husband. "I was just part of what we always heard: I went from home to college to marriage. I was groomed to be a housewife. I was not really groomed to work."

But Solomon, liberated by the divorce that ended her seventeen-year marriage, says she was sure to groom her daughter, also an only child, differently. Like her parents, Solomon says she encouraged her daughter to attend a black college. In contrast to them, though, Solomon insisted that her twenty-three-year-old daughter look at college as something more than merely a two-year endeavor to pursue cultural refinement and a husband.

Her daughter graduated from Louisiana's Grambling State University and is now a teacher in Columbus. She is unmarried and planning for graduate school next year.

The women Solomon and her daughter were raised to be are both absent from Armstrong's table. There are no cultured and refined homemakers or professional women with graduate degrees in the exhibit. Still, Solomon's life is not untouched by the legacy of the ideas inherent in the display. In many ways, the traditional values of her parents, which inspired them to raise a lady and a refined wife—grew out of their rebellion against bigoted views of what their lives could and should be. It was a racism that was reinforced by symbols like those that Armstrong spotlights. "I think, for me, this display helps to further decolonize your mind," says Solomon. "One that struck me the most was the black woman actually sitting on a big pot, like an outdoor toilet. This is the further devaluation of black women . . . I don't know if I am really a feminist, but I am a crusader for black women."

Emancipations are like birthdays in this southeastern Ohio county. They happen once a year and are synonymous with celebration.

That said, you can't find many festive faces among the gathering crowd as the opening of the 1994 Emancipation approaches on Saturday. Why should anyone smile? Rain threatens to melt the party into one that won't be talked about to grandchildren. A gray cloud hangs and the steady water falls onto the county's Junior Fairgrounds, the site of the Emancipation. The storm bars celebrating in the company of the sun and restricts the festivities to the interior of the fairgrounds' metal barns—not the best way to turn 131 years old.

Inevitably, though, the party persists into another year. Canceling it because of rain or even postponing until a sunny day is inconceivable in Gallia County, where the Emancipation is really too established to be surrounded by "Celebration of" and "Proclamation." Those words are for strangers. When many Gallia natives hear the word *emancipation* alone, they instantly think of the annual gathering that refuses to die with generations.

Victor Long, seventy-seven, helps immortalize the Emancipation. A retired Defense Department small-parts buyer, Long donates at least $300 annually to the Emancipation committee's coffers. He returns to his hometown for the event every year. "I just have to come back," says Long, who has lived in the state capital, Columbus, since World War II. "My genes are buried here and I just can't forget it."

Long traces his roots in the county to his great-grandparents, Jefferson Scott and Caroline Hockaday. They arrived in Gallia County in 1844, according to family records. The couple literally jumped the broom in Halifax County, North Carolina, where they had been slaves, according to Long. Caroline Hockaday was one of three daughters born to a slave and slave owner. In 1844, the daughters, their husbands, and their children were freed. Family stories of why and how they won their freedom are a mix of speculation, legend, and myth, says Long. One tale says that the slave owner was senile and guilt ridden. Another says that the nice owner didn't want his mean children to inherit the slaves. Whatever the reason, it is a fact that the couple made a new home in Gallia County, and Jefferson Scott lived to be 112.

In Gallia, Jefferson and Caroline joined a community that was pivotal to the Underground Railroad. Gallipolis, the county seat, sits on the Ohio River in the southeastern portion of the state. When Scott and Hockaday arrived, there was no such state as West Virginia. There was just Ohio and Virginia—North and South separated by a vast river. At least two routes of the Underground Railroad ran through the county, according to James A. Sands, a local historian. Gallia became the first and last stop for some passengers who settled in the county and whose descendants return today to celebrate freedom.

The first Emancipation was glued to the calendar and culture of Gallia County on September 22, 1863. On that day in 1862, Gallia residents heard the news: President Abraham Lincoln announced the Emancipation Proclamation to abolish slavery on January 1, 1863, in the seceded states of the Confederacy, where his authority was not recognized. Nevertheless, a tradition was born in Gallia County.

In Galveston, Texas, the word of freedom didn't come until June 19, 1865, and thus the big Juneteenth celebrations became a lasting tradition. June 19 is just another day here. In Gallia County, the ancestors celebrated first on September 22.

The customs of the Emancipation come and go with the times, but the event itself remains a lasting tradition.

Victor Long remembers the time when the thought of an Emancipation on a day other than September 22 seemed sinful. When Long was growing up in the 1920s and '30s, Emancipations were held on September 22—no matter what day of the week. There was even a time when September 22 was referred to as the "colored holiday" in Gallia County. In the minds of employers, it was extraordinary to expect a black employee to show up for work on that day. To children, it was inconceivable to think of school beyond noon, if at all. "As a little boy growing up down here, it was just someplace to go and have fun," remembers Long. "We didn't really know what it was all about."

The Emancipation no longer frees children from a day of school. "Wartime came," says Jesta Mae Payne Diggs, a seventy-something native whose father served as president of the Emancipation for decades. "People were then busy in the plants working. At that time, Papa started having it on Sunday so that would accommodate all the people, because our friends used to come from all over Ohio to the Emancipation."

Eventually, Emancipations evolved into two-day events held on the weekend closest to September 22. For some, this is homecoming weekend, attracting a couple of hundred natives and friends of the event from California, Alabama, Michigan, even Canada. The visitors board with relatives in the area or get rooms at the Econo-Lodge across the highway from the fairgrounds. They return to a county whose black population has dwindled to 871 out of Gallia's 30,000 residents—not even 3 percent of the population. In 1890, Gallia had 2,381 African Americans—10 percent of the county's total population, according the United States Census Bureau.

Long grew up in Little Raccoon, a black, rural section of the county. Most of the residents owned farms. "Farmers, that was about all," says Long. "I was born here on a seventy-eight-acre farm. We were all raised on the farm, four boys and four girls."

But Long's father couldn't support the family on farming alone. "He could do a little bit of anything, but he was also a coal miner. Back in the 1920s, he made fairly good money mining coal up in Meiggs County, the next county up the river. He mined coal there for the Pittsburgh Coal Company."

Long says that life in Little Raccoon was simple, rural, and conservative. The men worked and the women either did domestic work in town or tended to their houses full-time, depending on how much the man made. They were unknowingly poor, hard working, and proud—qualities that were tested on a day Long still vividly remembers. "If you don't mind me telling you a short story," he begins, "we kids were still on the farm. I couldn't have been more than ten years old. My younger brother and one of my sisters, we were out in the yard playing, and we happened to look up this little dirt road, it was County Road. And there came Dad walking down the road in the middle of the week. Well, we couldn't understand that. He always came home on Saturday evening after a week's work. He would leave the mines. Some of the younger men up there had cars. They'd all drive home. And here comes Dad walking down that dirt road. Well, we called Mom, 'Hey, Mom, here comes Papa.' She came running out the door and ran out to the road. And by that time Dad was right up in the front yard.

I remember this real well. She said, 'Jeff, William Jefferson Long, what are you doing home?'

"He said, 'Why, Sarah, they closed the mines down. The market crashed, they closed the mines and there was nothing to do. They just told us to lay down our tools and go on.'

"Now, when we were kids, Dad used to take us up there. We'd spend the week with him sometimes. Our mother would go along, and they lived in shanties. In those days, the coal mining company, Pittsburgh Coal Company, had shanties all over those hillsides.

"You know what happened during the Hoover administration: the stock market crashed. They closed down those mines, and matters got worse, worse, worse. Hoover was defeated by Roosevelt in 1932, and, as we used to say, Roosevelt was our savior. It was just that bad. I mean, all these blacks, many of them worked in those coal mines and made fairly good money considering the time. And when the mines shut down, it was awful."

Through those hard and uncertain times, one thing was consistent—the annual Emancipation. It survived the despair. The depression still shattered Little Raccoon, yet Long says that he never recalls anyone considering jumping from the roof of a farmhouse. Like many Americans, Long's neighbors searched for ways to survive. "Down here, this land is at the foothills of the Appalachian Mountains, and it's rough. Parts of it is rough, if you get what I mean. *Rugged* is a better word, I guess, rugged. Well, my dad came home, and he started farming full time. A year or two later, he sold that farm and put one of my older sisters through school right up the road here. Rio Grande University is right up here."

Despite the hard times, it was assumed that while men could still find work with their hands, women needed security and shouldn't be dependent on the whim of a husband's ability to support them, says Long. It was that thinking that prompted his family and others to make sure that their girls got off to college. "My sister went to school there. It was a two-year college. What did they used to call them in those days? Normal schools, that's right, it was a normal college in those days. Well, my sister graduated, and she taught school up at the black one-room schoolhouse. She taught school, and she got married halfway between the second year. In those days in the state of Ohio, married women were not permitted to teach school. The man was considered the head of the household, and that man is supposed to take care of you. Well, my sister was teaching, and she finished her second year, and they wouldn't permit her to teach anymore, so she was already married and she moved to Columbus.

"Dad died. He worked here on the county highways, anything he could do to make an honest dollar, that's the way black people were in those days, honest. Honest dollar. And a few years after he sold the farm, he had just worked himself to death. He died in April, my birth month. The extended family had to pay for the funeral. It costs us six hundred dollars. I never shall forget. The extended family members had to pay for it. We didn't have six hundred dollars."

His mother was left with a family to raise. "My mom told the older kids to begin to scatter—go their way. I was left at home with the younger brother. I was fifteen. Mom told me, 'I want you to go through high school.' Oh, she could talk rough. 'You're gonna finish school.' I made it on through high school."

Long, like many of his peers, left the area after graduation. The exodus of blacks would continue for years to come. Now, Little Raccoon is no longer called such, and is no longer a community of African Americans. Long joined the Civilian Conservation Corps, a Roosevelt New Deal program that trained workers for government jobs. He became a clerk for the CCC, a position he held until he was drafted and served in the Air Force during World War II. "I was lucky," says Long, who served at Wright Air Force Base. "I didn't have to leave the state of Ohio."

Ida Fulton is dressed in blond dreadlocks and a bright, colorful African-style headdress and robe. She sits behind her table piled with handmade jewelry, oils, perfumes, and T-shirts. She stands when a potential buyer is within the table's scope.

Fulton insists that she has never dyed her hair blond. "There's some whitewash in me," she says. "My hair has a tendency to blond. Now, living in Canton, Ohio, with dreadlocks . . ."

Fulton pauses and shakes her head. She says that some residents treat her like an outcast. "And to have blond dreadlocks is really taboo among black folks. I'm not talking about white folks—black folks treat you real bad. They can be a pain sometimes."

The color of her hair would probably look like a natural extension of her light-brown skin and hazel eyes if it weren't for the dreadlocks. She sometimes dyes her hair black to make the presence of her dreads look more natural. A few dark strands from a recent dye job are discernible.

As it is for Lois Solomon, this is Fulton's first Emancipation. "I didn't know black folks lived here. I'm serious. There's a whole group of people here. Last year, someone was telling me about this, and I said 'Wow, I'm going to check this out.'"

Fulton spends many of her weekends on the road at festivals, selling her merchandise, or at the two stores she owns in Canton and Youngstown.

She started her business in 1985, when she was a single mother trying to raise two children on her salary as a program coordinator of a drug-rehabilitation agency. Initially, it was a small, home-based—and part-time—button-selling operation at the time when kente cloth and the word *Afrocentrism* began to infiltrate popular culture. Her buttons captured the mood: "Save Our Black Children," "I'm Free and I'm Black," and "I Have No Alcohol in Me."

From the buttons, Fulton moved to T-shirts and clothes. When her job at the drug-rehab agency was downsized in a budget cut, her side business became a full-time endeavor. "This is a booming business, especially if we ever really get black folks to realize that being African is not bad."

Fulton also sells incense. One burns on her table. "I have a friend who's a local perfumer who makes them. He worked in a perfume factory or something like that up in New York.

"They are different from the ones you buy in the store—they're a lot stronger. I have a peach cobbler [scented variety], and you smell it and it smells just like peach cobbler. I have one that smells like a birthday cake.

"People use incense to make their rooms smell good. But I can remember when I was growing up, my aunt used them for meditation. They're supposed to be used for spirituality.

"See, I was raised by my aunts and uncles, my mother's siblings. My parents were from Alabama. But I was an orphan. There were three of us and we were passed around.

"My mother's siblings were all over. They were all over, in Buffalo and Detroit. I spent the school year in Buffalo and the summer in Detroit. I went to high school and college in Buffalo."

Fulton is the product of an informal adoption, which was more common in pre–Great Society African-American communities than it is now, according to sociologist Robert Hill.

"All of the brothers and sisters pitched in and helped us. They knew that we were dependents. You can't do that anymore."

Fulton's urban American childhood is similar to Long's rural experience; both are products of a resilience that transcended some of the horror of tough times. So, when Fulton appreciates the "good old days" of the fifties and early sixties, she is not mourning legalized segregation or any kind of forced separation of the races. Rather, she relishes the time when families "pitched in" in the interest of providing a childhood for children whose parents were, for whatever reason, incapable of handling parental responsibility. She sees welfare and government bureaucracy as impediments to such resilience. On the surface, she may sound like a Republican in Congress, or a Democrat like Bill Clinton trying to solidify his appeal beyond liberals. But it is a mistake to simplify, reduce, or typecast Fulton's conservatism in the strictly left-right terms that are so often misused to size up the American public. Her interest in dismantling welfare is born out of her childhood experiences and interest in sustaining self-reliance and a strong sense of family among African Americans. The pursuit of that self-reliance spins her politics and figures strongly in some of her ideas that the mainstream may consider irrational, including her unyielding opposition to transracial adoption. "Today, you got to go through all this welfare system to help anybody. You know, black folks, fearful of the establishment, an establishment that was set up for the empowerment of white folks. Now they using it to help us from caring for our own. I just don't think white folks should raise our children. I told my sons. They're twenty and twenty-three. If they get involved with a white girl and they have babies, I would have to go to court if they don't marry the girl and be with her forever. I would have to go to court and take the baby."

Fulton apparently sees the arch in my eyebrows. "You can agree or disagree."

She says that the strength of a family of any race blossoms through the ability to find a way out of a web of turmoil. She moved to Canton from Buffalo seventeen years ago because of the father who had been kept out of her life. Her father, whom she had never met, contacted her in Buffalo. "Now that's another story. He had looked for me. My aunts and uncles didn't want me to know. And I was working for the youth corps in Buffalo. He found me through the city directory, and I came here to be with him. We got to spend about fifteen years together before he died."

Victor Long wears a brown leisure suit covered by a khaki-colored trench coat, almost the same shade as his skin. City life in Columbus hasn't robbed him of his Appalachian Ohio manners and accent: even in the rain, almost everyone he passes gets a nod, if not a warm handshake and hug for special friends. The rain doesn't even seem to faze him. "On Saturday of last year, we had more than twice this many people," he says. "But we can't argue with the Creator. We have to accept his way of doing things."

One of Long's first stops at an Emancipation is the historical display in the lobby of the main exhibition barn. He unloads old newspaper articles, family documents, and old photographs onto a table. The collection always includes a picture of Emmet Bunche at the Emancipations of Long's youth. For years, Bunche, now ninety-eight and living in a Gallia County nursing home, always drew attention at an Emancipation because of his attire. From top hat to toe, he dressed in the style of President Abraham Lincoln.

James Dewey Keels, sixty-six, and his younger brother, Russell, sixty-three, walk briskly past the table. They don't have time for a history lesson. The Keels brothers, cousins of Long and also great-grandsons of Caroline Hockaday Scott, are president and vice president, respectively, of the 1994 Emancipation. For Russell Keels, a slight panic sets in with the rain: he fears that the storm may produce a first in his imagination—an Emancipation without Bernice Borden. By coincidence, the precedent would mark the year she was to be honored as the Emancipation's woman of the year.

Big brother James, though, isn't worried. He's certain that the eighty-something Borden will make it here in time for the award—even with the heavy rain. Few blacks as blood-tied to the event as Borden can miss the Emancipation; not even some of the old-timers who will come and complain that "they don't have 'Mancipations like they used to."

James Dewey Keels remains calm while Russell Keels searches the fairgrounds for Borden. He doesn't find her in the metal exhibition barn busy with vendors like Fulton setting up their Afrocentric goods. She isn't in the barn or makeshift restaurant, where members of the Paint Creek Baptist Church prepare the steak-and-rib combo sandwiches, chicken-and-rib dinners, and cakes. And she isn't in the exhibition area, where a portable stage, PA system, and an audience of two dozen people await the program's beginning.

Russell Keels decides that there is only one solution: call Borden, share the secret, spoil the surprise, and offer her a ride—if transportation and the rain are a problem. But just as he moves in the direction of the telephone, and seconds before the one o'clock drops of rain dissolve into the dirt, Borden arrives, saving her own surprise. "Sometimes I think, Lord, this might be my last year, the last one," Borden later told me. "And then I thank the Lord that I've lived and I get to go to another one."

Bernice Payne Borden, a slender woman with bleached oak–colored skin as smooth as durable satin with a few natural creases, was a schoolteacher for forty-one and a half years. "And Mama was a switchboard operator, for thirty years," she says. "That's the reason we keep jobs so long whenever we get them. Other people don't keep a job a very long time. We don't know when to turn them loose."

Borden speaks with the clean and crisp diction of an old-fashioned schoolteacher. But for at least one word, her tongue drops syllabic precision and marches with the linguistic liberty that naturally flows from the curling

Appalachian vowels of many Emancipation goers. With ease, they free the front of the freedom word of the sound of that bumbling *e*. "That 'Mancipation is something else," says Bernice Borden. "Oh the 'Mancipation, my goodness gracious. It was here when I got here. I've always gone. Mama took me before we started school, when we were babies. We never missed it.

"I don't know whether I felt the meaning of it. But we were always so happy when it would be time for the 'Mancipation," she remembers. "My mother and dad always made great preparation. We had all the kids to get ready, you know, clothes to make for them for the 'Mancipation.

"We'd all dress up. And you know how they used to dress, long skirts and all. And we'd have a parade."

"That was one of the last events of the year before the cold weather would set in," adds Borden's sister, Jesta Mae Payne Diggs.

Borden and Diggs grew up in a family of eleven children—ten of whom made it to adulthood, five boys and five girls. They do not know how and when their ancestors arrived in Gallia County. But as far as they can remember, the family was always heavily tied to the Emancipation. Growing up, they remember following behind their father, the Reverend Clifford Payne, the Baptist minister here who presided for years over the event in the way that the Keels brothers do this year. As adults, they were beside their big sister, Dorothy Lewis, now deceased, who presided over the Emancipation for a record forty years.

They especially remember their own household as well as others on the eve of an Emancipation. Kitchens across the county steamed with the aromas of all kinds of food. "Mama would stay up and cook all night," recalls Jesta Mae Diggs.

"We didn't have a food stand then, but everybody would bring their dinners," says Borden. "Mama cooked them dinners and packed them in a basket. Mama would have a great big coconut cake, and she'd have four or five pies stacked. A great big crock of green beans and potato salads and beets and baked bread. You see, we had all our flour. We had meat—all kinds of meat. Mama would roast up two big hens with the dressing. Oh, we would have all that food. And she would have a snow-white tablecloth. We would spread it out on the green when noon would come. Everybody would just pass around. And they would come to Mama's table the most."

"We used to ride to the Emancipation in the horse and buggy, in the surrey with the fringe around the top," says Diggs. "There was a number of us in the family. So Papa would ride the surrey. Papa would get in the front seat and Mama and the girls would get in the back. The seats were small at that time, but we all piled in."

"We'd have the preacher in the morning," Borden picks up, "and then in the afternoon we'd have this congressman. Tom Jenkins, he'd come every year, a white man. Oh, he was a dandy one. He knew everybody's name, yours and everybody else's. I don't know what his method was, but he certainly could call names. And he was a dandy fellow to everybody."

Today Borden lives in a ranch-style house on a street named for her father. Most residents of Payne Street in Gallia County's predominantly black hamlet of Bidwell are related to the family.

Like Victor Long, Borden and Diggs grew up at a time when college, particularly normal school, was a girl's thing in many black families, and work was for men. In some black middle- and working-class families, teaching and college were seen as tools of security for women who, unlike many of their white counterparts, couldn't be guaranteed the full financial support of a husband. The Payne family epitomized the idea: all five girls in the family attended college and became teachers, and none of the men went to college, according to Borden. "At that time, there wasn't much money in circulation," Borden states. "There wasn't any jobs or much of anything. But those fellows, it was just about farming. And the boys would just quit and just go to farm with their fathers. So many of them lost the opportunity that way. Whatever the dad did, these boys would just follow."

The result was many marriages like Bernice Borden's. She had more formal education than her husband, who was a mechanic and handyman.

As more Gallia women attended college and passed the teaching exams, the profession lost its security in the county as black schools closed. By the 1940s, only two black one-room schoolhouses remained in the Gallia County area, recalls Diggs. Most blacks in the county, like Borden, attended majority-white schools, where African-American students were welcome—but black teachers were not. So, in the 1940s, years before the *Brown v. Board of Education* decision, black residents of Bidwell battled not for integration, but for segregated schools, largely because they wanted jobs for black teachers, according to Diggs. Some also wanted their children taught by neighbors. Residents petitioned the county and won the fight for a one-room schoolhouse for black elementary students in Bidwell. Borden was one of the first teachers in the school. "I had all eight grades in one," she says. "I had never gone to a colored school."

"Initially, the kids in Bidwell were going to integrated schools," recalls Diggs. "At that time, people were needing jobs. We had a number of people who were teachers there, and none of us had employment. We had sacrificed. Our parents had sacrificed to send us to school. And then after we finished, and had gotten our education, then there were no jobs for us. So they decided to build a school so that the teachers would have employment. It made a living for these people. And I'm not going to condemn it, because it was a matter of survival."

Borden takes a seat in the front of the auditorium as the Emancipation program begins. "We were always taught to be there when it started and take one of those chairs and sit down on the seat and not to be running around outside," she says.

The audience of fifty early arrivals sees Borden's surprised face when she's named woman of the year. They hear her impromptu acceptance speech after the greetings of Harold Montgomery, a county commissioner.

As a white man, Montgomery is a minority at the Emancipation. But like the majority of whites here, he is a politician. And like any politician, he searches for some way to connect with the crowd and finds it through the Klan. "We had a most unfortunate situation happen in our community in the past year. I don't remember the date. Hopefully, I can forget the whole incident. But it was with the cooperation of your leadership and our leadership that we were able to avoid some terrible, terrible times in Gallia County. It was without invitation that a very subversive, divisive group came into Gallia County to speak on our courthouse steps. . . . We contacted leaders of your community and through their efforts we kept the crowds down. We kept everyone back, and, hopefully, this will never happen in Gallia County again. But we do commend you and we're certainly appreciative of your efforts in helping us through this tough situation."

Some among the crowd politely nod. Others, by the looks on their faces, drift away, obviously uninterested in the Klan today or almost any day.

The Klan is the last thing on Barbara Scott's mind. As historian of the Emancipation, Scott spent the morning setting up the display and passing out maps detailing Underground Railroad routes and lists of local conductors. She's also prepared a fact sheet about blacks in the county; it includes the name of an early black farmer who became a millionaire and the wealthiest farmer in the area, an executive once mentioned in *Ebony* magazine, and the name of the first black homecoming queen of North Gallia High School. In a few minutes, she will take the podium and read from the fact sheet.

Scott became interested in rediscovering the history of blacks in the county after she quit her job as a domestic in 1971. Her son was born the following year. A full-time homemaker and mother, she turned to other organizations, including an interracial group, Church Women United. The behavior of a member of the organization reminded Scott why it was important to become involved in the Emancipation organization, one of the few organizations in the county controlled and operated by blacks, with the exception of churches. That member, a former boss, never could see Scott beyond the role of maid or as an equal in the organization. "It was always 'my little girl, this,' you know?" says Scott. "She couldn't help it, I reckon. She would introduce me to the other women and say, 'Oh, this is my little girl. She worked for me.' It didn't make me mad, but I just felt sorry for her because she never grew up. She always had that little need to show off in front of the other women. The other women were nice, but it feels good to be away from that."

Throughout the opening day of the celebration, it was impossible to escape the sound of the wet taps knocking on the metal barn tops like the fist of a pesterous neighbor. They were a reminder of the world outdoors without sunshine. Eventually the drops became so constant that they seemed as natural as silence and dissolved into the day's events: they speak with speeches, sing with songs, act with dramatizations, chew with food, show off with vendors of Afrocentric books and paraphernalia.

By 6:00 P.M., the day settles into the finale—the performance of a Columbus, Ohio, dance troupe specializing in African dances. Minutes after the dancers parade onto the stage, the rain subsides into a drizzle. Seconds later, the director of the dance troupe breaks from his prepared remarks and declares the rain to be a blessing.

Minutes later, the sun steals back the final hours of daylight.

Day one of the Emancipation ends.

A Tradition's Feud

FRED Flintstone, Jesus, and O.J. Simpson share a table at the Emancipation. Versions of them have been shaped into a form that one vendor hopes will appeal to Emancipation goers. The vendor, Sarah Johnson Sow, sells the three, among other items.

At Sow's table, Jesus and Fred are brown dolls—Fred with dreadlocks. They stand above a ten-dollar silk screen of O.J. Simpson, whose face is surrounded by the words "O.J. Simpson Still Our Hero."

"Do you really believe O.J. is a hero?" I ask Sow, who is also selling a dark-skinned, permed Wilma Flintstone.

She looks at the tape recorder pointed at her mouth. She pauses for a couple of seconds and glances at Isaac, her ten-year-old son. She then looks me straight in the eye with an answer. "I still believe that," she says. "He's not a hero because he was a wife beater or a murderer. But if you look at the records he set, he would still be a hero."

He is a "hero" that the Gallia County native and University of Rio Grande Director of Multicultural Affairs clearly doesn't want her son to emulate. She refuses to allow Isaac to play football, which defies football-loving Gallia County's high school coaches, who sometimes stop the 143-pound boy and ask about his age and if he's training for high school football. "Yes, they've asked me does he play sports now," she says. "I only let him play soccer. He gets mad. He's not going to be some big, tragic, black athlete used up and unable to get a good education."

At forty, Sow, a fourth-generation Gallia native, is old enough to speak of those old Emancipations with a romanticism and nostalgia common to traditionalists of any sort or adults recollecting pleasant childhoods. It is a

much-heard voice among the small black community in Gallia County—yet
it is often applied to different "old" Emancipations, depending on the
speaker's age, and that ranges from Sow to Bernice Borden. Whether forty
or seventy, though, most of the descriptions of "old" Emancipations resemble the talk of veterans of wars before Vietnam recalling days of bravery.
Fond memories of the "old" Emancipations are similar to those of residents
of old segregated black communities: people selectively recall the cohesion
but, unlike Elaine Armstrong, may omit the era's comfort with the blatant
presence of a brand of tobacco called Nigger Hair.

For Sarah Johnson Sow, the "old" Emancipations didn't have vendors:
one couldn't find black Jesus dolls and T-shirts for sale; Fred Flintstone with
dreadlocks wasn't even in the imagination. At that time, the celebrations
were held at Bidwell's old Bush Park, which is now surrounded by senile
marsh and browning weeds that block the view of the old Emancipation
site from the road. "It was really wonderful back then. The worst thing was
the yellow jackets. Oh, the yellow jackets were terrible. One year, I was in
the seventh grade, I found out I was allergic to yellow jacket bites because I
got stings on my hand and my hand swelled up so badly that I couldn't
write. It was a mess."

Sow says the "old" Emancipations of her childhood—those in the sixties—reflected the times in the county. Emancipation goers were not drawn
to anti–Vietnam War rallies, yet many felt the pain of the war through loved
ones fighting on foreign soil. The civil-rights revolution and black power
movements were foreign to the annual gathering, according to Sow. "In
general, it was very quiet here during the sixties," she says. "We didn't have
the dissension that they had in Detroit and those places. Here, it's more of
the colored type. I call the people here dip, dyed, and colored."

For years, vending was a hobby for Sow. It matured into a business with
her second marriage, and she became the first to sell ethnic goods at the
Emancipation. She and her husband work as a team, with Sow spending
her weekends at festivals, rallies, and events in the Midwest where African
Americans gather. Her husband, a Senegalese, spends the week sewing
clothes and ordering Afrocentric goods, like the Fred Flintstone with dreadlocks. Married for five months, Johnson is now an orthodox Muslim, like
her husband, who makes all of her clothes. Today, it is rare to find her in
anything but African-style clothes. Mostly she wears momboys, the two-
piece outfits characterized by their deceptively wide pants. The momboy's
legs are so broad that you can't easily tell they are even legs—you could
easily mistake the bottom piece for a long skirt.

This woman who wears mostly African clothes (but has yet to visit the
continent) doesn't find pride only in her African heritage. She also doesn't

hesitate to tell me that she is a direct descendant of an American president. While she doesn't flaunt it like some members of the Washington and Jefferson clans do, she finds no shame in the fact that her great-grandfather was produced by William Henry Harrison and a slave mother, according to family records. The woman in a momboy accepts that part of her lineage, which, on the surface, may seem as shocking and awkward as Fred Flintstone with dreadlocks. But in actuality, the version of Fred for sale and Sow's comfort with the varied parts of her lineage reflects a peace with the multidimensional parts of a past and present that are as culturally diverse, distinct, and complicated as the presence of Fred, Wilma, Jesus, and O.J. Simpson at the same table.

Perhaps as complex as any such past is Sow's role in a feud over the present and future of the Emancipation. The orthodox Muslim woman, who as we speak sells Jesus shirts and dolls to a mostly Christian, church-going Emancipation crowd, has become one of the most vocal and earnest critics of the influence of the church on the Emancipation. On this issue, Sow's combatants are Bernice Borden and the Keels brothers, who preside over this year's Emancipation. "Some just want this to be a church service, that's all," explains Sow. "That's not the Emancipation that I remember."

Sow has become a defender of a group of Appalachian men and women who do not mark slavery's end by buying Jesus dolls or O.J. T-shirts, or by worshipping in a religious service. Their celebration in the back of the fairgrounds is comprised of cases of beer, uproarious laughter, and conversations that cover anything from politics to parenting to sports. This party is at the center of the debate between Sow and the Keels brothers. Sow says it is in the tradition of the Emancipation to respect the men who drink, while the Keels brothers contend that open drinking is illegal at the fairgrounds and have pressed a reluctant all-white police force to prevent the drinkers from congregating. "That definitely should not be a part of the Emancipation," says Russell Keels. "We've always had those individuals. I can remember back when I was a kid, we had individuals that would drink and stagger around. And they never really bothered anyone. They were just a nuisance, and that's the same way today. But I think it will create a problem that will have to be stopped." Keels says the Emancipation committee's contract with the fairgrounds stipulates that there would not be any alcohol drinking at the fairgrounds. "Now to stop it you may have to have the sheriff's department out there," says Russell Keels. "Of course that's going to offend some people, but we can't tolerate drinking."

Alliances produce unity but, at the same time, frequently highlight contradictions too. The battle of the Emancipation is no exception. It is a feud that mirrors the subtleties that often divide and sometimes unite African

Americans: it is a war between two devoutly Christian men and a Muslim woman who doesn't drink but defends the rights of drinkers. The fight pits Sarah Johnson Sow in her African-style clothing against the Keels brothers, who attend Emancipations in suits and ties; on one side is a college-educated woman connected to the local university, looking across the divide at two military men and high school graduates, who have sent their kids to college. The woman's complexion is dark brown, while the men are olive-skinned, straight haired, and have cheekbones that recall their paternal grandfather, a full-blooded Cherokee. Russell and James Keels say color consciousness among African Americans in the county has never been a problem as far as they see. Sarah Johnson Sow says that it was once big and still lives among some who would marry a distant cousin if it was the only way to marry light and close to white. The woman says that the young and old black men clutching beers at the back of the fairgrounds possess a hidden beauty that will never be seen by the shallow eye. The brothers counter that the drinkers should go to work and, even if they have jobs, still go to jail or off the fairgrounds if they refuse to stop drinking at the 'Mancipation. Sarah Johnson Sow grew up in the sixties and seventies. The Keel brothers came of age during the depression and World War II.

Moreover, the woman lives in the city—on Third Street in downtown Gallipolis at the time of this Emancipation. The two men live in rural Gallia county. But this apparent difference reveals a deeper similarity: Both Sow and the Keels display the values of family and land ownership in common ways. Acquiring land in the first half of the nineteenth century, African Americans in southeastern Ohio were among some of the earliest black landowners in the country. They quickly came to view land ownership as a tool for personal power in a racially hostile country. Today, Sarah Johnson Sow lives in a house that has been in the family for generations and was willed to her father. The Keels brothers live on 131 acres of farmland purchased by their great-grandfather. The land has been divided into four lots, on which they and two of their sons have built homes.

In some ways, too, this is a family feud: both sides are descendants of Caroline Hockaday, and thus cousins.

When asked about Sow, James Dewey Keels says that she is "nothing but an Uncle Tom" disguised in African clothing.

But with time, the differences between Sow and the Keels have withered. In fact, in 1999, five years after this Emancipation, James Keels and Sow began working on a project exploring Native-American heritage in Ohio.

• • •

You cannot see the sun, or any traces of the weather, from many corners of the windowless exhibition barns. Nevertheless, a consequence of the good weather is clearly visible in the dimly lit vending area: Like the rest of the fairgrounds, it is packed with people. In the afternoon, there is a standing-room-only crowd for the Emancipation keynote address by Dr. Barbara Ross-Lee, dean of the College of Osteopathic Medicine at Ohio University. Many in the crowd are not attracted to Ross-Lee solely because of her success as a black woman in the world of medicine. Some people admit they really just want to see the sister of singer Diana Ross.

Vendors like Sarah Sow and Ida Fulton don't have much time to think about seeing the doctor or the sister. Even during the church service and keynote speech, their tables are busy with browsers and shoppers. Vendors are eager to make up for yesterday's slow sales. At twenty-five dollars, Sow's Jesus dolls are among the best sellers, along with seven-dollar T-shirts featuring Jesus. Sow says Emancipation goers are captivated by the sight of a black Jesus because they are so accustomed to seeing Jesus in an image other than their own.

In the midafternoon, I leave the exhibition barn and travel to the back of the fairgrounds, passing the groups of youngsters playing football. I meet two men, Duke and J.C. As usual, they have bypassed any activity planned by the Emancipation committee, especially the church services. They are among the men and women who find freedom in the back of the fairgrounds, where they unload their liquor, lean their bodies on the sides of cars and vans, a beer propped in one hand, and talk about everything from politics to women.

"Man, look at them young kids over there," says the forty-something Duke. Three groups can be seen in the direction of Duke's gaze. There are the young teenagers who surround the hog pens, too cynical and cool for the games of football and kickball that engage younger children playing in the pen. Then there are the older teenagers and young adults in their early twenties, who drive on and off the grass in the back of the fairgrounds as if it's concrete, their speakers blasting the sound of hip-hop music. They ride with a pose and lean that pretends to be oblivious to everything—too hip to be aware of or moved by anything. They grab "forties" from their own arsenals and other cans of beer from the cases of the thirty- and forty-something drinkers congregated in the vicinity of Duke and J.C. "With the way it's going now, when the older generation here is gone, it won't be no more Emancipation," says Duke.

"They ain't gonna keep coming," J.C. adds.

In this respect, their mood echoes Sarah Sow's as they look at the future of the celebration that is as much a part of their life as any nationally established holiday. They speak with the sense of doom of those who've watched the deterioration of an old neighborhood. "They ain't going to keep it up because the only thing they can do out here is go to church," J.C. continues. "It's all right to go to church, but when the church let out, why can't everybody come over here and participate? If you're a Christian, you're supposed to go amongst the devils."

"This is what it's all about—black people being together enjoying themselves," says Duke. "See, the whole idea of the 'Mancipation is for blacks to come in and be heard and seen. And they stopped that, the church people. But I'm going to keep coming."

"You know, I believe in Jesus Christ," asserts J.C. "My grandfather, all my family, is Christian, and one day I'll probably be Christian, if I don't die first drinking the beers. But the people that go to church just done took the 'Mancipation over like it's a religious thing, like one of their church socials."

"See, the church people put the pressure on the police officers to watch the people in the back here," says Duke. "But, see, you can't do that."

But it did happen last year. "We had seven or eight cases of beer and food," says Duke. "And they came here with barbecue ribs and chicken. About six thirty or seven, they [police] came here, talking about we had to leave. I said, 'Man, it ain't over with yet.'

"But we respect the law. I mean, if the law come over, everybody hide their beer and stuff. So we left."

Duke and J.C. grew up across the river, in West Virginia. Duke now lives in Gallia County. Like many of the forty-something men gathered in the back, they are Vietnam veterans who have settled in the area and worked intermittently at area plants. Their real names are not Duke and J.C., but those are the names that have been with them since they were teenagers. "I used to try to sing all the time. They used to say, 'Well, that's going to be the Duke of Earl,' and everybody started calling me Duke."

"I got my name, Joe Cool, playing music. I deejay, and the next thing I know I was called Cool. And the next thing I know, I was called Joe Cool.

"Now, where I come from, they call me Joe Louis because when I was a kid I would take your lunch money. You know what I mean—I guess I just hung around with the wrong dudes, man. We all grew up together in the coal fields. And we'd throw pieces of coals. My grandfather would come and say, 'Boys, y'all got a half ton of coal out there on the road. Y'all thrown all that coal away.' We'd have to go out there and pick it up, put it in the buckets, and drag it back into the house."

There are unwritten rules that govern the 'Mancipation celebration in the back of the fairgrounds. "If you drink, you're supposed to be back here to show them, the church people, their respect," says Frank, who is in his mid-twenties. "You're not supposed to do it up there in front of them because they're the church people. That's not to say people here don't go to church also.

"Most of the people that are back here kind of give the people up front a little respect. Don't drink or curse around them or anything."

Frank, a car salesman, says that he has more in common with both the older drinkers and those on the religious side than he does with many in his Generation X peers: "I'm a country boy. I was raised on a farm; I have a farm now—I just bought a farm last week. Just small farming for personal reasons. It's never been no hip-hop in me. I'm straight from the country, a hillbilly. It's a good life here. It's a good place to raise your kids. I got three kids, a wife, and it's a good place to raise them.

"I like seeing black people in general getting together, having a good time, you know. Because it's not often people get together and do things as a community. . . . And this is about the only time of the year you ever see it around here."

Other than the churches and an NAACP chapter that encompasses Gallia and neighboring counties, there isn't much else, besides the Emancipation, within the cultural domain of the county's small black population. Aside from the NAACP, there are no chapters of the major national social, political, and fraternal organizations that cater to African Americans. But because so many residents live within close proximity to family and friends, they really don't need an organization to give them an excuse to come together. Who needs a networking organization when you wouldn't hesitate to go to a neighbor's house with an empty cup?

Of course, before most established black organizations were born, there was an Emancipation—several of them. Celebrations of the Emancipation Proclamation were practically universal across black America for decades after Lincoln signed it. In Texas, of course, Juneteenth celebrations have long honored the day that Texans learned that slavery was over. In 1867, New Yorkers celebrated the event in September, as Gallia County residents do today. But that gathering took place earlier in the month, according to a story in the *New York Times* on September 3, 1867. Under a headline reading: "COLORED EMANCIPATION CELEBRATION AT HUDSON—3,000 COLORED PEOPLE PRESENT," an article summarized the day:

About three thousand colored people are in the city to-day from the interior of the country and from cities and towns along the Hudson River, the occasion being the celebration of the anniversary of the freedom of the slaves. Early this morning crowds of dusky skinned lads and lassies made their way into town in all sorts of vehicles from the country. . . .

At various places in Warren Street the American flag was conspicuously displayed.

The scene in the city at noon was a curious one. Crowds of colored people thronged the sidewalks, filled the alley-ways, and lounged about stoops and hotels, all behaving themselves in a very orderly manner. The speaking took place at the Courthouse in the afternoon. Among those announced to be present were Fred. Douglass, Rev. H. H. Garnett, Rev. Mr. Logan and Prof. Day. All but Fred. Douglass were present. The speaking commenced at 3:30, and was continued until 4:15, all the speakers holding forth in an able intelligent manner to a vastly crowded audience. . . . Venders of spruce beer, ice cream, candy, and other compositions of nothingness did a thriving trade, for our colored brethren spread money with a lavish hand. At 6 P.M., many commenced wending their way to the cars and boats, preparatory to their departure for home. To-night there will be speaking at the City Hall, after which a splendid entertainment is to be given by the colored people, after which the day's proceedings are to end up with a grand colored ball. It is worthy of remark that not a single fight or disturbance has thus far been reported. The day has been a very pleasant one, and the white people here have enjoyed themselves over the affair quite as much as the colored people.

In Washington, D.C., the emancipation celebration was in April, according to an 1893 article in the *Indianapolis Freeman,* an African-American newspaper, which reported that strangers to the nation's capital visiting on April 17 were "puzzled to find that the colored people of the District of Columbia have an Emancipation day of their own," not on the day of the proclamation. It then explained: "The fact that the Emancipation Proclamation was issued by President Lincoln on the first of January 1863 is well fixed in the public mind, but outside of Washington very few people seem to know that the District of Columbia slaves were emancipated on the 17th of April before."

The same article reports that attendance at such celebrations declined as time established more distance between African Americans and slavery:

Emancipation Day is not what it once was. The slave generation, when it is not rich and respectable, is old and feeble, or getting so, and the rising generation which has never known slavery except as a tradition, seem rather ashamed than proud of Emancipation Day. Perhaps it is only indifference rather than a stronger feeling, but at all events many of the colored people, especially those who have been educated, do not take part in the Emancipation processions or festivities. Years ago all classes of colored people, high and low, rich and poor, took part in one way or another in the Emancipation Day celebration. Gradually the most important men among them, like Frederick Douglass and Blanche K. Bruce, dropped out, followed by the richer and more respectable of them until the celebration was left largely to the lower classes, especially as it was not taken up to any great extent by young graduates of the public schools. . . .

It is easy to see why this change has come with the great change which has taken place in the character and the circumstances of the colored population. The dead level of poverty and ignorance which prevailed for some time after the war has been gradually broken up, so that the colored population . . . [of Washington] is no longer of one kind but of many kinds. Some are rich, some well-to-do, some have regular incomes, and some are poor. Some are refined and cultivated, some are well educated, some are poorly educated, and some are not educated at all. Part of them are not educated at all. Part of them are just as respectable and some of them just as respected as though they were white, and part of them are entirely disreputable. They are divided into social cliques as exclusive and as apart as those among the whites. Frederick Douglass, Bruce Lynch, and their set are as far away from the colored people at the other end of the social scale as the most exclusive white society man thinks himself to be from the most humble white laborer.

A sharp generation gap divides the groups in the back of the fairgrounds. "Them little brothers over there," says J.C., pointing to the younger men and women in their twenties. "I got cousins and stuff over there . . . they don't listen."

"The opportunities that they had and got now, we didn't have," says Duke, who clearly sees an opportunity to a good life in a place that his ally Sarah Johnson Sow does not—organized sports. "When you got an all-black school, there ain't no scouts gonna come to an all-black school to check you out. But now they got opportunities because they got a mixed school, and everybody can see the team. You got a chance to make it now, man. And like I tell them, man, if a young black kid don't make it today, it's his fault."

"Instead of running around drinking a forty, go on in the service," adds J.C.

"Man, that's all you got do," Duke agrees. "If you ain't gonna go to school, go to the army. All you got do is four years, and they'll give you a scholarship—and you'll get your head on right. I mean, that's all you got do. The opportunities are out there. I'm not saying that he gonna get the same job that the white man got, but at least today if they don't give you something you work for, you can holler. You can get an organization to holler for you. And then I can holler myself if they don't give it to me. But when I was coming along, there wasn't nobody there to holler to. You know, if I try to holler, the white man gonna hit me in the head. But the kids can holler today. The man hit them in the head, they can take him to court."

"Yep," J.C. agrees. "I say take him to court."

The conservative streak that runs through some of black America is deep, and it reveals itself in conversations where some may express a preference for spankings and consider "time out" to be a joke. It reaches to the back of the fairgrounds, to be heard in the drinking men's calls for discipline in raising children, which the men say is becoming as rare as a good Emancipation celebration. Cast away the men's distaste for an Emancipation without beer and their desire for one without a long church service, and the ideas of Duke and J.C. would easily pass the comfort test at the Keels' table, or that of just about anyone else who wants to rid the 'Mancipation of drinkers. In many ways, the drinkers' beliefs are more allied to the Keels brothers' ideology than to Sarah Johnson Sow's. They may not want the church to be a big player in the 'Mancipation, but, as fathers, they want prayer in the schools—something that their ally, Sarah Sow, would not advocate. "I think the number-one thing wrong with America, man, is that they took religion out of the schools, and took responsibility away from the teachers," states Duke. "And when you roll an acorn downhill, sooner or later it's going to grow up to be a nut. And that's exactly what they trying to do to the black kids today. They say the teacher can't beat you. She can't correct them. And they ain't gonna put much time into them, no way. If he [a student] runs his mouth and all this, that ain't gonna bother them. They just kick 'em out. But with that white kid, they gonna say, hey—"

"They need counseling," says J.C., sarcastically finishing Duke's sentence.

"Yeah, they need counseling," Duke repeats.

"They'll counsel him, but they gonna suspend my kid, send 'em home for a couple of days. That's the way they tried to do my daughter down in Million. And she's the only black kid in that school in Million, West Virginia.

She had a fight with a white boy. And they raised Cain with her, man, put her on a two-week suspension. I went down there, and she was back in school the next day. I said, 'Man, if he's going to get to school the next day, I want my daughter back in school the next day.' The teacher said, 'Well, she started it.' I said, 'How could she start it? Her name is Angel, not nigger.'"

"I heard that," J.C. chimes in.

"That started it. That started the thing right off when he called her a nigger. And I told the principal that I told her—"

"To pop that head," says J.C.

"That's right. I said I taught my daughter, man, to respect everybody just like she want to be respected. I told her then, right in front of him. I said he call you that again, bust him in his mouth."

"Yep," J.C. agrees.

"You know, it's violence," Duke reflects. "I don't believe in violence, but I believe in making somebody respect me. That's what I was taught.

"There was five boys in my family and seven girls," he goes on. "Plus, my dad had to raise another six. My brother got killed in a coal mine, and my dad raised six of his kids. And man, it was always something to do. If I only had the knowledge to know what the future was going to look like. You know, the skateboard they got now: I used to take the steel skates and take the boat out of the middle of them and put them on a wooden board and ride up and down the road myself. But I didn't know what I was doing. The stuff they got now, they invent and make a million dollars off of it. I used to make that stuff when I was a kid to play with. My dad, he was a coal miner, so we couldn't afford a whole lot of stuff that kids have today. So we made just about everything we had. We would go up in the woods, man, and see them grape vines that grow around the tree. We'd cut that off from around the tree and swing on them. We would then cut them off and use them as a baseball bat.

"And in my hometown, I don't think there was ever any racism in the coal fields. Black kids and white kids played together all the time, anyway. So when they integrated the schools, hell, that was no big thing for us. When school was out, we'd always gather.

"I've been here in Gallia County since 1969. It ain't a bad place to live. Plus, the economy ain't bad. I'm renting a house. My yard is about two acres, and I got four bedrooms. Where else can you get all that for a hundred fifty dollars a month? So the economy ain't bad. It ain't bad here."

By now, two other men, Outlaw and Gill, have joined the conversation. Their right hands are only free and idle for a short time—as long as it takes to grab another beer. As they drink, they preach about those drinking-and-driving kids—and their sermon sounds much like one that would bring an "Amen" in a Baptist church. "They stand on the corner and drink a forty and lay the bottle right there on the corner. I mean, right upside somebody's house, in their yard," one says.

"And then, if they ain't of age, they will ask you to get them a forty," the other picks up.

"That's no respect," says Outlaw. "No respect."

"They done lost respect," says Chickadee, another man who's joined our little circle, shaking his head. "Ain't nobody raising 'em. That's the problem."

"When we was young, our parents carried us with them," says J.C. "They didn't leave us at home. If they went somewhere where we couldn't go, they didn't go. If they would go down to the bootlegger's house, that's where we'd go. Today, mothers are taking young kids, leaving them with kids."

The crowd in the back of the fairgrounds dwindles as the other celebration comes to an end. "Them people that was over there, they gone now," observes J.C. "See, if we stay—the law will come and tell us we have to leave.

"I mean, we used to stay out here until dark," he goes on. "I mean dark, dark."

"One of the best Emancipations I ever remembered was one that happened in Bidwell," says Duke.

Duke recalls an Emancipation not unlike the one Bernice Borden describes. "I mean, they brought food—I mean everybody. Everybody brung something, some kind of food. They brung macaroni salad, baked beans, fried chicken . . . you could go to each and everybody's car and they'd have it set out. And they'd put a tablecloth out, too. Set the tables and stuff up right at the car. Everybody just enjoyed everybody else. They had their fun, and they used the Emancipation as a celebration of freedom. . . .

"They just don't have 'Mancipations like they used to," Duke concludes.

Preparing for the Independence Day Parade

I n the overwhelmingly white Gallia County, African Americans created their own holiday to celebrate freedom, and they observe it on a rented space in the county. Contrast that with Lawnside, New Jersey, a historically black town, where the main streets belong to drill teams, marching bands, fire trucks polished to a mirrorlike shine, spanking-clean cars, and lines of spectators for the annual Lawnside Fourth of July Parade. In Lawnside, African Americans do not think to create race-based traditions that will sit on the margins of the town. And there isn't a need to claim any kind of centricity when you are the mayor, police chief, members of the local Republican and Democratic clubs, volunteer firefighters, and just about everyone with a stake in the town and a space in the parade. It's just an American tradition.

The festivities in Lawnside, located seven miles outside Camden, New Jersey, and fifteen miles from Philadelphia, are a step ahead of most other Independence Day celebrations: although it is called a Fourth of July parade, by custom the event is held on the last Friday in June, leaving July 4 free for small family gatherings throughout this town of nearly three thousand residents.

The parade is not simply all black, as bands and organizations from South Jersey towns with nonblack majorities are sprinkled throughout the lineup. Yet it isn't integrated for the sake of diversity—what matters is a festive atmosphere. The stately smiles of walking and riding town leaders probably would not create much festivity without the sounds of music accompanying them. The music also adds life to the stately veterans and firefighters in ceremonial attire.

The bands do not matter to the parade's most ardent viewers—parents with a child marching with a drill team or walking in a Little League uniform or riding atop a convertible as the winner of the Lawnside Scholarship Club award or as the King and Queen of the town's Warwick Country Nursery School.

In 1998, a year after my visit, the parade committee altered the custom and moved the parade up a couple of weeks, to catch the school year before it ended, and make it easier to attract more high school bands. The parade committee also changed the date to connect the event to Juneteenth celebrations, which have spread from Texas and become popular in many African-American communities across the country. Of course, by June 19, 1866—the first Juneteenth celebration—the tradition of Independence Day celebrations was already a decade old in Lawnside, known at the time as Snow Hill. At that time, the community would display flags and residents would march and culminate the day with a big picnic, according to *A True Story of Lawnside* by Charles Smiley.

It isn't surprising that Lawnside is just getting around to recognizing Juneteenth in its celebration. The town is sometimes unintentionally tardy in absorbing traditions of other communities, since it has its own customs with deep roots and its own established ways. "There are three main events in town," Lloyd Henderson, an attorney and Lawnside native who still lives in the town, tells me. "There is the Lawnside Scholarship Club luncheon, the graduation at the Lawnside School, and the Fourth of July Parade and community picnic."

In 1994, a resident tried to add another event—a Kwanzaa celebration. This annual program, however, has yet to attract a large number of Lawnside residents, according to Wayne Bryant, a state senator who grew up in Lawnside. Most of the participants are from other places and probably like the idea of celebrating Kwanzaa in a black town—despite the benign neglect of the holiday by many of the residents.

Perhaps Kwanzaa is a little too young for a place with one of the Underground Railroad's oldest known safe houses. It was owned by Peter Mott, an abolitionist and early black landowner who helped hundreds of runaway slaves gain freedom. The Lawnside Historical Society is raising money to preserve the two-story house built in 1845.

In Mott's time, Snow Hill was a tiny settlement of freed and escaped slaves living in log cabins that were hidden in the woods so as to keep them from the sight of bounty hunters. The community was buffered by a town with a large Quaker population. Like the small black community of Gallia County, the town of Lawnside has a heritage rooted in escaping the horror and brutality of slavery and creating a civility and community beyond the grips of bondage.

One of the town's most prominent families, the Stills, descend from the legendary William Still, a founding resident who was one of the most noted conductors and organizers of the Underground Railroad. Some estimates are that 50 percent of the town is related to the Stills in one way or another. Then there is the Arthur family, five siblings who escaped from a Maryland plantation to begin a new free life in Snow Hill in 1840. "I know that you could count it as rich history and that type thing," says the Reverend James Benson, sixty-nine, the great-grandson of David Arthur, one of the five siblings. "But for the most part, I just lived what I found in front of me day to day. I've never really gone back into history."

The Bensons have trouble seeing the town as unique because their own lives seem so normal, ordinary, and regular. "We didn't even realize that we were special until somebody like you came in to write an article," says Ellen Benson, wife of James Benson. "We've been in *Ebony,* we've been in a lot of the other black papers that aren't even in circulation now, because somebody looked and said, 'Hey, we don't have a black police chief, we don't have a black mayor, we don't have all this—you are unique.' We didn't realize that growing up. We thought that there were lots of places that were completely black governed."

On Saturday, June 28, 1997, Ellen Benson is up at 7:30 in the morning to begin getting her five granddaughters ready for the parade. When she steps outside her ranch-style stone-and-wood frame house, she revels in the good parade weather. There isn't a potentially disruptive cloud in sight. Like most Lawnsiders, she wants to make it through this day without an umbrella.

James Benson, a musician, retired music teacher and contractor, and now an African Methodist Episcopal (AME) minister, met Ellen in Sunday school. They have known each other for as long as either can remember. Ellen, a retired Lawnside postmaster, says that she doesn't know how her family arrived in the area, but she traces her ancestors' presence in South Jersey to the eighteenth century. Both James and Ellen Benson are products of old Lawnside Republican families. Her father, John Jackson, was mayor of Lawnside in the 1940s. James Benson's father, Leonard Benson, was school-board president during the same period.

James and Ellen raised three daughters who are now rearing their families in other places—Sicklerville, New Jersey; Randallstown, Maryland; and Mitchelville, Maryland. But the granddaughters always visit for the parade, and the Bensons use this opportunity to educate the children about Lawnside, which means teaching them about family. Today, for instance, James and Ellen will inevitably direct their grandchildren's attention to what is now the Warwick Country Nursery School. It was formerly the firehouse and was built by her father and grandfather, who were carpenters and builders whose work still stands throughout the town. In addition, the granddaughters rarely make a trip to town without a visit to the Mount Piscah AME church, where their grandparents met.

Founded in 1792, the brown wood-shingle church is the first building inside the town's limits if you enter via the Lawnside exit from Route 295 south. The turn places you on Warwick Road, one of the town's busiest streets. It houses most of the businesses that lend the town its character, while the other busy road, White Horse Pike, merely carries traffic through Lawnside and into neighboring towns. On Warwick, there's the Pit Stop Transmission Center, Artique Designs, the Lawnside post office, the Warwick Country Nursery School, and the old Lawnside School, which now houses the office of the town's doctor. The most commanding site is the tower of a church, not on the street but still in the driver's view. The church's original white building would be seventy-five years old, but is now just a memory. The new Grace Temple Baptist Church, built in 1984, is the tallest building in town. It might look odd in the same postcard with some of the aging stone-and-wood frame houses on Warwick, but such a portrait would accurately reflect the diversity in the hodgepodge of structures that defines Warwick's character. The houses are scattered among businesses like the Mademoiselle Beauty Shop and Friendship Barber Shop, the Carl Miller funeral home, and, with its red, black, and green awning, the Nile Valley Book store, an operation launched by a Philadelphia entrepreneur that closed a few months after the parade. Nearby, too, is Lawnside's two-story municipal building.

Ellen Benson probably knows the details of the 1.4 square mile town better than most. As the town's postmaster for thirty-five years, she oversaw the expansion of the town's postal system from the days when residents picked up their mail at the post office to the growth of today's delivery routes. Benson's career in the post office began in 1950, when she was a junior in high school. She noticed that the postmaster was busy at Christmas. "I just said to the lady, 'Don't you need some help at Christmas?' and she said, 'Yes.'"

Benson worked part-time at the post office through high school but didn't plan on a career there. Her eyes were on college, though at the time it was not easy for Lawnside youth to prepare for higher education. Like her Lawnside peers, she attended the all-black Lawnside School. Founded in the 1920s and operated by the Lawnside school board, the school goes to the eighth grade. After that, most students head for the predominantly white Haddon Heights High School, five miles from Lawnside. At Haddon Heights, Lawnside youth in Ellen Benson's time were routinely steered away from the college track and pushed into general-education courses. That held true until the sixties, according to Benson and several other residents. (It wasn't an uncommon pattern, actually, for black youth attending integrated public schools in the North during the days of school segregation in the South.) "Except for a few instances here and there, they [Haddon Heights guidance counselors] didn't encourage us to take a curriculum that would set us up for college," says James Benson. "And yet there were those who took college-bound curriculum anyway. But for the most part, they [school officials] were interested in our athletic abilities."

"It wasn't 'til later years that we began to challenge what was happening as far as our young folk were concerned," adds Ellen Benson.

Ellen Benson says that African Americans had to be well beyond above average to ward off the school's discouragement from taking college-track courses. Since she was near the top of her class, Ellen didn't face as many raised eyebrows as other peers might have when she chose courses like chemistry. Ellen was such a good student, in fact, that she won the coveted Lawnside Scholarship Award, an honor bestowed by a group of Lawnside women who formed the scholarship club in 1945. "They [the Lawnside Scholarship Club] grew out of a postwar group that had some money left over after the war was over, and they decided to give fifty dollars to the person from Lawnside with the highest-ranking academic average at Haddon Heights," Ellen, a member of the group today, explains. "And they gave that amount, fifty dollars, for at least six years until 1952, when I was the highest one."

Benson became the first to receive $150. "They were very proud to give one hundred fifty dollars," she remembers. "And that paid my whole tuition at Temple University for one year. Can you believe that?"

During the Christmas holidays of her sophomore year at Temple, Benson took a break from college that continues to this day. One of the full-time postal clerks in Lawnside became sick. Benson was asked to work full-time, and, seven years later, she became the town's postmaster.

Ellen Benson and others say that many Lawnsiders became accustomed to good jobs during the 1950s and were not as entrepreneurial as the previous generation. Most of the men worked in area plants, such as Radio Corporation of America, in nearby Cherry Hill, and Campbell's, in Camden, or in government jobs. Most of the women were homemakers or teachers, or took the bus from Lawnside into some of the neighboring towns to do domestic work for wealthy families.

The town was known to black outsiders then for Evesham Avenue, a popular strip called "the Park." There, one could buy corn on the cob at Delores Soul Food, or go next door to the L&J Barbecue Palace, or maybe to Hill Street Seafood. Across the street was the Cotton Club. That strip is gone. But, nearly a mile away, Lawnside's piece of White Horse Pike is still busy with a Pathmark, Radio Shack, Home Depot, Jiffy Lube, Kentucky Fried Chicken, Blockbuster, and McDonald's, among other commercial establishments. And the Bensons do not miss the park, for it attracted large crowds of outsiders on the weekends, and they appreciate the chain stores' boost to the town's economy. Of course, when the Pathmark and Jefferson Ward Stores opened there in the late sixties, their location was advertised as the intersection of Route 295 and White Horse Pike—without a mention as to the town in which the intersection was located, according to many residents.

Not all of the new businesses were welcome, however. In fact, in the late eighties, many residents were outraged at the opening of the White Horse Lounge, located on the town's border. When the white owner of the lounge applied for the liquor permit, he said that the establishment would be a "sports cabaret," according to town officials. It didn't take long after the opening for Lawnside residents to discover that there was a strip club in town. Members of one church picketed the club, and residents remember a couple of arguments between the black church "ladies" and the white strippers outside the joint. The club eventually closed for several violations discovered in a sting operation that originated in the state attorney general's office, at the urging of state senator Wayne Bryant, one of Lawnside's favorite sons.

Other changes in the town bother the Bensons. They miss the days when the town's government would check with the five churches before planning a major meeting or event to ensure that it wouldn't conflict with important church activities. They also cherish the time when a Republican-controlled Lawnside borough council was not as impossible as, say, an agnostic in a pulpit or, more realistically, a secularist with the audacity to challenge school prayer at the Lawnside School. Today, organized school prayer is banned, and teachers are not empowered with paddles. Those are two reasons why James Benson started a Christian school. He closed it a few years ago because of resources and declining enrollment, but he vows to reopen the school one day. "I had been on the school board, yes, and I knew there were discipline problems in the school. I know when they started . . . right after they came out with the law that teachers couldn't do this, couldn't do that as far as discipline was concerned—"

"You mean paddling," I say.

"Yes, yes. I was on the board when the government really started taking charge rather than allowing the community to deal with their children according to the way it was when I came through. I saw the changes beginning to happen then. . . . We were slipping away from ministering to the total person. We were losing the common touch. And then I began to realize why it was necessary for this Christian school."

"Every day, we had fifteen minutes of what was called morning exercise," says Ellen Benson of her own school days. "It began with 'The Star-Spangled Banner,' the salute to the flag, the Lord's Prayer, and reading of Scriptures. And then we sang some songs. Our grandchildren just laughed yesterday when I told them that one of the songs we sang was 'Oh! Susanna.' And we used to sing songs like 'Home on the Range,' and then, of course, during the war, we sang all those war songs, the 'Marine Hymn,' 'Anchors Aweigh,' all of them. We knew all of them. Sang them every morning. And one interesting thing—this is how ignorant we were: some of the songs were making fun of our race. One of the songs I remember singing was 'Old Black Joe.' We sang that . . . of course, we're only eight, nine, ten. . . . You raised your hand and asked, 'May I sing something?' And those were the songs that we sang."

"And you didn't know that the song was derogatory?" I ask.

"Oh, no, we didn't take 'em as derogatory," Ellen Benson says. "We learned later they were. But we were just so isolated, sheltered. . . . I always say our girls [her daughters] grew up sheltered. . . ." And Benson says her childhood was even more sheltered. "You were in your own little shell where everything was just beautiful. You were taken care of, you were fed, and that's why my husband said, 'We were poor and didn't know it.'"

"The bottom line was, we were Negroes then," James Benson picks up. "And Negroes had accomplished something down through the years. Negroes—Negroes who really had accomplished something. . . . What has the black accomplished? We have identified ourselves as a different species rather than being proud of who we are. We've separated ourselves. Why do I have to be separate? Let me be me."

I am initially stunned by James Benson's comments painting days of "Negro" life as progressive and "black" life as the opposite. What James Benson says seems to contradict what James Brown sang—"Say it loud, I'm black and I'm proud." But Benson is saluting the fact that with limited resources, African Americans in Lawnside built a town through discipline and resistance to the racist ideas permeating America. It happened when he was a Negro, not a black man. Today, he doesn't see the same commitment to community—though I've seen postmodern variations of it across the country. The lack of that commitment provides the foundation of Benson's appreciation of the days when the word—*Negro*—was just a reference to a people. Nowadays, some see it as a dirty word that signifies a superficial dignity resting on a contentment with a small, exclusive, and unequal piece of the American pie.

Benson's expressed disdain for separatism is also striking, given his choice to live in a town where 98 percent of the residents are of the same race. But Benson insists that there is no contradiction, explaining that the comfort of living in a hometown, not the fact that he shares the same race as almost all of the town's population, keeps him in Lawnside. That the culture of his hometown has evolved with a singularly African-American flavor wasn't his making, but largely the result of the tradition of racism in America—born before the Bensons. The horror of slavery, and the need to escape it, forced the founding of Snow Hill. Then, the legacy of slavery—its impact on American racial dynamics—compelled the eventual growth of the area into Lawnside, which was officially incorporated as a town in 1926. Indeed, several elements of the old Lawnside culture could exist in a multiracial community today—if members of the various racial groups were willing to overlook race and concentrate on their common conservative ethos. But such a community isn't the Bensons' beloved hometown, which provides a comfort that eliminates much of the Bensons' racial radar. "You're black, I'm black, okay, fine, but I don't have to make an issue of it," says Benson.

The Bensons have lived nearly all of their lives in a town where blackness was never much of an issue. It is the absence of racism as an overt and continuous intrusion that helps to produce a community with many people who don't see race as an issue or a stimulant of bitter feelings. That is how "Old Black Joe" could become just another song to many residents and not a piece to the tune of Elaine Armstrong's racist collectibles in Gallia County. But even as the children sang "Old Black Joe" at the Lawnside School, counselors at Haddon Heights High School steered Lawnside students away from college-track courses. I can't help but wonder if the obliviousness to the degrading lyrics has anything to do with the lack of protest voiced over such academic steering, which didn't really become contentious in Lawnside and Haddon Heights until the sixties. I also wonder if the "poor and didn't know it" attitude breeds naïveté and produces an acceptance of the status quo that does little to nurture activism or even an intolerance of subtle forms of racial injustice. Such an outlook, sometimes reeking of pride and nobility, nevertheless seems to blind one to covert fists of inequality that can't be equalized by the virtues of independence and an unyielding work ethic. As Melvin L. Oliver and Thomas M. Shapiro note in *Black Wealth, White Wealth: A New Perspective on Racial Inequality*, the white middle class has inherited economic advantages through very friendly government policies, of preferential treatment from the Southern Homestead Act of 1866 to the Federal Housing Administration, which offered loans in the 1930s and '40s that were mostly distributed to the emerging suburbs—many of which had covenants that banned black families. Lawnside was born without the help of favorable government policy, which is one reason why the town, while solidly middle and working class, doesn't boast the kind of upper-middle-class wealth and amenities that is common in the neighboring towns of Haddonfield, Tavistock, Cherry Hill, and Haddon Heights.

Those inequities are not mentioned when James and Ellen Benson reminisce about the old Lawnside. Their longings parallel the nostalgic views that many African Americans express for old segregated communities, some of whose social and economic stability eroded with the flight of the middle class. But the Bensons are not products of a dying place or one whose glory lives through landmark-status buildings that coexist with signs of socioeconomic decline. While Lawnside does not possess the wealth of some of its neighbors, the town has not changed for the worse, economically, because of integration. Thanks to a larger professional class, Lawnside is more prosperous today than ever before. Most of the town's high school graduates go on to four-year colleges, and most of the other graduates go to community colleges. That wasn't the case when James and Ellen graduated from high school.

The town's growth parallels the expansion of the black middle class as it grew from the blue-collar jobs of the postwar era to the much larger and still-evolving professional class today. Lawnside has been able to hold and attract a middle-class population in the face of integration without the lure of "executive" housing that draws scores of professional families to suburban neighborhoods in DeKalb County outside Atlanta and in Prince Georges County, Maryland.

What the Bensons miss is their own version of a Rockwellian America. While they admire the civil-rights movement, they scorn many of the other social changes that came with the sixties and transformed the social fabric of their town. From their perspective, those changes came when the word *Negro* became derogatory. So, to the Bensons, an appreciation for the term

Negro is not a valuation of that term or even what it represents to many African Americans. Instead, it represents the couple's desire for a return of the old culture of Lawnside—largely religious, extremely conservative, and devoutly cohesive. In the Bensons' view, that culture was a chief ingredient in the town's ability to be itself, a place that they and the generations before them built and sustained by often ignoring the odds of American racism. "This might sound crazy, but it's real," asserts James Benson. "So many people have come into town now and have adopted ways of other cultures . . . that in itself is enough to start changing the foundation of who we really are. This is not a put-down for 'em, don't misunderstand me, but those who have come have come, for the most part, from various schools are have, let's say, Egyptian teachers. And they come with Egyptian ideas. And that's pulling away from the basic fundamental ways of the folk who were originally here in this town."

"A new, or just a different, type folk came in. There was a feeling [of] who was old Lawnsiders and who was outsiders," says Ellen Benson. "So, you see some progress because as more people came in, you became financially able to do more things here in town, but then that oneness just disappeared."

The Parade Today

L AWNSIDE'S quiet and residential Tillman Avenue is the organizing point of the parade. At 8:00 A.M., the street doesn't seem possessed by the rush of a parade that is scheduled to begin in two hours. The only sign of something grand on the way is a few papers and an electronic organizer on a card table on the corner. Morris L. Smith, the parade's marshall, stands at the table and grips a walkie-talkie. His youngest son, Stephen, twenty-five, sits at the table. The father and son study the parade's lineup and draw one conclusion: too many cars. "The problem is, as people get older, they want to ride instead of walk it," says Morris L. Smith.

Dallas Grundy, twenty-five, Stephen's best friend since their days as high school classmates, joins them at the table. He will help organize the parade once again this year. "I think in about half an hour more it'll become a little bit more hectic as people start to fall into the back and we start to actually kick the parade off," says Grundy, a graduate student in business at Rutgers. "But even that is not hectic. It's just a lot of excitement, a lot of energy. And it's always a smooth day."

Grundy, who grew up in Lawnside, says he never knew the parade defied an ugly stereotype until he left Lawnside for college. At Rutgers, he learned that many people—black and white—consider blacks and violence to be inseparable and trouble an inevitable consequence when large crowds of African Americans gather. "It is a common school of thought that [states] when massive groups of people, especially of African descent get together, it can't be a peaceful and fun-loving day. And in the twenty-four years that I've grown up in Lawnside, there has never been an incident at a parade," he tells me.

Tillman is a street of tidy and modest homes, many of them prefabricated. Few houses in Lawnside are gaudy, or even tastefully plush like the colonials or Victorians that one may find in Washington's Gold Coast, Prince Georges County's Mitchelville, Detroit's Palmer Woods, or in the neighboring majority-white New Jersey towns of Tavistock and Haddonfield. This is clearly a proud town of middle- and working-class homeowners—many of whom exude a comfort with simplicity.

Tilman borders Warwick Hills, one of the newest neighborhoods in Lawnside. It was developed by an African-American entrepreneur. The houses there are a little fancier, and it is easy to discern that the community was built in the seventies, as most of the homes are ranches or split-levels with brick foundations and aluminum siding. A few of the newcomers who purchased those houses didn't really want to live in Lawnside. Some had seen their inner-city neighborhoods decline in ways that characterize the American perception of a community that prefixes itself with the word black. A black town wasn't what these folks had in mind when they moved to Lawnside, and this was especially true for those who moved onto a street bordered by a fence separating it from the country club next door in upscale Tavistock, according to Benson. There, the family median income is $150,001 per year, compared to $41,429 in Lawnside. "That's how those builders got them to buy, saying, 'You're going to be neighboring the Tavistock Country Club,'" says Ellen Benson, referring to the newcomers who came in the seventies. "They were even told that that was going to be their address—Tavistock. One lady was putting Tavistock on her mail, and I said, 'You're going to have to change this. You live in Lawnside.' She said, 'Oh, no, the builder told me I live in Tavistock.' And then she came back to the post office and said, 'Well, how come you're getting my mail?'

"One group of people even went up to Tavistock and tried to vote and they were told, 'No, you live in Lawnside. You have to go back to Lawnside.' They wanted to come in thinking they were better. . . . They kind of thought that Lawnside was a dumb little section of black people who had never gone anywhere. . . .

"It's sad, it's sad. People can be swayed by something like that. They wanted to better themselves. . . . so I can halfway see how they were thinking, coming out of those areas in Philadelphia that they came."

Before Warwick Hills, Benson says, there were not really neighborhoods in Lawnside. "No, no special neighborhoods," she states. "We were all just Lawnside."

• • •

At 8:30, Walter "Butch" Gaines, fifty-nine, is cooking hot dogs in the tradition of the "oneness" that James and Ellen Benson mourn. His station is the Lawnside park, where the parade ends. When it is over, the participants and spectators can count on a hot dog cooked by Gaines and other volunteers and paid for by the Lawnside Fourth of July Committee.

Gaines, a former mayor and retired teacher, says that one big change in Lawnside is the bus he remembers seeing nearly every day when he was growing up in the fifties. "During that time, there was one bus to take you from Lawnside to Haddonfield," says Gaines. "A lot of women would go to Haddonfield to get housework. They don't have to do that today. You've got black people here who've got people coming to clean their houses. Our lifestyles have changed."

By now, I am accustomed to idyllic descriptions of a Lawnside childhood. Gaines describes his youth with some of the same bucolic terms as the Bensons: he too was "poor and didn't know it." He recalls one television in his neighborhood—every child on the block would crowd around after school. As Gaines describes how children in Lawnside used to make their toys, my mind travels to the Gallia County fairgrounds and the drinkers at the Emancipation. J.C., Duke, and others there told me the same thing: beat-up tires would be shaped into scooters; likewise, as in Gallia County, pigs and chickens wouldn't get a second look on a Lawnside street. In both places, it was the days of preserving and canning, of "yes, ma'am" and "yes, sir."

"It wasn't anything about unhappy childhood and all of this kind of stuff and [going] hungry . . . Hey—you could always get something to eat," remembers Gaines. "In the summertime . . . my mother would always put up preserves, peaches, pies . . . made applesauce and put all that stuff in the jar for wintertime. That's how we got through the winters, man. We don't do that stuff no more. We would work in the kitchen all day long putting all that stuff together, and we'd go out and pick blackberries, get a pot together for blackberry dumplings. We could eat of that pot all day long, man. If we're going to make applesauce, we'd make some apple dumplings and we'd pick some peaches, or they'd buy peaches from the farm or somewhere, and they had peach dumplings, peach cobblers. Cook that stuff in the pot, man, eat it all day long. Talk about hungry? I didn't know I was poor until I grew up to be an adult."

Still, for all that Gaines's recollections share with so many others I have heard, they are the first that appreciate the complexity of what many others simply see as the "good old days" in Lawnside and many other pre-sixties African-American communities. He tempers the romanticism when he recalls the ways in which elders may have unintentionally reinforced ideas of black intellectual inferiority as they prepared youth to compete at Haddon Heights High School. When Gaines reached high school, Lawnside residents were just beginning to question academic tracking and encouraging more of their youth to pursue college-preparatory courses. Gaines says that the elders, in the process of grooming African-American youth to compete with whites in high school, may have indirectly sent the message that whites were inherently smart and blacks had to work extra hard to compensate for the white advantage in intelligence, which, of course, was really only the advantage of power predicated on racism. "I always had the impression that all white kids were smart. I don't know if that is something they [Lawnside's elders] instilled in me when I left Lawnside School for Haddon Heights. They would say, 'When you go to Haddon Heights, you've got to do this and you got to do that and you're going to be around white kids.' So I always had this impression that white kids were smart. And when I got down there, I said, 'Shoot, these kids are dumber than I am.' And not a whole lot of them were smarter than I was."

Gaines received the message that many African-American youth received when going into what could be racially hostile arenas: Do everything right by the book. Out of twenty Lawnside students in his class, only five—Gaines being one—pursued the college-bound track. And those five were more than in previous years, he recalls. Then, even after graduation, many school officials didn't expect him to go to college. Around the time he entered Winston-Salem State University in North Carolina as a freshman in September 1955, his mother received a call from a Haddon Heights guidance counselor who was looking for someone to wash windows. "My mother said 'No, sorry, he's not here, you know, he's in college.' It was like silence on the phone . . . she [the counselor] couldn't believe it."

When Gaines graduated, in 1959, he returned home and soon began what would become a thirty-seven-year career as a teacher at the Lawnside School. He was now an adult citizen of the town, in possession of the kind of young, homegrown energy that the two local political parties saw as an asset. The Democrats were riding a high, as they would soon enter the Kennedy years, while the older members of the Lawnside Republican club were starving for fresh faces and ideas to boost a group that had once been the dominant player in the town's politics. Gaines himself doesn't know whether he grew up in a Republican or a Democratic household. His father, a clothes presser, died when Gaines was a sophomore in high school, and he and his mother, a homemaker, didn't discuss politics. In the end, Gaines settled on a party in the way he chooses a favorite football team: "I always root for the underdog. It's just me. I joined the Republican Party because they seemed like they were the underdog."

The Republicans' days as weaklings in Lawnside were indeed relatively recent when Gaines joined. There was a time when most blacks who voted were Republicans, preferring to associate with the party of Lincoln, and, naturally, the GOP, with its connections to the abolitionist movement, would have a rich heritage in a town with deep roots in the Underground Railroad. But by the time Gaines was ready to pick a party, those roots were distant enough that he was free to make a choice in which race needn't figure. He didn't think to become a Republican because the Democrats were perceived as racist, or vice versa. Today, the partisan choices in the town are not as removed from the larger political and racial landscape that compels many African Americans nationwide to choose the Democratic Party, and Lawnside is a Democratic town. Residents have overwhelmingly voted against Republican candidates in every modern presidential election.

"We had a club and clubhouse here," Gaines says, recalling the party's stronger days in Lawnside. "I don't know how we lost it, but we lost it. We would have dinners and dances."

You could call Gaines a Clinton Republican, because he admits to voting for the opposition party's candidate over Bob Dole. Still, Gaines, like the Bensons, insists that he's devoted to the local Republican organization. Interestingly, many of the town's Democrats proved to be more loyal to him than their own party when he ran for mayor during the Reagan and Bush years. "The first time I ran, I ran against a lady, and I don't think we were ready for a lady mayor at the time."

Gaines served two terms as a Republican mayor, with a Democratic borough council. "Black Republicans catch hell here. And they [Democrats] use it."

In elections, Gaines could never count on Reagan's coattails for help. In fact, it behooved him to keep a little bit of distance between himself and Reagan. "When I was running, they [Democrats] said, 'Oh, he just wants to spout Reagan's philosophy and all of that. If you elect the Republicans here, they're going to cut your Social Security.' And people believe this stuff. That's what happens when people don't think for themselves and let somebody else do their thinking for them. How can we, here, locally, a little black town, a mile and a half square, three thousand people, how can we cut their Social Security? But you have some people who believe this."

When it comes to social spending, Gaines is a liberal when compared to his political archrival, state Senator Wayne Bryant, an attorney who is the town's leading Democrat. While Gaines differs from fellow Republican leaders across the country who supported President Clinton's welfare-reform bill, Bryant was the author of New Jersey's controversial welfare law, proposed nearly two years before Clinton was even elected to his first term. In many ways, the president's bill was modeled on the New Jersey law, which cuts off benefits to mothers if they have additional children while on welfare. "What I did on welfare reform was not very creative," claims Bryant. "It's much of what I learned in Lawnside about family. I come from a community that believes strongly in family. Man, wife, and children. That's how I was raised. That's what Lawnside was all about. That's where I learned it all. Second, you go out and you produce something. You just can't say, 'I love my family,' and not be willing to do anything about it. Why should poor folks or any set of people have other choices the rest of us don't have? I can't sit there and say I want to enlarge my family: I have to think about work every day. Can I afford it?"

"It was wrong," says Gaines, referring to the Bryant and Clinton bills. "I thought the climate was wrong. I mean, twenty, twenty-five years ago, yes—there were plenty of jobs around then. . . . But what kind of jobs can they do now that would replace welfare and allow them to raise a family? Everything is downsizing. They're closing up. They're moving out of here. You have people out there who have two degrees and can't get a job. Now, what kind of job are people on welfare going to be able to get? The majority of them are dropouts and everything else. To me, I just thought it was twenty-five years too late. Twenty years ago, you had places where people could work. But today we've become a service economy. We don't make things anymore. You have a lot of people on welfare who would gladly take a job over welfare, [but] they can't get jobs."

While Gaines is cooking hot dogs, Wayne Bryant arrives on Tillman Avenue, shaking hands and joking with residents. As a seventh-grader, Bryant was a student in Gaines's first class at the Lawnside School. By then, Bryant's family had fled the Republican Party. Bryant's grandfather was an old Lawnside Republican, but now the state senator is one of New Jersey's most powerful Democrats. In Lawnside, he's more powerful than his younger brother, Mayor Mark Bryant, who is also a chief operating officer of a health-care company. Still, Mark Bryant, the part-time mayor, will ride in the front of the parade, and Wayne Bryant will walk. His explanation for doing so is fashioned in terms fit for a politician: "One of the reasons I walk the whole route is that I was born and raised here. My family has been here since the late 1700s, and it's a town that nurtured me. . . . The town . . . deserves to see a homegrown boy."

Wayne Bryant, a founding partner of a law firm boasting a roster of *For-*

tune 500 clients, is the first lawyer in the family, but he's not the first politician. With a bit of braggadocio, Bryant doesn't hesitate to share the black firsts that Lawnside has produced for the county and state's political history—most of them happen to be members of his family.

"The majority of African Americans live in Camden City, but I don't think it's by accident that this town produced the first black freeholder in this county, which is about seventeen percent African American . . . "

That freeholder was his Uncle Horace.

"I became the second freeholder. Lawnside produced the first African-American assemblyperson in all of southern New Jersey. That was me. Then the first African-American senator outside of Essex County, and the first African-American senator who won in a majority-white district."

That senator was also Wayne Bryant.

"This town has belied all the mistruths that they have said about African Americans over the years," he says. "They say that African Americans don't vote—we vote more than any other town in the neighboring communities. We are always in the top three for turnout in the county, even in off year elections . . . "

Without a doubt, Bryant loves his hometown. But his affection doesn't prevent him from chastising residents in ways that contradict some of the praise for the town that he spills into my tape recorder. Some residents describe a few borough-council meetings in which Bryant did not admire their citizenry, but rather scolded some for "having a welfare mentality" when they requested funding from the town for such things as a fence around the Lawnside park. Bryant counters that he was merely trying to remind them of the self-reliance that is inherent in the town's tradition. "I think there are times when we forget about our heritage and what has made this town. It wasn't government."

The debate between Bryant and Gaines on welfare illustrates the ways in which partisan politics in Lawnside has evolved in its own unique way, with leaders of both parties celebrating the virtues of self-reliance. The Republican version sees the values in entitlements and social engineering, while the free-enterprise Democrat says welfare recipients don't need a check to pay the bills but free tuition so they can "go out and produce something" in the market and take care of themselves and their families. Just as Gaines often finds himself in ideological sparring with fellow members of the GOP outside of Lawnside, Bryant's attacks on welfare often grow into relentless criticism of blacks in his own political party. "I'm going to be very candid here," Senator Bryant says. "African-American politicians may want to keep people uneducated and nonthinkers so they may not vote them out of office. Even the Black Caucus is absolutely one hundred percent wrong on the welfare reform. They had a prescription to keep people poor, and I disagree with that.

"If you give five hundred dollars a month in welfare, then the kind of jobs you give them couldn't allow them to live like that?" asks Gaines. "So, it doesn't make sense to me. Welfare reform is good, but what are you going to do for jobs? Where are the jobs coming from? . . . What are they going to do? You're talking about people who have a high school diploma or a couple years on a degree, they don't have a job . . . I'm telling you, man, everything is going up. Food is going up and everything else. The one good thing about welfare, at least they [the welfare recipients] . . . get health benefits and things. What's happening now is that places like Pathmark, they work them people twenty-two hours a week, just under the minimum so they don't have to pay them health benefits and all that other stuff, man. Part-time jobs. What about these people on welfare who have three and four kids? What kind of job is going to help them take care of all those kids." He pauses. "Man, how many kids you got?"

"Two," I say.

"You got two kids and you work, and you still catching hell, I bet," says Gaines. "So, what're they going to do? Most of the time you're talking about a welfare recipient, it's usually one parent in the house, typically the mom.

"I think the people out there who are on welfare, it's basically a temporary thing until they get themselves back on their feet. Somebody might be having a hard time and they'll say, 'Let me get on welfare until I can get back on my feet.'"

On the other side, "African Americans for too long have allowed too many folks to fall into poverty," Bryant argues. "And I don't believe you can survive as a race when you have this big disparity between the haves and the have nots. And we're doing nothing about it. We're sitting there just saying folks needed more money."

"Does racism still create poverty today?" I asked Bryant.

"Sure."

"How do you deal with the impact of racism?"

"Education. I mean, you got to give the people the opportunity. That's what it is . . . you can't take racism and say okay. . . . Race impacts poverty, so, therefore, since you happen to be black or Hispanic or some brown person, that's all right for you to be in poverty and not to change your lifestyle, and race is the whole cause of why you're in poverty—[that] is not true. Race is one of the factors. . . . Race or racism is going to be one of the factors; it's not the total factor, (especially) if you're sitting there with a third-grade education. [Then] education is a bigger factor than racism. My thing was to put the opportunity out there to help them [welfare recipients]. Let's not talk about loving your kids—how can you love your kids and sit there and not do anything about it? How can you not go back to school? Yes, school is tough work. It's hard. But if you love your kids, that's what you have to do.

"I can't make a prescription to make you successful, but I can tell how you're going to fail on the market. If, in fact, you're uneducated, you will fail on the market.

"If you are on welfare and you want to go to community college or four-year college, we'll pay for that too. People don't tell you about all these kinds of things. . . . That's part of the law. That's how progressive it was. I took welfare reform and even said to conservatives, 'If you're about families, then this is how you got to do it. You've got to put families on the right track. You've got to help welfare recipients go to school so they can get off welfare.'"

By 9:00, the Bumble Bees have arrived on Tillman Avenue. They wear short, yellow pleated skirts, white boots, and white blouses. The Bumble Bees are a drill team composed of eight- to twelve-year-old girls. Some of their parents stand on the sidewalk with clicking cameras as the girls practice. The parade hasn't even started.

Members of the Smith family are making their way up and down the street, taking cues and directions from Morris L. Smith, the family patriarch. Smith left the Garden State for college in the late fifties, receiving a degree in chemistry from the University of Michigan. He eventually settled in Lawnside and landed at the Scott Paper Company. There for thirty-three years, he rose up the scientific hierarchy and holds three patents on sanitary paper products. In 1994, he retired as technology manager and now runs his own product-development consulting business.

Of all of Morris's three sons, the youngest, Stephen, takes the most active role in organizing the parade. His father is still the marshal, but Stephen is the parade's chief soldier. He is clean-cut, with a neat goatee. His manners are mild and, on the surface, bespeak an upwardly mobile, churchgoing family with a mother, an educator and a father, a retired company man. He is the son of a father who, as the president of the Lawnside school board, didn't use his influence to overturn the school suspension of one of his sons for using profanity in the school yard. But the elder Smith didn't depend on a school system to drill in the consequences of such unruly behavior: he credits homemade switches from the family's backyard.

Today Stephen J. Smith lives with his parents, and there is no need to ever tear a bush. Yet Smith does take road trips. "I just bought a new Jeep," he says with a chuckle.

Stephen J. Smith, Jeep driver, occasionally cruises down some streets and blasts one of his favorite riding companions—the hip-hop music of his generation, music he wouldn't dare play at the table or anywhere near a Lawnside elder. "I love all the music," he says, "I can just make the distinction between entertainment and real life. My girlfriend has a small child, and I understand that she shouldn't be exposed to certain lyrics, certain videos, certain atmosphere, and that's fine with me."

Admittedly, Smith doesn't have much time for idle cruises in his Jeep. He works full-time, forty hours a week as a supervisor of a group home for victims of head injuries, and is also a full-time student at Temple University, majoring in business administration. It's his second try at college. He's only a few credits away from graduation, but not close enough to ward off the comments of some family "outsiders." They look inside and see his two older, high-achieving lawyer brothers. In a small town, he isn't free of sibling comparisons. "It was never anything that my family would bring up. Other people would compare or make casual comments about it. I would think about it for a minute. . . . It was always in the back of my mind, always has been. I guess part of my desire to complete college comes from my family. Well, I know they would support me if I didn't; my father would be a little disappointed. . . . "

At eighteen, Smith left Lawnside for the other coast. He started college as an engineering student at USC, but dropped out during his second year and worked full-time at United Parcel Service.

After six years, he left California, and his Lawnside network of friends helped to make the transition to home easier. The director of the Bumble Bees, a classmate, tipped him to the job opening at the group home. Still, Smith returned home considering several options, one of them to be an entrepreneur. So why wouldn't he immediately forget about college and throw himself toward that goal, à la Bill Gates or Puff Daddy or a twenty-something white boy without a college degree but with visions of big bucks to be made in places like Silicon Valley or Alley? Tossing college aside is a risk that violates the Smiths' way of thinking, characteristic of upwardly mobile black America, which regards a college degree as a weapon against racism. A degree is also a big source of pride in a town with a heritage of youth encountering guidance counselors who didn't consider the town's teenagers college material. "African Americans are forced to see it that way," says Stephen Smith. "They won't always get the breaks or small opportunities that normally other cultures may attain. We have to kind of strive extra harder and work twice as hard to prove ourselves . . . because we have a stereotype that's been put on us and that's still there."

The stereotypes extend from the collectibles on Elaine Armstrong's table at Gallia County's Emancipation. The legacy of those items helps to perpetuate the idea that African Americans must jump higher than whites to succeed, an idea that permeates the black side of the racial divide: blacks must be "twice as good" to receive just treatment in the professional world. An opposing view on the white side expresses itself in perceptions of blacks as unqualified beneficiaries of affirmative action and preferential treatment. Those ideas push matters to another level: now many blacks say that they must also be doubly qualified to ward off white perceptions of blacks as mere affirmative action tokens. It is all enough to drive many blacks to hop off the white American swing altogether and try to create their own opportunities through entrepreneurship or working for black-owned companies, but these are not plentiful enough to employ the majority of African Americans. Some merely settle their personal lives away from the racial divide, in places like Lawnside. But Stephen Smith disagrees with fellow residents who consider Lawnside a refuge from racial issues. "Race did matter here to me," he says. "I always remember growing up knowing this was a black town. It was not something that we said to one another every day, but it was always understood that this was a black community, even in the positive sense."

Smith says that Lawnside is an open black town that doesn't burden its small white minority with the kind of discrimination blacks might find in a town that was 98 percent white. "We have a few white residents here. We've always been willing to accept anyone who wanted to be a part of the community. We have Puerto Rican residents here."

It was not always that way, if it ever was. According to a 1972 article in *Philadelphia* magazine, a young white couple teaching in the Camden school system had a difficult time buying a house in Lawnside, due to discrimination. Today, town leaders deny that whites are ever excluded. Of the town's 2,835 residents, 25 are white, many of them married to black residents. Town leaders say that there are so few white residents because few whites want to live in a majority-black town.

Stephen says that the idea of racial isolation is foreign to him because most of his friends are not black. He tells me of a basketball game the night before with white friends from Haddon Heights High School. The camaraderie, however, is different from what he will experience today: "There's a different outlook on things, especially being a white male. I don't have a problem with their outlook because I understand where they're coming from. . . . We talk about the things we both have in common—sports, work . . . [But] there's a level where you cut it off, certain things you can talk to people about, certain things you can't."

Smith says race is one of those things that he avoids discussing with whites. "It's naïve to say that we ignore it because we don't see it . . . but you've got to keep your sanity. If we have a relationship where we can talk about things we have in common, there's no need to go further or deeper and aggravate things. . . .

"There shouldn't be, but there are limits, and I probably do self-impose a lot of those limits, just because there is only so much I feel comfortable talking about because I think I can see his [a white male's] situation better than he can see my situation. I would be extremely surprised if a white man were understanding, not so much of my own personal situation, but our [African Americans'] situation as a whole. I would be surprised if he [a white male] could see a black man in this society and not pigeonhole him into some type of stereotype. I would probably get bothered by that . . . there's no need to even go there. . . .

"I went to a predominantly white school . . . and I spent more than enough time with white families in their homes and on vacation. . . . I know, to an extent, how some white children grow up and their advantages. I know that there are things that they would not understand from a white perspective about black society and growing up in a black atmosphere."

"What are those things?" I ask.

"It's a lot of things. The struggles that black men and black women have to go through, the kind of attitude that's given to people who have darker skin and the unwillingness to even sometimes just be talked to or interviewed for a job because of the way someone looks, and things like that. And those are the things that a white person usually does not have to think about. . . . They would look at my situation and say, 'Well, you don't have to look at that. You don't have to feel like that because of your situation,' because I have my parents here, because I've been able to work in good atmospheres. So they may not understand. . . .

I pose a question. "But what you are saying, in some ways, is antithetical to what President Clinton says he wants to accomplish in the Initiative on Race he has created. Do you think it's necessary to have this national conversation on race that Clinton has launched?"

"Well, I think if the idea trickles down to the base, to the smaller community levels, it may actually be good. Those people at Clinton's level, the politicians, have already worked out their ways and how to work with other people, to an extent."

Still, Smith doesn't want the conversation to trickle into his world. Race relations are not a priority in his everyday life. He's more absorbed with reconciling his commitment to Christianity with the moral values of his generation. "In past years, people were just accepting of God's word and just knew that you just had to be married if you had a child. . . . If you were pregnant, you had to get married . . . and nowadays, people are questioning that.

"I think it really has to be the parents who implement the understanding of the sexual act and sexual relationships and things of that nature. Even if a young child hears certain things through church, a young child may not understand those things. . . . And many young children may not always hear that sexual relationships should take place within the confines of marriage. They may not understand it, so I think it's the parents' responsibility to go back home and reimplement that—"

I interrupt. "Do you believe that? That the sexual act should only take place within the confines of marriage?"

"Yes," he replies.

"You do?"

"Yes," he repeats.

As a tail-end baby boomer, I am surprised to meet someone who doesn't see premarital sex as an inevitability. My own morality sees sex before marriage as a given, and marriage before children as the ideal. While religion does run deep in African-American culture, hormones are human, and this motivates my next question: "Do you live that—no premarital sex?"

"I try to. I believe sex should take place inside a situation where it's a loving relationship. It should be a relationship that is building toward . . . marriage. I'm in a stage where I'm still trying to work that out with my Lord, with my God, and understand that fully. . . . My parents say, 'That's something you need to work out between you and your God.' I'm not saying that everybody doesn't have the same God, but you have a special relationship with God. But that's a hard question. I know there are many people who don't even think about marriage, but they are in a monogamous relationship with one person, and they're good people. That's hard to get into . . . that's dangerous water to tread. You see a lot of cases where it's the single parent raising the child and is successful to a certain extent."

Smith says his girlfriend, Sara (not her real name), twenty-one, is one such person. She is, like him, a college student, but she is also a single mother and has very little contact with the father of her child. Smith hopes he, Sara, and her daughter will eventually become a family, reside in Lawnside, and build a future. But those dreams are not couched in naïve ideas about raising children in a black town to shield them from racism, stereotypes, and negative peer culture. While Smith says that the majority of his peers went to college, he can readily point to people "who I was in high school with who are now in prison . . . and who have basically fallen victim to that stereotype. They were choosing to lead that lifestyle that is stereotypical of our people and our males, and they got caught in stupid situations. . . . Lawnside is no different from the rest of society when it comes to that. We still suffer from the same sort of things that society suffers from."

At 9:15, Tillman Avenue still doesn't seem busy enough for a big parade, but crowds are forming and Morris Smith's rush is as familiar as the occasional complaints from leaders of organizations about their places in the line. This year, the Lawnside Democratic Club's members don't appreciate being too many cars behind the elected officials. "I rotate the Republican Club and the Democratic Club alternating years so that one is not in front of the other."

By 10:00, the streets of Lawnside finally do look like something extraordinary will soon happen. Tillman is a hectic rush, and spectators are finding the standing spots on other streets. The parade is scheduled to begin now, but some parents still rush children into lines while one adult scolds a few boys in Little League uniforms who've strayed away from their line and onto a well-manicured lawn.

At 10:22, the police chief sits in his car at the foot of Tillman, at the head of the parade. With the cue from Morris Smith, the siren on the chief's car sounds a few seconds and the blue light above twirls. The police car moves. The parade has begun.

The uniformed members of the Lawnside chapter of the Veterans of Foreign Wars march behind the police car and are followed by the Ladies' Auxiliary. The riding mayor, Mark Bryant, and his walking brother the state senator lead the rest of the parade—everyone from the bands to the Bumble Bees. There are twenty-three entries into the parade—it is truly a small-town parade.

From lawn chairs set out on the yards of houses on the parade's route, residents and friends sip lemonade and point to the children they know riding in the Warwick Country Nursery school car or walking with Little League teams, Boy and Girl Scouts troops, and other youth groups.

Hilda Picou's yard is one of the first on the parade's route. The matriarch of the Bryant family, Anna has a spot in that yard, as usual. She stays inside the house to avoid the heat until she receives word that the parade is moving her way. "Help the mayor's mother into the chair," Hilda Picou instructs younger relatives as Anna Bryant exits the house.

They help, smiling at the mayor's mother, and then turn their attention back on the crowd.

You can hear screams of "Hey, baby!" throughout the street as elders spot the children they know. Children who are not in the parade cheer the town's volunteer fire fighters on their trucks.

Most spectators, a few with video cameras, are on the streets in front of businesses, churches, and houses, standing as they would in their own yards. And most dress casually, in picnic clothes. That is why Juanita Gibson and Donica Venable are noticeable. All they need are crowns, and they could easily ride in one of the convertibles. In less than two hours, Gibson and Venable are scheduled to walk down the aisle as bridesmaids in a friend's wedding at the Mount Zion United Methodist Church, only a few blocks away, but they couldn't miss the parade. So, draped in long gowns, they stepped away from the wedding preparations to cheer their neighbors, relatives, and, most important, their seven-year-old daughters, who are stepping with the Bumble Bees.

"We're going dancing at eleven o'clock," jokes Donica.

"No, but seriously," says Juanita. "This is a nice tradition. Everybody comes back. You see people that you don't usually see, and it's just something that you grew up with, so you just keep coming back for it."

Only one of the town's seven police officers is on duty at the parade. It is an easy job watching over a peaceful parade; Augustus Wilmer rarely has to blow his whistle. It becomes difficult when I ask him what he thinks about the Fourth of July celebration.

"Ah, see, I'm getting ready to go into something I really didn't want to go into. . . ."

Finally, he sighs. "Well, first thing, the veterans that walked through, they salute the flag. When it becomes equal and everything is fair in this country, then I'll salute the flag. Not until then, you know what I mean? So the Fourth of July Parade is really nothing to me, not until things become more equal for us and white folks."

The tinge of bitterness in Wilmer's comments is piercing because it is so alien from virtually everything else I've heard from Lawnside residents on the subject of race. It is ironic (or even, perhaps, sublimely cogent) that the first person to share the most cynical and caustic interpretation of racial equality is the man guarding the celebration.

The After Party

THE parade empties into the Lawnside park. Art, book, clothing, and food vendors from Philadelphia and neighboring New Jersey towns tempt the crowd with displays. The Bumble Bees and other drill teams, though, don't have time to browse. Most get a free hot dog from Butch Gaines and rush toward a free spot of grass to keep practicing: a drill-team competition follows the postparade ceremony of prayer, "The Star-Spangled Banner," and speeches from the Bryant brothers and other officials.

Outside the park, Lawnside now looks naked to any eye who saw the street packed with people and teeming with noise just a few moments ago. The sidewalks are bare, and only a few cars pass through on the way to some other place. After walking the deserted streets for a few blocks, I hear another party near Borough Hall.

The hall is a two-story red-brick building that sits on a corner. It houses the borough council chambers as well as offices where the town's forty-two employees work. Next door is the firehouse, with its typical wide steel door lifted out of sight for the moment. Two fire trucks, hoses, and equipment rest in their spaces. A kitchen, dining room, and sleeping quarters are tucked away upstairs.

A radio at the firehouse booms a station playing hip-hop and R&B music. A police scanner plays as loud while some twenty volunteer firefighters, their wives or girlfriends, and children feast on ribs, potato salad, and a roasted pig, and drink from a keg of beer. The volume of the radio goes down at the sound of anything from the scanner that could signal an end to this party and the beginning of a mission.

By now, the men wear their formal volunteer firefighter uniforms in casual ways. The collars of their white shirts are open; their dry-cleaned blue jackets are on hangers. It was an early morning for them, preparing the three trucks for the parade. Most made an appearance at the park, but their main after-parade party is at the firehouse, and it is much like the gathering in the back of the Gallia County fairgrounds that belongs to the drinking men at the Emancipation. Minus the scanners, there are similarities in the sounds of both gatherings—uproarious laughter, loud talking, and jokes that get funnier with every beer. Both are parties of working-class men and their families that are separate from the larger established gatherings. Yet the Lawnside men gather in an official space in town. They are not in violation of anything. They do not gather with the threat of being dispersed by white folks in charge of black folks. Their behavior and its noise are probably as robust as a party of volunteer firefighters in any other town; here there is the freedom to be male, robust, and black without any stares or peculiar mock admiration of such behavior. That opportunity pulled Derek Johnson, twenty-seven, a paralegal at a Haddonfield law firm, past two towns to serve as a volunteer firefighter in Lawnside. Johnson, who grew up in and still lives in Voorhees, two miles from Lawnside, says that he never even thought of joining the fire department in his hometown. "I have had friends who joined this fire department," he says. "It's one of the best departments in Camden County, in my opinion. . . . My father is a firm believer in living in an integrated society . . . but . . . keeping a strong tie with your respective group. That's what I think. That's why we always have a strong relationship with Lawnside. And it's no different from all of the other ethnic groups out here."

Johnson's town of residence sometimes stirs jokes in the firehouse. "They always just want to joke around with you. You're a black white guy. You didn't grow up in Lawnside, so you don't know what's going on around here. That sort of thing. But it's all just jokes, though . . . if you get your feelings hurt easily, don't join Lawnside Fire Department, because if you can't take the heat, you will crack. But that doesn't bother me any . . . it's all in good fun."

Most of the men here are Lawnside natives—some are second- and even third-generation volunteer firefighters. Some grew up with this atmosphere, like the children here now for whom the fire trucks are giant toys that they climb on and off, under the eyes of elders. Days like this silently, subtly help to perpetuate the department, help to shape the youngsters into tomorrow's volunteers. A generation or two ago, many of today's—and yesterday's—volunteers played on the trucks and with the equipment when their parents gathered for social events at the firehouse. At home, they watched their fathers rush to scenes where Daddy's presence could prevent a tragedy. "Our whole family is just fire-department oriented, from my parents on down to my sons now," says Franklin Harper Sr., a Camden County sheriff's deputy and deacon at a Lawnside church. "Two of my sons are Camden City paid firemen and, also, volunteer firemen here. So we've been in it quite a while. It's a family thing."

Harper says that he learned how to fight fires from the elders in town. He recites the names of his teachers—last names only. They are familiar names to the Lawnside ear, so well known that the speaker, by habit, would not insult their memory by stating the full name of the Benson or Johnson of whom he speaks. "In those days, the old way of teaching was on-the-job training. That's how it was, and nowadays you've got schools to go to. You've got different schools: You've got pump training, you've got firefighter one, you've got firefighter two. Different things like that."

Harper is a sit-down storyteller. His hand rests on his knee. Younger firefighters sit for a minute and listen, then rush off and focus their attention on something else at the party. Harper's stories reach back to the more primitive days of Lawnside fire fighting, when he wasn't old enough to carry the water. Those were the times when bells were rung to signal fires. "They had a bell that they used to ring at Emlen Avenue and Bryant Avenue, and they had one up here at Ashland Avenue. They used to come out here with a steel hammer when they had fires, and the people would get their shovels and buckets and stuff and go out and fight brushfires and house fires with their buckets. After a while, they got a chemical truck—it was a horse-drawn chemical truck. When they got that, they were fighting fires with chemicals, [using] dry chemicals to extinguish it. And as time went on, they purchased a ladder truck. I think it was a hundred dollars or fifty or something like that. They used that. And as time went on, they just progressed and progressed.

"When we had the old firehouse, Mrs. Miller [of Miller's funeral home in Lawnside] would get out of her bed when we had fires. They would call her house and she would go across the street so that she could blow the whistle five times for fire, three times for the ambulance. It was all hours of the night.

"We fought a lot of brushfires back then—a lot. It's not as dangerous as a house fire or brushfires now. We had a lot of open brushes and open fields then. . . . We would get out and maybe take us all day to put out a brushfire. We'd get to the back end of town. When we would have a dump fire, we would just have to shuttle water from Charleston Avenue."

Now Harper's story and voice fall into a cadence: "Go to the hydrant, go to the fire. Go to the hydrant, go to the fire. Go to the hydrant, go to the fire."

Harper motions to the equipment in the house. "See that piece of equipment here? Top-notch. Rescue tools? We do our own rescue, we do our own fire fighting. We have home alarms, pagers . . . we have an automatic alarm system here. But the biggest thing is volunteerism—it's hard to get volunteers. It's just hard to get volunteers now in a world where everybody's got to get paid. Volunteering is a dying breed, definitely a dying breed. Because two people have to work for the family now, and they just don't have the time. And you have to spend quality time with the family."

Harper's eyes wander around the house and he refines his outlook on volunteers. Maybe half of the men here are in their twenties and thirties. Overall, the ages range from mid-twenties to late fifties. For many, events like this have become a way to spend quality time with the family.

A tragedy helped inspire Omar Higgs, twenty-seven, to volunteer. When he was twelve years old, his four-year-old sister and five-year-old cousin were killed in a fire at his grandmother's house. "It was real hard. Sometimes it is still hard. It's something I had to learn to live with. My family had to learn to live with it. It's still rough sometimes, thinking about it.

"Back then, things in the fire service weren't as good as they are now. I still believe in my heart that if we had the same resources and people we have today, they could have been saved. But that's not to blame anyone. No one's getting the blame. Things were just different back then as far as firemen and methods of fire fighting.

"From what I know, it wasn't painful to them what happened. It was smoke inhalation. So it wasn't painful to them."

Without a doubt, Higgs's family suffered. "It was rough, it was rough. It had a little something to do with me joining. I wanted to try to help other people not go through that. But, truthfully, I think that I would still have joined if that didn't happen, because I enjoy this. It's volunteer. I don't have to get paid for it. I really, really enjoy it."

Like Ellen Benson, Terri Wright, a Lawnside native living in Willingboro, New Jersey, brings her two children to the Fourth of July Parade to expose them to their family heritage. Wright also makes a stop at the firehouse every year. The daughter of Franklin Harper, she grew up playing in the firehouse. But she says that she never considered becoming the first woman firefighter in town, that she's more comfortable sticking with the jokes, ribs, and beer at the house. "I never even thought about it or really wanted to be one," she says, adding that she feels as much a part of the life of the department as do her two brothers who are members. "My whole family is in this department."

Wright lives in a black neighborhood in Willingboro, a majority-black, middle-class suburban town which, unlike Lawnside, was once nearly all white. The houses in her neighborhood are more contemporary than most in Lawnside. But for Wright, there's a difference in the two communities beyond appearance and economics—one is home. "I miss my friends and my family. Yes, I do miss living here. No matter what block I'm on in Lawnside, I'm probably related to somebody on the block."

Wright's distinction between Lawnside and Willingboro exposes the limits of using race as the defining and primary thread that ties her and other natives to their hometown. If Wright only wanted to live in a black world, she would be at home in her Willingboro neighborhood. But Lawnside, whose founding was rooted in race, has branched beyond that. Its ability to grow in such a way, ironically, has much to do with the fact that nearly everyone in town is of the same race. Today, Lawnsiders are bonded more by mutual traditions and experiences than they are by race. Wright doesn't yearn to live near her Lawnside friends and relatives simply because they are, like her, black: she misses them because of the past she's shared with them.

Wright's views on race carry the same innocence that I hear from so many other Lawnsiders—most notably from James and Ellen Benson. It is a perspective that precludes them from seeing the world through the prism of race. "I wasn't exposed to it, racial stuff, as a child because I was always among black people. I guess people who are exposed to it as a child, they're often saying that white people are against them, but I wasn't in that kind of atmosphere. I don't feel the prejudice, any hostility toward me as a person. I don't see it because I don't look for it, maybe. Others do. They see it."

Wright says that she has become most aware of her outlook toward prejudice at the hospital where she works as a billing clerk on a staff of some sixty employees, only three of whom are black. "Like if a black person and a white person apply for a job, our office perhaps is more prone to hire a white. I didn't see it that way at first. The other blacks do. I just thought they hired the best person."

Frank Cook, thirty-nine, a firefighter, Lawnside native, and police officer in Camden, joins the conversation. He says that most blacks are conditioned only to see racism against them, but not to see their own bias. Yet he claims to see as much prejudice among blacks as whites on the police force. "Mark Fuhrman doesn't only come in white. Mark Fuhrman comes in black. . . . It's a two-way street, that's what you have to understand. You still have blacks who are prejudiced just as whites are, and that's a fact of life. We are just as prejudiced as any white man can be. Prejudiced against whites, blacks, whatever. I've seen some black officers treat blacks just as bad as many whites."

Cook says he too remembers the absence of race in his life growing up. He says that the golden days of his childhood have convinced him that the separation of the races may be the only way to produce peace in America. "The majority of the black race of people should live within their own communities, should live amongst themselves," he asserts. "There are white established communities in this country that can choose to remain white, and we blacks should not live in those communities because those communities are hostile. It goes all the way back to when slavery was abolished, forty acres and a mule. It should have been done. We would have had our separate identities, formed our separate black communities like Lawnside.

"The problem with impoverished black communities is they were not created by blacks themselves. Many were created by the immigration of blacks from the South to the northern areas or into the southern areas where whites moved out and put their businesses out of the black communities.

"There are areas in a white community that will accept blacks, and there are white communities that do not accept us. And do I respect that they don't want blacks to live over there? Yes, I do. They have a right to live among themselves, and I don't think it's prejudiced. And I have a right to live amongst blacks, and I don't feel I'm prejudiced.

"That's the way we naturally are. In my opinion . . . when I say 'naturally,' if you look at the structures of the world, the way God set them up, Africa is Africa, Asia is Asia, Europe is Europe."

But Cook lives in America. And the contradictions in his separatist philosophy become obvious when I learn that he no longer resides in Lawnside, but in the integrated neighboring town of Magnolia. "We are all Americans," Cook says. "But we blacks are the true Americans. We are the American blood. We are the American blood of Indians, the American blood of blacks, the American blood of whites, we have them all in us—so we are the true Americans."

In praising blacks as "the true Americans" because of our blended lineage, Cook extols a part of us that is directly contrary to the racial purity he lauded in another breath as God's nature.

Up from the River

THEY are playing cards, three to a table. They are not silent. Eleven white men and one white woman sit and slap cards on tables. Wordless, they communicate via grunts that almost erupt into screams. Silent frowns dance on their faces: they are angry. You see it in their eyes, which widen with frustration as cards hit the table. Occasionally, a card thrown sets off a tug-of-war, with two sets of hands violently pulling as though they both own it. The strongest or most persistent hand of the moment wins the card.

Gallia County's Sarah Johnson Sow, a black, orthodox Muslim woman, circles the card players. She wears her usual momboy. She walks among the tables and smiles at the frowning players.

After three minutes, Sow puts an end to it. The game is over. The players can speak. She goes to the board and charts their feelings.

"I was aggravated," says one man.

"I wanted to just scream," says another.

"I want to just smack her," says yet another man, sitting at the table with the only woman. "I wanted to just smack her."

"What else?" urges Sow. "Come on. Tell us how you felt."

"That pretty much sums it up right there," a fourth man says. "After a while, I didn't care."

"I wanted to smoke, Marlboro . . ."

Sow pushes for more comments. "How did you react?" she asks. "You were frustrated; to hell with it." One of the men mutters something under his breath. "I don't know what he said," Sow says, jokingly pointing to the man. "But I do know we can't write it down."

"Now, I'm going to let you get, like, a five-minute break; you can relieve yourselves, go out and get a smoke, scream, whatever you need to do to get yourself back together so that we can finish the rest of this."

The men and woman are training to be state troopers. They will be stationed in a five-county southeastern-Ohio area that includes Gallia. Tonight, Sarah Johnson Sow is moonlighting, conducting a diversity training workshop for the troopers to be.

Sow leads workshops for public institutions like the state police, businesses, and school systems on coping with cultural diversity. Despite the sometimes heavy criticism leveled at it, diversity training is a growing industry. Companies of all sizes now contract so-called diversity experts to lead workshops in which employees learn how to function effectively in a culturally diverse work environment. Some turn to large contractors, while others use consultants, like Sow, who took a three-month course at a multi-cultural-training institute in Columbus, which, she says, helps qualify her to sensitize state troopers to cultural diversity.

This is the kind of workshop that Lawnside native Frank Cook would not rush to attend were one held in Camden, where he is a police officer. He told me that he's not opposed to such workshops, yet his machismo seems allergic to such forums. Diversity workshops would not be a priority for one who believes that racial and ethnic groups should follow the model of Lawnside and build their own communities. In those alleged utopias, Cook says, there would not be a pressing need to teach residents to be tolerant of racial differences.

Other critics of the workshops mount the typical complaints: They charge that the diversity-training programs cost business and government too much money. Others say that the workshops merely highlight differences among workers and impose "politically correct" values on the work environment, which is a simplistic and reactionary response to attempts to deal with issues surrounding differences.

Sow begins each session with Barnga, a card game intended to introduce participants to the challenges of cultural diversity. "I put them at tables and give a different set of rules to each table," she explains.

On one table, high cards win. On another table spades may win. "I let them practice and play by those rules."

Then Sow takes the rules away, makes the players switch tables, taking the rules they learned with them, and orders silence—no talking. The results are tables of people with each person playing cards by a different set of rules, and they can't talk about it. This leads to chaos. Sow says that it is analogous to what happens when people of different cultures can talk but can't understand each other because of cultural differences. "I want them to feel what it's like to be different under a different set of rules, because each culture is basically playing by a different set of rules. . . .

"They start snatching cards, glaring, and the whole business. That's what we want them to do—to feel uncomfortable. I once had one young man who had just quit smoking. And [Barnga] drove him to the point where he got up and he ran out of the room."

Sow claims that she knows practically every black person in the county and knows of only two others among them who regularly wear African garb, as she and her husband do. Some residents don't know her by name—they know her only if you describe her as the woman in African robes who works at the University of Rio Grande. But when she leaves the county, it isn't the garb that often attracts attention: it is the accent. Some people apparently see it as unique among people of her skin color. She remembers a trip to Cambridge when, as she sat in Harvard Square conversing with a relative, a stranger interrupted her. "He said, 'Oh wow, a black hillbilly,'" she recalls. "Of course, I was ready to attack him, and my aunt is trying to calm me down."

Sow says that the white stranger's remark reinforces the need for diversity training, to help, among other things, dilute ideas of black exoticism.

The state troopers are coming back into the room. Many of them have been outside the two-story building, smoking cigarettes. They are all in their early twenties.

Sow now stands next to the blackboard. "Gay and lesbian versus heterosexual. City versus country. Rural verses urban. Appalachian versus non-Appalachian. All these things you're going to run up against. Okay, cultural differences. Almost all of you are of the same culture; all of you are from southeastern Ohio. Okay. You're in this four- or five-county area, so, basically, you don't have much exposure to any cultures that are that much different from you. But then, you take me. I'm just a little bit different because of the color of my skin. But we do share the same culture in other ways. We are Appalachians. Appalachians are the people you probably feel very comfortable with. But let me tell you, when you're dealing with people from other states, like Colorado, Arizona, and California, and you're talking about Appalachians, they may say that all of us are just dumb hillbillies, that we're barefoot and pregnant and educated maybe past the fifth or sixth grade always, and we're all inbred."

Some stare intensely while others laugh. "That's right, we run around in the woods, eat bugs, and have no electricity," Sow goes on.

"Like people in Kentucky," says one trooper in the back, laughing.

"No—that's what they think about all of us. We're not in their comfort zone. They're not just talking about people from Kentucky; they're talking about me, and you are an Appalachian, too. They're not only talking about Kentucky Appalachians. See, we even think we're just a little bit better than they are."

Sow goes through a list of categories—regional, racial—into which we group people and asks the group if people from particular categories are in their own comfort zones. "New York. How do you feel about people from New York?"

"I hate them," says one guy.

"I do too," another man agrees.

"Do you know anybody from New York?" Sow asks.

"No, I never did, and I don't care to."

Sow turns to me. "David, where are you from?"

"New York," I reply, with hesitation.

Everyone laughs.

"Why would you not like someone just because of their state, and you don't even know them? You're not looking at someone as an individual."

Sow moves on to discuss cultural differences between groups as diverse as Jamaican Americans and Greek Americans. In some ways, her presence itself is part of the exercise: some class members admit in the discussion that they've never had a conversation with a black Muslim Appalachian woman in a momboy.

Two young men in the back giggle like seventh-graders in a sex-education class. They crack jokes about every group—except, interestingly enough, African Americans. Others begin to roll their eyes in frustration at the two men. Sow tries to ignore them.

In some ways, the session is largely a roll call of various groups, with the troopers uttering their feelings and, sometimes, expressing their ignorance, concerning those groups.

"How do you feel about immigrants?" Sow asks.

"Personally, I don't believe in them," one of the gigglers in the back says.

"You don't believe in them?"

"I hate them," says another man.

"Why?" Sow prods.

"All these ones that are coming in."

"Okay, but why do you hate them?" she digs.

"Because."

"Because why?"

"Just save them from the water," says the other giggler.

"They're dangerous, they'll put you in danger," a more-serious class member states.

"How do you know they will put you in danger?" Sow wants to know.

"I saw it on TV."

"Because you saw it on TV," Sow repeats. "Do you know some of the most violent things and stereotypes that you've ever seen come from television? Some people think that black people are dumb, ignorant, and crazy. That's what they think, because that's what they see [on their television programs]. Some Japanese people think all blacks are lazy, because that's all they see. Some have told me this. They think we're all crazy, and then I meet foreign guests at the airport for the university. Well, the first thing they find out very quickly, if they don't come to me, they don't get their money converted into dollars. It's what you call culture shock for them. And I do mean *culture shock*.

"Now, some of you have never seen somebody like me before. And I did have braids until last week, and I got my braids out. Long braids, kind of dreaded down. My height, my weight, and I'm standing at the airport, saying welcome to the university. How do you think they feel?"

"Their mouths drop," says a trooper trainee.

"That's right, because I wasn't in their comfort zone. Now, you're going into law enforcement. How are you going to deal with these things that aren't in your culture, comfort zone?"

The two men continue to giggle as Sow resumes her list and discussion of stereotypes. Italian Americans are the final group she brings up. One of the nongiggling trainees says, "Don't they always keep guns under the table?"

That comment sends Sow into yet another explanation of the problems with stereotypes and why such a characterization of an ethnic group is inappropriate for someone entering the state police.

At the end of the seminar, the one woman trainee offers an apology to Sow for the behavior of the two giggling men.

"That's okay, don't worry about it," the teacher says as she packs her brief case. "That's just their ignorance; they can't help it."

It is my last day in Gallia County and before dark, Sow wants to see an old church with an operational outhouse in northern Gallia County. So we leave right after the session, at 6:30.

The church sits in the middle of an important stop on the Underground Railroad. Sow says that a trip like this would be beneficial for participants of a diversity workshop because it would expose them to sides of African-American history and culture that they probably never think about. It is her dream to expand her workshops to include something like the trip we are taking.

As we ride, I ask a question. "It seems too easy to just dismiss the laughing as ignorance. What if one of those laughing troopers runs across your son in six years?"

"Hopefully, something I said has helped, even though it did seem that it didn't help for those two, or the one who listened and would still think all Italians keep guns under the table. I can't worry about people who won't be helped, but I can help those who are willing. Most of the time we as African Americans don't always reach out to help and educate. I don't think that's good."

Sow would not agree with Lawnside's Stephen Smith, who would find the conversations of the workshop to be outside his comfort zone when socializing with white friends. I wonder if the differences between the Smith and Sow perspectives on race represent the vast differences in the racial compositions of their native communities. A product of a black town, Smith comfortably makes friends with whites—aware of differences but uncomfortable engaging in lengthy conversations about them with those friends. In Gallia County, Sarah Johnson Sow's career is devoted to promoting tolerance and directly confronting the thorny issues that come with diversity, while Elaine Armstrong sees the need to directly confront and challenge the racist past by collecting its most offensive remnants. I can't imagine anyone in Lawnside taking up such a hobby as hers.

We take the main artery through Gallipolis. The city was founded by a group of upper-middle-class Frenchmen and -women escaping the wrath of the French Revolution in the late eighteenth century. The influence lives in some corners of downtown, in the names of stores, like Bastille. Then, out of the city, we pass the massive Bob Evans farm and open fields that hug the sun's glare.

Eventually, we arrive at one of the state's oldest churches. Sarah Johnson Sow was a member of this church before her second marriage, before she became a Muslim.

Bethel Baptist Church is a one-room structure sitting atop a steep hill that is a good test for any automobile clutch. On Sundays, most people park on the shoulder of the road and hike up to the worship service. It is a freshly painted, white wood-frame church. Inside, there is a sparkling-brown old wooden floor that according to Sow is mopped by church members after each service. There isn't an organ here, but a piano. And, of course, there isn't running water: there's a new outhouse, which surprises her. "It's really something to see," she says. "I never could use the old outhouse. I have a good bladder."

Ten years ago, when membership dwindled to three and the pastor died, the church refused to die. The three living members, all widows, decided that they couldn't keep up the building, so they took the church to their homes, rotating among the three homes every other Sunday. Eventually, the three found a new pastor, who helped recruit new members, and the services gravitated back to the historic church. Only one of those three widows is still living.

Sow found refuge here from the established black Baptist churches when she was battling those churches' leaderships over the Emancipation.

For a visitor, the main attraction at this church is not its outhouse but the rich history of this area. Historians say that the houses surrounding the church sheltered and hid many runaway slaves traveling the Underground Railroad to freedom. Generations ago, words and noises carried codes that were only understood by escaped slaves and those working to help them. The vocabulary included terms like *paddy-rollers,* which referred to patrollers on the hunt for escaped slaves near the Ohio rivers. Underground Railroad conductors altered the route that came through this strip of the county several times because of bounty hunters, according to James Sands, a local historian.

"There were bounty hunters flooding this area as they looked for escaped slaves," says Sow. "A lot of our ancestors started a life here in hiding."

The Seekers

JOSHUA slams down the phone. His adrenaline races with time—all because he's heard the name of a baseball team. "Sometimes you get, like, a cue, like certain things that give you an indication that your man's going to be caught today."

In this case, the cue is the name of the baseball team: the Chosen Few. "For the team that he's playing with to be called the Chosen Few, we know he's going to be caught today."

Joshua, in his Elizabeth, New Jersey, home, calls Rock, a trainee working the case. He unloads information about the team, slams down the receiver again, and loads his gun.

Within the hour, Joshua and Rock are armed and speeding down the Garden State Parkway, south to Keansburg, New Jersey. Rock drives the van while Joshua sits in the passenger seat and takes another look at a Polaroid picture of Rich, a white man with dark curly hair. It is not a good picture—you can barely see the man's green eyes. "Sometimes we get pictures worse than this," says Joshua. "Sometimes, the eyes are closed altogether."

Rich plays baseball but, more important than that, he was arrested recently for resisting arrest and possession of cocaine. Released on $25,000 bail in Perth Amboy, New Jersey, he missed a court appearance and presumably jumped bail. A bail bondsman wants him back and has turned to Joshua, the leader and founder of the Seekers, an organization with more than 1,200 captures in its sixteen-year history.

• • •

Rock is silent. The only thing I hear from him is his right foot periodically slapping the gas pedal. His hand casually tilts the wheel a few inches as he races by Sunday-morning drivers leisurely obeying the speed limit. Rock, twenty-nine, a brown-skinned man, is over six feet and muscular, while Joshua, thirty-seven, with dark skin and light-brown eyes, is five feet eight and stocky. Rock seems oblivious to my questions and Joshua's answers. He is attuned to the Al Jarreau tape playing in the van.

Joshua takes on my questions while reviewing the folder on the case. Now is the time to talk, he says, because you don't know what's ahead. "There isn't a typical day," he tells me. "That's what's so sweet about this situation. You don't get bored."

The folder, containing the facts of the case, is from the local bail bondsman, who is one of the Seekers' biggest clients as well as a fan.

Joshua and Rock started the case yesterday with only the bad picture of Rich and the name and address of Rich's girlfriend, Sue.

Joshua has detailed notes of his conversation with Sue. He studies them for the purpose of consistency—he may have to fall back into the role of "John Benson," a name he pulled out of his imagination when he first called her. Since Seekers work on more than one case at a time, it wouldn't be implausible to occasionally mix up aliases from one to another.

The Seekers are known as bounty hunters, but, officially, they are licensed private detectives who specialize in catching bail hoppers for a fee of 25 percent of the bail. As bounty hunters, they employ many of the surreptitious investigative techniques that private eyes often use to get information. Joshua, for example, discovered that Rich was playing baseball today through a series of telephone calls to Sue. Posing as John Benson, a potential employer with a job for Rich, Joshua told Sue that he had met Rich at a bar. Sue said that she would pass on the message.

Joshua followed up with another call last night, leaving a message on Sue's answering machine. When he phoned in for a routine message check this morning, he found a message from Sue, returning the call. He immediately called her. Joshua recounts the conversation:

"Rich isn't here now," says Sue. "I told him you called. He said he doesn't remember meeting you, but was interested in getting a job."

"Well, I'll be dropping my son off at my ex-wife's house near that area today," said Joshua, who is really married to a schoolteacher and has a six-year-old son. "Maybe I can drop by an application."

"He's not here now. He had a baseball game."

"Oh, what team?" Joshua asks, as though he, too, played in a league.

"The Chosen Few. They play somewhere in Keansburg."

   The seven Seekers, three full-time and four part-time, rely on a philosophy and a "spiritual" way of life that connects them to a "sixth sense," according to Joshua. That extra sense discerns clues, signals, and hidden
messages in things that may seem innocuous to others, things such as the
name of a baseball team—the Chosen Few. For Joshua, the team's name,
with the word *chosen,* was enough to make him forget about working on
another case today.

Like all Seekers, Joshua and Rock have two names. Their real names are
private. Joshua and Rock are their names for the business of bounty hunting. They acquired their group name, the Seekers, in a way similar to that in
which Macon Dead Jr. became "Milkman" in Toni Morrison's *Song of
Solomon,* and in the way Theo Huxtable's best friend on *The Cosby Show*
became "Cockroach." Or maybe the way Gallia County's Duke and Outlaw
acquired their names. The name was dropped spontaneously in a conversation, and it stuck because of its unique relevance. In some northern New
Jersey neighborhoods, residents grew accustomed to seeing Joshua and his
flock asking about people's whereabouts. "One of the street guys, he said,
'You are always seeking someone, the Seekers, who you seekin' today?'" remembers Joshua. "I said, 'Oh, shit, *Seekers.*' And, uh, it sort of like just carried on from there."
   Hats sporting the name followed: black baseball caps embroidered with
gold script lettering: THE SEEKERS. They often leave the hats behind on days
like today, when they are role-playing, but the hats and black jackets are
uniform in familiar places where the Seekers are known—places where
Joshua wouldn't play John Benson or any other undercover game because
it wouldn't work. Still, few people in even those places know the Seekers
by their official affiliation with the Ranger Investigation Protection, a private
investigative company that Joshua took over in 1980. Then, it was a part-
time operation owned by a postal worker who was retiring to go south. He
met Joshua through a mutual acquaintance and eventually turned the company over to Joshua, who was twenty-three at the time and had spent the
previous five years as a commercial fisherman in Alaska.
   Before Joshua, Ranger Investigation Protection provided security
guards for businesses and nonprofit agencies, which is how many detec-
tive agencies across the country turn a profit. Joshua didn't foresee
enough pleasure in making sure guards were at the right place at the right
time: it didn't promise enough adventure for a New Jersey native who had
packed up for Alaska at eighteen. I also can't imagine Joshua chasing to

catch cheating spouses in the act, another source of profit for many agencies. Spying on adulterers seems too soft and soap-operatic for Joshua. After all, he grew up on *Shaft,* the black urban PI from the seventies who became a cult hero. Shaft didn't chase cheating husbands or watch over security guards. But when Joshua took over Ranger Investigation Protection, no one flocked to him for help in tracking down the "real killer" or liberating black slaves from white owners, as Richard Roundtree did as John Shaft in *Shaft in Africa!* seven years before Rhodesia became Zimbabwe. But Joshua did get a call from a bail bondsman, who was looking for someone to catch a bail hopper. "I felt it was a natural. It was a clean transition. You get the body, you hand the body to the police, you get your body receipt, take it to the bondsman, you get paid, and you keep moving. It was a very, very clean and simple transaction. I could groove with that."

So could other young men, he says, and word quickly spread among those with visions of machismo. "The gun, you know, the badge when you need it, the whole thing about bounty hunting is intriguing to people, getting a permit to carry a gun; if you don't have an agency behind you, or your own agency, you just don't get a permit to carry a gun . . . some of the brothers started to hear about this brother that was doing this work. . . ."

It looked like the perfect opportunity for men to realize boyhood fantasies; it was legal yet separate from a force dominated by men often perceived as the enemy of the justice they are sworn to uphold. Unsurprisingly, a flood of calls followed Joshua. Think about it, as perhaps the American male callers did in an unconscious way. Action, yes. Guns, yes. Legal, yes. An exam perceived as biased, no. An ultimate boss like Frank Rizzo or Ed Koch, no. The calls didn't stop.

But Joshua wasn't willing to easily hand over an affiliation with the company, its accompanying badge, and the right to openly carry a gun to anyone. There had to be a standard for Seekers. So he created it—body building, training on a gun range, and a test, which grew out of the Seekers' philosophy. "I thought a philosophy was necessary in knowing who I could trust," Joshua explains.

The ever-evolving philosophy is a homemade mixture of Egyptian metaphysics, mild Afrocentrism, and some of Joshua's favorite books—*The Way of the Warrior, 12 Million Black Voices, The Art of War,* and *The Prophet.* "In order to have any control, there had to be some type of philosophy behind it, or else we would be just like anybody else out here trying to snatch people up and do their thing. Our approach with nature, and the philosophy, is that we try to think out the capture before it happens. So if we plant the seed of the capture in our minds, all we have to do is follow through with what our mind has already set forth. And it becomes a very easy capture. It's just basically mind over matter. We've had somewhere in the area of twelve hundred captures, and we've never had to kill anybody, or beat anybody down, or none of that kind of crazy stuff. And it's because we have put our minds out first, and then we've let the physical follow that, and everything falls in line."

The Seekers' philosophy turns the pursuit of bail hoppers into an exercise that bonds the seven into an organization or fraternal order modeled loosely on an Egyptian secret society. The Seekers' numerology, which may seem foreign—even crazy—to most people, guides the organization, according to Joshua. Seven becomes a number of significance in many ways: there are never more than seven Seekers; the required reading list contains seven books. "Numbers are very, very important in the way that things are played out, be it events, be it organizations, be it money, be it whatever, numbers are very, very important. We believe in seven seekers, sharpen them, sharpen them, sharpen them. You know, you got seven sharp guys; they can do the work of a hundred incorrectly sharp guys. You know, we get applications for people wanting to join like crazy, but we got the magic number seven for us."

It is an eclectic seven: Rock, an unemployed construction worker; a teacher, even a CPA. They are among the few dozen men and one woman who have begun training, which entails reading the books and working part-time, like Rock does. The overwhelming majority have been black males. Others have included one black woman, one Cuban American, and one white male. Some finish the training and eventually drop out of the organization because of the time commitment, organizational feuds, and disagreements; some never get through the couple of months of training. "If you want to stay a part of this, you've got to read the seven books, you've got to train, you got to work out. You've got to examine your life."

It was not that requirement—"examining the life"—that eliminated many potential Seekers: many adult men didn't like the reading requirement. "Some people were like, 'Well, fuck that.' They didn't want to read. And they didn't really come right out and say that. But I knew that's what they was all about. I said, 'Well, no book, no gun. Ha. No book, no gun. No more to even talk about. No book, no gun. See ya.'

"To call yourself a Seeker means just that, that you're seeking. And what you're seeking is more control of your time, a better understanding of your life, of those around you, of their lives, and helping to try to make things better. . . . Most of us follow that philosophy because it makes so much common sense. And you can't fight common sense because it's there, it's right there in front of your face. You can't fight it. When truth hits you, man, you can duck it and dodge it, but it's like an odor—it'll stick to you. You can't get around it. So we all follow that philosophy."

Joshua is not yet Joshua—he is years, even decades away from that name and bounty hunting. He is a fourteen-year-old at the dawn of the seventies, and the new decade brings one of the first clues that he might become something like the creator of an organization that meshes homespun philosophy, Egyptian metaphysics, and the capture of bail hoppers to pay his bills. The clue isn't a clear prediction that he would form the Seekers, but merely bespeaks the possibility of an unorthodox future. His attitude toward recreation violated the stereotype, or the norm, or something in between the two for a fourteen-year-old boy: at that age, he developed an uncompromising distaste for the pastime that is synonymous with the rugged joys and bravado of American boyhood. "I think the last time I watched a sporting event, I was thirteeen or fourteen years old. I don't follow none of that shit. To me, it's all a big waste of time. It's a shame that we're caught up into this bullshit. It's a diversion, and I know it's a diversion because we spend so much time watching it. Some of us know so much more about sports than we do about our own family heritage and where we come from, and all that other kind of good stuff. It is a big fucking waste of time. Sorry to be so straight like that, but if you try to get a conversation with the average brother and you're not talking about the game, just any game, you can't carry a strong conversation."

Joshua connects his distaste for organized sports to reading Kahlil Gibran's *The Prophet* at age fifteen. "I just didn't want to engage in the killing of time. I wanted to spend time, and killing time is sitting in front of a tube and watching some guys either chase, kick, or run a rubber ball. It had nothing to do with being macho or tested. My father took me to martial-arts school at a very young age. I engage in weight training, heavy-bag, and speed-bag training for my profession."

Joshua links blacks' fascination with sports to an inability to escape defeat in other aspects of American life. "Deep down within our psyche, [sports] gives us the chance to win at something. But we're not really winning: to win is to straight up confront the system. Instead of taking that on, we would rather engage in our team winning—you know, 'my team beat your team,' that kind of bullshit."

But can't African Americans enjoy leisure without being accused of neglecting or being distracted from racial responsibilities? Must our lives be reduced to a perpetual confrontation with American evils? These questions travel through my mind as I listen to Joshua. It is understandable that many blacks would be attracted to rhetoric such as Joshua's, even when they are closely intertwined with the system they speak of confronting. Such talk is often the residue of the rebellion present in African-American culture from its beginning. By necessity, the heritage of racism and the nobility in assuming responsibility for battling its evil impact have been deeply embedded in the collective values of African Americans, from Brown to Douglass to Tubman to Du Bois to King to so many others. So, today, in postintegration America, many African Americans speak rhetorically, sometimes by mere habit, of confronting a "system" in which they are more entrenched than ever before.

On the surface, is it peculiar for Joshua or any Seeker to speak of "confronting the system"? If so, what system? Is such confrontation even in the mission of the Seekers? The Seekers are independent wheels of the criminal-justice system; they do not directly confront or seek to eradicate police brutality or racial inequities in sentencing. They are, for the most part, helping to put more black men behind bars. Though Joshua and Rock seek a white bail hopper today, Joshua admits that roughly half of the men he captures are African Americans, and they're usually not wanted for murder or violent crimes. Joshua isn't bashful about taking on the question: How is he confronting the system by putting more black men behind bars? "The individuals that we're going after are drug dealers. So, it's like, would you prefer to have me in your neighborhood or a drug dealer? Those are your choices. I mean, plenty of times I've gone out at two, three, four, five o'clock in the morning and have diverted stickups, muggings, because I was out there at that particular time, prowling, looking for fugitives, and just happened to run into someone getting their pocketbook snatched, or getting beat or jumped or whatever. So if you ask those persons whether or not they would prefer to have a Seeker in the neighborhood or a drug dealer in the neighborhood, I'm quite sure the answer is going to be a Seeker."

Why wouldn't that be an answer in a neighborhood of mostly law-abiding people frustrated with the behavior of those who wear the face of the race so often shown in the media and for whom their sons could easily be mistaken by those of another race with a badge? Why wouldn't the law-breakers incur the scorn of the majority who've managed to find straps to pull themselves clear of the wrath of racism, especially since those law-breakers are more likely to violate a law-abiding American of their own race? In fast, short-answer America, why wouldn't many among the law-abiding black majority fume with an anger toward black lawbreakers? For some, the anger they do harbor does not easily dissipate with reminders that the black victimizers are also victims of the larger society, and also likely to face harsher penalties than whites who commit the same crimes. Why would the hearts of the black majority bleed for the pain of the victimizers in this climate?

Indeed, Joshua's presence threatens those lost to the world of crime and drugs. But beyond the threat, his power is limited. It takes more than the number seven to compensate for the shrinking job base in the inner city, which sociologist William Julius Wilson and others cite as the leading impetus behind many of the social problems in urban America.

We take exit 117 off the Garden State Parkway and are in Keyport, a town on the New Jersey coast only a few miles away from Keansburg. The first thing past the welcome sign is an amusement park. The Ferris wheel can be seen from at least a mile away. Joshua notices something else. "Man, these guys down here got plenty of tattoos," he says. Rock nods a yes.

The mission is to find the right baseball field. It is a sunny August day in 1994. Exactly twenty years ago, Joshua was on the road to a new world—a place he had never seen—Alaska.

His parents were not thrilled about his journey. His father was a welder and his mother a teacher. They had moved to Elizabeth, New Jersey, from Georgia in the fifties, following the migration pattern that helped transform America's cities. For many, it was the beginning of a boom: in the fifty years after World War II, according to economist Peter Drucker, the economic position of black families improved faster than that of any other group in American history. Sixty percent of African Americans rose to earn middle-class incomes—but not always middle-class jobs, because a good half of these people occupied blue-collar jobs that paid upper-middle-class wages. They were the kind of families that formed the comfortable working-middle-class community and who raised a large share of the contemporary generation of black professionals.

The jobs that provided a good life for many of the parents in Joshua's neighborhood, and in places like Lawnside, have disappeared with the decline of America as a heavy-industrial and manufacturing economy. But, as Joshua notes, his parents and others typically didn't want their children to reach for the same jobs as they had, the jobs that had given them entree into their version of the American dream. His parents, for example, wanted their only child to become a professional, maybe a doctor or lawyer. "They wanted me to go to school, like all the other parents—you know, further your education, education. Get your degree in something and make something of yourself. School or the military, those were the choices. Everyone was pointing toward school."

It was clearly possible in 1974. College enrollment of blacks was soaring. By 1976, when Joshua would have been a sophomore, 33.4 percent of all African Americans between the ages of eighteen and twenty-four were in college, compared to 33.1 percent of all whites, according to the U.S. Census Bureau. By 1985, though, just as President Reagan began his second term, the numbers for African Americans had gone in the other direction— only 26 percent of all eighteen-to-twenty-four-year-old African Americans were enrolled in college, while the figure for whites had grown slightly, to 34.4 percent.

Joshua came of age when that window of opportunity was open with possibilities. For many in his and my generation, the choices were clear: college for good students; the military for bad students and good students without college money. Joshua freely bypassed both. "The military was too structured. And I developed a belief early on, when my older cousin had died in Vietnam, that I wouldn't fight for any man unless I got a piece of the pie . . . and if I can't get that, I'm not going to go fight. And I had seen too many people go to college and come back, disappointed, with nothing but a piece of paper stating that they had completed some courses. And they learned nothing about wisdom: They knew nothing about self-control. They learned nothing about how to deal with people, how to deal with life. I mean, some of the most basic issues on how to survive in this system are not taught in college; you can't get that.

"I never wanted to be rigid. I never said, 'Well, I want to be a doctor or a lawyer or this.' I just left it open. Because as you get out of school, particularly high school, you have a sense now that people are looking at you and you have this newfound freedom that you must fill now."

The freedom seems fresh in June 1974, for Joshua at least. The world and country are more tense—President Nixon's resignation is two months away; the fall of Saigon ten months away. Yet for Joshua and many of his peers, this is the month when James Brown's "The Payback" rocks basement house parties.

Joshua is in the basement of a friend's house—not for a big party, but a game of chess. The crowd grows as other friends drop in, and a low-key party is born. Some play poker, some just talk and listen to music. Most of them, like Joshua, have just graduated from high school. The atmosphere is jovial as they joke about the past and dream about the future. One friend produces a newspaper article on the Alaska pipeline. Some predict there is money to be made, and everyone is ready to go west. The party ends with a pact that everyone will go—together. Like Joshua, some pledge to forget about college and the military. Horace Greeley, look out: the class of '74 is going west to make a fortune together and to return home one day with big bucks.

Two months later, just about everyone else is either off to school or on Uncle Sam's payroll. Others are left looking for the jobs that were plentiful in their parents' youth but will decline in the coming decade, leaving some to choices that could one day lead to the grip of a Seeker's handcuff. Joshua is the only one embarking on his own date with manifest destiny. He's on a bus en route for Alaska.

Joshua sees a police officer and asks him if he knows of any area parks and baseball fields. The cop says that there is a field near the high school where summer baseball is played. Joshua doesn't introduce himself as a bounty hunter. Once again, he conceals his identity. He might as well be John Benson. "Police in the southern states salute us, which is very strange, you know. Alabama, Arkansas, Mississippi. In those places, they salute us. You're coming to get some bullshit that just crossed the border into their area. . . . So if you snatch someone, then they know someone is out of their hair, they're back where they belong. So they salute us. The northern cops just find it hard dealing with brothers with guns, even if they are on the same side. They just find it hard. That's been our experience."

"What do they do to show they are not on your side?" I asked.

"It's not what they do; it's sometimes how they look. Or what they won't do for you that you know that they might do for someone else. We tested this with the white member. Once, they said that there were certain things that they couldn't give us by law, but when we sent him in, they gave it to him. So we were able to put them on the spot and say, 'Hey, he's with us, and you gave him stuff you said you couldn't give to us.' And I would call them over and say, 'Hey, let's talk, we gotta talk. You know, what's up, you gave him a photo, I came to get the same photo two days ago, you said you couldn't do it, what seems to be the problem?' And when they would see us and realize that 'Oh shit, they're together.'

"And this is in what cities?" I ask.

"All over Jersey. It was almost as though they didn't trust us at first."

The conflict, however, is not all rooted in race. Tensions between law-enforcement officials and bail-recovery agents are sometimes based in the reputation of bounty hunters, most of them white, among police officers. Few states require bounty hunters to be licensed, and many police officers contend that recovery agents lack the training and experience to do what often amounts to police work. And the dangers can be fatal, as in the case of a Tacoma, Washington, recovery agent who was shot and killed while trying to arrest a suspect wanted for cocaine possession in 1994.

Despite the danger, it is a growing and profitable field. There are more bail hoppers than police departments can handle, and bail bondsmen say they couldn't live without bounty hunters. There are seven hundred bounty hunters registered with the National Association of Bail Enforcement Agents, and in 1993, bounty hunters apprehended 25,000 fugitives.

We follow the directions to the baseball field. It is empty, bare but dusty. A game could have been played here.

Rock drives off. What now? He slows down at the sight of a green station wagon coming toward us. Two men are in the front seat. A sandy-haired boy, who looks about ten years old, is in the backseat. Rock stops and blows his horn. The car stops at Rock's window. Rock asks the driver about baseball fields and games. They give us directions to another field. The ten-year-old disputes the directions. Rock and Joshua thank them all and follow the child's instructions. "There they go," Joshua says. "Adults think they know it all. Kids go all the places."

We follow the child's directions and arrive at another field in less than five minutes. But once again, there are no players, just an empty field. Joshua and Rock speculate that the game may be over and that the Chosen Few could be drinking in one of the local bars, so we drive back to the main strip. A bar on the corner catches Joshua's eye as a potential fountain of information.

I wait in the car with Rock, who has said nothing to me since nodding a greeting at the beginning of the journey. He looks straight ahead, engrossed in the music playing on the radio. Despite the music, I feel an uncomfortable silence. So I interrupt Rock's serenity and ask him how he got involved in the Seekers. "I met Joshua and the Seekers about three years ago when they came to lock up my brother."

"What?" I ask with surprise.

Rock explains that he had never heard of the Seekers until they came after his older brother two years ago. His brother, out on bail, missed a court appearance and fled to South Carolina with Rock and another brother, to visit relatives. "We were down there maybe about an hour before we found out that some bounty hunters was looking for my brother. I thought the only bounty hunters was on TV. I never knew it was like really actual bounty hunters, you know, going all over looking for people. And so to send somebody from Jersey way down to South Carolina to look for somebody and pick them up, I just thought that it was far-fetched."

Joshua and another Seeker found one of Rock's relatives and convinced the relative to talk Rock's brother into a peaceful surrender. Rock was impressed. When he returned to Elizabeth, he decided to join the Seekers. "They were pretty cool. I'm still training with them, not working with them full-time. I'm doing the reading and trying to live by everything they want you to go through."

Joshua comes back in the car. Nobody in the bar had heard of a team called the Chosen Few, but they did have directions to another baseball field. As we ride, I ask Joshua about Rock's brother. "Rock's unique for sure. That's very rare for something like that to happen. Very rare. We came to lock up his brother. Most people in that situation wouldn't think about joining us. You'd be a little pissed at us. But it wasn't the case."

The eighteen-year-old who will become Joshua sees the enormity of America beyond Elizabeth from a Greyhound bus's window. It takes several days and nights on a bus to reach Seattle. There, he gets a room at a YMCA, finds a job as a waiter at a Japanese restaurant, and tries to save money. His mornings are spent walking near the docks and looking at the boats. His imagination carries him on a boat to the unknown state of Alaska.

There is a familiar face at the docks. He doesn't know the man's name, but the two begin to see each other so much that they automatically speak. On one morning stroll, the white man strikes up a conversation. The older man offers to take him on his boat, where they play chess and become friends. The man claims to have been a Nazi as a youth and is now beyond racism. "He actually trained me on his boat," Joshua recalls. "He taught me a lot about boating and surviving outdoors."

Eventually, he also takes his two sons and Joshua with him to Alaska, where Joshua finds a job as a commercial fisherman.

Joshua exits from a second bar with the directions to yet another baseball field. It is five minutes away—and empty. Joshua and Rock discuss options. Joshua does most of the talking. He doesn't want to keep calling Sue. She might get suspicious, and Rich would run away for sure. Time is already running by them. All baseball games will surely be over soon.

"Why wouldn't you go to Sue's house and grab Rich?" I ask. As bounty hunters, they are free of some of the restrictions on police—they don't need search warrants, and an 1873 Supreme Court ruling allows them to detain and arrest, as well as knock down any door—as long as its the door of the right person. They can be sued if they mistakenly grab the wrong person and infringe on the rights of an innocent person, and the price can be high: in 1995, a Connecticut bounty hunter discovered that the wrong move could land him on the other side of the law when he was charged with attempted murder for shooting a man he mistook for a bail jumper.

Joshua says the Seekers' philosophy keeps them from busting through doors. "We wouldn't storm the place," says Joshua. "We don't really do that. That's the cowboy TV way. I might walk up, knock on the door, with my hat flipped backwards and ask 'Yo, is Rich home?' And then, we can take it from there. I would take my cap and raise it out. And Rock would know that's the sign, *pow,* he's home. And then, he would come out and take position. Either at the back or whatever. When positive ID was made, he would just snatch him."

The reluctance to snatch by any means necessary is the parting point for the Seekers' philosophy and the raw machismo that might initially appeal to wanna-be Seekers. Through the philosophy, the Seekers also manipulate negative stereotypes of African Americans to the advantage of a capture. Joshua says that organization in black men throws black and white enemies off guard, because its violates the stereotypes that are implanted in many Americans. "They see an everyday terror in us, but now you have something that's organized and trained—you don't want to mess with that . . . I don't think that there's anything more threatening to . . . the establishment, be it whites, or even be it blacks, than a sense of union and organization."

Now I am beginning to see how Joshua might really "confront the system." The system he confronts isn't a government body, police agency, or any arm of a criminal-justice system, but a set of beliefs, stereotypes, and unfounded ideas of black inferiority. He defies that system by creating the Seekers, an organization that allows him and others to define their values and humanity largely on their own terms. What makes his challenge formidable is its relative freedom from an explicit desire or need to disprove any specfic idea or racial notion—even as the Seekers may disprove such ideas by example in the process of a capture. Their mission is merely to win a surrender through intelligence, not to show that black bounty hunters are as good as whites in the field in the way that Lawnside's Butch Gaines was instructed to show that he could do as well as whites at Haddon Heights High School. "Now, when we normally step into a situation and people see the symbols and they see that there's a union there and a connection there, they don't want to fight that because they see no win. This is not a thug or a hood; this guy is coming to you and explaining to you that you got to go. They are not going to fight that. They are not going to fight that because they see no win. They see no way of outrunning us, or outfighting us, so they submit to us. They don't want to fight that. When a gun is coming at you organized, you don't want to mess with that. I think they are saying if I can't outshoot them, outfight them, or outrun them I might as well go ahead and submit to them."

For now, there is no one to outrun. Joshua and Rock decide to return to the main strip one more time. Another bar becomes a stage for Joshua, he enters and his eyes alight on three men in baseball cleats at the bar. Joshua sits by the bar, in a stool next to them. He catches their sobering stares with a friendly but tough-looking nod. They return it with caution in their eyes.

Joshua doesn't normally drink, but he needs a prop to help ease his entry into the good old boys' conversation. He orders a Budweiser. He fakes a few sips and waits for a pause long enough to allow a black outsider's entree. It isn't a long wait—beer and a friendly smile that doesn't violate a macho pose go a long way among men. That shared space carries Joshua over the temporary halt in the conversation. It is enough to take him beyond the seconds of discomfort and the silent stares. Perhaps suspicion is replaced with intrigue, curiosity about the other. Soon, he's part of the game.

"How did the game go?" Joshua asks.

"We lost," one man says, giving a friendly, but reserved look you would expect for a stranger.

"Well, lose on the field and win at the bar," Joshua says with a chuckle and a raise of a mug.

They laugh and joke about bad plays.

Joshua soon asks if they know of the team his friend plays on—the Chosen Few.

"Oh, they played earlier today," one of the men says.

Joshua smiles and abandons the mug full of beer.

Joshua decides that it's time to drive to Sue's house, a few blocks away from downtown Keansburg. I ask Joshua about the bar. "It's a lot easier for them to deal with just one black guy," he says. "It's only difficult with a group."

With that, Joshua offers another rule of black life in America: you can successfully infiltrate anything white by blending in as much as possible in a nonthreatening way. This bit of wisdom extends from the other lessons of the days of segregation, when many African Americans strove to look as neat and well suited as possible in order to distinguish themselves from "the rest of them" in the white mind. To do so could prevent a simple trip to a clothing store from becoming a demeaning nightmare—but not always. My mother once described trying to buy a hat in a department store when she was in college in a Southern town; all of the women at her college were required to wear dress hats. She was dressed "properly," yet a shabbily dressed white clerk followed her and slapped a rag on her head to protect the bonnets she was trying on. The rule was often passed down by black teachers, who stressed that their students shouldn't speak in public what may be called Ebonics today—especially in front of whites. You should look like a professional, even if you are not a doctor or lawyer. (I heard another version of this rule from Bernice Borden in Gallia County, three months after I rode with Joshua. She criticized blacks who visited white churches on special occasions taking them to task for "singing loud" and showing off. "Don't go into someone else's church and try to take it over," she told me. "Come in quiet and look around and see how things are first." Of course, Borden's credo clashes with the does-for-do and baggy-pant rebellion of hip-hop culture.)

Anyway, back to Joshua, and now to Sue's house: hers is a modest green wood-frame dwelling on a tree-shaded street. Rock parks across the street. There are two cars in the driveway: predictions place Rich inside. "He's in there," says Joshua, who speaks slowly in a voice almost as low as a whisper. "He's asleep, or just laying back, chilling. After playing baseball for four or five hours, you know, and doing a little bit of drinking. That sun will beat your ass, make you lay down."

The plan is to wait for him to exit for a night out. "You gotta have patience sometimes, you know . . . if you don't have patience, you're not going to be in this game long at all."

Joshua has time for more questions. I want to go back to Alaska. "I developed a sense of independence from being in Alaska because I was somewhat self-employed working on a fishing boat. You are your own entity, in a sense. And the only thing it required of you was to be just a very hardworking person. It's not like, you know, 'I'm your boss and you do this and you do that.' You had a job to do, and as long as you did your job, you never received any slack. So, in a sense, it made me feel like I was self-employed. I worked eight months out of the year and then [had] four months vacation, so I came home to visit friends and family and whatever."

On one visit home, Joshua was outside washing a car when an old friend drove up—a friend who had promised to go to Alaska a few years ago. Today, he takes Joshua to a Harlem bookstore.

There, Joshua is introduced to books that are outside of the American mainstream but popular among African Americans. Many conservatives and so-called liberals will discover some of those books in the eighties, when Afrocentrism becomes a popular, and then controversial, issue in social, political, and academic circles. He reads Frances Cress Welsing, John Henrik Clarke, and others. He develops a friendship with the owner of the store, who begins sending him books. "It was consciousness-expanding. He awoke that part of me. I was sort of reborn. I had almost forgotten a lot of what was taught to me early on in life.

"It was seeing the world for what it really was and not for what other people were telling me it was about. I think that's one of the major factors on why we're not where we should be today—because we're living according to someone else's definition [of us]."

Joshua became Afrocentric before it was fashionable. His consciousness was awoken, and he continued to read until, by the time black nationalism became commercialized in the eighties, he had outgrown it. Just as kente cloth began appearing on street corners, he was beyond Afrocentrism. "The consciousness-expanding material that I read tells me, or dictates to me, that when I leave this life I won't be an African American. I don't think I came into this life as an African-American man; that was taught to me because of the nature of my color and the definition of the reality that was given to me. Now, what was I before I came here, and what will I be when I leave? That's the question. So I'm more into the soul, that part of the nature of man that we don't quite understand yet, and I've tried to link myself to that and . . . and not so much on Afrocentric kind of things.

"Afrocentricity is cool," he continues, "but there's no growth action involved in that—as I heard a brother say, being black and proud. You won't be black and proud and knowledgeable, or you won't be black and proud and have wisdom in the things that we need to pull ourselves out of the dirt. You'll just be a person standing on the corner, black and proud.

"I see myself as being universal, per se. You know, when I leave here I don't know what I'm going to be or where that energy is going to carry over. And so I try to stay focused on the energy, the energy that came and the energy that I will leave with. And not so much on the color of things."

It is four o'clock. We've been in the car for forty-five minutes—three black men in what appears to be a predominantly white neighborhood. Joshua isn't too concerned about what most of the residents may fear or assume: he is worried about what Rich and Sue might think. He wonders if they will notice us, consider us to be out of place, and assume that we must be tied to law enforcement or something else. "No, they might think we're about ready to do a B-and-E [breaking and entering] somewhere. People who are doing dirty are very conscious of what's around them."

Joshua looks around and finds a decoy. A FOR SALE sign with a realtor's number sits in front of a house a couple of doors down from Sue's. An elderly white man is working on the lawn of the house next door to it. Joshua tells Rock to ask the man about the FOR SALE sign and to tell him that we are waiting for a realtor. "That will throw them off in case anybody gets suspicious," Joshua says. "Motion or point to the house."

Rock exits and chats with the man. "There goes the neighborhood," Joshua jokes.

Through the window of the van, we see Rock and the old man sharing a laugh. Rock points to the house a few times. Rock returns to the car. A woman exits from Sue's house. She looks to be about three hundred pounds and has a short black haircut. "That's Sue, I bet," Joshua says. "She looks like a royal pain in the ass."

Sue, or possibly Sue, gets something out of one of the cars in the driveway and goes back into the house.

Joshua continues to talk. He says, in recent years, that he has developed an intolerance for black whiners who complain about racism and exclusion from the white world. "Shit, yeah. Shit, yeah—whining all the damn time. Whining, crying all the time about the white man."

The man who says that he isn't a sports fan uses several sports metaphors to explain his disdain for whiners. "It's like if the whites—four white boys over here are playing, and you and I come along, and they exclude us from the game, we can do one of two things. We can bitch and moan about 'let us in the game,' or we can go down the block and create our own game. Now if they see us having more fun than them, what do you think they're going to do? They're going to want to roll down, 'yo, can we get in the game?' And then it's our choice to say yea or nay. And if we do the same thing in our adult situation, we'll be good to go. But we keep running to their game, running to say let us in, let us into your game. So they let us into their game, and they've already created another game, so they just move on. Here, you got an old game, they got a new game going any damn way.

"It's not about equality, it's not about justice, per se. . . . We still think it's about A, B, and C, and they've moved on to X, Y, and Z. That's how far behind we are to them in technology and understanding and control, that's how far behind. We're just followers now, followers of the reality that they set forth for us. So, we get mad that they don't share with us. They do not have to. Why should they share with us? It's not going to come out of the kindness of their hearts. Nothing else has come out of the kindness of their hearts. . . . So we start screaming about equality, this, that, and the other. . . .

"We need to back up off their [whites'] reality. Sit back." Joshua pauses and once again offers a sports metaphor to make his point. "You know, when you're fighting a fight and you're a boxer, in between rounds you sit and you do what? You contemplate your next move. I don't think we contemplate our next move. I think we're just steady trying to catch up to white folks, steady trying to catch up. They get the big car. We get it. They want the big house. We want it—everything they have, we chase, we chase.

"Here we go with Snoop Doggy Dogg and Ice-T, and the rest of these fools who incite a misunderstanding of the system altogether. You know, there is no need to incite people if you're not going to train and educate them, too. So you incite them over the white man, and now what? Now we're standing around mad at the white man when we should be concentrating on forgetting about the white man, saying fuck him. You know, he's doing his thing, let's do our motherfucking thing."

But the self-reliant ideas that Joshua praises pervade the message in much of rap music, along with the commentary on the social ills of inner-city life. And wouldn't hip-hop be a "game" that whites and Asians, particularly the youth, who are major consumers of the music, are anxious to play? Joshua blasts artists in the same way he disdains athletics. "All those big-name individuals—entertainers, singers, rappers, dancers—court jesters, I like calling them, because back during the times of the king that's all they were. You know, the king would call out the court jesters, and they would make him laugh, do some dances, singing, some music; that's all they are, court jesters. I mean, straight up."

The conversation stops. The woman who may be Sue and three men leave the house. Joshua and Rock study the picture of Rich and look at the three men. The picture of Rich resembles one of the men: he also has curly hair like Rich's, but it is lighter. Joshua and Rock look carefully at the man.

"He could have dyed his hair. I don't know," says Joshua.

Neither Seeker is absolutely sure that they are looking at Rich.

Two of the men get a tire from the trunk of one of the two cars in the yard and place it in the trunk of the other car. They all get in the car, and Rich, or his look-alike, drives.

Rock follows them at a pace that keeps us as far behind the car as possible without losing them. The journey takes us first to a gas station. We pass it—pulling in would give us away. We circle the street a couple of times. Then Joshua decides that it would be better to return to our original spot outside Sue's house before they return. We assume the same spot. Minutes later, they return and reenter the house.

Joshua's imagination is vast, an obvious prerequisite to creating an organization like the Seekers. His unorthodox inventiveness becomes more apparent as he offers his opinions on how human life was created. "I have a real deep belief that we were created by extraterrestrials. I have a real deep belief about that. And that the Egyptians that we know, they had a direct tie with these extraterrestrials, who taught the Egyptians the technology of the stars . . . and the pyramids and the marvelous things they did back then. . . ."

Truly American, I guess: free to think, believe, and, more important, utter with little or no scientific support—even while a tape is recording. Extraterrestrials create human life and wonders in Egypt . . . Elvis and Tupac are still breathing somewhere . . . Nancy Reagan says yes to the stars . . . conspiracy-believing militiamen run free . . . and Hillary talks to Eleanor.

Joshua's homespun prophesy is interrupted by Rock.

"Guys are about to roll out again!"

Rock's voice is louder than ever—so loud that I am stunned. Five people leave the house this time, go to the car. The fifth and new person says what looks like a temporary good-bye. He is wearing a baseball uniform. His face is turned away.

"Turn around," Joshua commands the man in the uniform, who obviously can't hear him. "I'm not sure whether or not it is him."

For a few minutes that seem like an hour, the man remains turned away, his face averted from our eyes. He talks to the woman who could be Sue.

Finally, his identity becomes clear. He turns around, revealing his face to Joshua and Rock. Rock's voice is loud again. "Oh, okay. Okay. Fantastic."

"Thanks, baby," says Joshua. "So long. I think we hit paydirt. If I had to put my life on it, that's him in that crazy fucking stupid-ass hairdo."

"He got a baseball uniform on too," observes Rock.

"Ha ha ha."

The man in the dusty uniform leaves the other four, who drive away. The man who is surely Rich walks down the street. Rock starts the van. Joshua jumps from the passenger seat back to the second seat and crouches down. He instructs me to move to the third, hindmost seat and do the same.

With Rich in sight, Rock creeps slowly down the street. He is driving far slower than the motorists who earlier had frustrated him on the Garden State Parkway. After a few blocks, Rich turns onto a commercial street of neighborhood bars and small stores. Rock drives past Rich and parks up ahead, close to the street corner. Then Rock jumps out of the van, stands on the corner, and looks around like a lost tourist. Rich walks past the parked van as if it's just another car on the street.

After Rich passes the van, Joshua slides open the side door. Rich doesn't hear a thing.

Rock is now ahead of Rich on the street corner. Joshua is behind him— still bent down in the backseat. Rich appears to be heading for the corner bar. Rock stops him with a question.

"Hey, man?" Rock asks. "You know where Main Street is at?"

"Oh, yeah," Rich answers casually. He points the directions and turns away until he hears another voice.

Joshua has risen in the second seat and is in the side doorway, a few feet away from Rich.

"Hey, man, come here," Joshua says.

Rich looks his way. Joshua flicks his private-investigator's identification badge and license. Rich runs off in a flash. Rock takes off after him.

Joshua jumps out of the van and pulls out his gun. A few eyes on the street turn to this spectacle: Rich and Rock running and Joshua on the street with a visible .38. Joshua looks in frustration. He doesn't see Rich or Rock.

"Damn," he says.

He jumps back in the van. He starts it and takes off with squealing tires that leave rubber on the street. On Main Street, he slows down. He sees Rock, T-shirt torn, walking with one hand firmly around Rich's arm.

Joshua gets out and handcuffs Rich. Rock had dropped and lost his handcuffs in the chase.

Rich is breathing heavily. Rock slides behind the wheel, silent again. Rich sits in the second seat, Joshua close to him—so close that their shoulders can't avoid touching.

"If I didn't fall down," Rich says, "Damn."

"I guess I can't even change, huh? Yo, money, can I go home and change?"

Joshua's stern face answers the question. He doesn't even need to utter a no.

"Damn," Rich says. "Another day, man, you wouldn't have got me. Oh, fuck. Shit."

"Man, you fast for a white boy," Joshua teases. "Where did you play at today?"

"We played up in, uh—" Rich pauses, then laughs. "Did you watch me play the game?"

"No."

"You say you wouldn't have been caught had it been another day—why?" I ask.

Rich looks to the back at me and my tape recorder for the first time. "I'm not talking. What you recording for?"

I explain that I'm writing a book. He turns away in disgust.

Rock explains that he jumped three fences in pursuit of Rich, tearing his shirt in the process. But he didn't have to wrestle Rich to the ground. Rich's pace slowed as Rock persistently trailed him, and a tired Rich eventually fell on his own.

"I didn't stop because you called me, I stopped because I couldn't run no more. The cigarettes. I guess I won't be watching the game tonight. Damn. Damn."

Rich pauses, apparently struck by a curious thought. "Who pays you to do this?" he asks.

"Bail bondsmen," Joshua answers.

"Bounty hunters?" Rich says.

Joshua nods a yes.

We arrive at the jail. A woman jailer comes to the door.

"What the hell is this?" she says with a chuckle, eyeing Rich in handcuffs.

They explain, drop Rich off, and get a receipt for the body.

"He's more concerned about baseball than getting his life together," says Rock, speaking of Rich's interest in catching the game tonight. He gains a nod from the boss, who sees Rich's desire to see a game as part of his problems in life. Whatever.

Rock is speeding back to Elizabeth. Joshua talks about the future. "I mean, I'm going to move in the next couple of years . . . I want to take more control of my environment, my immediate environments, [with things] such as power, water, land—you know, the growing of my own food . . . you need land for that. Not a lot, but you know, fifty acres, forty acres. I want to become less dependent on the system.

"What we have been discussing is setting up our own community in the South. I'm doing this because of my worldview. Now, if someone else comes along and, you see, wants to gain more control of their environment, they're welcome to come. If you don't, see ya down the line.

"This way, no matter what happens, we will be able to not only cultivate a stronger community but defend it also. Because if you cultivate and develop a neighborhood and you don't have the means of protecting it, you don't own that neighborhood.

"What's the use of buying and cultivating if you can't protect, if anybody could just run up in your neighborhood and do whatever and then roll the hell back out? Doesn't make any sense. When they come into your neighborhood, they ought to know that there is a force to deal with. There's men in the neighborhood that will defend the neighborhood, that will protect the neighborhood, and that will cultivate the best from the neighborhood. That's what we had during the [nineteen] fifties, forties."

There are some holes in Joshua's patriarchal romanticism of the good old segregated days. Who protected Emmett Till and countless others from their horrific endings in America? A woman named Ida B. Wells tried to, in a campaign launched years before the Till case.

Still, Joshua raises some legitimate questions that have been posed before: How much control of African-American communities did blacks lose with integration? Is the loss partially responsible for social breakdown in some communities? How do African Americans gain more control of their communities in a legally—if not socially—integrated society? Should they? Should that be the mission? How does such a mission collide with American individualism? These questions haunted me throughout my own journey across the country, from even before my time with the Seekers, and beyond.

Joshua says that we can't go back, so we must create new communities that keep street corners free for children and free of the enemies of the community who, according to him, are not usually white or institutional—unless one believes that the government took an active part in spreading drugs in African-American communities, or doesn't consider the Tuskegee syphilis experiments to be isolated. Regardless, the Seekers' overriding message centers on personal responsibility for community and does not absolve black Americans of such responsibility through the crutch of any conspiracy theory.

"Money flows, and everyone turns their back to it now," says Joshua referring to drugs. "You know we always say, 'Well, they [whites] don't give us any other way of making money.' So you do what? You come back in your neighborhood and you destroy it because you want to move up, and you take maybe twenty other people in your neighborhood down? You destroy twenty for one to survive. [That] shit don't make good arithmetic. You know, it don't sound good, it's not logical.

"Drug dealers will not be allowed to stand out on the corners," continues Joshua, speaking of the utopia he envisions. "They'll be some brothers to step out on those spots and say, 'Yo man, what you doing on the corner here? Selling drugs?'"

Joshua says that if the answer is yes, force should follow. "Beat down, chased after, and it's over with. We will always need a means by where we can legally move and groove with weapons."

But, of course, Joshua says the mind is always the most winning weapon.

The Town's Elite

IN some ways, Lawnside is a model of what Joshua seeks to create. Yet he doesn't know that there is such a model right in his own state. That isn't surprising—Lawnside is a quiet place that doesn't show off as a paragon of black life in America. Perhaps that is why William Young had never heard of Lawnside when someone suggested that he open a medical practice there upon his graduation from Howard University College of Medicine. It was the early 1950s. "He said he'd stay two years," recalls Young's wife, Flora. "We've been here for forty-two years."

"Doc Young ain't never been young to me," is how one Lawnside resident describes William Young to me. Young delivered many of the town's residents into the world, and his career was devoted to extending the stay of others. He is a slender man who built a home in Lawnside and operated his practice out of that residence when he wasn't making house calls. In 1989, the Young family purchased the old Lawnside School and turned it into a medical office. William Young retired two years ago, and his son, William Mark Young Jr., forty-two, now operates the practice. William Sr. and Flora's daughter, Marie, forty-four, is an anesthesiologist at University of Pennsylvania.

While Lawnside's neighboring towns have wealthy business communities to drive civic life, Lawnside lacks a chamber of commerce. The town does not house the headquarters of any major corporations, and its professional community is relatively young. Here, like in many other older African-American communities, the physicians play a civic role similar to that of a business elite in many predominantly white communities. "Black physicians had to play a major part, along with ministers and teachers, of being mentors and motivators for young blacks to go forward," explains

Flora Young. "You didn't have any comparable business community. You couldn't go to a corporate structure for help."

When they moved to the town in the fifties, the Youngs almost instantly became Lawnside aristocrats. Within a year, they had started a Lawnside youth group that took children on educational and field trips to black colleges in the South and urged them to ignore the guidance counselors at Haddon Heights High School. "Now, you see we [blacks] have a problem with letting other people define who we are," says Flora Young, echoing sentiments I heard from Joshua.

Flora Young says that these definitions rarely encompass models of success. "So then everything we do is wrong, is bad. My father went to Howard University. My husband went to Howard University College of Medicine. I went to Howard University undergraduate. . . . My daughter went to Howard University undergraduate, Howard University Medical School. Now, we've lived through African-American talent. My son did too. He went to Morgan State and Meharry. I don't care if it is all black, if it's all orthodox. Whether it's green, whether it's gray, if it's quality, you can make it. . . . But some of us have to go to call Mr. Charlie all the time and ask him, 'Is this all right?' Well, I'm not calling him."

A decade after the Youngs became Lawnside residents, black nationalists ridiculed the idea of blacks doing what Flora Young says her family also refused to do—to live by a credo that always seeks the acceptance of whites. But aristocrats like the Youngs were not in style when the black-power movement spread across the country. It touched Lawnside, as a group of high school students formed a group called Young Blacks. To some members, the Young family was part of the problem, not the solution. The Youngs' youth group fell from popularity despite the many goals and ideas it shared with the Young Blacks and the movement. Tensions heightened to a point where Doctor Young was punched by a member of the Young Blacks at a meeting to discuss problems at Haddon Heights High School.

For the most part, though, those tensions are behind the town now. Today, Flora Young, sixty-four, like her husband, revels in a new pace of life. She's no longer racing to the library or to class at Rowan University, where she was a professor of sociology and education. Nor is she in the middle of Lawnside civic life or presiding over meetings of the South Jersey chapters of the Links and Jack and Jill—two organizations that are staples of service or snobbery, depending on one's perspective, in the African-American community. Like Gallia County, Lawnside is not a strong base for many of the national black social and civic groups. The few residents who belong to those groups are members of regional chapters.

Flora Young says that the organizations are strong models of charitable and civic good, even though one doesn't need to dig deeply to discover the less-attractive sides of either. "If you're white, you can have three good outfits and wear them to different events all year and be told how nice you look," says Young. "If you are black, you need several to keep people from saying, 'Isn't she tacky.' You see the same people at the same meetings and conventions. We have so many organizations—the Links, the Girlfriends, and the Boule, the fraternities and sororities. It is so expensive to be black in America. Whoa. I'm now through with it all. I'm wearing my warm-ups."

Today she wears a fuchsia exercise suit and her hair is perfectly coiffed, her café au lait complexion highlighted with delicate touches of rouge. She sits in the study area that once served as the waiting room of her husband's practice. A picture on the mantle snatches my attention—Howard University's class of 1950 at its fortieth-year reunion. David Dinkins is sitting in the front row. "Oh, yeah, I made Joyce, you know," Flora Young says, referring to the fact that she pledged Dinkins's wife into her sorority.

William and Flora Young met at Howard through their respective Greek-organization connections. "He was in medical school and I was on line for Delta. He is a Kappa. We've been married almost fifty years. A long time. Three more years to go."

They began their life in Lawnside shortly after they were married. "They had a doctor in the next town, Magnolia," recalls Young, referring to the one black doctor in the predominantly white town. "But they didn't really have their own physician in Lawnside," says Flora Young. "So when we got ready to get married, Judge Kenton asked us where were we going to settle. He's dead now. He wasn't really a judge but that's what they called him. He served in the capacity of a magistrate.

"He's the one who asked daddy about asking my husband if he would consider coming here when he finished medical school.

"Judge Kenton and his wife were good friends of my parents. . . . They were domestics that worked for the very rich, so they acquired the taste and habits of the wealthy. He was a butler and she was a maid. They had a beautiful home then. . . . During the summertime, he and his wife delighted in having a social affair where they would cater and invite the black professional families from Philadelphia to their home. And I came from the time I was a little girl to this affair."

For William Young, settling in one town for such a long period is a marked change from his childhood. "My earliest recollection is Lewis, Delaware. My father was principal of the school in the black section in Lewis. Both my mother and my father taught at the school.

"We would travel a lot. We drove to Kansas a couple of summers. I always liked to ride. You remember the rumble-seat days? We had the rumble seat where the trunk would be. There was a seat with a handle on it, and you could roll off the thing, pull the backseat up, and you called it a rumble seat. You could use it for luggage or passengers. I hated to see the rumble seat go. I rode all the way from Los Angeles to North Carolina in the rumble seats."

For several summers, his father did graduate work at Harvard during the week and worked on the railroads on weekends. "He would go from Bangor, Maine, to the Northwest, past Chicago. He worked as a waiter on the trains while he was working on his master's. . . . Harvard had listings of the various schools that needed black teachers . . . so he would stay a couple of years at one school and then go to another until he got a position at St. Augustine's College in Raleigh, North Carolina, an Episcopal college."

Young grew up on the St. Augustine campus, which also had an elementary school at the time. When he reached high school, his parents sent him to Cambridge, Massachusetts, to live with family friends so that he could attend the well-regarded Cambridge Latin School. While many African Americans praise segregated schools, Young says, his parents were keenly aware that resources in many of the schools were limited. "It was a trend in those days. If the professional people could afford to send their kids to a school in New England or private prep schools up North, then they did."

Like her husband, Flora Young is also a product of a pre-1960s professional black family. But hers was a different world from his entirely. While William Young grew up under the influence of the black college life, Flora Young was a child of Philadelphia's old black society, an upscale urban world that was well established when she was born in 1932. Springing from a community of freeborn blacks and ex-slaves who made up an estimated 10 percent of the black population between the mid-1800s and mid-1900s, its roots are chronicled in W. E. B. Du Bois's *The Philadelphia Negro*. Excluded from white clubs, libraries, and hospitals, they created their own elite bases—much like African Americans in many other cities did. The way of life was steeped in Victorian values and the Puritan ethic.

Flora Young lived in the center of it all, on Christian Street, which was often referred to at the time as Professional Row because of the large concentration of black undertakers, lawyers, doctors, and dentists—her father being one of the latter—who practiced in the area. "It was kind of interesting, given how I grew up in Philadelphia, and what was around me," says Young. "The transition to come and live here was not difficult because, ostensibly, it was the same kind of environment. It was not as many social clubs and professionals or what have you, but the value system was the same: Get a good education. Be self-reliant. Be responsible. It's nothing rais-ing children in this kind of community. It's really a safe haven."

Despite their privileged upbringings, as both children and parents William and Flora Young have had their encounters with American bigotry. There's the yearbook at Haddon Heights High School that abandoned tradi-tion and failed to picture the valedictorian of the class of 1971—the year that their daughter, Marie, happened to have earned the honor. Several banks refused to give them a loan to build the kind of house they wanted in Lawnside, one that was not lavish, but comfortable and large enough for Young's practice. William Young never forgets the time when he was a stu-dent at Cambridge Latin and white Harvard students vandalized the con-vertible of a friend who is now a doctor in Greensboro, North Carolina. Young says that they ripped the car apart when they noticed that a black teenager owned it. But the Youngs do not recount those stories with bitter-ness, emotion, or excitement: such tales are merely conversation pieces that can serve as small talk with friends who will shake their heads and offer a sarcastic smile or some other mild expression of indignation. The stories can also be easily shot at a conservative who wishes to sweep racism into a column of rare and abnormal American experiences.

There's more excitement and glee in their eyes when the Youngs share stories of the lives of the black elite before integration, or their experiences in Lawnside and at Howard. They speak a language with words that only those who've been through that world would understand—"lines," "Ques," "Deltas," "AKAs"—and cite trends in those worlds today that only those who've been there would grasp. They talk about the changing population in some of the groups and professionals forgoing graduate chapters, espe-cially if they have demanding careers or join groups such as the Links, Guardsmen, and the Boule.

The minute details of their social heritage are not as interesting as the mere existence of the social world itself and its role in enhancing a self-reliance that guided the Youngs' lives through a society with legally sanc-tioned racial injustice. Just as the legacy of that injustice can be thrown at conservatives, the examples of self-reliance can counter liberals who may prefer to see blacks as totally deprived people who were saved by the goodness of the left in the sixties. "I wasn't as worried about racism, be-cause I had a very fine community in which to interact, and my own house-hold had its own expectations as to what I was to do and what I was to get out of it," says Flora Young. "My parents were very very active in the com-munity, the NAACP. So I had people in and out of my home who were well trained and had high expectations.

"You had a whole environment of people who were all going in the same direction. The kids in our circle went to college. You dwelt upon them getting an education. You were supposed to be literate. You were supposed to be articulate. You had the social clubs, you had churches. The schools were as discriminatory as they could be, but you had parents and their friends serving as role models, and you felt motivated to keep on going. Your reality was this very tight-knit kind of situation. That was what drove your reality. You didn't have as your reality these people who were always trying to knock you down."

Flora Young's "sense of reality" in pre-sixties America provides the basis for a postmodern perspective on race that is increasingly common among black Americans and extends beyond descendants of the black elite. It is a view that isn't held hostage to the left or the right but tacks to the rational center, acknowledging racism as a pernicious but nonfatal force in American life. It is a perspective that does not regard racism as the totality of the black experience, but as an inevitable barrier that can be partially overcome by refusing to allow it to halt personal initiative. For some, independent schools and rites-of-passage programs, rooted in black nationalism, enhance that initiative. For others, professional associations and social networks serve the purpose. Such a perspective—perhaps not so explicitly articulated—helped to sustain racially encased worlds like Philadelphia's Professional Row and Lawnside.

Flora Young doesn't answer questions with only a verbal response. She frequently jumps up, leaves the room, and returns with something to amplify her answers. She's a collector. In one afternoon, I've seen things as diverse as a program from a theatrical performance of *Othello* starring Paul Robeson to a French first edition of the late Howard University sociologist E. Franklin Frazier's *Black Bourgeoisie*. "He never thought this would get read, you know," she says, placing the copy of *Bourgeoisie Noire* in front of me. "He never thought anyone was going to translate that book. I was his student."

The book had its critics, particularly from families like Flora Young's, for its scathing attack on the values of black aristocrats. Yet she defends Frazier. "It wasn't unsubstantiated. It was his life. He was my mentor. I knew E. Franklin Frazier. . . . But the main problem of the book is he didn't make a clear distinction between the Aristocrats and the Nouveaux Riches. He put them all in the same pot . . . it was all mixed up together. You had the Aristocrats, the Nouveaux Riches, and then you had the Shadys, and they were the ones who had made their money pimping and gambling. He put them all together. And everyone was angry when he wrote it. . . . He should have broken down the groups."

Young quickly exits the room. She returns with a copy of Frazier's *Negro in the United States* and flips through the pages. "He did better with that in *The Negro in the United States*. It categorically describes your upper class, your middle class, and your working class and your working poor," she says, trying to find a passage. "It's lifestyle—it's not income. For example, somebody who is like these fighters and these ballplayers who are making all this money: they would have never been accepted in old Philadelphia black society, believe me. They wouldn't have let them in the door because they don't have the manners. They don't have the bearing. They don't have the knowledge about books and reading and music.

"It goes back to 'bagitis,' where they [whites] put us all in one bag. They never did want to accept that we had an upper class and a middle class in black America. The upper and middle classes were different from the white upper and middle classes in America, primarily because of the longevity of traditions and what have you. But in terms of carriage and deportment and dignity and lifestyle and ideology, you had definite proof of an upper and middle class, and the traditions that have been handed down, occupational and all of that kind of stuff. But the white world never wanted to admit to all of that, because then they would have to differentiate among us and see us as equals. As long as they could put us in a bag and make O.J. Simpson on the same level as you and me and everyone, then they have the whole race in one bag. Simpson could not have walked into a house in Philadelphia and been accepted before or after the murders."

Young is not a cheerleader for the black elite and has a fierce impatience with those who promote a hush-hush approach to all corners of black life, those who only want to examine the positive for fear of letting dirty laundry out into the open. One of those hush-hush issues she discusses with great frankness is prejudice within the black community based on the shade of one's complexion. "It's a reality. It was certainly a very important reality in Philadelphia. Color played a very important part as far as Philadelphia society was concerned and as far as African Americans are concerned.

You had a very stable, solid, upper-class black group in Philadelphia that came out of the domestic class. They had worked for the rich, and their lifestyle was just like the rich. Many of the old aristocrats who were maids and butlers for the very rich were mulattoes, and so they were able to travel between two worlds. They had some access to the larger society and the accoutrements of the rich for whom they worked. So it became very natural in the way they carried themselves, the way they kept their homes."

Young says the parents of that upper class often raised their children to join the professional class. She picks up *The Negro in the United States*. "It's all in this book. There was a cohort of them, and even though they were not professionals as we were, they had knowledge about the proper behavior and so on . . . and many of their children were encouraged to maintain their light-color line. When they ran out of them, they began to encourage them to engage with some of the browner professionals. But that was the wrong darn color! If you go through the history of Philadelphia, you will find some very accomplished brown or dark man married to some light-skinned woman. And Washington was like that. And Boston was like that."

"Yeah, that was very prevalent," agrees Dr. Young.

"The domestic side ended up being the upper class, or the foundation of much of it. A lot of people don't like to admit it.

"Many of the professionals had to go through an academic process before they could become professionals. But the aristocrats who had taken on this particular lifestyle of the people for whom they worked had stuck in there and saved a little bundle all by themselves, and they began to enjoy or look toward enjoying classical music, literature, traveling, the whole scheme of things. Now, the professional class was black. They were academics and doctors. But these others had to assume a posture so they wouldn't be embarrassed. . . .

"It was very interesting, last week on the Internet," adds Dr. Young. "We pulled up all of the first black graduates of the University of Pennsylvania, and they had the rundown on every one of them."

"They were not all fair skinned," says Flora Young. "Some were. Some of the professionals were part of that old group. But it was reluctantly that the mulattoes allowed themselves and their children to marry black or darker people unless, eventually, they were accomplished. The mulattoes didn't have to have a Ph.D. to go to the dance, and here you had many professionals, many of whom were dark skinned, were accomplished—and all of them have women on their arms who were mulattoes."

Flora Young steps out again. She returns with a set of books—the annual yearbooks of the Pyramid Club in Philadelphia. Founded in 1945, the men's club purchased a building, where they held meetings and events and rented space to black organizations. The members were professionals: doctors, lawyers, morticians, and educators. Her six yearbooks from 1945 to 1951 provide a glimpse of the active life in the old Philadelphia society. There are pictures of annual Yankee Doodle Banquets, Fisk and Lincoln University alumni luncheons, the sorority and fraternity luncheons, meetings of the Girlfriends, and outings and activities of the daughters and mothers of the members. One is captioned CUTIES AT THE PENN RELAYS.

"Look at the women in this book and look at the men."

In the portrait of the "cuties," and in most of the other pictures, almost all of the women could be mistaken for white, while the men, including the founding members of the club, are of various skin tones.

Flora Young says that Lawnside is not immune to the color conflict. In fact, she says, there are traces of it in the political rivalry between Democratic state senator Wayne Bryant, who is fair skinned, and Republican leader Walter "Butch" Gaines, a darker-skinned man. "The power play between the Bryants and the rest of them have some elements" of the color conflict, she asserts. "The Bryants represent the fair-skinned ones. They would not admit to that, but that is a reality, and they've been in power here for a long, long time."

Flora Young isn't the only Lawnside resident who shared the light/dark interpretation of Lawnside politics and culture. Some residents even suggest that one had to pass a paper-bag test to attend some of Wayne Bryant's teenage parties.

I visit Butch Gaines again after my interview with the Youngs. His face grows stern when I raise the color issue; he declares it a nonissue in Lawnside and that he is unaware of Bryant ever showing any favoritism for fair-skinned people. Wayne Bryant also denies that it is an issue and cites his many friendships with people who were not fair skinned. Either the issue is too hot and sensitive for politicians like Gaines and Bryant to address or Young and other residents are inventing it, which I doubt is the case. Regardless, Gaines and Bryant are much more comfortable taking jabs at each other on other issues: Bryant built a glistening, modern four-story office building in Cherry Hill, New Jersey, to house his law firm and in which other professionals rent space from the Bryants. Gaines wants to know why Bryant's firm isn't headquartered in Lawnside. "When it comes to using your dollars to develop businesses and buildings . . . I guess I believe in basically the free market system," explains Bryant. "There are people who are going to always tell you what you should be doing. . . . My question is, what are they doing? I ask them, what have they put in Lawnside? And I have no qualms about giving back to Lawnside much more than Lawnside has given to me . . . I've hired a lot of students that have gone on to college in my firm. A young girl who's now the judge started here. . . .

"If you look at Lawnside, this small town, people have left here and gone all over the world. I still live in Lawnside, and I love it. But you don't have to live here or work here. You can stay there and make it better or you can go in the world and use what you learned in Lawnside to make the world better."

• • •

Cord Whitaker, seventeen, rode atop the Lawnside Scholarship Club's car in the Fourth of July Parade. He was among the twenty-five Lawnside students who graduated from high school in 1997, most of them finishing at Haddon Heights High School. Cord was third in his graduating class at Haddon Heights and first among his Lawnside peers. Like Ellen Benson, he received the Lawnside Scholarship Club's first-place award. I spoke to him a few weeks before he was planning to enter Yale as a psychology major. "I tend to be a very academic yet artistic person. I'm into all the fine arts . . . I act, sing, and Yale exudes that—a lot of emphasis on art. I applied to Harvard, Princeton, Yale, Penn, the University of Rochester, University of Chicago, Temple, Rutgers, Hampton, and there are probably a few others in there. But I chose Yale for the artistic environment there."

Though he has lived in Lawnside since he was seven, Cord could be considered a newcomer to the town. He isn't a Still, Arthur, Benson, Bryant, or one of the few other old names in town. The Whitakers moved to Lawnside from Philadelphia in 1986, when Cord was a second-grader. "We just moved here partly because our parents wanted to get out of the city. They found the house my mother always wanted. The vibes were right."

Unlike some of the new families cited by Ellen Benson, the Whitakers knew they were moving to Lawnside. "My father does say he likes the fact of living in a black community. After we moved here, we found out my grandparents had come here back in their heyday. You know, when they had all the barbecue places.

"When we first moved over here, it was culture shock . . . I was going from the city to the suburbs and then from private to public school all at once. But I began to adjust. Lawnside is not bad. . . . Sometimes it blows hot, sometimes it blows cold. . . . This town breeds a lot of solidarity, I think. It also breeds a lot of . . ."

Cord pauses. "Well, let's just say the opposite of solidarity—sometimes."

Cord says there are divisions among youth in the town, but he doesn't see the same differences that some old residents described between the old and new ways of Lawnside. He also says that the divides are not based on upper-middle versus middle class in the way that class factors cause rifts among whites at Haddon Heights High School. Cord believes that the social factions are formed around common values and academic interests, which vary among Lawnsiders regardless of the depth of their roots in the town. "Lawnside School is very cliquish, and I had my clique. Believe me, those are the people who I still hang out with."

People outside of the clique made Cord feel like an alien when he first moved to town. He says he confronted charges of "acting white" because of the way he talks: he speaks in an alto with naturally crisp endings to all of his words, nothing forced for the sake of sounding proper. And he isn't the only young Lawnsider I've heard with strong g's on words like *starting* and *ending*. But Cord is the only one so far who says he was chided by peers for speaking with an intonation that defies the stereotypes of black speech. "It really, really bothered me. But, later, I came to find that it meant absolutely nothing. In the end, the people who were saying those sorts of things were just saying them because other people were saying them. Eventually, I found out a lot of those people admired me."

Cord says his speech followed the model of his father, a public-relations executive who doesn't even jokingly speak so-called Ebonics when he is away from the corporate world and in the comfort of his home in a black town. Cord's is a family in which once a week at dinner, he and his younger brother were expected to discuss the family book of the month—Steinbeck's *Grapes of Wrath,* Wright's *Native Son,* or Buck's *The Good Earth,* among others. "I've been raised by my parents, one being an English major, and both being very literate people. I speak proper English, which is the way I believe the language should be spoken."

Cord recalls whites at Haddon Heights High School who took pride in talking and acting in the ways that some of his peers at the Lawnside School pressured him to speak and behave. But "acting black" is apparently all right for white kids. Conversely, black teenagers in any town face criticism from black peer critics for any apperance of "acting white," according to numerous scholarly and journalistic accounts of the phenomenon. Cord suspects that pressure on African-American youth to conform is greater in a public school of a black town, but he also says that it is much easier to resist the pressure in such places as Lawnside because of the diversity of the population. "Lawnside is reflective of the general population—some good, some bad. You've got your top, you've got your bottom. A lot middle of the road. There are choices for friendships. Generally, birds of a feather do flock together."

Cord says that his flock has similar views on racism. They mirror the postmodern perspective expressed by Flora Young and Joshua the Seeker: it isn't a race-blind perspective that dismisses the presence of racism today in the way that some conservatives do when they eulogize the country's most racist days, but it also doesn't let racism deter them from their goals. For Cord, bigotry doesn't stop him from forming strong bonds with people who are not black, nor is it an excuse for failure. "I think there's a little too much complaining about racism and not enough action. I'd prefer less complaining and more action. I wouldn't even care if there was as much complaining if there was more action."

Cord cites a racial dispute at Haddon Heights High School this year as an example of black inaction. The trouble centered on the school's winter musical, *The Wiz*—the black version of the classic *The Wizard of Oz*. Most of the cast was white, and Cord, who played a lead role in the show, says he disagreed with some Lawnside students, who make up the overwhelming majority of blacks at the school about how to react to that. "The director tried to get more African-American students to try out, which they very well could have, but not as many tried out. So the cast ended up being mainly white. It turned out just fine. It may not have been Stephanie Mills on Broadway . . .

"The usual people, they didn't try out, but were saying, 'This is bad and you shouldn't do this and that.' And I'm like, 'I didn't see you at auditions.'" Many residents celebrate Cord's success because he is a product of the Lawnside School. Since the late seventies, when test scores there began to decline, many parents in town, particularly newcomers, have chosen to send their children to private grammar schools. A member of the Scholarship Club, studying the list of the club's most recent awardees, privately notes that unlike Cord, some at the top did not attend the Lawnside School during the elementary school years. In 1980, 11 percent of all Lawnside elementary school–age children attended private schools, and 10 percent did the same in 1990—twice the New Jersey average for any school district. Some, like the Bensons, prefer the old ways of the paddle and prayer in the school and can at least find prayer in area Christian schools, but others choose secular prep schools. A generation ago, it was rare to find a family avoiding the Lawnside School. But new teachers, values, and standards force many to look elsewhere.

Cord says he doesn't know if he will settle in Lawnside as an adult. It is a big world and Lawnside is a small place, he says. But a Lawnside perspective will touch all of his destinations.

Two

FISHING

Morning in Hampton

ISHING has grown into a Father's Day–weekend tradition for the McKoy family. The fathers gather in Hampton, Virginia.

Hampton, a city of 138,062 on the Chesapeake Bay, is home to the school that educated Booker T. Washington. Now Hampton University, it was called the Hampton Agricultural and Normal Institute when Washington arrived on the campus in 1872. For him, it was a five-hundred-mile journey to Hampton from Malden, West Virginia. He walked much of the route. He also worked along the way so he could pay the fare for the other legs of the trip. "Perhaps the thing that touched and pleased me most in connection with my starting for Hampton was the interest that many of the older people took in the matter," wrote Washington in *Up from Slavery,* his autobiography. "They had spent the best days of their lives in slavery, and hardly expected to live to see the time when they would see a member of their race leave home to attend a boarding school. Some of the older people would give me a nickel, others a quarter or a handkerchief."

At Hampton, Washington was immersed in a bootstrapism that became the foundation of his focus on building institutions rather than screaming for entry into a place where he wasn't wanted. Washington founded the Tuskegee Institute, in Tuskegee, Alabama, a black school where he taught and modeled his politics of accommodation and black self-sufficiency. Both Tuskegee and Hampton grew into colleges, but both began as multipurpose boarding schools that stressed agricultural and vocational education over studying the classics. Washington said he lacked patience for schools of the other type—those that didn't teach his people to see the value in labor. Some historians cite a contradiction in what Washington preached and

what he practiced in raising his children. He sent them to Fisk and Welles-
ley, liberal arts colleges clearly not of the make of Tuskegee and Hampton.
He still never failed to publicly praise Hampton: "At Hampton," he said in
Up from Slavery, "I not only learned that it was a disgrace not to labour, but
learned to love labour, not alone for its financial value, but for labour's own
sake and for the independence and self-reliance which the ability to do
something which the world wants done brings."

Eight decades later, Clarence McKoy, sixty-five, took a different route to
Hampton, coming from Hoke County, North Carolina. By then, the school
had changed with the times and grown into the four-year, fully accredited,
and reputable university. Nevertheless, it hadn't at all shed the influence of
Washington; it had kept "Institute" in its name until 1984. "There are still
some people who won't say Hampton University and still look for things to
buy that say Hampton Institute, if they can find them," says Clarence, who
majored in agricultural science and minored in education and social sci-
ences. "And Booker T. Washington stood for working with your hands as
well as academics. He stood for both sides. I like that. I was disappointed
when Hampton did away with the trade school."

McKoy wasn't a student of the trades, but while he was at Hampton, the
school had departments for bricklaying, plumbing, and welding, among
other trades. Those trade departments—another part of the Washington
legacy—existed until 1958. "A few of the buildings on campus today were
built by students at the trade school," says McKoy. "We are short electri-
cians, carpenters, bricklayers, and plumbers. It's hard to find a black one
today."

McKoy didn't plan on attending Hampton. "I applied for the Tuskegee
Airmen—and got accepted. But I was too young. They finally asked for a
birth certificate, and then they kicked me out. I was sixteen; you had to be
eighteen.

"I went to Hampton because my principal at my high school was a
Hampton graduate, and he told me about it. During that time, nobody from
our area was going to Hampton."

In 1948, Clarence met Irene, a freshman coed who would become his
wife. Clarence and Irene McKoy remain fiercely loyal to the school, and
they sent their daughter, Tanya, to Hampton in the mid-seventies. They live
on property that was actually part of the campus when they were students,
in Granger Court East, a quiet, residential neighborhood of forty-five ranch-
style homes that sit on what was once Hampton's School of Agriculture.
"Which means this was a farm," says Clarence McKoy. "There were no
houses out here. And then they began to sell the property off to people

who had some connection with the university. Either you worked there or graduated there."

In 1962, McKoy purchased a half-acre lot for $1,500. With the help of one of the school's professors of architecture, McKoy, like the area's other residents, built a home customized to his taste. His rural roots required a large kitchen that could also function as a living room, because the latter is too formal to really *live* in. Much of the house, then, grows out of the kitchen, which opens into the family room and wet bar on one side and a closed-in porch on the other. "And you see the size of that kitchen," says McKoy as he points to the twenty-by-twelve-foot room featuring a dining area almost as large as the formal dining room. "Where I came from in the country, the kitchen was sort of the social center. That's where you sat. So we decided we wanted a big kitchen. Look at that kitchen. You don't see a kitchen that size anymore."

On this Saturday morning, Irene McKoy loads the kitchen table with Wonder bread toast, sausage, bacon, and eggs as her husband is gathering the fishing rods, three Igloos, sodas, beer, and cheese-cracker snacks. The younger McKoy fathers—his nephews, Henry McKoy and Willie Artemus McKoy, along with James McMillan, Willie's brother-in-law, and Jay Jeffries, the boyfriend of Willie and Henry's sister—are on their way.

The younger men arrived at the Marriott in Hampton from Raleigh, North Carolina, last night. They are up early and rushing to make a 7:00 A.M. call for breakfast. The music of their youth rides with them to Clarence and Irene's house. It doesn't blast: a roaring car speaker doesn't complement Marvin Gaye, Tammy Terrell, and the Supremes; too much volume could easily defeat the relaxing energy of Motown. "I drive a lot in my job," says Willie McKoy, a human-resources manager. "I have eleven locations in the eastern area of the state. So when I get tired of trying to flip the stations, I put that tape in and just let Marvin take me down the road."

At 7:10, they are parking in Uncle Clarence's driveway. Marvin Gaye is in the middle of a soulful rendition of "The Star-Spangled Banner." It obviously wraps up Henry and Willie. They hum and, occasionally, their heads slowly sway like a flag waving on a pole through a slow breeze. They turn off the car after Marvin's "home of the brave." But the song stays with them into the conversation over breakfast. "We ought to take that to the chancellor and ask him to play that when Central plays A&T," says Henry. Henry, forty-nine, and his younger brother, Willie, forty-four, are both graduates of North Carolina Agricultural and Technical State University, a historically black state college in Greensboro, North Carolina.

Willie nods as he slices his sausage.

"You talking about that Marvin Gaye thing?" Clarence asks.

"They played it at one of Hampton's basketball games," says Irene.

"How did the crowd react?" asks Henry.

"The old folks don't like it," she says. "I don't like jazzing up the national anthem. I like it to be sung the old-fashioned way."

A generation gap opened over "The Star-Spangled Banner" places Henry McKoy on the liberal side, for a change. In contrast, two weeks ago, he was more at home on the conservative side in another intergenerational flap over music. His daughter was blasting music in his own backyard, and it wasn't Marvin. "Marcia had a graduation party that Saturday before she graduated," Henry remembers. "She had about fifteen or more young people. And she was playing some of that Snoop Doggy Dogg stuff. People talking about 'I screwed so and so' on the record and some slow songs. One of the songs was 'Between the Sheets.'"

"Yeah?!" blurts Clarence.

"'Between the Sheets,'" Henry repeats. "And my daughter's playing this stuff. I called her over, and I said, 'Marcia, you're going to turn that thing off and you're going to put something else on, or I'm going to tear that tape up.' She walked over there. She turned it off. She didn't say another word. And I told her, 'You are not going to play that stuff and invite children, sixteen, seventeen years of age to our house.'

"But let me tell you what the most beautiful part of it was: I looked and they were taking a picture. Every one of those kids was going to college. And I said it is remarkable. You got seventeen young black kids sitting out here on my deck and graduating tomorrow. And every one of them going to college. Five of my classmates went to college. Five. When I graduated, it was close to one hundred in the class, and five of us went to college. And on my deck, seventeen young black kids."

"And all of them were going to college?" asks Clarence.

It is refreshing to hear African-American adults and elders who grew up in the segregated South speak positively about African-American teenagers when comparing them to the youth in the "good old" segregated communities. The further we grow from the era of segregation, the more those days become romanticized as the time when Negroes were so polite and genteel to one another. Today, the young and the old alike argue that integration eroded the essentials of family and community and created the need for role models to be called such. I ask Henry McKoy if his observation at the party contradicts the idealized perceptions of the segregated past and fatalistic predictions of the future of the race. Uncle Clarence jumps in and offers some argumentative protection for his nephew. Essentially, he says that there are two black societies—one extends neatly from the past and one is lost. "All right, let me give you a scenario there: Henry is dealing with kids who know his daughter, who may go to college. Go to the East End here [in Hampton], and the guys are going nowhere but on the block. Look where I live. Everybody in Hampton and Newport News does not live like I live. The people I associate with, their children and grandchildren are going to college. My daughter teaches school, and the kids she teaches are going to college. But I can take you where these other kids have no vision. I mean, they have no future. They stay there and survive, just survive."

Henry McKoy jumps back in with a footnote that coincides with the theme of the weekend. "The majority of the kids on my deck had fathers living with them," he says. "About ninety percent of them had fathers in the home."

"It's two different societies out there, even for blacks," says Clarence.

Humor this weekend is often driven by friendly rivalry. It starts with the annual five-dollar bet over who will catch the first fish and spills into jokes that boast about and berate everything from the inconsistency of New York Knick John Starks's three-pointers last season to the three rival college fraternities that still hold the loyalty of the three McKoys. Henry only intensifies the sparring this year by wearing a black-and-gold hat bearing the Greek letters of his fraternity. Then there's the big rivalry over their alma maters: Hampton and A&T.

Willie and Henry McKoy's families are as committed to North Carolina A&T State University as Clarence McKoy's family is to Hampton. Both Henry and his wife, Katie, are A&T graduates. In May, his oldest daughter, Kara, graduated from the university. His youngest daughter, Marcia, is entering the school in the fall. Willie McKoy's eleven-year-old daughter is on the same path. "She already says she wants to go to A&T," he says proudly.

"I belong to the Hampton Boosters," says Clarence McKoy. "I pay five hundred dollars a year. I get two seats with my name on it. I get a parking space with my name on it. I get reserved seats for the basketball games."

"Do you get all of that for five hundred dollars?" asks Henry jokingly.

"Yeah," Clarence replies.

"That's mighty nice, mighty nice. I need to join that club," says Willie with sarcasm in his voice.

Clarence McKoy shakes his head. "I can't wait until we play A&T."

"I can't wait either."

"Our first five games are away," says Clarence McKoy. "They play More-

house, they come back to Howard, they go to the Meadowlands to play
Grambling. Then they go back to New Orleans and then to Florida."

"*They* play in Florida?" says Henry. "Who?"

"Bethune Cookman, FAMU. You know, Hampton is leaving the CIAA and
going into the MEAC."

Father's Day weekend fishing began six years ago, in 1989. Then, the gathering was primarily a way to bring together two brothers—Clarence and
Harvey McKoy, Henry and Willie's father. The elder McKoys were the last
two living siblings of their generation in the family. Fishing wasn't the main
draw for Harvey McKoy. "We couldn't get him on the boat," recalls Clarence
McKoy. "He wouldn't go fishing, but he'd come up with them."

When Harvey McKoy died in 1990, the weekend's importance grew. "All
of my brothers are dead, and their father's dead," says Clarence, pointing to
Henry and Willie. "And the boys adopted me. I call them boys, you know.
I'm the only male image for them of the older age. That's why they're here.
And they do that every year. Around Father's Day every year."

Clarence McKoy, a retired school principal, always has been an influen-
tial model in the family. His life reflects a transition in the family: Through
Clarence McKoy, the family moved with the nation, from the end of the
agrarian era to the modern industrial society. He was the youngest of his
siblings, and the first in the family, as well as the only one of his generation,
to attend college. During the late fifties and early sixties, he would return to
his old home in Hoke County, North Carolina, as the graduate living in his
new home of Hampton. Back then, Henry and Willie were children working with their father on the farm in the summers and studying during the
school year. Their eyes were focused on achieving a future on the model of
Uncle Clarence. "I remember when he first brought Aunt Irene home," says
Henry. "It was the first time I had seen someone dressed up like that on a
weekday. My parents would dress up on Sundays, but during the week they
were basically farming. But Uncle Clarence, every day he had a nice set of
clothes, and his wife had pretty dresses. He had a Cadillac. I remember, as a
young boy, that is what I wanted to do, so I worked hard. Every morning
the sun would shine on our cinder-block house. I would sit outside and
read about people like Marcus Garvey."

Today, Henry McKoy values segregated schools for the black teacher
who helped him secure a scholarship to A&T. "My parents wanted me to go
to college, but they knew they could not afford to send me. I remember
whites would get mad with my father because he wanted his children to

stay in school. And that is who ran the farm. But five of the six children graduated from college."

The Father's Day weekend has evolved into its own routine. The business and fun of fishing come first. After a few hours on the boat, the men eat, drink, talk, argue, and laugh away the rest of the day back at Clarence's house. They leave early Sunday morning with fish wrapped and ready for their families on Father's Day. "You give a man a fish, you feed him only temporarily—for a day," says Henry McKoy. "You teach a man to fish and he can live forever . . . You see, our tradition is, we grew our crops. That's a tradition that we learned as children. And the loss of that rural tradition is a part of what I think has gone wrong in America: We have created a generation of people that we have given the fish to. We haven't taught them how to look out for their own."

Last year, the conversation of the trip was dominated by Henry McKoy's mission to carry the old tradition of Harvey McKoy, Clarence McKoy, and, perhaps unknowingly, Booker T. Washington into electoral politics. In the home of Jesse Helms, Henry McKoy ran a campaign to become the first black Republican elected to North Carolina's state senate since Reconstruction.

Chapter 10

Campaign '94

I T is Friday, November 4, 1994. The Republican Party's drive to take as many statehouses as possible and to own both houses of Congress is more than a decade old and close to fruition. America is four days away from the 1994 electoral revolution that turned Newt Gingrich into *Time* magazine's Man of the Year. Henry McKoy is one of the few black candidates across the country pumped up by the muscle of the GOP's resources targeting state legislative races. While he's raised less money than his Democratic opponents, he can count on the party's massive effort to bring out the vote in predominantly white and Republican precincts. He also has his own team of white volunteers in those precincts.

McKoy now sits in the heart of his challenge. The people surrounding him are all African Americans. McKoy hovers over a plate of food at Le Counts, a cafeteria-style restaurant in mostly black southeast Raleigh. "The Democrats can amass a whole group of people . . . to make sure blacks come out and vote Democratic. So I'm not only competing against my two opponents, I'm competing against the leadership of the black community."

The presence of Senator Jesse Helms surely helps the competition. Helms isn't actually in the restaurant, but he haunts McKoy's campaign. The senator was once a Democrat, and his switch of parties inversely mirrors that of many black Americans. Most old Lawnside families, for example, were once members of the party of Lincoln—there was a time when most black voters were members of the GOP. But then came the popularity of Franklin Delano Roosevelt, which stirred a realignment among blacks that accelerated when the anti–civil rights Southern Democrats of the sixties—the Dixiecrats—Jesse Helms among them, defected to the Republican Party.

Today's Willie Horton and Patrick Buchanan were merely continuations of the Republican Party's Dixiecrat heritage of offending blacks to draw whites. Even Colin Powell isn't powerful enough to counter the party's Dixiecrat past—and present.

Today, most—not all—black Republican candidates win only in districts that are overwhelmingly white. Lawnside's Butch Gaines is an exception. On this Friday, Oklahoma's J.C. Watts is four days away from a historic victory in a congressional district that is 92 percent white, and Connecticut's Gary Franks is fighting to hold on to a House seat representing a district that is 91 percent white. McKoy is trying something different: he is running as a black Republican in a district that is 22 percent black. It is a tight race, and he needs a good chunk of the black vote to win. His chances turn on his ability to nurture a coalition of two seemingly incongruent voting blocks—conservative whites and blacks.

McKoy stops eating and stands when the hand of a voter is in shaking distance. He knows it is highly probable that he is pressing flesh that has never pulled the lever for a Republican. In Wake County, there are roughly 1,500 blacks registered as Republicans—4 percent of all black registered voters in the county—and straight-ticket voting is common among blacks across the state. For many blacks, race is thinner than party membership if the choices are a black Republican and a white Democrat. But McKoy insists that culture—not race—is the bond that could tie black voters to his candidacy. He says that his values are rooted in the same conservative culture that nurtured those who are standing in line for the plates of fried chicken and macaroni at Le Counts. McKoy's campaign stakes a black claim to values that are commonly associated with conservative whites.

McKoy's challenge, though, is taller than this one-story restaurant and wider than the 1.4 square miles of Lawnside that Butch Gaines traveled in his campaign for mayor. McKoy must show that a black Republican is not always an alien to African-American culture. This seems to compel him to remind people of his roots. "I grew up in a black neighborhood, finished an all-black high school, went to a predominantly black college. I am the black experience."

Many blacks and whites are guilty of imposing the urban experience on the whole of African-American culture. But not Henry McKoy: he loves to talk about his rural American experience, taking pride in being a country boy. "I was born in 1946, nine months after my father came back from World War II. My mother and father started a home in Hoke County running along a lumber river about four or five miles from where their parents lived. I spent a considerable amount of time with my grandparents. When I grew up, you got up when an elderly person came into the room. When an elderly person came to the table, you stood up and gave them their favorite chair."

The men and women for whom he stood in such instances couldn't count on commanding the same level of respect outside of their homes, facing the mood swings of Jim Crow. For blacks in that era, independence and seclusion were two of the best shields from racism's intrusions into their authority as adults. Yet that wasn't always possible for proud, but poor, families like the McKoys. The family owned thirty acres of land—eight of which were farmed by Henry McKoy's father. The farm didn't generate enough income to support eight McKoys, so sharecropping made up some of the difference. In the winter, his father looked for other ways to support the family. "My father made money selling wood. He would go to the local sawmill and gather up slabs of wood. We would saw the wood into smaller chunks and sell it at the general store. My father was also a barber and a welder."

As he describes his father, I am reminded of Gallia County's Victor Long. Though McKoy is a few decades younger than Long, the politician describes his father in ways that echo the Ohio man's recollections of his own family. "Anything for an honest dollar" were Long's words as he described the credo of life in the black community of Little Raccoon; it was the principle that guided the Longs through a depression—and the McKoys through the post–World War II era. Through it all, many African Americans lived in racially separate worlds that they only left when economics necessitated that they venture outside. McKoy says that the elders of that era whom he knew were fiercely independent and proud.

So were the good old days really that good? Or is McKoy merely engaging in his version of the old American pastime of doomsaying the contemporary and praising the past with the showers of nostalgia? Whichever, McKoy says that black expressions of independence or individuality in the political arena are undermined and severely inhibited today by the paternalism of white liberals and moderates of the Democratic Party. He argues that blacks are strapped to the donkey in a similar way their ancestors were chained to the plantation. The Republican McKoy, like the Lawnside Democrat Wayne Bryant, contends that blacks often ignore an important side of their roots: the independence and tenacity required to survive in a racist society. "It wasn't welfare," he tells me. "Under segregation, we had fewer millionaires and fewer in the middle class, but we built Tuskegee, Shaw University, St. Augustine, Bennett, and on and on and on. We used to build hospitals, private schools. David, we're off track."

Are we? First of all, who has the power to determine the track for a diverse racial group that exists in a larger culture predicated on the values of individual liberty? McKoy doesn't want white or black Democrats to exert paternalism or dependence by telling him to join their party for race-based reasons. Should black millionaires or middle-class African Americans, given their means to do so, feel more obliged than anyone else to build or contribute to a black college or a race-beneficial cause or institution? (Of course, many apparently do contribute to such causes, according to recent studies on black philanthropy that document giving among the African-American middle and upper-middle classes.)

As for schools, more than four hundred private schools have been launched by African Americans since 1990—many of them developed by black churches concerned about the same failures of public schools that trouble Americans of all races and complexions. McKoy surely knows this, as he bases his support for school vouchers, in part, on the success of black private schools.

McKoy's calls for self-reliance are couched in political rhetoric likely to draw cheers from many corners, black or not. Who doesn't talk about self-help, self-reliance, and independence in these days of welfare reform? It certainly is familiar rhetoric to me after hearing it at stops across the country—mostly from black Democrats. But McKoy's version ties the perceived failures of black self-reliance and independence to white Democrats, and that helps to sharpen his aim to win over black voters who are habitually inclined to vote for a white Democrat over any Republican. By highlighting his own negative encounters with paternalistic Democrats, McKoy creates a space in which his choice to become a Republican may be viewed as a move of militance and quixotic insurgence. He portrays his presence in the GOP as an act of black bravado in the face of exploitative white liberals and their co-opting of black Democrats. His choice of party becomes a move to embrace the values of self-reliance, self-help, and even patriarchy at a time when responsible black fatherhood is popularly viewed as the cure to most American pathologies. Through his rhetoric, McKoy's Republicanism flirts with Afrocentrism as he carves a niche at an intersection between black culture and the version of self-reliance and family values popularly associated with the GOP agenda. It is hard to offend anyone with calls for a stronger black business community and for black millionaires to put their money in the inner city. It easily wins the agreement of both Republicans and Afrocentrists. As for his attacks on white leftists, how many voters in North Carolina are likely to care at all if you offend white liberals?

There is often a contradiction in the calls for self-reliance among blacks, whether it is McKoy at the podium or a black Democrat or an Afrocentric advocate of a black political party: they all often see the "self" part not as an individual but a racial group. The do-for-self talk seeks to set an agenda actually based on *racial group*–reliance. But again, how do members of a large and diverse group rely so heavily on one another while living with the freedoms that came via the civil-rights and black-power movements? It is a difficult balance to attempt—much less maintain. Of course, a common culture produces some group loyalties. So does the persistence of racism, because it perpetuates the searches for ways of life that can either eradicate or evade discrimination. Those loyalties often impose ideas of white advantage and privilege while bestowing more responsibilities for blacks. For example, African Americans often expect one another to pursue goals and interests that benefit the group, while whites have the luxury to merely pursue individual goals and interests; McKoy himself has couched his attachment to the GOP in terms that define his loyalty to black culture or his racial group. But one could argue that whites, too, such as Dixiecrats and Willie Horton–inspired Republicans, clearly make partisan and electoral choices based on racial considerations. It's an American thing.

There are strong pockets of communal reliance among African Americans, including an organization that visibly promotes black economic independence and conservative values: the Nation of Islam, with its deeply conservative approach to life and social issues. Does McKoy see the Nation as a potential ally? The question provokes a mild twitch of McKoy's eyebrows. After a second of silence, he offers a careful answer. "I have great respect and admiration for the Nation of Islam and its belief in independence . . . I am real concerned about what a liberal direction for the country has meant. I think that Farrakhan realizes that [that] has crippled us . . . Minister Farrakhan has found that blacks are being trapped in this dependency-producing mode . . . where I part with Minister Farrakhan is where he, in his need to explore the independence and thinking of our people, finds it necessary to put down other people and their cultures."

Polls show that black voters are generally more conservative on social issues than the liberal politicians they elect. Just look at the rising numbers of black parents sending their children to schools characterized as conservative Christian: 71,000 in 1994, nearly double the number than in 1991. That doesn't automatically translate into good news for McKoy, however. Signs of black conservatism show up almost everywhere but in the voting booths. The perceptions of the Republican Party and white conservatives as hostile, racist, and, in an unchristian way, lacking compassion for the poor continue to nurture the bonds of such strange bedfellows as blacks and white liberals, who are often viewed, rightly or wrongly, as more open on the issue of race. So, even if the values and lifestyles of many upper-middle-class African Americans are closer to those of country-club Republicans than those of Pat Schroeder, and even if many working- and middle-class blacks are more attuned to the morality and values of Ralph Reed than those of Ted Kennedy, liberals can still pull in a black vote as easily as David Duke can turn one away.

McKoy's mission is to erode those black partisan perceptions so that African-American conservatives can be comfortable voting for black Republicans. Toward that end, he points the finger at liberals, like Supreme Court Justice Ruth Bader Ginsburg, for a dismal record of hiring blacks. And he brushes off Republican opposition to affirmative action: "I don't agree with everything the Republicans support and am not afraid to say it. . . . I have to answer to everything Jesse Helms has ever said. But what about racism on the left?

"The feminists of America went after Clarence Thomas. And George Bush stood by Clarence Thomas. Bill Clinton deserted Lani Guinier."

Yes, Bush stood by Clarence Thomas—but I don't think Bush would have ever nominated Guinier or someone with her politics to a high-level civil-rights post. I wonder how Republicans would have reacted had Bill been loyal to Guinier. Anyway, according to McKoy's logic, if both parties have racist elements, then a voter shouldn't choose a party based on race, but on values. If racism is eliminated from the picture, which party is more compatible with your interests? McKoy, of course, says the GOP. As for Helms, McKoy says, "Most black voters see Senator Helms as a formidable political enemy. But I can't be swayed by that. I refuse to take the position that just because Senator Helms takes the views that he may take on race [that] I've got to sit over there in the Democratic Party and take all the crap the Democrats heap upon our people.

"Senator Helms didn't create this welfare system that's got my people dependent. He's not in charge of the criminal-justice system that's locking my brothers up in jail. He's not in charge of an educational system that's trapping our kids by labeling them unfairly, calling them, basically, mentally retarded, slow learners, and just making them drop out of school in the first ten or twelve grades. So my answer to you, David, is there is far more damage being done to my people by liberal Democrats and the programs they have founded than by anything Jesse Helms has ever done."

"But some would argue, though, that Helms helped create, or at least contributes to, the climate where some of those things you talk about occur," I point out.

"That's what liberals think. I'm not willing to allow Jesse Helms and his views of the world to dictate and determine how I must participate in politics. Every election, the mentality of most black people is we've got to vote the Republicans out. That's the only opportunity or purpose we find in an election. It's a narrow approach to politics."

McKoy checks his watch. He has to pick up his daughter Marcia from school. McKoy pays his bill and leaves some campaign flyers with the cashier.

McKoy is driving to the magnet school that his daughter attends. It's on the tip of Southeast Raleigh. On the way there, we pass old neighborhoods of wood-frame houses. Some look unkempt, while others have lawns of shining green grass. The ride takes us past neighborhoods of newer and older brick homes—ranches and split-levels. McKoy doesn't live in South Raleigh, which 68 percent of the city's black population calls home. McKoy balks at the attempt of a few black Democrats who have tried to make an issue of his residence in a white neighborhood. Still, for McKoy, residence does become a natural question since he so often talks about his closeness to his culture. I ask a question about it. "You spend so much time talking about how you enjoy being around your people. It's one thing to be with them at an A&T football game. But why do you choose not to live around them?"

"My choice of living when I came here was to look for a predominantly black neighborhood where my wife and I could live. [But] there were no houses—homes—like the ones that I was looking for, because there was not a substantial amount of development in southeast Raleigh at that time. I could have moved at another time. But I don't believe that I have to live in southeast Raleigh to think and be and act like an authentic African American. Southeast Raleigh is ten minutes away from me. I have breakfast over there two or three times a week. I go to church. My daughter's friends live there. I visit friends there.

"I like where I live. I enjoy my neighbors. Living there has given me a unique understanding of my own culture. [And] it's given me an understanding of Owen, my neighbor, and how he thinks and looks at the world, and what he values. [I get that] when we're talking across the lawn, or over the lawn mower, and he's expressing what his children are doing and what they're going through and what he's hoping for them. Joe and Gail's kids are in my kitchen playing. Joe is an executive at IBM, a white male, and his wife, Gail, is a homemaker. Their children and my children grew up together, playing together. So that experience—my pride in my own Africanness lets me know that not only are we different in many ways but we're similar in many ways. And that hopefully Joe and Owen have a sensitivity about African Americans that may have come with their relationship with me.

"By the way," he adds. "My white opponents don't live in this part of town. Black Democrats don't ask them why they live where they live."

McKoy is one of three major-party candidates running for the two seats apportioned to Wake County in the state senate. His two white Democratic opponents—J. K. Sharon, a moderate Democratic incumbent, and Ruth Cooke, a liberal member of the state house who has a long record of support among African Americans—are running as a team to take both seats.

McKoy shocked some of his critics and supporters by winning the endorsement of a local black political organization, the Raleigh-Wake Citizens Association, whose leadership is dominated by black Democrats. The Association distributes its list of endorsements at precincts with black majorities, and those on the list usually carry those precincts with ease. To win the endorsement, McKoy didn't court the group's leadership. Instead, he and his wife strategized to win over the rank and file. On the night of the group's vote and debate, McKoy counted on black Southern, genteel manners to blow the dirt out of the process. "I invited my wife to sit through the debate with me. I wanted them to stand up in front of her and trash me. Many of the leaders consider themselves to be ladies and gentlemen. They would have to look her in the eye and say bad things. I trusted they wouldn't, and they didn't. They did bring up the Contract with America, but they didn't say a thing about me.

"I won the endorsement because it was a secret-ballot vote. We don't think as a free people. We are still somewhat afraid. There are many people who support me but are afraid of the white liberals who will see them doing it and of the blacks who will run back and tell the white liberals."

Now McKoy is talking to individualism again—self-, not group-, reliance. "You have the freedom in America to be anything you want to be. . . . So being a senator, being a businessman, being the head of a civil-rights agency, working for a governor . . . Being a Republican is no different to me than being any of those other things, because those are the choices a free man can make. What's difficult for me is understanding why I'm finding the limitations in the black community to my exercise of a freedom of simply being self-reliant.

"Our history has taught us that there is a consequence for breaking away from the mainstream of expectation. When you stood out against the establishment, even during slavery times, you were punished. We as a people are very careful to get permission to do some things because we don't want to lose our jobs. That kind of thing still exists today. This is a capital city, so many of the people here have government jobs.

"On the positive side, I think that what slavery did to us is make us believe that we needed to band together—all for one and one for all—that we needed to stick together because we wouldn't have been able to have survived if we hadn't. But the negative side of it is that it creates a mentality, a kind of plantation mentality, that makes you believe that everybody has to stay in the same place and be the same. And when one breaks away, that there's something wrong with that person. He's rejecting us, his people, when he moves away—even though that is not true. I think it's part of a mentality that has developed, that is an outgrowth of slavery. And I think that there are political leaders who know how to manipulate that so that when one steps out of line, everyone will view that person in a negative way.

"I am sometimes chastised for having a relationship with the mayor, who is a Republican, because many of the blacks have some difficulty with some of his policies. They want to limit my associations that are crucial if I'm going to be a good senator for this district. But there has never been any question about limiting J. K. Sharon's associations, or Ruth Cooke's associations. They have freedom to move around and ally with whomever they need to ally with to produce whatever product they need to produce for the community. . . . So we very often are programmed to limit ourselves and limit our associations, and not take full advantage of all associations to maximize our advantages. And liberals have done a very good job of courting that, in the sense that they have always wanted to be the ones that blacks go to. And hell has no fury like a liberal's scorn. If you want to create the ire of a liberal or even a moderate Democrat, go after the black vote and they'll come after you. Because they see you taking away from them something they perceive they own. There's an ownership issue there."

McKoy came to Raleigh as a Democrat in 1978, appointed by Democratic governor Jim Hunt to head the North Carolina Human Rights Commission, the state's chief agency for fighting discrimination. Even as a Democrat, McKoy expressed his independence. In 1984, for example, he did not vote for Jesse Jackson, who captured the vast majority of black support in the Democratic presidential primaries. Nor did he support Walter Mondale in the primary. Mondale won the backing of a good share of established black elected officials. "My candidate got in trouble three years later because he got caught on the back of the boat with a female."

"You supported Gary Hart?" I am surprised.

"I was a Hart delegate at the convention. I stood on the floor at the Moscone Center in San Francisco about fifty feet from Jesse Jackson, looking up at him when he gave that "Lord hadn't finished with me yet" speech at the Democratic National Convention."

At the time, McKoy was also working his way up in the Hunt administration, eventually becoming deputy secretary of administration. But Hunt gave up the governor's mansion for what would be a losing run against Jesse Helms in 1984. Republican Jim Martin won the governor's race and asked McKoy to stay on in his job as deputy secretary. McKoy agreed, and some Democrats were furious. "They called me a traitor . . . they said I was being used. Whites remained; they didn't say that about them. . . . Whites do it all the time. They move back and forth and cut deals. In the major development companies, one partner is a Democrat and another is Republican. That's how they stay politically attuned. There is a sophistication in the political machinery in the South now that allows whites to come together and go from party to party when it serves their interest."

McKoy did not immediately switch parties with the change in administrations, though. It happened four years later in the fall of 1988, after he went to Harvard for a summer program in executive leadership. In Cambridge, he met real white liberals—the kind who were not ashamed of it, who were not running from the label and calling themselves moderates to please conservative Democrats. McKoy says he refused to suppress his black rural independent streak in the face of what he saw as rampant white-liberal paternalism. "I found myself kind of out of sync with a lot of the ideas and beliefs of a lot of the Harvard professors I had. They had sort of a mentality that says, 'I've got to rescue you. I've got to save you.' They were nice people, and it was a great experience—but their mindset didn't see or acknowledge the strength of the individual or self-reliance. That's the mentality [they had]. It says, 'Let me take you to fish,' and as long as I can have that feeling that I'm doing something noble, benevolent, and good for mankind, we can forget about what I may be doing to keep you from achieving independence."

While at Harvard, McKoy also watched Jesse Jackson tumble through another Democratic presidential primary. "Jesse Jackson placed second in votes to Michael Dukakis. Jesse Jackson found out who Dukakis picked for his running mate in an airport when a reporter walked up to him and asked him if he knew that Dukakis had picked Lloyd Bentsen. A few weeks later, something happened that really troubled me . . . on television, Dukakis stood there with Jesse Jackson, Coretta Scott King, Andy Young, all standing there holding hands singing 'We Shall Overcome' in a church with an audience of mostly black people. I made the decision then that I was going to change and become a Republican."

Four years later, in 1992, North Carolina Democrats won back the governorship. McKoy was out of a $76,000-a-year job on the day of the inauguration. "Now I'm fighting with some of the same people who fired me and thought I was finished in politics."

Out of work, McKoy did what many professionals do when they are downsized: he became a consultant, launching a firm that specializes in team-building exercises for businesses and school districts. He also made his first run for office after he lost his state job. In 1992, he ran to become state commissioner of labor and didn't get past the Republican Primary. Still, there was a sign in his defeat that directed him to this race for the state senate: "I got forty-seven percent of the statewide vote in a party that is ninety-five percent white. And I carried this county."

McKoy pulls into the busy parking lot of William G. Enloe High School as students hop onto the orange school buses parked on the side of the street. Marcia sees her father, walks past the buses, and jumps in the car. She has his darting dark eyes, her mother's fair-skinned complexion, and her own ponytail.

On the way home, McKoy stops to drop off some literature to a supporter while I talk to Marcia in the car. Within minutes, I discover the rural McKoy in Marcia's life today as it has come through in Henry McKoy's parenting. Marcia shares many stories, including the time her father embarrassed her when she went on a beach trip sponsored by a social organization for black teenagers last summer. "We went to Virginia Beach just for the weekend. It was chaperoned, though, so it wasn't just us. My father would never let me go by myself. No way. He almost didn't let me go then.

"It was, I'd say, forty teenagers on the bus. Someone said, 'Marcia, isn't that your parents beside us?' And I looked up; he was following the bus. I was like, 'God, I can't believe he's doing that.' I was so mad at him.

"He claims they were going to the farmer's market. I've never seen them go to the farmer's market that way. I was so embarrassed. They followed us for thirty minutes. They turned off eventually, and I just ignored them after a while. I just waved once. And then I acted like I didn't see them."

Political parties don't mean much to the teenager. She says that some people take party membership too seriously, citing a black teacher at the school who taunted her because of her father's affiliation. She also tells me about the daughter of a prominent Democratic politician who had a party for black classmates after a football game last year. When Marcia arrived with a date, the Democrat's daughter told Marcia's date that he was welcome. Marcia was not. "She was like, 'You can come in, you can't.' I was more mad at her parents than her. Her father was standing right beside her. I think that's rude for a parent to let their child do that. I know my Dad would get mad at me if somebody came into my house and I said, 'You can come in and you can't.' My Dad would say, 'No, Marcia. If you're going to have a party, people can come, unless you give out invitations.' And she didn't give out invitations. But my Dad wouldn't let me point to somebody and say, 'You can't come in.' Not unless it was somebody that might get into a fight or cause trouble. I've noticed if I'd ever been rude to a child in this neighborhood or something like that, he'd make me go over there and apologize and invite them over."

One of the toughest issues she sees in the campaign is abortion. "I feel like it's a woman's choice. And then I feel like it's not right. I have never been able to stick with that decision. I don't think I'll ever choose a politician over whether he was pro-choice or not . . ."

Her father's position on abortion has lost him the endorsement of the local chapter of the National Abortion and Reproductive Rights Action League. Henry McKoy says he's against abortion but supports a woman's right to choose—that doesn't bother NARAL. But he's opposed to abortions without parental consent and to federal funds for poor women to receive an abortion, unless it's a case where the pregnancy can harm the woman's health.

Marcia was born in 1977, when the edges of school desegregation were still rough and rather fresh. In that year, my mother was teaching history at the school Marcia now attends, and I graduated from another school in the county. It was the anything-for-integration time, and there were no debates among NAACP leaders over busing. Those who argued for court-ordered racial balances at all schools didn't sound so out of touch with everyone else as they do today.

In those days, Enloe High School was predominantly white and surrounded by white, integrated, and black neighborhoods. It was just another high school—not the magnet school that it became as the area became largely African American and the school district decided to add special academic programs to attract students from north Raleigh neighborhoods like Marcia's to achieve a racial balance more reflective of the district.

According to Marcia, there are two schools at Enloe. There is one school of regular classes, with large numbers of African-American students from

southeast Raleigh. Then there is another school of enriched magnet programs and college-preparatory classes that are composed largely of whites
and Asians. Marcia says that she is among the few dozen black students
who go to both schools, taking magnet and college-preparatory classes in
which they are in the minority, but also sitting on the same side of the
lunchroom as students in the regular classes, gossiping over the same people, often going to the same parties, knowing the same dances, and listening to the same music—sometimes behind the backs of their strict parents.

There are obvious differences in the country that Henry knew as a
teenager and the America that Marcia knows today. Henry McKoy was
forced to attend segregated schools; Marcia chose to attend an inner-city
magnet school for its strong academic programs, and also because the
school, at 40 percent black, had a much larger population of black students
than her overwhelmingly white neighborhood school. Henry lived in a segregated rural community; Marcia grew up in a predominantly white upper-
middle-class neighborhood. Later, McKoy explains that Marcia is a product
of values that span the generations of his family and transcend many of the
social upheavals that erupted in the sixties.

"When the *Brown* decision came down in 1954, I was a youngster. When
the civil-rights bill passed in 1964, I was a senior in high school. I'm a product not so much of the sixties, when the laws were passed—I'm a product
of the messages I got in the forties and fifties . . . those black family messages that came up through the sixties, that I heard from my grandfather in
the fields. He would say, 'Boy, you go out there and get some girl pregnant,
you're going to have to be responsible for her. You're going to have to take
care of that girl.' Is that conservative? Is that liberal? Is that radical? No, it's
what I believe. That's what my father taught me. That's what I believe we as
a society should believe.

"By '68, when the fair housing law was passed, my values were already
set. What happened after '64 had about as much impact on my life as what
happened between 1946 and 1964, when I graduated from high school. In
that time, I had lived in a little rural North Carolina county, and all of those
messages up to that point had come from my father, my mother, my grandfathers, my grandmothers, my church, my community. So when I went away
to college in '65, my views were all shaped around that.

"I think civil-rights gains were appropriate and needed, and I enforced
some of them as head of the state commission and believe today the laws
need to be strengthened. But beyond that, I have some grave questions
about all this helping stuff under the guise of doing good and what it has
actually produced in real benefits. Those are the things that go against what

I learned between '46 and '64 about hard work and self-reliance, about families taking care of families. . . . Today when I see all these homeless people, the question I'm asking is, who are these people? Who are their sisters? Who are their brothers?"

McKoy insists that his grandfather's values resonate with his white neighbors too. Those values, however, are not enough to build strong friendships across racial lines—at least not in Marcia's life. Though she lives in a predominantly white neighborhood and attends an integrated school, her social world revolves totally around African Americans, as did her parents' social world when they were teenagers in a rural segregated community. While her father speaks of her closeness to her white neighbors, she says that when she entered her teenage years, she became socially distant from her neighbors. "We all speak," she says. "My parents haven't raised me to hang around all black people. They've asked me why I don't hang around any white people. It just ends up that way. But they didn't raise me to pick any color. I'm sure they really prefer me to hang around black people. Like I doubt if white parents teach their kids to hang around black people.

"Like the people in my neighborhood, it's not that I stopped hanging around them because they were white. When you play in the neighborhood, you eventually just get older. It's not like you're trying to dodge white people, but . . . I don't know, I guess you have more in common with black people.

"I think white people are wilder than black people, regardless of what the media says. Like, white people at school, they're always asking me, 'do you drink, do you do drugs' and stuff. And then they're like, 'you don't?' They actually can't believe you don't do that, that you don't smoke. I don't know. To me, they're more wild than black people. But the news and media say otherwise, so I don't know. Black people, we have some wild ones, but they're not too wild . . . I've never seen any of them drunk. Like, on the way into school, you might see boys or black guys smoking weed or something like that. You see that so much these days, it's like smoking a cigarette. You just walk on to school and that's it. I mean, they don't ask you to. They don't bother you about it. Half the time, they're your friend.

"I don't really see white people smoking weed in the morning. But I always see them every morning smoking cigarettes out in the front, and they do all the drinking a lot at the games. I don't drink, and I can't stand cigarette smoke."

But her distaste for alcohol and tobacco does not explain her social distance from white peers. It is the baggage of history that makes it easy for people of different races to politely live next door, go to school together, work together, but to exist in totally different social worlds. This is most striking to me now, as I see that Marcia and her white neighbors appear to have much in common, based on her and her father's descriptions. On the surface, she has what most of them have—a comfortable house, a loving family, and parents who tend to be recent Republicans. McKoy tells me that the white neighborhood teenagers are not as wild as Marcia's descriptions of her white classmates. Like Marcia, they are not products of families that overtly encourage separation, McKoy says. Marcia herself clearly doesn't carry any racial grudges, animosity, hostility, or tense feelings. She does not choose black friends because she was rejected by whites. "I haven't run into any problems where somebody was racist to me where I noticed it right on the spot."

But even without racial anger or the hostile racial experiences that beset many in the generation of African Americans before her (and still some in her own generation), Marcia is more comfortable with black friends, as she suspects her white peers are comfortable with their own as well. Perhaps it takes something extra and bigger to compel one to leap beyond racial boundaries within the culture and comfort of middle-class American youth, which already has its share of discomforts beyond race. And perhaps such a leap would make Marcia less of the typical teenager than she is, concerned about grades, strict parents, parties, beach trips, boys, gossip, and excitement over going to North Carolina A&T, her parents' alma mater, next year.

I ask McKoy about the social distance that Marcia keeps from her white peers. "Marcia would feel comfortable walking across to see Christine or Jennifer . . . but I think we as a society are held apart by some of the stuff we're talking about, and I think some of it starts to occur at about thirteen or fourteen. They [teenagers] start to seek out their own then. One of the most fundamental relationships for a young person is a relationship with a member of the opposite sex. At whatever stage in their life they want to begin to think about that, we in America, our tradition still is we seek someone of our own culture, our own race and background."

McKoy says adolescent girls establish friendships with female peers of their own race in the interests of forming relationships with boys. "Growing up in a conservative environment, when my daughter's young friends wanted to meet young boys, they found their parents were more accepting if they said, 'Dad, I want to go out to the mall with Latasha,' or whomever else in their circle of four or five [girls]. Now, my belief is that the bulk of those young girls would call some of those boys they're interested in being with and say, 'Well, we're going out to the mall between one and three,' and they had a chance to have their little crushes and those little relationships that young people have at that stage in life. But I think . . . they're simply reflecting what they see in their parents, and I think the young whites do the same. They also look at who their parents socialize with to a large extent. In growing up, Marcia saw my peers and old college friends, fraternity brothers and their families, and they all were mostly young black professionals. We would take trips together and do things of that nature.

"But she never saw me treat whites in a negative or superior or inferior way because they were white, and that's why she is comfortable with whites. I myself have had only one bad racial incident since I've been out here. When I first moved out here in the late 1970s, early 80s, I received a racist call one night from someone who said if I stayed in this neighborhood, I would be dealt with. I told the caller, 'It's a coward who calls out of the darkness—it takes guts to meet me out in the middle of the cul-de-sac,' and if he wanted to talk to me, meet me out in the cul-de-sac on Saturday at noon in full daylight so that everyone can see. We can do whatever we wanted to do, say whatever we wanted to say. I never heard any more from the caller."

McKoy lives in north Raleigh, on a circle of brick homes and well-manicured lawns. He parks his car and Owen, a neighbor watering the lawn, waves and yells, "Good luck."

"I'm hearing good things, Henry," he says.

McKoy immediately checks messages and finds a call from a white National Rifle Association member who saw him on television and says that he'll vote for him and is glad to see a black in the party. There is a call from a black man who says that he's glad to see that McKoy "isn't just some old Republican." He offers to pass out flyers at his family reunion.

After McKoy gets off the phone, we sit on the front steps in the face of a North Carolina fall breeze. McKoy says that he expects both of his daughters to go into politics. "My oldest is majoring in computer graphics communication. She talks about politics more than this one. Marcia is more outgoing and talkative—she's a typical teenager who likes to be on the phone with her girlfriends. My oldest daughter had been a student-council representative . . . she was thinking about running for Miss A&T. And so she came home one day and said, 'Dad, I'm going to run for Ms. Senior.' She and four of her girlfriends from A&T came, and we sat at the computer and worked out a strategy and designed a brochure for her. She took about a thousand or so flyers back, and, actually, we had a flyer for every dorm room on campus. And we talked two days before the election: 'Have your rep in the dorm slide this flyer with your picture in the dorms. On every main walkway on the campus put up a picture of yourself.' And then one day she called and said, 'Guess what, I won!'"

I pose a question. "Now, some people would say that pageants and contests like that are sexist."

"Nonsense. I think any way that we can keep our children out of the streets in a productive track in a winning position. And my daughter has a feminine side that she cherishes because her mother is a very feminine woman. But just like I asked my wife to go to that meeting that night . . . and sit among this group of people, some of whom would take her husband's head apart, I had more confidence in her ability to defend her family, because my wife is like a cat with kittens if you attack her family. Hell hath no fury. She may be quiet and unassuming and easy going, but she is a strong, strong woman, and my daughter is the same way. So I don't pay attention to all of those kinds of labels about what women ought to be. I teach my daughter to be strong, be feminine, use what you got to your advantage, and try to achieve in this world as long as you're moral and you don't dishonor yourself or dishonor people . . . it's okay."

"Do you worry about the sexism that your daughters could face in the political and professional arenas?" I ask.

"Yes. I think that is a problem in our society that we have to overcome. And I tried to be the kind of father to my children that no matter what they faced, they never questioned whether they were valued, loved, or cared for. I think that becomes the foundation of what I can offer them. And that's the tragedy of moving toward a policy that pushes fathers away: it creates situations where families are breaking up and young people are out here searching for acceptance and approval. Young ladies out here searching for men who will tell them that they are okay. My daughter does not have that problem."

"But wouldn't you say a contest or pageant, in a way, is still a way of women seeking validation for their looks?"

"What's wrong with being validated through your looks? I would look at that as healthy. When we get up in the morning and we put on our best clothes and we put on our suits and ties and we comb our hair and wash our face, the women put on their makeup, we want to look nice, we want to look good! If intelligence is your thing and you're the smartest person in the world, we don't condemn someone for being the best scientist in the world. We don't condemn someone for being the best looking. If somebody has a gift from God and they are beautiful and there are pageants, what's wrong with that? We manicure our lawns and paint our homes. That's society that has that problem. I don't have it. Once again, let's use what God gave you to help you.

"I have a history that shows I've never done anything that would put women in the backseat. I'm a father of two daughters, and I want them to be whatever they want to be, and I want no male to get in the way of their being what they want to be. But I don't want them with weak men, men who have been beaten to death by a society. I want the fathers of their children to be there by them, just like I'm there for my children."

Final Plays

O N Saturday morning, Henry McKoy struggles with his schedule. The problems begin with a 6:45 A.M. call from a talk-show host at a local black radio station, who invites McKoy to participate in a candidates' forum at 10:00. McKoy can surely reach a large share of black voters that way. But he already promised a fraternity brother that he would speak to a group of community leaders in Holly Springs, a rural town in the county, this morning.

McKoy decides to try doing both. He'll go to Holly Springs and rush back to Raleigh. For safety's sake, he calls Teresa Peoples, a supporter and community activist in southeast Raleigh. She agrees to arrive at the station at 10:00 and be prepared to represent him if he doesn't make it back from Holly Springs in time.

Why are there so many appearances in the black community and so few among whites in the final days of the campaign? Is McKoy trying to avoid white crowds? Does he fear that if white Republicans discover his race, they will go for white and against their party in his case? Could race interfere with the appeal of conservatism among white voters? After all, this is the state of Jesse Helms. Did Dixiecrats and Reagan Democrats flock to the GOP with the thought of one day voting for a candidate like McKoy? Of course, it's hard to talk about whites flocking to the GOP without thinking again of Willie Horton. Mention that name and McKoy throws back his usual answer: Racism on the left, Lani Guinier, and so forth.

So do two wrongs make a good black Republican?

As for the suggestion that he's avoiding whites, McKoy says "of course not" and points out that his face is on flyers and will be on the large newspaper advertisement that will reach the seventy thousand subscribers of *Raleigh News and Observer* on Monday. "This is where I am," McKoy begins as he chews the last of a sausage biscuit and his hands negotiate a cup of McDonald's coffee and the steering wheel. "Starting yesterday, I decided that there were three different things that needed to occur in the closing hours of the campaign. The first one was I needed to get flyers out to the churches. The second thing is that I want to attend the Gospelfest tomorrow afternoon. The third thing is the ad."

McKoy pulls onto the gravel parking lot of the small brick church in Holly Springs. Inside, he is the lone Republican among the five candidates for various races. His two Democratic opponents are absent.

A dozen community leaders sit on the folding chairs, and the candidates are seated behind a rectangular table. At times the other four—three white and one black—candidates sound so much alike they might as well be one voice. Their messages center on fairness, civil rights, crime, and their records on those issues. They also attack the notorious Contract with America. They speak casually from the table.

McKoy is the last to speak. He stands out by standing up straight and formally, as one would if reciting a part in a Baptist church pageant. He speaks in a professional baritone tempered with an occasional emphatic twang of tenor that stirs grunts of agreement from the crowd. He doesn't talk about civil rights. He focuses on schools that track black children and how school-choice legislation can free them from racist school environments.

McKoy also talks about how both parties fail the black community. After traveling with him for a day, I feel I know the speech by heart but, by the looks of the leaders, it is a fresh and intriguing message here. His solution is to look beyond the parties and the politicians: black mothers and fathers have to come back together and save black children in the way that his parents worked hard to raise their children. Of course, he goes after welfare and dependency too. His attacks on welfare and social programs are not couched in the promises to save taxpayers' money. Instead, like Lawnside Democrat Wayne Bryant, McKoy slams welfare on moral grounds, declaring that it destroys families and, ultimately, the black community. McKoy translates the conservative agenda into terms that easily win an 'Amen' in this black rural Baptist church in North Carolina. And then he casually drops A&T in a reference and gets a few nostalgic smiles. By the time he finishes, there are no tough questions. Most of the hands that go up have comments that echo his message.

• • •

"I go to churches and I ask for five or ten minutes," says McKoy as we drive away. "I leave people startled with the degree of frankness. I'll say, 'Our children might as well put a sign on them saying HEADED TO JAIL. I'll look out into the room and I see the mothers shaking their heads. And when I see mothers start to shaking their heads, I realize I'm tuning in with them. And at that point Republicanness and Democraticness start to fade away."

The radio show is over. McKoy goes straight to Theresa Peebles' house. It is a modest and immaculately kept split-level home in southeast Raleigh.

"Henrrrrrryyyyyyyyyyyyy," she says as soon as she opens the door. "They tried their best to tie you to Jesse Helms."

She rushes him in the house. She must have been in the middle of folding clean laundry, as clothes are neatly stacked on the couch above a half-full basket of more clothes. Her son's soccer uniform is set apart from everything else. Peoples speaks rapidly about the black Democrats and activists who called the radio station to attack McKoy while Peoples was left there alone to defend him. "But someone called said, no, you were the only Republican running currently that distanced himself from Jesse Helms. That all the others were running, like, on Helms's same agenda. . . . So I thought he was saying something positive. Wasn't he?"

"Yes, Yes," confirms McKoy.

"You would think you was running up on Jesse's family values. I said Henry has his own values. I didn't know Mrs. Murray was going to be the host. If I would have known that Mrs. Murray was doing this show today, I would have told you to be there yourself. 'Cause I know, I know the people that listen to her. I know that Mrs. Murray has a strong listenership."

"You know when I found out that they wanted me on the show?"

"When?"

"At six forty-five this morning."

"What? Oh, she just pulled it up this morning?"

"Yeah. And the first thing when I heard it, I said I bet you that Ruth Cooke will be among the first people on the show. I bet she knew before. That's—what I suspected was they were called before."

"You think so?"

"Oh, I believe that."

"But, you know something—Mrs. Murray is a last-minute person."

Perhaps the biggest surprise of the morning didn't come from Mrs. Murray but from the wife of Dan Blue, who in 1990 had been elected the state's first black Speaker of the House. McKoy says that he helped Earlene Blue secure a state job, and in preparing Peoples for today's show, he told her to mention the help: it would illustrate that McKoy is rooted in helping African

Americans in the city. So Peoples dropped it on the air—and a furious Earlene Blue called to say that she didn't get any help from Henry McKoy.

"She said she had her own contacts and Henry McKoy never helped her."

"That's not true. About twelve, fourteen, fifteen years ago, before Dan was Speaker, when I oversaw one of the agencies, she applied for a position. And when the information came to me for purposes of hiring, I acted favorably. I said, fine, this is a fine person; I would like to see her hired. And she was. Now as a public official I could have said no, we don't want her."

"These people are something, Henry."

"Well, let me run. Are you okay?"

"I'm fine. It's these people that are the problem. They on the plantation still."

"In the speeches given by a number of the white Democrats, they start off by saying, 'I want to help Dan,'" says McKoy, now driving on the expressway. "'I want to protect Dan.' That's what they say. That's designed to send a signal to the black community, 'Keep me, and I'll help him. He needs me.'"

The implication, McKoy says, is that Dan Blue needs a great white Democratic father to survive in the legislature and to vote for a black Republican will deny Blue the parental guidance that black Democrats require.

"If you lose, what will you do?" I ask.

"I don't know. It depends on how much I lose by. I'd like to serve at least two terms in the Senate. I am not real certain about after that, exactly what direction I will take. I might decide to retire and teach. Or I may decide to run for higher office. I think we have shortchanged ourselves with all of the divisiveness. The Black Caucus fussing at the Republican Caucus and vice versa.

"If I find that it works, I would not mind taking a chance at lieutenant governor first and then other things later on. Right now, I think that the action is at the local level, not the federal level. More and more dollars are flowing from the federal level down to the state and the local government. And that seems to be the battleground of the future."

Only twenty minutes ago, we were riding by the diverse neighborhoods of southeast Raleigh. A quick journey on the expressway takes us to Cary, a plush and wealthy suburb. We pass several entrances to subdivisions of executive homes on at least three-quarter-acre lots. From the street, they all look similar; each bears a white sign on a post shaped like a fork of grass.

Finally, we turn in to the subdivision where McKoy's campaign manager, Calvin Bunker, lives.

Bunker, like McKoy, is an A&T graduate. He also holds a graduate degree in engineering from Harvard and now is the general manager of a radio station. "There are a lot of young, outstanding, talented blacks who have been trained and schooled at places like Harvard and Yale and other places here," McKoy says. "They are not tapped by the established black community because they don't know how to find them. They live out in the suburbs and places around the county and associate mostly with each other. They want to get involved, but they don't know how. And they aren't accustomed to going through this kind of political baptism that I'm receiving. They come around this kind of thing and they see it and they shy away.

"I've had to assemble a team of people like Calvin and other people who live in similar neighborhoods like the one you see here."

McKoy now drives at a slow pace; it is a fall day made for grooming yards, throwing and bouncing balls, or just running around. And there are children playing in the yards of the homes. A wooded area surrounds the subdivision, and these trees look ripe to be replaced by another neighborhood of colonial-style brick homes for this booming area.

I see only white children playing in yards and riding bicycles—until we reach Bunker's house. I am reminded of Marcia's social distance from white peers when we drive into Bunker's yard. It is Bunker's ten-year-old son's birthday party. African-American children play in the backyard and run in and out of the house as their parents mingle in the kitchen over hamburgers, hot dogs, beans, punch, beer, and a birthday cake, waiting for the moment of song and candles.

Bunker, in a polo shirt and white shorts, has clipped some more newspaper articles that mention the campaign. McKoy briefs the parents and relatives on this morning's latest.

Then McKoy and Bunker huddle and go over the volunteer and poll lists.

"Move him."

"Where do you want him?"

"You should put him at Precinct thirty-four."

"Year?"

"I asked him why did he prefer to cover that one. He said, 'Well, Henry, my children have gone through this community, many of their friends are here. I know their granddaddies, their daddies. And when I'm standing there and I tell them to vote for you, they're all Democrats, but they're going to vote for you. So I want to take full advantage.'"

"Okay."

"I wanted to put my daughter at that one—you have a lot of young families there. They care about children. And she can say simply put a sign on, saying 'I want you to vote for my daddy.'"

They rush through the list and break when it is song-and-cake time. McKoy leaves after the candles are blown out and makes a promise to Bunker's son that he will "take him to the hoop."

"Are you ready?" McKoy teases the youngster as he pantomimes throwing a ball toward a net.

McKoy says that it is not easy running a campaign where a large number of supporters and volunteers are not natives of the community. Many do not know the inside details of the voting precinct's they're responsible for. "There are some neighborhoods in this city where it is absolutely crucial to have someone there whom the people know," he says as we drive out of the subdivision. "And if that person says, 'I'm supporting Henry,' it goes a long way. That's important, David, in older, established neighborhoods where people have been involved for fifteen to twenty years. In some of the neighborhoods where people are newer . . . many of them do not even know their own neighbors. So you can almost put anyone there who has a good professional demeanor about them and knows how to greet people.

"My opponents taught me these things."

McKoy chuckles and names the city's first and only black mayor and the first and current black sheriff. "They taught me these things. I was their pupil, among the older people here in this city—many of those people who are now spearheading the campaign against me. They are dealing now with a pupil who learned the ropes from them. And they're forgetting that. It's like a coach who teaches a young man how to be a coach, and then that young man comes back one day and plays against his coach. That happens."

Chapter 12

Fishing

F OR Henry McKoy, Monday night blurs into Tuesday morning—Election Day. At sunrise, smiles and handshakes become automatic, each as unchanging as the face on the flyers that volunteers distribute. Still, the smiles can't melt the uncertainty that hangs over a candidacy tied to an untested coalition—one without a history to formulate any predictions. He is a black candidate hoping for white Republican and black Democratic votes, but unsure if either block will come through. So he didn't know whether to cheer or cry when, by midafternoon, the word on the street describes the turnout in predominantly white north Raleigh as high and modest in predominantly black southeast Raleigh.

McKoy arrives at the Hilton Hotel that evening and is joined in a suite by family and friends huddled around a television. Downstairs in the Hilton's ballroom, hundreds of GOP members cheer as they learn that their party will control both houses of the United States Congress for the first time in nearly fifty years. But it's still early, and the numbers in McKoy's race look too close to call. After an hour upstairs, though, McKoy receives a call from the party chairman: "It's time for you to come down and make a victory speech."

McKoy was a decisive winner, running overwhelmingly strong in white-majority precincts, but only pulling 25 percent of the black vote—a record for a Republican in a state legislative race.

It is seven months after the election. Henry McKoy is in another state, in Hampton, Virginia. It is Father's Day weekend and the McKoy men are almost ready to cast their lines into Chesapeake Bay. They climb aboard

Marc II, a twenty-five-foot boat owned by Bernard Lovett, a retired Hampton postal worker and a friend of the McKoy family who loves boats, water, and fellowship, which is why he relinquishes a Saturday morning every year for the McKoys.

The boat is docked at a marina on the Hampton Roads River, which empties into the bay. Once aboard, Clarence McKoy, Henry McKoy's uncle and the trip's elder statesman, immediately turns to a white bucket of bait and pulls out worms, one by one, piercing them with the fish hooks.

"Everybody put their life jackets on, all right?" Uncle Clarence commands.

The orange life jackets go on. Lovett starts *Marc II.* A serenity beguiles us when the motor roars and the boat bounces and moves steadily above water; it detaches us from the rest of the world or everything we wish to leave on land. Politics, however, rides with us: to leave elections, racial issues, and the problems of the poor at the dock would violate the peace that allows the McKoys to argue, agree, and debate in the comfort of a boat of family men.

"He shook up the world," says Clarence McKoy, referring to his nephew's election. "And that's great. The first Republican elected to the state legislature since Reconstruction."

He's also the first Republican elected anywhere to win such an enthusiastic cheer from Clarence McKoy. Blood must be thicker than partisan ties. "Having a black in Jesse Helms territory, winning on a Republican ticket, is sort of unusual. You doing something right. I don't know what it is, because you got to get out of that fraternity."

Henry McKoy shakes his head in disagreement and laughs.

"Bernard, how you feeling?" asks Clarence, turning from Henry.

"Doing great," comes the reply. Lovett, a father himself, isn't shy when it comes to talking about his adult daughters. "My oldest daughter is in the Hampton school system," he tells me. "She graduated from Virginia State. My youngest daughter is in Atlanta. Works with Coca-Cola. She got her MBA from Duke. Doing good. Proud of both of them. Married good men."

"I vouch for all of that," says Clarence.

The Virginia June heat dissipates with a breeze that flows with the speed of the boat. "When we get out there, you're going to see a bunch of brothers, hanging out in different points in the bay," says Henry McKoy. "The first time we came, I wrote a poem about it—'Brothers in the Bay.'"

"Yeah," Clarence chimes in. "You're going to see some big boats."

"Right here together," says Henry.

"You're going to see some like this boat," Clarence continues. "But you also going to see some commercial boats out there, where there's maybe eighty people on."

"I didn't realize this," says Henry. "It's an undiscovered place. If you want to find where some good brothers are on a Saturday, you come up here in the Chesapeake Bay. It's a way of life that these guys have every Saturday. I just like to come here once a year. I wish I could do it more often.

"When we spend Saturday together, we're talking about one generation communicating with another generation. One of the things that I admire about my uncle and Bernard and those guys is that they lived to be old men. That's something a whole lot of black men don't get a chance to do these days."

"I remember when I was growing up, people died when they were about forty-five," says Clarence.

"Now they're getting shot," says Henry's brother, Willie.

"Yeah, at age seventeen and eighteen."

"Let me interrupt you a minute," says Clarence. "We're passing Hampton University."

"Is that that little school over there?" jokes Henry.

Clarence ignores him. He points to a huge, old English–style grandfather clock, enclosed in burnt-red bricks. "That is the clock at the center of the campus. All of what you see is Hampton University. People fish off the pier . . . there's something going on under the tent. And that's the power plant there. And the Veterans Administration is over here. One of the most famous restaurants in the area is Fisherman's Wharf, on your right. Fort Monroe is over here. We're going by there. I'll show it to you."

Lovett eventually slows the boat and we settle on the waves. This is one of his favorite spots for fishing, a place where the ocean's bottom is grassy and rich with fish. Clarence passes around the poles. It is time to fish, and the first man to land one wins the pot, to which they've all contributed five dollars. It translates into a twenty-five-dollar prize.

"I'm going to catch Moby Dick," jokes Willie. It is not Willie's pole that gets the first jerk, though.

"I got it," says Jay Jeffries, Willie and Henry's sister's boyfriend, less than ten minutes later. He reels in a croaker.

Bernard instructs everyone to bring the lines in, and he drives to another spot. He passes a tall post planted in the water with a light at its top. It marks the end of the river as it empties into the Chesapeake Bay.

Clarence McKoy was a public-school educator who in the late sixties helped write the Hampton school district's desegregation plan. Now his nephew the state senator is cosponsor of a school-voucher bill that the North Carolina Association of Educators, the teachers' union, vehemently

opposes. Critics say that it would severely jeopardize public-school education. Similar legislation has been passed in seven states. The bill would allow low-income children to receive a voucher of four thousand dollars to
attend a private school, and it would also offer a tax credit to all parents
who send their children to private schools.

Some predict that the bill would lead to private schools that resemble
the public schools that educated the men on the boat—segregated institutions that Uncle Clarence helped to outlaw. But that doesn't bother black
conservatives like Henry McKoy, who see the anything-for-integration posture as a liberal thing. In this regard, black political conservatives are
aligned with black nationalists who sometimes out-right even Newt Gingrich. "One of the reasons we need to [allow vouchers] is that we need to
build some of our own schools, put our own teachers in them to teaching
our children—and that is one of the ways to do that," Henry tells Clarence.

By now, after an hour on the water, everyone has caught at least five fish.
Henry McKoy rests his fishing rod and tries to convince his uncle of the value
of vouchers. Clarence McKoy stares straight out over his pole and listens.

"See, in Wake County, four thousand dollars would follow a child, each
child that went in," Henry explains. "If you got twenty-five children in a
school and we could find a guy like you to head the school, you could educate some more children."

"We debated that one night," yells Willie, who still has his own line in the
water.

"Yeah, I had some problems with it then," says Clarence, not looking at
his nephew.

"What about now?" pushes Henry.

"Still have some reservations about it," Clarence replies.

"One of the things they'll do is it will allow a guy like you to head the
school and teach the children some of the values and things," says Henry.

"But it also allows everybody else to head a school," says Clarence.

"That's okay."

"But I'm not sure if that's okay."

"It's okay if the guys over there in that boat decide that they want to
open that school," Henry says, pointing to yet another boat of black men
fishing in the Chesapeake Bay. "As long as we got help with our children.
And we got to do that."

"But I'm not sure."

"But it can't be any worse than what our children are experiencing now.
Anything they can do with those vouchers, anything they can create can't
be any worse than the inner-city schools we've created, the rundown buildings we've created, the tracking of our children—they're forcing them out

of schools—the suspensions. All that stuff is going on in the present system. And our boys are falling out like flies."

"I'm worried about opposite groups taking advantage of that situation, and we're taking resources away from public education. That's my concern."

"But don't you think we're going to have to give up something to get something?"

"I'm opposed to public money for private ventures. That's my objection. Anybody can go out here and start a school. Six people can get together and say, 'We're going to start a private school.' And then they get public money for their tuition. I'm opposed to public money for private schools."

"But that's the only way, Uncle Clarence, that we are going to be able to get money in the hand of people like you to open up the school . . . Listen to what you said before: eighty percent of the elementary-school teachers—"

"Are white females," Clarence completes the sentence.

"And that's who's teaching our black boys," says Henry.

"She does not understand him," says Clarence.

"That was my problem with integration," Henry states.

"Well, look a there." Clarence is momentarily diverted as he reels in a nine-inch bass, one of the most attractive catches so far. Everyone admires the fish until Clarence turns their attention back to education. "I wrote the integration code. It was a no-thank-you kind of position. White folks say you're going too far; black folks say you're not going far enough. And you're in a Catch 22–type situation."

"When you think eighty percent of the teachers in the elementary grades are white females, the road we took to get here has not been the right road," says Henry. "And it's going to be . . . anything that took us to the point of eighty percent white teachers says that blacks have been dumped off, thrown off the ship at some point along this route. And blacks are not in the schools. They're not the role models. The teachers now can't teach our children. They can't teach our children the kind of values we want them to have. So we got to rescue them. If they're going to get saved, we're going to have to save them. We can't depend on the system to do it."

Clarence pauses. "I agree. The system will not do it. I have forty years in public education, and I watched almost every change that you can name— from totally segregated black high schools where kids were disciplined and hungry to learn to an integrated, undisciplined situation. I mean, I went from one extreme to the other. I went from where there were two-parent families to where it was single-parent families with mostly women heading the households. I went through all those changes."

"Since 1960, the number of single parent female households has doubled," says Henry. "I'm telling you that my children would not be as wholesome without the love of two parents. They would not be as full if I weren't there. There are too many things that they can be exposed to, that a father being there makes a big difference. I'm not criticizing a female head of household. I'm saying she's doing the best she can. The male walked out on her in many instances."

"Or she kicked him out," adds Clarence.

"But I'm saying that when we started to get in trouble in America, two things were going on: welfare was introduced into our lives and fathers started leaving home. When those things happened—"

"Let me tell you what I had to go through," Clarence breaks in. "I saw a young girl one time sitting on the stoop outside the cafeteria. I call myself a tough principal. I went out there and said, 'Look, you don't sit out here. You're supposed to be in class. Now you get up and go to class.' The girl started crying. She was about thirteen years old."

Clarence recounts the conversation:

"What are you crying about?" he asked.

"I thought I should stay home today," she replied.

"Why did you think you should stay home?"

"My little sisters are home. One of them six, one of them seven."

"Who's home with them?"

"Nobody."

"Why aren't your mother and father there?"

"They [police] came in the house at four this morning and arrested my mother and left all of us in the house."

"They arrested her for what?"

"She shot her boyfriend."

Not that we haven't heard worse, but the story leaves us all stunned. These stories always surface when the African-American middle class takes up its pastime, discussing and analyzing the problems facing blacks who are economically disadvantaged.

"What did you do?" Henry asks.

"Carried her home and got social services to go get the children. And that's what I'm required to do."

There is a frustration in his voice, a dissatisfaction with the regulations that required him to turn to a bureaucracy rather than try to solve the problem in the old-fashioned, community-centered way. In many communities of the segregated South, or, really, before such a thing as "social services" was known to rural black America, a teacher or principal could call an elder with a room and resources to take the youngster in and maybe even give her a new home. It is a voice similar to that of Gallia County's Ida Fulton.

"Let me give you a statistic," Henry says. "In the Wake County–Durham area in a four-year period, there were three hundred eighty-six blacks murdered. For the same period, there were seven whites. And do you know who murdered the blacks? Blacks . . . And they're killing their own families. The black guys. Yeah, and we talk about racism. We should blame our national leaders."

Politicians of any shade should not be spared the health that criticism produces. But how can one hold black "national leaders" (elected or civil rights and the like) responsible for something as complex as black-on-black crime? Should we hold white politicians accountable for hate crimes or mass-murder school shootings? To ascribe blame so loosely is as careless as condemning *all* whites or *all* blacks for America's racial problems, or holding welfare mothers responsible for most major social problems, or finding a conspiracy to fit every social dilemma. Fast and facile finger-pointing suits the tastes of a contemporary political climate in which the comfortable can be more easily placated with glib solutions like bringing back the old-fashioned black schoolteachers to clean up the contemporary mess of inner-city schools. It reflects the American affinity to sometimes look to a never-to-return past for ways to fix the future. Even the idea that segregated neighborhoods can restore the glory of black capitalism in a global economy carries a whiff of the American fling with nostalgia. It reminds me of Republican congresswoman failed television anchor and Harvard professor Susan Molinari's descriptions of her great-grandfather in her keynote address at the 1996 Republican National Convention, almost a year after this fishing trip. "Gaetano Molinari lived a simple dream. It was the same dream shared by a generation: Find a job, marry your sweetheart, have children, buy a home, and maybe start a business. . . ."

Regardless of what it has in common with Molinari's, Henry McKoy's message is attractive because it affirms the way blacks have traditionally pursued lives that defy the stereotypical perceptions of beaten-down soulhood, fate at the mercy of racism, and an outlook bordering on fatalistic nihilism. As Lawnside's Flora Young noted, those perceptions, so prevalent on the left, never acknowledge the triumphant and self-reliant traditions that nurtured her upscale family, or the working-middle-class family that produced Lovett's daughters, or the farming families that raised men like the McKoy fathers. Their stories, so normal, often are regarded in American mainstream thought as special or the exceptions. In reality, they describe the black majority, which refuses to submit its destiny to the approval of someone with views rooted in a collective consciousness that considers African Americans subhuman. Such a refusal is a human, and, maybe, very American impulse, for what product of contemporary American culture wants to be ascribed a fate that requires one to continually extend the hand across a divide for help rather than clutch the straps of a self-directed, upwardly mobile course? Not many Americans, black or nonblack, would choose such a destiny unless there is political or economic capital in it. So it is only natural for the dogmas of self-reliance and self-help to assume much of the place occupied a generation ago by the civil-rights agenda.

Henry McKoy doesn't dismiss racism as a force in American life. But he says that public assistance and most inner-city public schools have failed as responses to the legacies of discrimination. "I think that those who wanted to stop segregation thought that the best solution was to integrate our kids with the majority culture. In doing that, we gained the benefit of the materials and the supplies that would not come to us in a segregated setting, but we also lost, when you look at a statistic that says eighty percent of the elementary teachers are white females. And you look at the high suspension rate of our kids, the number that are dropping out, once again you have to ask, isn't it time to shake up that system, try something new? . . . Conservatives have come to a point where the solutions we have seen emerge are not working . . . we're the ones raising the new ideas, while Jesse Jackson, Kweisi Mfume, and that group of liberal thinkers are fighting to hold on to welfare . . . screaming about all the pain that's going to be caused without it. And, obviously, the things that they've proposed haven't led us anywhere.

"One of the problems in America is that we are afraid to say that fatherhood is important . . . too many people feel that saying that is putting the black female down. And it is not.

"Tell him the story that we talked about earlier. Uncle Clarence was talking about his daughter. . . ."

"She underwent a turbulent divorce," Clarence picks up. "The guy wouldn't cooperate and whatnot. She told me she did not even want to go back to live in that house. She was living there before she got married. The divorce was so turbulent that she didn't want to live there anymore. So I built her another house."

"He physically built the house," says Henry.

"I got some help with it now, you know. And so she lives there now."

"Talking about houses, I own a second home," Henry tells us. "And I bought it so that I could take the equity from the home later when I sell it and split it between my two daughters and help them get their first homes. A lot of times men do things that women don't understand. My wife didn't understand it and thought I should wait. My children didn't understand my way of helping them."

After three hours, three chests are full of fish, which will be equally divided. By now, the men are sipping beer, talking about O.J., and sharing old jokes—many that were told last year. "I was talking to my doctor," says Clarence, "and my doctor told me to stop drinking. So I looked him straight in the eye and said, 'Look doctor, I know more old drunks than I do old doctors.'" Everyone laughs.

"I'm going to drink a little beer today."

After fishing and returning to Clarence's home, the schedule falls victim to the impulses of the fathers. Some visit a street fair; others talk in the kitchen. Clarence eagerly shows off his wife's creations. Irene McKoy describes herself as a folk artist, and her paintings are on the walls and the porcelain dolls she's made sit in the wet bar and in her daughter's old bedroom. "I sell some of my dolls," she says, "but basically it's just a hobby thing with me."

"She's an excellent seamstress too," says Clarence.

"Yeah, I've been sewing since high school," says Irene.

"She can make anything." Clarence opens the closet and pulls out a long, beaded white dress. "This is my daughter's wedding gown. She made that."

Irene McKoy picks up a fluffy paper pumpkin. "This is a papier mâché pumpkin I made."

Clarence leaves the room and comes back in with a fruit basket of shining porcelain replicas of oranges, apples, and bananas. It normally sits in the living room, and is also Irene's work.

By dusk, Clarence and Irene's house has a break from guests. Clarence joins Henry, Willie, James McMillan, and Jay Jeffries back at the men's hotel room to drink, watch the quick fight, talk, and, inevitably, engage in an emotional debate. It starts with a suggestion from Henry that he and Willie organize a drill team to help instill discipline in troubled teenagers—the kind poorly served in inner-city schools. From there, they reminisce about Clarence and Henry's ROTC days, and the conversation eventually turns to Vietnam. Henry McKoy was drafted in 1970. He was a graduate student studying political science at A&T, with one semester left. But days before Christmas and his wedding, his unit received a new set of orders that saved him from going over. "I had been struggling with the idea that I had to come home and leave my new wife for Vietnam. You remember Christmas Day," he says to Willie.

Willie nods a response.

Henry McKoy insists he, unlike a certain working-class, upwardly mobile white boy from Arkansas, was willing to fight for his country in a war that stirred turbulent protests at home. "That's one of the reasons why I don't respect him, because a lot of men my age were faced with the same dilemma that he had, and he got out of it. And what I don't respect about him is his attempt to pretend that he is so promilitary. He's constantly around the military. He should go back to the square in Russia where he protested and blasted his country. When he was overseas, he was a part of that hippie movement that condemned his country."

"There are requirements for being president," Clarence observes. "I don't think that having had a military career is a necessary requirement for being president."

"I don't disagree with you," says Henry. "I don't disagree. But I don't respect what he did. The way he did it—"

"I was protesting it too," says Willie.

"Yeah, but, Willie, you didn't go over on foreign soil while men of my age range were dying in the jungles of Vietnam.

"You should know what it feels like to be in the military and have a bunch of people back in your country or in another country burning your flag. . . . These rich white kids back here—longhaired, rich white kids, hippies . . . free love . . . on drugs . . . with needles in their arms. I'm not talking about a black man or woman in this country who was protesting racism."

"Why were we in Vietnam?" asks Willie forcefully. "That ain't our fight. That's not our fight."

"Why were we in Iraq? Why go to Bosnia?" Henry counters. "Why do any of that? Why go to Somalia? Why go to any of those places? Superpowers have responsibilities to help stabilize the world."

"I would say that's not our fight either."

"Sometimes it is more of a humanitarian issue rather than fighting a war," says Clarence. "But you want to know something that makes me feel good sometimes? The one thing that makes me feel good about the president— now, I'm not totally happy with him, but you got two Rhodes scholars out there. Both president and vice president are Rhodes scholars. And that makes me feel good."

"Being a Rhodes scholar doesn't mean anything to me if you're a phony," says Henry.

"I don't think a Stormin' Norman should be in the White House," says Clarence. "You don't have to be in the military to understand it."

"Ronald Reagan was never in the military," says Willie.

"Suppose your daughter ran for president," says Clarence. "She ain't been in the military, ain't fought no war."

"You're missing my point," says Henry. "I don't hold it against a person. I agree with you—a person doesn't have to be in the military to be a good president. I have a difficulty with an individual who did what he did and denounced his country while men died that I know, died for the country.

"Once again, a soldier does not understand the burning of his flag. College students back here burning the flag. . . . During the sixties, people were burning buildings down in the inner city. . . . Black folks were burning them because of racism. That's different. The white kids, they were out there in the street, a bunch of these free-love hippies, Clinton's crowd. They were burning flags. They were doing all these things at a time when America was in its fight against the spread of communism."

Willie McKoy takes a break from the heat of the debate and goes to the store for more soda to mix with Jack Daniel's. I tag along. Willie McKoy says, in his view, America is not far beyond the sixties in terms of race relations. "If I married a white woman and I went to work, it would make a dramatic difference. I've seen that. Even as a manager, if I were to marry a white woman, it would change everything. We still deal in a predominantly white-male management environment. And if you're in a predominantly white-male environment, they set the rules. And that means that they have to be willing to accept a black man and a white woman together. And I think that if you talk about all the things that cause people to feel the way they do about race, it all comes down to one word—*s-e-x*. And whenever you get black men and white women together, that is a problem. I hear in conversations, you'll hear people say when you talk about race things, you'll hear people, your peer level or the people above you say, 'Well, you know, I don't know if I agree with interracial marriages because the kids, the kids, they suffer.' You hear that: they say it. They tell you how they feel. [But] that's not the real reason, it's not the kids—it's that they don't want those people together in interracial marriages. It makes us guarded-in when we're around white women. You're always making sure you don't say the wrong thing or you don't do the wrong thing that can be perceived as being aggressive toward her. Even when she's aggressive toward you, you've got to be extremely careful of how other people perceive that, because it could affect you. If she's coming on to you, then you've got to keep things aboveboard. You can't afford to let some kind of relationship develop because it'll have an adverse impact on you. This guy worked with me. He'd been to Germany. He married this girl in Germany, this white girl, and he brought her back here when he came back. He was in the service. . . . And one day his wife came out to the job to pick him up or something, give him some kind of message—something she had to deliver. And you know, I could detect the knives. They looked at him, like, kind of stuck their noses up, you know. And a few weeks later they said, 'Oh, we can't use you no more.' And it's that kind of stuff going on. . . . A white guy told me. He says, 'You know why they let him go, don't you?' I said no. He said, 'Well, they didn't like the situation with his wife.'

"You have kids going to school together now. Before, you could say black men had tails or black men had big, you know, sex organs or whatever, but now when you grow up together and you interact together on a daily basis, you see [blacks are] smart, they're intelligent, they're bright, you can have fun with them. They're attractive. They have nice features. All those myths of the past are no longer valid. They've been invalidated. So black children—[black and white] girls and boys become attracted to each other now, and the old guard is threatened by that. You have intelligent black people in corporate America now. Before, we weren't there. And the white women who were around us or the white men around the women who are in these positions didn't see this person as a leader or had all those skills that the white man had. And now they're saying hey, she's all right or he's all right and I'd like to get to know that person. We're infringing on what they see as their power. They're accustomed to having power, and they don't want it taken away from them."

Willie McKoy is four years younger than Henry and extremely loyal to his brother. He was thrilled to get a job offer so he could leave Teaneck, New Jersey, where he was also a human resource manager, to live closer to his family. He moved to Raleigh last September—just before the election. "I was glad to be there then and help. I wanted to get back. I got a sister in Durham, and I got friends there. It's not far from A&T. It's only an hour and fifteen minutes from A&T, so we can drive back and forth. I wanted to be closer to A&T. I like Raleigh. It's a good place to live."

When we return to the room, Henry and Clarence are in the middle of the discussion on taxes. "Who controls that? Who controls the amount of taxes you pay?" asks Clarence.

"Well, we're trying to give you some money back so you can control your own," says Henry.

"*We* who?" says Clarence.

"Legislators. Republican legislators like me are trying to give you your money back, but I have people over here who want to take your money and give it to somebody else. I guarantee you, you're going to see some of your money come back if the Republicans stay in control of Congress."

Clarence pauses, pours a splash of Jack Daniel's into his glass and takes a gulp. He then speaks slowly, like an attorney beginning the cross-examination of a hostile witness. He asks a question, certain that everyone knows the answer. "Have you all ever heard of George Bush? A former president?"

"Yep," all answer.

"Now, you said the Democrats control what happens to your taxes," Clarence continues.

"That's right," says Henry.

"What did he, Bush, say when he ran for president?" Clarence asks.

Henry catches the trap. "You know what he did?"

"No, no, answer my question," says Clarence.

"The biggest mistake George Bush ever made was striking a deal with the Democrats."

"That's not what I asked you, Henry."

"When he raised taxes," says Henry, "George Bush made a compromise in his presidency, and it killed him."

"Sure he did."

"He was stupid," says Willie.

"He was stupid for making a deal with the Democrats," says Henry.

"He underestimated the intelligence of people out here, you see," says Clarence.

"I don't disagree with you," says Henry. "And I think what Newt has come to realize is that he cannot make the mistake. He has to rise or fall."

"I think Newt's a joke," Willie states. "Do you know what Newt said about the black festival in Atlanta, the black college thing?"

Willie is referring to what has become known as Freaknik, a gathering of black college students in Atlanta that city leaders and many residents dread and have tried unsuccessfully to end. "Newt said he was going to send a camera crew in there to televise and get tapes of these kids having fun so that he could go back and show it and determine that we shouldn't be giving them aid to go to college. To publicly make a statement that way. That pissed me off. That pissed me off. Newt is a racist."

"I don't believe that," says Henry.

"Newt said it, Henry. He said it. Henry, Newt is a racist. Newt said that."

"It is very, very easy to take something a person says in the media and misconstrue. I spend most of my time trying to answer this question: How can you be a Republican? How can you beat that?"

"That doesn't bother me—a Democrat or a Republican—that doesn't bother me at all," says Willie.

"Those black kids who went to Atlanta and those black kids who came up here to this beach up here, Virginia Beach, the things they did—Somebody needs to say something," Henry asserts.

"No, let me tell you something—" says Willie.

"I had to turn the tape off so my daughter wouldn't play a bunch of vulgar mess in my own backyard," Henry cuts him off.

"His [Gingrich's] motive is to show the world that we are funding these black kids to go to college and they're going down here to Atlanta tearing up the place," says Willie. "That's Newt. And that's racist. Newt is no different from the guy we were watching on TV, what's his name?"

"Rush Limbaugh," Henry answers, then continues. "What about the president? He said have midnight basketballs and let them go out and play basketball and everybody thinks that's love. President proposes a program to deal with inner-city kids by saying let's open some gyms at midnight and give them some basketballs and let them play to two and three o'clock in the morning."

"But you just said something needs to be done. Recreation," says Clarence.

"That's about as bad to me as what you're saying Newt is saying."

"Newt is Rush Limbaugh," declares Willie. "Incompetent. Simple."

"I think Newt has a lot of intelligence," says Clarence.

"He's not stupid, but he's just a joke," says Willie.

"But you know what," says Clarence. "About those disturbances—and I'm not sure about how much in Atlanta, but when it came down to the nitty-gritty in Virginia Beach, most of the disturbances was started by the hoodlums in the city. Very few were the college students."

"They weren't the students," says Tanya, Clarence's daughter, who has entered the room.

In perhaps "talented tenth" fashion, everyone protects the black college students from the criticism and pours the blame on the non–college bound, inner-city youths—the alleged troublemakers, or "riffraff" as they are frequently called—for preying on mass public gatherings of young blacks. You can't even let your kids have a little bad fun in the street these days or else they'll be corrupted or shot by those bad inner-city kids, or so the thinking goes.

"Don't condemn the students," says Willie, "but look at these white kids had gone down to Florida and Myrtle Beach for years and trashed the whole damn town and nothing is said about it."

My mind goes to Ann Arbor, 1989, when University of Michigan won the NCAA basketball title, as well as to other college towns and to the "celebrations" that lead to vandalism. I decide to enter the conversation and cite those examples of youth violence.

"Yeah, they tear the town up," says Willie.

Henry turns the conversation back to the original subject.

"What we do to people like Newt is what they do to us," he states. "Exactly what they do to us."

"How so, Henry? How do we do that?" asks Willie, an impatient tone in his voice.

"We take individuals like [Newt] and we condemn them off the bat, anything they say, we single them out, like they single us out. But we're not talking to each other. They are to us, what we are to them. They single us out, we single them out."

"He's [Newt] got diarrhea of the mouth," says Willie. "He doesn't know when to shut his damn mouth."

"I don't always agree with him, but I listen to people condemning Rush," says Henry. "They never say anything about Geraldo. . . . They never say anything about all of these other people who put so much garbage in front of us and painting it as all right."

"Henry, I think you got three liabilities as a party," says Clarence. "Jesse Helms is a liability. Newt is a liability, and Patrick Buchanan [is]. When those guys keep running their mouths, they're going to turn voters off. They're going too far to the conservative side. They're going too far."

The discussion of politics winds toward an end much like its beginning, for Henry McKoy is a big player in the conversation. He cites examples of racism in the Democratic Party to counter the "liabilities" Clarence raises.

Politics has exhausted the room, and the subject naturally changes. There isn't even a need to acknowledge that it is time to move on to a topic to save the character of the weekend. Without even saying it, or perhaps even consciously thinking it, everyone knows it's time to talk about something else. It is time for a conversation that preserves the energy of the remaining moments of the Saturday night with Jack Daniel's in a hotel suite without wives and children. In their minds, responsible fatherhood has earned this night—an evening where it's okay to sit on the floor and lean back on the side of a couch rather than sit upright and posture-perfect in the chair to set an example for others or to merely ruffle the automatic assumptions of strangers who don't know any better. Who would want to drain the energy out of an evening like this with too much Vietnam, Bill Clinton, and Newt Gingrich?

Clarence does most of the talking now. His nephews throw him a series of questions about their father and uncle's generation. Clarence McKoy tells them the stories of the youthful days of men and women that Henry and Willie know only as adults. There are also new stories about Clarence, or old ones that hold interest as though he's telling them for the first time. There's the story of the fifty white parents who walked out of the school with their children when Clarence McKoy walked in as principal. There's also the stories of Uncle Clarence's days as an amateur boxer and his experiences as a country boy who traveled to Harlem in the fifties. And, of course, there are jokes—many from the nephews. "Uncle Clarence went to the doctor not too long ago with Irene," says Henry. "Uncle Clarence wasn't feeling too well. After examining him, he asked Uncle Clarence to go out 'cause he wanted to talk to Irene.

"The doctor says to Irene, 'Now, Irene, Clarence is in bad shape, but he's going to be all right. But there's some things you're going to have to do.' And Irene said, 'What is it?' He said, 'Now, you're going to have to wash his feet every night.' And she said, 'Every night, Doc?' He said, 'Every night.'

"He said, 'You're going to have to cook him three square meals every day.' She said, 'Every day?' He said, 'Every day.'

"He said, 'Now here's a final one: you're going to have to have sex with him every night.' And she looked at him and said, 'Every night, Doc?' He said, 'Yeah, you're going to have to have sex with Clarence every night.' And the doctor looked at her and said, 'Now, do you have this clear? Do you have this clear?' She said, 'Yes, I got it clear.'

"So she left the room. Uncle Clarence was sitting out there kind of anxious. He didn't know what was going on. So when Irene came out, he said, 'What did he say? What did he say, Irene?' Irene took his hand and looked him in the eye and said, 'He said you're going to die.'"

Early Sunday morning, the visiting fathers pick up their fish and get another one of Aunt Irene's breakfasts. Clarence and Irene watch them as they drive away. Clarence returns to their hotel room and checks out for them. "I am their role model now," he says again. "They miss their father, and they need me in their life. I guess I need them too."

Chapter 13

The Real McKoy

A few months before Marcia McKoy's graduation party and the Father's Day–weekend fishing trip, Henry McKoy is at the dining-room table with a few papers in front of him. His attention bounces between a fight with black Democrats and Marcia's persistent requests for permission to go on a date that her father considers too unorthodox for his taste.

First, the black Democrats: they are fighting to preserve funding for an educational program for low-income children. Nearly all of the contracts associated with the program go to white liberals, McKoy says; black educators are invisible to the program. In the middle of his explanation, Marcia comes downstairs from her room.

"Daddy, have you decided?"

McKoy looks down at his papers and then his eyes flash to Marcia.

"No, Marcia, I'll decide later."

She exhales a sigh louder than a whisper and a soft spoken word that I don't catch.

I hear the rush of her feet going upstairs as McKoy explains that she wants to borrow the car for a date tonight. Her friend either does not have a car or is having car trouble, which brings up the part that McKoy doesn't understand: his daughter driving the guy on a date.

"He's a nice young man," says McKoy. "But I don't understand. A boy his age should have a car if he wants to take a young lady out and be organized enough to have these arrangements in place. He seems to always have some kind of car problems that he needs to work out."

Then McKoy is back on the Democrats—the liberals, he says, who want to control blacks and are uncomfortable with African Americans who dare to be independent, and dare not believe that everything white and liberal promises a sacred and protective political path. Those liberals would probably think it was a sign of progress for the girl to drive on a date.

Liberals seem to be targets for McKoy in all of our conversations. I am beginning to see his distaste for the white liberal as a manifestation of his struggle against the Southern tradition to revere white benevolence toward blacks even if it degrades at the same time that it benefits. In the past, who wanted to reject a feeding gesture even if the crumbs claimed the cost of some dignity, when so few hands offered true justice and equality? In the old South, white believers in true equality for African Americans were not the norm or the expectation. So, anything that hinted at such was exalted. Even outside the region and past the time of Jim Crow, the white man or woman who treats a black friend with decency and humanity is too often admired—for doing what should be taken for granted. The racial do-gooders sometimes are mentioned in sentences with words such as "racial tolerance," a concept that should be too minimal for the expectations of the experiment of a multiracial democracy. To merely "tolerate" people of a different race implies that one endures their presence and does not live with a natural acceptance of a common humanity regardless of racial differences.

Three years after my conversations with Henry McKoy, I see evidence of the black tendency to worship white racial "tolerance" in the polls measuring black support for President Clinton during the Lewinsky sex scandal. Blacks are among his most devoted supporters. The loyalty grows out of the high-visibility relationships he maintains with African Americans: He golfs with Vernon Jordan. He seeks spiritual guidance from Jesse Jackson. He plays the saxophone and taps his feet to good jazz. For all of that and more, Toni Morrison and comedian Chris Rock call him "the first black president."

Some African Americans suggest that Kenneth Starr and the relentless Republican attacks on Clinton are racially motivated: It is the bad white boys again, goes the thinking. They can't stand to see so many black appointments and employees at the White House. They are out to get the white man who is too good to blacks for generic white taste. The good white/bad white black orthodoxy casts race and American politics very narrowly. In it, whites are cheated of their individuality with the same simplicity that makes whites see blacks in only two classes—those who mug and those who go to college. The legacy of racism, slavery, and legalized segregation in America sustains that conformity among many blacks. But Henry McKoy refuses to be beholden to the good white/bad white orthodoxy. He says he's motivated by individuality. I wonder if his motives are of pure opportunism. It's probably both.

African Americans, especially those called black leaders, historically have been gracious in acknowledging that white decency required the courage to challenge some of the norms of racism. The most famous graduate of Clarence McKoy's alma mater, for example, has much praise for white support in his autobiography and speeches: Booker T. Washington's self-reliance was built largely on the foundation of his associations with white benefactors.

McKoy doesn't see the need to be overly grateful for white support today, but he easily identifies with Washington on the issues of self-reliance, which he sees in the values embodied by his father on the farm and Uncle Clarence in the classroom. However, his vision often misses the impacts of the black-power and civil-rights movements, which greatly enlarged the arenas in which to employ the values he praises, as they pushed openly racist extremism far enough out of the mainstream that McKoy doesn't have to hear what some of his partisan allies might really think of him. The sixties produced new relationships between blacks and whites. McKoy's rhetoric often doesn't appreciate the connections between the movements of that decade and his freedom to make political choices that some might consider unorthodox.

It sometimes takes an outsider to grasp the essence of change unfolding. James Baldwin's eyes were new to the South when he made his first trip to the region in 1961. Writing about the experience, Baldwin focused on the new tensions developing in relationships between blacks and whites in the South as the civil-rights movement burst through the old order. McKoy was fifteen years old at the time of Baldwin's trip. Perhaps the writer could see a Henry McKoy forming as he looked at the strained relationships between blacks and Southern, white liberals. "Men do not like to be protected, it emasculates them. This is what black men know, it is the reality they have lived with; it is what white men do not want to know. It is not a pretty thing to be a father and be ultimately dependent on the power and kindness of some other man for the well-being of your house."

Marcia comes back downstairs.

"Daddy?" she asks.

She exhales another windy sigh that drops her shoulders an inch.

"Okay, Marcia," says Henry. "This time."

• • •

Some white Democrats and Republicans consider McKoy's victory in 1994 "a fluke," an accident of the strong Republican wave that made McKoy's race irrelevant in the minds of white voters: they were pulling levers against incumbents and for a new set of bums.

A year and a half later, in July 1996, it seemed clear that white Democrats were ready to exploit McKoy's race with the kind of race-baiting that helped build the Republican Party in the South. In one instance, the campaign of Eric Reeves, one of McKoy's white Democratic opponents, conducted a poll in which four hundred voters were thrown a series of negative questions about McKoy and then asked if they knew that he was black, according to some white McKoy supporters who were called. Reeves denied that the campaign conducted a "push poll," but refused to release the questions.

As the Democrats moved to exploit race, McKoy forged an alliance with the North Carolina politician noted for using race in the nastiest of ways. In 1996, Jesse Helms and President Clinton haggled over an appointment to the United States African Foundation, which makes recommendations to Congress on the distribution of aid to African nations. Eventually, Clinton and Helms compromised with the appointment of Henry McKoy, whom Helms recommended to Clinton.

Ridding the United State Senate of Jesse Helms has been the goal of many black and Democratic voters in North Carolina for several years. In 1984, they backed Jim Hunt, the white governor in what became one of the most expensive Senate races in American history. Helms won. In 1990, Helms faced the historic challenge from the campaign of Harvey Gantt, a black architect and former mayor of Charlotte. Helms won again. Now, in 1996, Gantt was trying again to unseat Helms. As usual, the campaigns for and against Helms generated enormous energy across the state and contributions from across the country.

McKoy avoided the Helms-Gantt race for most of the 1996 campaign season. It posed delicate issues for his own campaign: supporting Helms would insult blacks; backing Gantt would offend fellow Republicans.

The issue finally confronted McKoy two weeks before election day when he went before the Raleigh-Wake Citizens Association, the powerful black political organization born in the thirties to fight for the hiring of black postal workers. Two years ago, McKoy's campaign received a tremendous boost with the surprise endorsement of the group. The organization's leadership voted against him, but the rank and file overruled its leaders in their own vote. There was, however, not a Jesse Helms race in 1994. Now, in 1996, McKoy couldn't escape the question of Helms. When asked if he supported Helms over Gantt, McKoy answered yes to the nearly all-black audience.

His problems didn't stop there. Two years ago, the presence of McKoy's wife at the meeting shielded him from the attacks of enemies who didn't want to berate the candidate in front of her. But when Katie McKoy and Teresa Peoples, a McKoy supporter, arrived at the meeting, they were forbidden to enter. "She thought she had attended enough meetings that she could take part in the endorsement process," said Jannet Barnes, president of the RWCA. "But she had not been to enough meetings."

I met Barnes, a stout woman wearing African-style clothes, for coffee at Hardee's, a fast-food restaurant, after the election. She told me that the organization had enacted a new rule stating that in order to vote, each member was required to attend at least six of the organization's twelve yearly meetings. "We had the meeting rosters, and each individual signed their own name and address to the roster passed around at each meeting. We had the meeting rosters from the last endorsement meeting to this one. She had not attended a single meeting except for the endorsement meeting the last time. Our philosophy is, if you're interested in our organization . . . then you should be willing to [attend] six meetings a year. We only meet once a month. It's not like you have to attend twelve meetings."

Katie McKoy and Teresa Peoples became enraged, argued, and eventually went home. Peoples later called the black radio station and went on the air blasting the RWCA as a "white-controlled organization." I am not surprised that such an accusation made it into the feud: black-on-black political disputes quite often have one side throwing the so-called plantation charge at the other. This time, it came from the Republican side, which is the one more commonly on the receiving end.

Without his wife in the audience, RWCA members were not bashful about criticizing McKoy. "We also found he passed out two candidate handouts," says Barnes. "In the black community, he had a handout with him and some little kids and everything. In the white community, he had one with him and Bob Dole on the front. . . . Now, you tell me what kind of games he's playing."

It sounds like the normal game of American politics and marketing to me. I'm sure that all of the white candidates' campaign literature picturing them posing with blacks didn't arrive in my hand by accident. But when asked about this, Barnes disagreed. "No. They don't do that. The handout we get is the same one they pass out in white communities," she says and starts naming some obscure white politicians who she's positive haven't sent out separate materials to black and white communities. "This was the first time we found this to happen."

Whatever.

McKoy lost the endorsement. Two weeks later, he lost his seat. Gantt was also a loser. Helms won again.

Predicting the black vote has never been too difficult. The legacies of Franklin D. Roosevelt and the civil-rights movement tied African Americans to the Democratic Party. And while the bond—always fragile—has loosened, Henry McKoy's experience shows that it is still there nevertheless.

McKoy argues that blacks will never be free politically as long as they are locked into one party. His argument portrays black loyalty to the Democrats as a failure to fully engage partisan politics due to a fear that imagines one party as a monster. Fear of the Republican fangs translates into a black weakness that bestows upon the white masters of the other party the power to patronize and posture as protectors of a race that can't face the evil Republicans on its own—much less negotiate a place for its people in that party. African Americans, according to McKoy, merely become subordinates on one side and not full players in the game.

Six weeks after McKoy's defeat, I visit a black North Carolina politician who is considered a true player. Representative Dan Blue, forty-eight, sits in a reclining chair behind a cherry-wood desk in his downtown-Raleigh law office. He divides his working time between his law practice and the state legislature. Like Henry McKoy, Blue too has made legislative history. In 1990, as a Democrat, he became the state's first black speaker of the House. But when the Democrats lost their majority in 1994—the same election that swept McKoy into office—Blue lost the position.

Blue sees little value in celebrating African American firsts in politics—unless they produce something of value to the electorate. "What's so exciting about the first black Republican getting elected to something? If you've got Colin Powell as president, maybe it matters. But if you've got somebody just working on the party theme, it probably doesn't matter a whole lot.

"Did having Henry McKoy in the senate cause Republicans to vote the way the masses in our communities thought that [they] should vote? No, not in any significant way."

Blue grew up in rural Robeson County, only a few miles away from McKoy's native Hoke County and his descriptions of a rural North Carolina farm childhood in the late fifties and sixties are similar to McKoy's. "My mother was a homemaker," Blue says. "My father was a farmer. I had very supportive parents whose major goal was to ensure that we were educated. Education was very important to us. We had instilled in us a sense of self-sufficiency. They instilled a work ethic. A very, very strong work ethic. . . . I had parents who taught me that there were no excuses."

Also in common with McKoy, Blue attended a historically black state college—North Carolina Central University—the rival of McKoy's beloved A&T. From Central, Blue was among the first African Americans to attend Duke University Law School. But Blue isn't possessed by the kind of black-college spell that dictates the college choices of his offspring. His two oldest children are at Duke. Nor does Blue look back at old segregated black schools with the romanticism that colors McKoy's vision of the black past.

"You hear people talk about that halcyon age of old. I mean, make no mistake about it, I went to elementary, grade, and high schools that taught me how to achieve in this world. It was the best that segregated system had to offer. But don't make any mistake and believe the high school I went to had the supplies that white high schools did. It was a small high school, very homogeneous school body . . ."

Blue also describes Republican claims to values like self-reliance and self-help as "a lot of bullshit": "They're American values. I feel that very strongly. I don't think the Republicans represent them any more than the Democrats do, and in many instances, not as much. You know, I get tired of hearing all this stuff about self-reliance. Everybody here embraces what Franklin Roosevelt did as president with Social Security. . . . We didn't want old people out in the streets without any level of support. Republicans supported that fully . . . If you're going to argue that's not self-reliance, then that means neither party believes in self-reliance and believes if you didn't save enough when you were farming, or 'cause you didn't save enough when you were working for the textile mills, you should starve.

"Medicare is something everybody supports. Lyndon Johnson came up with it and Richard Nixon expanded it. Everybody supports Medicare. Well, I guess, if you're really self-reliant, then you really ought to be able to pay all your own medical costs, there ought not be any governmental intervention to help you pay that. Same with Medicaid: if you're really self-reliant, then you ought to be able to pay for your own medical care. . . . Those programs go to the real strength of this country. Each of us is responsible for ourselves, but we're also responsible to the full body. . . . In order to have a healthy country, we have to have a healthy population, so we support Medicaid to ensure that kids aren't going to be sick, they aren't going to have diseases. . . .

"Now, I've played with budgets and I've played with tax policies. If you really favor self-reliance, you ought not have any tax policies that favor anybody over anybody else, and one of the greatest favoritisms we play is tax policies to benefit people who claim to be self-reliant.

"People embrace these ideas of self-reliance and self-help as if they just thought about them and they just came into existence. These things have always been an integral part of my black experience. I sometimes get offended, because there's a certain feeling that these ideas and beliefs that people espouse are somehow foreign to us as a group and, specifically, blacks in the Democratic Party.

"As a community, we believe in community action. You look at it. Although many of the black institutions were initially supported by white philanthropists, we supported them over the years as best we could, whether they were church based or [based in] various other institutions. We are self-reliant. We have a history of it. But you have to have a playing field that allows you to be self-sufficient and that gets us to the ultimate issue. You can talk about self-reliance; you can talk about being independent and believing in these things all you want. But when you tilt the playing field such that you're spending all of your energy trying to stay on it and you're constantly going uphill, you don't have the same resources and energy to do the things that indicate your self-reliance as some other folks do."

Blue and McKoy's rhetoric share a refusal to allow terms like *self-reliance* to be separated from black culture in the popular imagination. Both know that the black American experience is heavily layered on values of self-help and self-reliance. McKoy claims those values by joining the party that assumes them, preaches about them, and has become associated with them in the political sphere. Blue claims them directly, by unraveling the fallacies that place them with any party and outside of a culture that couldn't survive without them. In the process, both men battle the remains of the Reaganite notion that welfare queens define the whole of black culture. In a large sense, they confront the extensions of the collectibles at Elaine Armstrong's table at Gallia County's Emancipation—the stereotypes represented by those items.

Henry McKoy is in his driveway, waxing his black BMW on the Sunday morning after Christmas 1996. It is seven weeks after election day, and the campaign sticker is still on the bumper: THE REAL McKoY.

"A lubricant was invented that helped the trains roll—before that, they kind of smoked. The lubricant was invented by a black man who's last name was McKoy and he called it 'The Real McKoy.' It works. It gets the job done. It's the real thing. That's what I want people to think about me."

McKoy now spends his time working with the U.S. Africa Foundation. He's also building his consulting business, which continues to focus on diversity training and conflict resolution. "One of the techniques I employ is I ask people when we first get into a room, what are some of the things we have in common? I'll put some of those things on a board. How many of you are born in the South? How many of you are parents? How many of you are grandparents? How many of you have teenagers? How many of you are going through the empty nest? How many of you have kids under two? Talk about some of the struggles about sending young kids to school. People start laughing and talking about baby-proofing the house . . . people start bonding and so on. I'll say, 'Out of these ten things, pick the ones that are the most important to you. What would they be, let's list them.' And most times people pick five or six things they have in common. And it crosses all kinds of lines. Then we move to the things we disagree on.

"But when we talk, blacks and white conservatives, the dialogue always seems to be what we don't have in common. What we disagree on, which is affirmative action, sometimes welfare reform. But we never can get to the things we have in common. For example, many white conservatives are real concerned about the educational system and what it's doing. Most black parents will tell you that they are not getting a good shake from the public education system. Many of our children are being tracked . . . they're in trouble. Blacks will tell you, 'We're rethinking this whole integration thing, this busing thing.' Conservatives are saying we really need to rethink this, but there's a core group of people who want to keep things the way they are, and they will tell blacks, 'Don't pay attention to the conservatives' belief in charter schools and school choice because it's aimed at resegregating and getting away from you. That's what they really want.'

"In the meantime, David, they [educators] segregate our schools every single, solitary day that our kids go to school. If you don't believe it, go into these schools and see who's in the most mentally retarded, the severely disturbed classes, and go and look who's in the gifted and talented classes. You will find segregation in an integrated system. And the two groups of people who were talking about changing the educational system are blacks and conservatives, and they can't talk because the people in the middle say to blacks, 'You don't want to talk to those people.' About home schooling, charter schools, tuition which will allow the kids to go to religious schools or to another kind of private school created by blacks! These things might be worth considering when you look at the public school system. But we never get to that discussion because we're so busy talking about what those conservatives are doing over there. Volatile, flame-throwing issues are often used by people who want to keep the conversation from occurring."

The conversation *has* occurred in some places. In Wisconsin, Polly Williams, a black legislator, joined with white conservatives to enact a school-vouchers program for low-income children. She was the black toast of white conservative think tanks in the early nineties, but the lovefest didn't last long. In 1996, Williams was blasting the original supporters of the program for only pushing the parts of the program that benefited whites.

Katie McKoy comes outside while Henry is waxing the car. She offers me a cup of coffee, and McKoy interrupts our conversation with an observation about me that actually crystallizes the sincerity in his values. "He loves his daughter and son, Katie," McKoy yells. "He carried his daughter all the way to Hampton for the fishing trip and all across the country."

I've never really discussed my own family with McKoy. My son, David, was born shortly after the fishing trip. I carried my daughter, Lynnette, to Hampton to give my wife, Valerie, a break. My mother and sister traveled from Raleigh to Hampton to watch Lynnette while I followed the McKoy men. On Father's Day, Lynnette and I rushed home to join the rest of the family. She never even met Henry McKoy.

His observation of something so seemingly small over a year ago confirmed for me that the value he places on family is authentic. It is not manufactured to suit the "family values" debate, but genuinely reflects his politics. I still have problems with his attacks of racism on the left: it is not that I object to his argument—I actually think it is a healthy addition to the conversation on race and politics—but his vision is too orthodox, just like that of the black diehard liberals on the other side. Too often, he merely switches the good and bad tags that the black mainstream has placed on white liberals and conservatives.

McKoy's wax job turns his car into a black mirror—the closer you stand to the BMW, the easier it is to see yourself. He steps back and gives the car a final look. I stare at the lonely and aging campaign sticker on the bumper. It's chipped and looks out of place on a car shining so brightly.

We go inside for a cup of coffee, and the scent of wax is carried in with the rag McKoy carries. He says that despite his loss, he is not a defeated man. "If I move forward with a sense of despair and depression, then everything that I propose, everything that I advocate, every position that I take, every new idea that somebody else advances, no matter where it may come from, I'm only going to be able to judge it from my perception of depression and despair. And I think one of the problems with America is that a lot of its leaders are looking in the twentieth century at black America, and when they see black America, they see depression and despair. I don't believe that group of people is going to lead the kind of people I grew up around, people who believe they have some responsibility and control over their destiny, who would tell their children to get up and go to work. People who look at black America with despair are not going to be able to look at those young black males and say, 'Young man, it is your responsibility to get out and work'; they're going to see that young man's despair. They're going to see that young pregnant woman's despair. They're not going to be the ones to say, 'Go out and go get a job.' Their answers are going to be desperate. They're going to send them to midnight basketball. They're going to say, 'Let's give kids needles.' They're going to say, 'Let's not change welfare.' We're in a crisis, and the crisis is around vision: a vision of where we need to go and who's going to come up with the idea to tell us where we need to go. It will not come from the people who look at our community and see all our solutions are about desperation and despair. It will not do it."

In 1998, McKoy ran again and lost. The Republicans on whose coattails he rode in 1994 also fell as America expressed frustration with the Republicans and the costly obsessions of Ken Starr. In 1998, control of the state house of representatives returned to the Democrats.

The change kills the hopes of those backing school-voucher legislation. Still, a compromise charter-school bill actually did became law in McKoy's term. In 1998, nearly two years after his defeat, the coalition McKoy envisioned—blacks and conservatives—became reality in North Carolina over the issue of diversity at charter schools. In a battle against the state's teachers' union and many black Democratic legislators—who happened to receive campaign contributions from the union—the black charter schools–Republican coalition teamed to eliminate diversity requirements for charter schools. The diversity clause, which required the schools to "reasonably reflect" the demographics of the school districts they serve, was born out of a fear that charter schools would become white-flight academies. But as the schools opened for the second year, in 1998, those in violation of the clause were overwhelmingly black and faced the threat of closing because they failed to attract white students.

The charter-school fight was two years away when I spoke to Henry McKoy in his driveway weeks after his defeat. At the time, the bill had passed and educators were in the process of applying for charters. Then, McKoy predicted that a flood of African Americans would start and enroll in charter schools and, indeed, in 1998, 50 percent of charter-school students across the state are African American, while blacks comprise 30 percent of public-school enrollment.

Three

TRUE
COLORS

The Norm of No Color

FOR some artists, the city famous for American cars and a trademark sound commands another distinction. "I'm an artist in New York because of Detroit," says Al Loving. "For some reason, Detroit has a much more sophisticated cultural whatever-it-is than any city in the United States."

Detroit? "The reality is there. Detroit has been bad-mouthed in the national press. But the measure of a culture is the capacity to expend people who can make art and support them. That . . . reality measures the culture more than any other thing. Detroit has clearly become a primary center that way.

"To the national art world, New York might be the center, but for us, Michigan is."

Ed Clark agrees and disagrees. "I'm not a Detroit person. I don't know the city," he says, but goes on to note that he sells twice as many pieces there than anywhere else. "And I have a gallery in Hamburg. I have a gallery in New York. I live in Paris and have a gallery there. I'm not putting down Detroit, but not many people are flying into Detroit like they fly into Manhattan or Paris to buy art.

"It has to do with who the dealer is," Clark explains. "Galleries open and close all the time. A talented dealer is as rare as a talented artist. That's what makes Detroit the market that it is."

The talented dealer didn't know the names Romare Bearden or Jacob Lawrence in 1968 when someone offered him a Bearden for six hundred dollars. A college student at the time, he couldn't afford it. Today, he scolds himself for not finding a way to buy it, but eases his regret with the knowledge that youth isn't always smart. And, regardless, he has Loving, Clark, Nanette Carter, Herb Gentry, and David Driscoll, among others, who help to sustain a thriving enterprise in a field where failure is as common as a bright color in a painting. He strives to maintain a gallery where taste isn't compromised by the need for profit. He stirs a market for high art in a midwestern city that outsiders associate with crime and economic decline, and his Detroit collectors keep some New York artists from having to teach to eat. "He supports a lot of us out here because he can sell the art," says Loving. "The money that he sends me monthly is enough so you don't have to worry about working for a living—you know what I mean?"

Nanette Carter has been living off of her art in New York for twelve years and 85 percent of her collectors are African Americans who spend between $1,000 for small pieces and $15,000 for canvas size. "I have just never seen any place quite like Michigan in terms of the numbers of blacks who are buying and seriously buying, not just the Romare Beardens and the Jacob Lawrences. But they are also getting the Ed Clarks you know the abstract artists like Al Loving, myself, and what have you. When I go to these homes, it's a wonderful thing. I'll never forget the first time I visited this couple's home, he was an attorney and I believe she was a judge. They were not more than maybe late thirties, early forties, young couple. I walked in and saw Emma Amos's work going up the stairwell. And I saw Ed Clark over the sofa, my work was over the fireplace, and Al Loving was in the dining room. It was like, oh my god, all friends are in this home. Since that time I've gone to other homes and the people are just so excited about having a part of their culture there, and again this abstract work. We're not seeing black faces on the wall. And I think that raising families and having children to grow up with this also makes a difference. I've actually talked to some of the children and they said, 'Oh, yeah, I know you, you're on the wall and mummy got this, that, and the other. And we've got this piece and that piece.'"

The GR N'Namdi Gallery isn't in Detroit proper. It is a thirty-minute ride from the Motor City to suburban Birmingham, Michigan, which has more merchants and department stores than downtown Detroit. Birmingham isn't SoHo, and Detroit is known for cars and Motown while New York is home to the Whitney and Metropolitan Museum; but the Birmingham zip code is in a socioeconomic league with Scarsdale and New York's Upper East Side. With its collection of high-end galleries downtown, Birmingham is as close to SoHo as one can get in Michigan.

Still, survival has grown tough for gallery owners in Birmingham, where business generally booms. The white-shoe Donald Morris Gallery, for example, one of Birmingham's oldest, closed in 1995. GR N'Namdi, however, is untouched by downturns in the industry. Its owner was doing so well, in fact, that he opened a second gallery, now operated by his son, in Chicago's River North District, another center for high-end galleries.

GR N'Namdi owner and founder George N'Namdi is a former psychologist who left the chair and couch for art ten years ago. Now, with several well-reviewed exhibitions behind him, he is known more for his acumen as a fine art dealer than he ever was for counseling troubled minds. He is also known for adorning his face and head with art of a different kind: on this summer Saturday in 1995, a pair of small, red, rectangular-rimmed spectacles sits closer to the edge of his nose than to his eyes, and, as usual, he wears a tailor-made, pork-pie hat. At home, there's a collection of flat-top, low-brim silk caps that have outworn their periods on his head. When N'Namdi is ready for a new hat, he goes to Nashville to commission one from a hatter known to the gallery owner simply as "Jew the hat man."

"Jew the hatter, that's all I know," he says. "I'm not trying to be derogatory. I don't know his name. Everybody calls him Jew, and he's not Jewish.

"I had a person do it here, but I felt he didn't do it correctly to my specifications. I also thought he might mass-produce his hats, and then other people will be wearing my stuff, you see."

The walls of N'Namdi's gallery, meanwhile, are adorned by the art that is his first passion. There are few faces in the frames: most of his artists are abstractionists whose works would not be at home in an exhibition of folk art. Unlike folk artists, says Loving of his contemporaries, "There's nothing innocent about us. There's nothing accidental about us. We're all professionals. No pop artists in the group. Nothing like that."

Of N'Namdi and his mission, Loving continues, "He doesn't want to sell you one picture—he's looking for players, people who want a lot of pictures, people who will successfully and eventually be able to go to auctions and go there with some authority. He's actually building something that has never existed in America before: a conscious black audience of people who are conscious of the art beyond its visual information."

You would never hear George N'Namdi refer to the gallery or its collectors as black or African American. Yes, the gallery is one of the only businesses in Birmingham owned by someone of African ancestry. But to use either term—*black* or *African American*—violates a tenet of the N'Namdi family philosophy, which considers such racial references as impertinent and subtle rejections of one's humanity. For the past two decades, George

and Carmen N'Namdi and their children have lived by a homegrown philosophy, called the "norm," that originated in one of George's graduate-
school papers. According to the norm, when someone, particularly
someone of African ancestry, refers to an artist as "black" or even "African
American," the speaker implies that such artists are abnormal. When you
think of yourself as the norm, the philosophy goes, there isn't a need to arbitrarily identify your race. The norm forbids celebrating Toni Morrison as a
black writer: she's merely a writer and Nobel laureate, not the first black
American to win the Nobel Prize for literature. "It's a beautiful concept isn't
it? It really is," says George.

N'Namdi pauses for a second. The dreamy look on his face does the talking—he may have just glimpsed utopia. He shakes his head, then speaks
just above a whisper. "Its like, damn, we could be normal. I can have a
mother—I don't have to say I have a black mother or a black father or a
black woman or a black kid.

"I think the concept in itself is unique . . . because most of us don't think
of ourselves that way."

When one's race is relevant to a conversation, the N'Namdis refer only to
the person's ancestry. The words *African* and *European* are more common
in their conversations than *black* and *white*. They use the color words
strictly to describe objects or things that are truly black and white. References to their family philosophy also come with a casual familiarity and understanding. "The norm" is uttered in the way some people might say
words like *Freud, God, Baptist,* or *Afrocentric.*

The GR N'Namdi Gallery, founded in 1981, isn't the first family enterprise
to exercise the philosophy. The norm actually grew up with a school
founded by Carmen N'Namdi in 1978, when Henry McKoy was still a Democrat. Decades before *choice* became the buzzword in educational jargon
and before McKoy launched his campaign for vouchers, blacks across the
country were starting a new generation of private schools. In the late sixties
and early seventies, many of the schools were secular and pan-African; by
the early eighties, the majority of them were Christian schools affiliated with
black churches.

Some of Carmen N'Namdi's first graduates have either reached or are a
few years beyond that age when they unabashedly share the philosophy of
the norm. Still, the norm makes a deep and lasting impact. In the late eighties, one of them, while a student at Howard University, mounted a solo
protest against a university event and its advertising because of its title: it
was called a "black" arts festival. The student, calling on norm thinking,
questioned why an event at "a predominantly African" school would have

to be described with the word *black*. Then there was the seventh-grade student who was reading Pearl S. Buck's *The Good Earth*. After finishing the book, he asked his teacher, "Is she European? Wow, she's as good as James Baldwin."

"So, it's like Paul Laurence Dunbar, Toni Morrison, those are your norms for writers," says George. "So then you're good or bad compared to how you come up to them. That's your frame of reference. You don't have to put down Steinbeck, you see? You don't have to put down T. S. Eliot. You can read all those things. But what's the frame of reference you use when you read them? That's the issue here, with the whole norm: it's establishing your frame of reference and not just the acquiring of information . . . the norm doesn't just present information, it also speaks to how you absorb the information."

"We really don't make any big deal out of being African, that's the whole big deal about the school," adds Carmen.

George and Carmen distance their school from Afrocentrism, but not out of any fear of offending whites. "It goes back to identifying yourself," explains George. "I think [saying] 'Afrocentric' is almost like saying 'black.' I think what happens is a lot of times when that term is used, *Afrocentric,* it has political connotations to it. Usually, it's a reactionary term—it's reacting a lot of times. Race is an issue in the sense that you're reacting. You're trying to overcome something that has been said or done. . . .

"The concept of the norm, first of all, is not African. The norm is a philosophical construct. It's how you look at life and the way you look at life and how that has established the norm of the people. So, if you're Japanese, you have a different norm, but the philosophy that guides you is the same thing as the norm. So, when we speak of the norm, we are not saying use African people as the defining force. That seems to be, like, Afrocentric. We're not the norm for Europeans. We're not the norm for Asians, okay? But so many of us see ourselves, again, in relation to Europeans so our definition comes from how we think they perceive us. You know, as opposed to defining ourselves."

George and Carmen say that the norm also influences the way the family responds to racism. "There's something called institutional racism. That I tend to acknowledge. Then there's personal racism—you can't acknowledge that. You've got to acknowledge that more as a sickness or insecurity in that individual. If you don't, you give that person a certain power."

But, regardless of race, "that person" has power if he or she signs paychecks or drives cabs. The effect of that power is minimal on an individual who owns his own business, operates her own school, or even drives his or her own car. Such independence frees one of the worry over the root of a slight and provides the space to live as "the norm" and to see little value in loud protests over racism—which are almost irrelevant to the experience of one whose created his own means by which to live in America. "You give it [racism] more credence by responding to it," says George. "And do you remember the O.J. picture on *Time*? I mean, people made a big thing about it. I don't believe in all that. See, that's one of our philosophies—like, if you believe in something, do it yourself. If you want a decent article, write it yourself. Start a magazine, you know. If you want a gallery to showcase art, you do it yourself. Don't go to protesting about it. I don't believe in that. I believe in doing it yourself."

So did Booker T. Washington and so does Henry McKoy. Despite the similarities, though, N'Namdi isn't a neat ideological descendent of Washington, for his thought also has much in common with Washington's ideological and intellectual rival W. E. B. Du Bois. As an art dealer, N'Namdi markets the work of artists who are steeped in classical traditions, and he's strengthening the opportunities for a class of high-end artists who would surely have been part of Du Bois's Talented Tenth.

In some ways, N'Namdi's perspective reflects an emergent black (pardon the norm violation) line of thought that guides the way many African Americans live. You would not find N'Namdi running behind whites with a fist, poster, and cries denouncing his exclusion from a mainstream. It would be just as rare to see him seated next to Armstrong Williams on *America's Black Forum* calling the problems of the poor self-inflicted, announcing the end of racism, or extolling the achievements of Clarence Thomas. There are both liberal and conservative pieces of him that manifest themselves in the way he lives; they're not manufactured merely to win white approval. He isn't a "race man," but he does acknowledge the vestiges of racism, which he sees as slight but powerful enough in his world to inspire him to stand among one million men in Washington a few months after my visit to the gallery. "Like, I'm not a person who will go hear Farrakhan speak," he told me a few weeks after the Million Man March. "I mean, I've done that. I heard him speak in the seventies. It's not like I'm anti-him or anything, it's just something I wouldn't think to do.

"For me, it was a mental, spiritual release, in a way. You know, to be able to have people around you in a similar situation—[to] see it's still there, still that little frustration . . . like a little suppressed rage or something like that."

As N'Namdi describes his participation in the march, I sense a small and subtle ambivalence in him about his own success—something that he shares with many accomplished African Americans. It is something that is as

eternal as racism and penetrates even the norm. "I found that large numbers of participants [in the march] that I knew were people like myself who
were self-employed. They could be attorneys with their own practice;
physicians or dentists, you know, with general practices. But I had a whole
lot of people like that . . . who had heavy means, very successful, but they
were sure there. . . . We have these businesses, and we seem successful and
all that—and we are successful in some point. But, a little level of frustration
is still there. Like [when] you know if somebody else is doing the work
you're doing, [and] they benefit in a much bigger way or something. Okay,
so for me with the art, if I was white or something, on the level that I oper-
ate—oh, man. The museums would be knocking down the door to be part
of it, you know. 'Let's be friends,' you know. . . . Like, race does say things,
although you don't let it hinder you. In this group, it's not hindering us.
We're not letting it stop us. But at the same time, you know it's there . . . and
just a little pain in the butt sometimes. You're like, 'Damn, I can be drawing
ten million as opposed to two hundred thousand.' That's how you feel. It
may not be totally true, but that's a little level of frustration because of race.
It has nothing to do with the quality of your product or what product you
bring."

In 1976, George and Carmen N'Namdi and their two children drove into
Detroit to live and open a school. The family of four, with a baby on the
way, had a three-figure savings account and even less money lining their
wallets. The GR N'Namdi Gallery, which would open years later, wasn't
even a thought.

Many friends thought that the mission was made of the kind of dreams
and thinking that would inspire someone to quit a good day job and move
to New York or Hollywood. It wasn't quite the initiative expected of a
thirty-two-year-old man with a Ph.D. in psychology or of a twenty-nine-
year-old woman who had an undergraduate degree in early-childhood
education but had been a homemaker since college.

Carmen sits in the front passenger seat of their green Datsun as the couple drives onto the Lodge from I-94 east. The doubts of friends zoom in and
out of her mind. "My friend in Ann Arbor said, 'You can't just go to Detroit—you don't even know anybody in Detroit. How does one just start a
school?' And so I started really feeling uneasy," remembers Carmen.

George, her husband and a psychologist, had told Carmen to discontinue
any conversations that dwelled on the impossibility of their mission.
"George kept saying, 'It's very important that you not hold conversations

like that.' He said, 'That's true for them. They're speaking the truth for them, but they don't know you, and they don't know your realities, so you're not to listen to stuff like that, or your realities will disintegrate and theirs will start coming in.'

"But I still thought, why am I so sure I can do this and nobody else is? Is there something I don't know?"

The Ohio natives ignored the fact that they had never operated a school or taught full-time. They disregarded the fact that they had no idea how they would finance the operation or who, with the exception of their own children, would attend this school. All they had was a basement furnished with collected furniture and old schoolbooks donated by friends—many of whom thought that the mission was crazy.

Nevertheless, the school with only three definite students and without a building had a name and an opening date. It would open in two years, after Carmen completed her master's degree in education at Wayne State. The school would be named for their daughter, Nataki Talibah.

It is easy to tell that Nataki Talibah is the daughter of George and Carmen. In the pictures, her skin, the color of a fall leaf, is the precise shade of Carmen's complexion. Her face derives a unique character from its round cheeks, and its shape seems destined to grow into the form of her father's, which at age forty-eight, still retains a touch of baby fat. Yet George and Carmen will never know if Nataki's features would have grown in maturity to resemble her father's or if they would form into a slender and angular cast like her mother's. Carmen's face only seems big when her full, toothy, and infectious smile flashes and stays long enough to fully absorb a moment. Carmen smiled and cried on November 3, 1974: it was the day that Nataki first walked and the day she died.

George and Carmen were a young family, with two-and-a-half-year-old Kemba, fourteen-month-old Nataki, and Carmen pregnant with their son Jumaane. They were in the middle of the morning routine in their apartment in Ann Arbor, Michigan. George, a Ph.D. student in psychology at the time, was working as a teaching assistant on campus and was getting ready for work. Carmen, a homemaker, was getting her daughters ready to go to the University of Michigan's William Monroe Trotter House, a huge meeting place and social center for African-American students.

"We had a play group at the house," says Carmen. "All the mothers would come together, and we would teach the kids little things. That day we were having dress-up dinner in adult clothes and a lot of role-playing and stuff."

Carmen was gathering clothes and props in between cooking breakfast when Nataki surprised her. "She's fourteen months and she wasn't walking, and so it was a big joke about how this girl was going to be thirty and not walk. All of a sudden, I'm in the kitchen trying to get some breakfast together, and I come in the living room and Nataki is just coming. I said, 'George, she's walking.' I'm sitting on one end of the living room and he's on the other, and she starts walking back and forth between us. So we're just cheering and everything. We got her walking back and forth, and she's just laughing, like, 'I got this.' So I started calling up everybody, I said, 'I want you to know who's walking . . .'"

Eventually, they left the house and arrived at Trotter. "I'm carrying all this stuff and Nataki is just so irritable," Carmen recalls. "She kept whining and whining. So, I thought she must be sleepy still. So I put everything down and put Nataki down for a nap."

It was the last moment Carmen would see her daughter alive. An hour later, Carmen went into the room and saw Nataki's arm hanging through the slat of the crib.

"What goes on in your head at a time like that?" asks Carmen rhetorically. "I kept thinking, 'This is not what I'm thinking.' I looked over at her; she's totally blue, foaming at the mouth and blue. She's completely blue. I don't remember the rest of it. I remember picking her up and running to Marcia [another parent]. I remember saying, 'Would you tell me this isn't true,' and then I ran away. I left her with Marcia and just ran."

Carmen ended up in a car in the lap of the director of the center and watched George's arrival through the front window. He would jump out of his automobile, leaving it running in parking gear with a door flung wide open. He would extend his arms, clutch the back of an ambulance, and nearly collapse with his face soaked in tears.

Nataki Talibah died of strangulation. A string around her pacifier caught on a slat of the crib. It happened when the nation was less enlightened about accidental crib deaths. "She had a pacifier around her neck because we used to play this thing where she would throw it up and I'd go fetch it like a dog, you know. So then I said, 'We'll put it on a string, and that way, she won't do that.' The night before, I said to George, 'Don't let her sleep with that pacifier around her neck.' He said, 'Oh, I let her do it the night before,' and I said, 'Why, don't do that, I don't like that.' And then I said, 'Oh, let her do it. It's silly of me. I'm just always thinking something's going to happen to these kids.' So we left it on.

"I get to the hospital, George is on the floor, and he's got his head in a chair and he's crying. I go up to him and I say, 'George, this is my fault. I put the pacifier around her neck. This is my fault. I have killed our daughter, this is my fault.' George comes out of all of this and says, 'Don't you ever acknowledge you did anything like that.'

"Do you know how special that was at a time like that? There are not many people on this earth that at a time like that when you're looking for something to blame that can do that. You can come out of your own pain like that and be there for somebody. That's incredible. He says, 'There's nobody that loves her more than us. This is painful, it is a tragedy, but you don't do that to yourself.'"

"Kemba came in the house that day," recalls Carmen. "My friend brought her home. She went straight to her room and got into bed. They slept in the same room. Kemba did not say a word. She was two and a half, she did not open her mouth, and she was just sitting. Nataki's crib was right across from her. She doesn't say a word, no questions, nothing."

But she would eventually ask a question that was too difficult for her parents to answer. George, Carmen, and Kemba arrived at the funeral home, and it was the first time that Kemba would see the body of her sister. The funeral home director offered advice on how to help such a young child cope with the tragedy.

"Tell her Nataki is asleep," the director said.

"No, I'm not telling her she's asleep,'" Carmen replied.

"Oh, you have to or it will frighten her."

"No, I'm not going tell her that. I don't know what I'm going tell her, but I'm not telling her she's asleep."

The family entered the room where the body of their fourteen-month-old lay in an open casket. "George was carrying Kemba. We did this by ourselves because we didn't want other people around—we didn't want her dealing with the reactions of other people. So we stood there looking at Nataki laid out. I put a sweater on her, and I had one jean leg rolled up and wild socks on and gym shoes. And I had her hair all like it used to be all messed up like a birthday party, you know. So Kemba is looking at her, and she doesn't say anything. And then she looks at me and she says, 'Make her get up.' I said, 'No, that I can't.' And she started screaming, 'Please make her get up,' and we all fell apart at that point. We couldn't pull it together, so we went outside and we sat and then we started talking about how Nataki had died and how she choked and everything."

Nataki was buried in Cincinnati, Carmen's hometown. Carmen's family has been in the city for generations. She suspects that some of her ancestors crossed the Ohio River, taking a route similar to that traveled by the first African-American settlers in Gallia County. Coincidentally or not, her great-

h word of mouth. They moved with Nataki Talibah as the
ed locations three times in the first two years. It was the time
from George's second job was rushed into the Nataki account
nses for the school.

ataki found a building—an underenrolled public school that
chool system was closing. George and Carmen eventually pur-
wo-story red-brick building.

insides have been renovated, the grounds are much the same.
ataki Talibah Schoolhouse is situated among an acre of green
l blossoming bushes, and a couple of maple trees.

April Monday in 1994, Nataki students are in their uniforms—
, green ties, and a green sweater for boys, and a white shirt and
for girls. I visit a class of the eighth grade students, who will be
ourney to New York in a week for the senior class trip. They will
Catcher in the Rye character Holden Caulfield's steps on one day;
m and Rockefeller Center; tour the United Nations; see *Les Mi-*
nd, of course, visit an art studio and some galleries. "A lot of times,
read novels and you read about different places," says Brandi
ou usually don't go visit them. So it makes it different and more
f you go visit after you've read about it."

around with my cousins in public school. They're going to Wash-
ve're going to New York," says Justin Brown. "When you go to
ces and you say you are from Detroit, people think you are rough,
they are surprised when you're not.

Detroit a lot. This is where I want to live when I get older. I want
lawyer because everybody in my family is a lawyer—a defense at-
here, like my father, because I like to argue."

ke some private black schools, particularly the growing number of
hristian schools, the educational philosophy of Nataki is liberal—de-
e uniforms. In fact, some would even characterize it as progressive,
hole language as a major method to teach reading. The school also
s the lifestyles of George and Carmen as the philosophy of the norm
pins the curriculum and students also have TM time—transcendental
ation. The school started with an eclectic collection of families—
nationalist, some working class, some middle class. By 1990, the
lation was largely upper-middle-class children whose parents were
rs, judges, lawyers, and psychologists and whose children traveled all
the world—Ghana, Denmark, Paris. "We've got two-career parents
work hard so the kids can have things, and that's normal for us," says
en N'Namdi. "I've gone places with the kids, like New York, we've

grandmother founded and operated a school in Cincinnati named The African School.

Nataki's death consumed the couple's moods for months—probably years—after November 3, 1974. "It's just a very strange, strange thing, very, very difficult. For George, it would hit him and he would have to leave work. They would call me and say, 'You're going to have to come and get him, because he can't really function.' It's like, 'I feel so good today and this is the first day I feel like I could be really right and George is depressed. So now I've got to help George.' Or George says, 'I'm so happy, I feel great, I can function' ["not that you're ever happy," she says in an aside to her husband]. You're like, 'I can function, I can get out of here and function, but . . . Carmen has to rest all day. So I've got to go now and join her.'

"If you come through those things, it's really a special relationship."

The sadness lingered into another tragedy three weeks after Nataki's death: George's father died of a sudden heart attack. "He was on his way to work," says Carmen. "He stopped at a friend's house and he said, 'I just don't feel good. I keep having all these chest pains. I've been so depressed because my granddaughter just died,' and he died just as soon as he said that. Just died. So, we were really out of it."

The two deaths made the couple realize the importance of living in the present, of pursuing their dreams and ideals. For example, they had talked about officially changing their names to reflect their African heritage in the late sixties; their children were all given African names. Now, however, they decided to act, so before they moved to Detroit, they offcially changed the family name from Johnson to N'Namdi, which in Ibo means "the family name lives on."

"We really took our life real seriously after that," says George. "I mean, we were like, 'Baby, nothing is guaranteed here, you know.'"

"I can remember sitting on the bed and saying to George, 'I don't think I can make it. I really don't.' I just can't imagine how I'm going to live through this; I was pregnant and the whole thing. And I went to bed that night and I thought, 'You have the baby inside of you and you can't lose yourself right now, because you have a baby to think about.' And then my girlfriend, I called her that next day and she said to me, 'Carmen, not only do you have a baby, you have a two-and-a-half-year-old that lost her sister. Your daughter lost a sister. Then I sat down, thought about this, and I said, 'I have to subdue this grief a bit for the baby that I'm carrying and this two-and-a-half-year-old, because I'm so consumed.'

"So then I started looking at Kemba and thinking—this was so hard for me because I had no philosophy on death, none. I decided to focus on this opportunity to give Kemba a philosophy on death. And so George and I started focusing totally on her and how to think of death, what to do when a person dies, how do you remember them. I remember sitting her in front of me and saying, 'I want you to think of every little thing you can tell me about what you and Nataki used to do together. We're going to keep all of this stuff all written down because one day you're going to be big and you won't be able to remember everything. We're going to keep her memories, the memories you have together all together on this paper.' We did that. We did all kinds of things that gave us a direction. That's when I started getting into karma, I started thinking about reincarnation."

The couple turned to books like Kahlil Gibran's *The Prophet* and joined meditation groups. "We did a lot of reading, and we had more of a spiritual approach to it," says George. "We were doing meditation. So we just looked, we learned. We ended up with the perspective that death is part of nature. It ended up, ultimately, an easier acceptance of it, you know, and not thinking we had done something wrong."

"I didn't realize it until years later how we were transforming ourselves into different people. We became very spiritual," says Carmen.

In the process, they became detached from a chief source of their parents' ethics and spirituality. Both Carmen and George grew up in Christian households that dictated both families' places on Sunday mornings. "I realized that the religion I had known had absolutely no place for me," says Carmen, who grew up in an Episcopal church. "It was not in any way able to help me with this because it just didn't make any sense to me. . . . It just didn't work for me. I go to funerals now and I hear the minister stand up and say, 'God loves her more than we did and that's why He took her,' and all that. I don't understand that kind of conversation. Your child is no more important than a shrub, you know, or a little bird out there or whatever. It's all a part of life. And dying is okay. Everything does it. So I need to learn how to acknowledge death in the same way you do life, and I wanted Kemba to be able to be comfortable with it.

"So we would go to Cincinnati to Nataki's grave site. Kemba would take every doll and every toy she could find and go to the grave site, and she would sit there and say, 'Nataki, look at the doll we have' and 'Look at this.' We might cry, but we would try not to let her see it. She was so up, and she was excited because she felt she still had the essence of her sister."

Ultimately, George and Carmen decided to honor Nataki's memory: her name would title the place where Kemba and her two siblings would receive their elementary education and where Kemba would teach twenty years later. "We were either just absolutely going to die ourselves, or we're going to find a purpose for this. And [...] in her name."

"The impact of the death was so str[...] feel like the only way I could accept it [...] know what I mean? You know how y[...] and you say, 'This is too much' and th[...] thing to something,' and nothing will st[...] this into something?' You are so very dr[...] about things like you have no money, yo[...] None of those things came to the forefron[...] driven as I was."

Before Nataki's death, George had a dream [...] Ph.D. "My plan was to live in D.C. I had alwa[...] I knew I could do well in that kind of env[...] wanted to be in D.C. where it's warm.

"We thought of starting the school in D.C., [...] We could never afford a school there, 'cause w[...]

"When you saw the Detroit paper, they ha[...] dollars, you know, twenty-five thousand dollars[...] Detroit. We had no jobs, or anything."

George and Carmen found an eleven-room e[...] district for $28,000, three blocks away from Ber[...] years ago, they sold the house for $160,000. After[...] son, Carmen went to graduate school and George[...] a professor of psychology at Wayne State and an[...] coordinator for Wayne County.

Many of the traits that turned Detroit into one [...] ugly cities made it ideal for Nataki Talibah. Rampa[...] the wake of the notorious Detroit riots in 1967 and [...] imposition of court-ordered busing in the seventies [...] auto industry. As whites fled many of Detroit's affl[...] more black and upper-middle-class families rushe[...] Palmer Woods and Sherwood Forest, sometimes buyin[...] $100,000. Though it wasn't part of the plan, Nataki Ta[...] ally serve many of the city's black middle-class parents[...] ternative to public schools, and it would also capture [...] followed the white rush to the suburbs only to find the[...] in suburban schools.

In the beginning, there were a few loyal families who [...]

been stopped and the people comment on the children, how well behaved they are. They'll ask where we are from. I'll say, 'We're from Detroit,' and they'll say, 'How did they get here.' And we'll say, 'We just flew.' And they'll say, 'How did you raise the money?' And we'll say, 'Their parents paid for it.' And they'll say, 'You're kidding, that's wonderful.'

"They just marvel at that. Now this is an independent school and independent schools travel whether it is Country Day or whatever. . . . I'll go to other independent schools for meetings and headmasters will say, 'Oh Carmen, you're doing such a great job and you have such nice families.' Why wouldn't we have nice families?

"I don't get upset about it. And sometimes I'll say, 'So do you. Your families are just so nice.' And they hear it and I think they'll catch it and learn, which is good. But you can't carry around hostility."

Carmen says freedom from racial hostility is sometimes stressed in the school's parent workshops.

"There was an incident in a store with one of our parents when the little child was looking in a mirror and the saleswoman said, 'who's that little monkey in the mirror?' Well, the mother said she had to stand there and think to herself, 'now where am I going with this' . . . Well, freedom is being able to move on in one respect.

"The mother said 'I had to stop and think through this because my first reaction was to grab her and go and then I thought that "monkey" is also an affectionate term people use with children. And then I couldn't decide whether I'm putting stuff on this woman because I'm so full of what I think somebody else thinks about me,' which is so burdensome. She thought 'that could be what I'm really reacting to. I never could decide.'

"She said to her daughter something like, 'Oh come on, Sweetheart,' you know. 'Just because you're pretty doesn't mean you can stand in the mirror all day long,' or something like that. But she was groping with that, you know, because she said it was really difficult.

"Well, we also had three of my old fourth-grade boys and a fifth-grader who were learning how to tie a tie. So they put it around the neck of one of the kids and said, 'This is how they hang people.' So one of the teachers comes to me and says, 'What in the world' and they hurry up and get it off of him. There's a rope burn on one of the kid's neck. So we write a note home to the parent and everything and we're like, 'Oh thank goodness this was a parent we're very close to. So the mother said, 'Carmen, that was the most inner-city incident for me,' she said, 'because I knew if he had been at a suburban school, I would have had the newspaper out there; I would have said, 'These two boys tried to lynch my son.' She said because she was at Nataki she could just say, 'These kids are nuts,' he and his friends, to play around with something that is dangerous. She said, 'Because I could trust the environment, I could deal with the real issue. When I can't trust the environment, I'm dealing with all kinds of things that are real and unreal and everything. Well, to me being able to trust is freedom. Do you know what I mean? Being able to say it's okay.' She said, 'This is my turf. This is my thing. I know these people . . . I know these kids.'"

Brandi Barton, an eighth-grader, and her brother, Brandon Jr., travel forty-five miles from the affluent suburb of Bloomfield Hills to Detroit to attend the school. "She's been in a public school and a Catholic school and teachers were scared to really challenge," says Brandon Barton Sr., a dentist, of his daughter. "They would let her get away with a lot. I think they were scared of being called racist if they were tough. She wasn't getting the education I wanted her to get. And I didn't want my son to fall into a trap."

"The people, our clientele, are primarily—at least half of them—Detroiters with a sense of pride in Detroit," says Linda Casselles, a teacher whose daughter was also an eighth-grader at the time of my first visit. "Some had sent their children elsewhere and they noticed some damage, psychological damage . . . like they thought that all this discrimination was finished business . . . They're [from other] private schools here—Country Day, Roper, and a few others that historically enrolled upper-crust African Americans— but they have now come here. A few of these people are now even grandparents of kids who had gone there for a few reasons and are now here."

"The thing I want to do now is move away from an image of building self-esteem," says Carmen, "because I've grown over the fifteen years to figure out that people think that's synonymous with being African American, that you need your self-esteem built up. And it never occurred to me over those years. So then it means give me your tired, your poor, you know, your hungry to be free. It translates to people saying 'now this child of mine should go to Country Day, not this one. He's just not quite sure enough of himself. I think I'll send him to Carmen.' So it's as though we associate wounded and healing with ourselves, and competition and rough, rough, rough academic rigor with Europeans.

"Then there are some upper-middle-class parents who would never look at us," she adds. "Now what's interesting to me too is that the people who are products of the African colleges send their kids to the European high schools and elementary schools, the ones who pay twenty-five thousand a year for it, but they want to make sure they go to the African colleges. Now, I think they are thinking, I want you to sing and dance and also do work, because we don't think you do both at an African school, right? So it's like, I want to make sure you can read and write and do the math, so that's why you're going to the European schools. And then in the end, I want you to know how to party and you've got to find a wife or a husband, so therefore you go to the African college."

In fall 1995, Kemba N'Namdi, fluent in French, began teaching at the school after receiving a graduate degree in education from Louisiana State University and spending a summer in Mexico studying Spanish while working toward her goal of being fluent in five languages. In 1995, Carmen took a big step in redefining Nataki Talibah. It became a charter school from kindergarten to fifth grade, eliminating the middle school. It is no longer a private school, charging $7,000 a year for tuition, but receives $5,500 per student in state money. Enrollment jumped from 50 to 125 students and the population became more socioeconomically diverse, creating some rumblings among a few Nataki parents.

As a charter school, Nataki was required to publicly define its mission and admit students through a lottery, which didn't preclude existing students from attending. Carmen says she welcomed the opportunity to define the school's purpose. "Everywhere I go," she says, "people have interpreted the school to me, and I'm always surprised at a lot of the interpretation. We've been called Afrocentric. We've been called the black school. We've been called the school that only teaches black history. And those things just don't fit. So I thought I better define. And so as a charter school, I'm calling it Social Studies and Immersion, which is still focused on people and their relationships with one another and with culture, history, and land, and so forth. And then, the traditional subjects will be taught as we do, but with a slant. So if we're studying science, then we'll also deal with the water problems or environmental issues in a particular country. Or if you're studying math, you'll also acquire certain math skills that might apply to a population problem. If we're discussing Rwanda, we'll have a Rwandan person here at night for discussion with parents. Or we may assign every family to have a dinner at an East Indian restaurant."

In June 1999, the school made a headline in Detroit: "DETROIT SCHOOL IS MODEL OF SUCCESS: MOTHER WITH A MISSION TURNS NATAKI TALIBAH INTO A LABORATORY OF INVENTION." While N'Namdi appreciates the publicity, she is concerned about how the article measures the success of the school. The piece highlighted the students' high standardized test scores in comparison to other charter, public, and private schools. "I think if I can move parents out of thinking that high test scores are the mark of an educated person and get them to understand that [it's] knowing different kinds of food and sitting in a library and letting their children choose books and going to the eastern market and noticing the prices and who's selling peaches for the market."

The article will inevitably help N'Namdi's $15 million capital campaign launched in 1999. Kwame Kilpatrick, a former Nataki student who is now a Michigan state assemblyman, is a major player in the campaign. "We're a young school," he says. "So we don't have old money to draw on, but we're going after corporate money and individuals."

The dreams of the campaign are a long distance away from Nataki's beginning.

"We would never have this school if we wrote out a business plan to do the school," says George. "None of it would make sense. It would not make economic sense. The same with the gallery, too. I would never have a gallery if I had to write out a business plan or if I had a lot of money because it wouldn't make sense.

"We came here with nothing. In two years we have a school, and, in five years, we've got a school and a gallery. Cream always rises to the top."

Chapter 15

Mansion of the Dolls

THIS is the best place to be in the country," says Margaret Betts. "This is a well-kept secret."

If Detroit is Utopia, it is indeed a secret to most Americans. Of course, so many pieces of the African-American experience are both secret and elusive to the American mind, blocked by the thick wall and tangled web of race, media images, history, stereotypes, and statistics.

Detroit isn't Utopia. Yet I am listening to two more residents extol the city that Al Loving and Nanette Carter treasure for its contribution to their independence as artists.

Dexter Fields and Margaret Betts are natives, and they are among the collectors who've helped to make Detroit a magnet for artists. The walls of their home are covered by more than half a million dollars' worth of fine art, with Nanette Carter, David Driscoll, Howadena Pendell, and Al Loving well represented. The couple, married twenty-four years, vow to live nowhere else.

"I made a couple of attempts to leave," says Dexter. "The first year of medical school I went to Howard, then returned to Detroit to finish. Then I made another attempt the first year of my psychiatric residency. I went to Boston for a year and came back to Detroit and finished the residency. I've been here ever since.

"Detroit is a great place, number one. And none of the other places, D.C. and Boston, really compared. Now, Boston, you know, they're a lot more openly chauvinistic in terms of their city, but it was really strange to go there because the black population is so small.

"But I enjoyed Boston. I took in as much as I possibly could, but I was glad to get back. It really helped me to appreciate home more."

"There are a lot of things I like about Detroit," Margaret says. "That I'm in it. That I'm involved in it being the city that it is. I was raised here. It's not a bad city, but perception is a truth unless proven otherwise, and we can't prove it."

"But you do prove it every day, one person at a time," adds Dexter.

"We prove it every day to ourselves, but not to the person who lives in D.C. or Boston or wherever," Margaret breaks in. "Until you come here, you don't know what Detroit is. I travel a lot, at least once a month. People always ask me, 'Oh, how do you live in Detroit?' They think we have to duck bullets every day. I've never dodged a bullet in my life."

From the window of Dexter and Margaret's Palmer Woods home, it is difficult to picture the check-cashing establishments and stores with bullet-proof partitions that are less than a mile away on Seven Mile, the nearest commercial strip. From here, you can almost erase the view of Detroit that many who've never been here see when they think it. The city does look bad on paper, though, thanks to some harrowing statistics: it is the first major American city to see its population dwindle below the one-million mark, and 70 percent of all of its children are reared in single-parent homes.

In Dexter and Margaret's window, it is impossible to miss the accoutrements of a lofty lifestyle, or, in their words, "gracious living." It isn't euphemistic to call their home a mansion, a description that would also be appropriate for most of the other Victorian estates in the Palmer Woods neighborhood.

On this August Sunday in 1995, the streets of Palmer Woods are sunny and quiet, unless you are within earshot of the basketballs dribbling in a couple of driveways, or are a part of the conversation of the women in warm-ups walking at an exerciser's pace. "Life in this neighborhood is pretty isolated," Dexter comments. "We know a lot of our neighbors, but it's not the kind of neighborhood where you go over to borrow a cup of sugar or talk over the fence. It's a working neighborhood. A lot of the city's movers and shakers live in here. As a matter of fact, the mayor has a home on the next block. Lots of people here work very hard and play very hard. It's a very attractive and peaceful place to live."

Dexter, a psychiatrist who wears gold-rimmed glasses, and Margaret, an internist, are inside lounging in African robes and literally sitting among dolls. They have two sons, ages thirteen and fifteen, but Margaret has several other children, or "babies," as she calls them. Unlike the teenage boys, the babies are motionless until Margaret decides to move them. "Sometimes I think they move on their own," she says. "They are always in a different place."

I try my best not to bump into them or knock them down as I make my way into the parlor room. Who would want to knock down Thurgood Marshall standing in front of the stairs?

The first floor of the Fields-Betts home could pass for a doll museum. Margaret collects them: more than one hundred figurines sit, stand, and stare throughout the living room, dining room, foyer. On this day, children with hats and glasses sit in the windows above both staircases, including the winding one that leads to the basement rooms. The dolls are in all ages and sizes and outfits; there's a bride in her white dress as well as a farmer in his overalls. Others are dressed in everything from elaborate evening wear to casual chic to antebellum finery.

In one wing of the second floor, the dolls have a storage room and another where they are on display. In the other wing, there's a master bedroom, two studies, and another sitting room. The top floor of the house, originally a full servant's quarters in the house's early days in the late twenties, is home to the teenage boys. It also contains a large, empty room on the east end, where the family hopes to eventually build an exercise room. "That is one of our fantasies," says Dexter Fields.

Like many of the residents living in the neighborhood today, Dexter and Margaret moved to Palmer Woods in the seventies, after the notorious 1967 Detroit riots accelerated the white flight that had begun in the fifties. Property values declined in the wake of the unrest and continued to fall during the seventies' collapse of the auto industry and court-ordered busing. Many black middle- and upper-middle-class families eagerly took advantage of the depressed market and became beneficiaries of the young men and women who took to the streets in the sixties and scared many whites off to the suburbs. Now, in fact, home ownership among African Americans is higher in Detroit than in any other American city. Dexter and Margaret purchased their home for $69,000. Even today, while the property values have appreciated in Palmer Woods, they are still comparatively low: Dexter and Margaret's eight thousand-square-foot home was appraised at $315,000 in 1995.

Across a commercial strip from Palmer Woods is the Palmer Woods golf course, with mansions on the green. The strip running in between the two, Seven Mile, can be described as depressed at best. That is where you find the clerks hidden behind bulletproof partitions.

A stunning contrast between a decayed commercial artery bordering an upscale residential area isn't a shocker to any eye that has looked carefully at African-American neighborhoods across the country. The prevalence of such disparities is visible from Harlem's Striver's Row to southwest Atlanta. The phenomenon is perpetrated by the tendency of many wealthy residents to live in the neighborhood yet shop elsewhere—in the nearest up-scale suburb, for example. Saks is one of the first businesses to openly cap-italize on the trend, as it recently opened its first-ever store catering exclusively to upscale blacks. The store isn't on the commercial strip next to Palmers Woods, though—it's in a suburban Detroit mall where African Americans frequently shop. The company's research found that a large share of residents prefer to shop at that mall outside the city.

The contrasts in Detroit—the mansions juxtaposed with the check cash-ers—are stark because they are so extreme. Still, even less-extreme con-trasts in the city frequently shock visitors to Detroit who expect to find the city to be everything but "the best place to live" in the country: Detroit is home to several communities of well-kept brick bungalows boasting lush green lawns that are within walking distance of decrepit commercial prop-erties. When probed about the contrasts, many loyal Detroiters blame everyone, including themselves:

"Your question seemed to suggest that because one has a well-kept lawn and owns their home, they're politically savvy and have control over their community and knows what's going on," observes Margaret. "I don't think that's the case at all. One often surrounds oneself with their cocoon and they basically remain there.

"It goes back to the struggle—and we struggled for voter registration, civil rights, and that was it. We didn't struggle for economic power. Even though we have political power, many of us don't play politics well, and that drives all this other stuff. Many people say, 'Yes, all I want is a house. I will keep my house nice. I'm going to mind my own business.' But if you breathe, you can't just mind your own business, because breathing is politi-cal. It goes into the concentration of air."

Political or not, it's only natural for a first-time visitor to the Fields' home to expend air on dolls and art. To miss them would be like not seeing the mansions and partitions. Both dolls and art are plentiful, and perhaps ex-cessive, but not gaudy or distasteful. I ask them if they remember the first original piece of art that they purchased. "I can't remember," admits Mar-garet. "I just have to go around the house and see if it touches me."

A Jacob Lawrence in the parlor doesn't touch them as the first original. But it speaks to me. It's called *To the Defense*. A judge sits before two lawyers in suits. One of them confers with an unkempt-looking couple.

The piece strikes me because it is one of the few examples of figurative art in a house where abstracts are visibly the preference. "Initially, I was go-ing to buy it for a friend of mine," says Margaret. "But then I found out how much it cost. I said, 'Nah, I'll buy it for me in memory of him.'"

Margaret looks at the men. "There's a prevailing feeling through them all that has to do with community, community itself," she says. "This lawyer is helping African Americans. This lawyer is helping people who probably have less than him and probably would not have any representation if it were not for him.

"I think if you look at it and you stay there for a while, you see this lawyer is even bigger than life. So, you're seeing someone who is less fortunate being helped by this person in the legal arena."

The lawyer reminds Margaret of the friend who almost received the piece as a gift. "This represents this guy. I mean, he takes a case, and he knows [the client] won't pay him. He wants to help everyone, almost to a fault. So this was a perfect celebration of my friend, a gentleman that I have known since I was about sixteen; we went to Wayne State together. He became Michigan's youngest elected official. He was elected to the state house and he represented the city of Detroit in the early seventies.

"During that time we went to Wayne, he was going to school to be a lawyer. I was going to school to be a doctor. He wanted me to go into politics, and I wanted him to stay in school. So I promised him if he one day finished law school, I would consider politics. In '91 he finished law school, and in '91 I became a member of the board of education, which shouldn't be, but is, very political."

"The accusations of being 'too black,'" says Margaret, "or being a 'racist' or coming on 'too strong'—those are all phrases that you hear when you decorate your house or surround yourself with comfort."

"With yourself," says Dexter.

"Really, with yourself," Margaret agrees. "The total love of self and the total display and recognition of it. When you come into this house, you know an African American lives here—not Chinese or Jewish. If you go into a lot of homes, you will see art that may be attractive, but has no real meaning in terms of who the residents are and where they came from."

"That's fine if that's fine for them," Dexter picks up. "I think it all really depends on the individual, because there are individuals who could have these same images. . . . If they still see themselves as 'the other,' I think it's very hard to comfortably be in any arena, be it your home or your business or your church."

Surprisingly, Margaret, the collector of black dolls, says that had she been given a Kenneth Clark doll test as a child, she would not have chosen a doll that looks like those on display in her house. "I always share with my husband and some friends that when the Mustang came out, I could see this red convertible Mustang and this woman in it with blond hair and blue eyes. And I wanted a red convertible Mustang. After I grew up and thought about it, what I really wanted was to be white at that point, [though] not necessarily wanting to discount my race or my mother and father.

"I do think in order for me to appreciate European Americans or any other race, I've got to be solid in my appreciation of my own culture, and then I can share. I cannot share or enjoy myself or appreciate anyone else until I can appreciate myself. And sometimes it's real difficult to know and accept your heritage in this country. It evolves. If you are a child of God, you cannot believe that he put you here to suffer. Or that God just developed this slavery with nothing connected to it. Eventually, I could not believe that life for African Americans or people who looked like me was just that, slavery. There had to be something else. It wasn't until recently we realized that the first woman who walked the earth was a black woman.

"Our oldest son, when he was about three, said that he thinks the better race is the white race, even though there are more blacks in this world. That's the way he saw it living here in Detroit: more blacks in the world, but it seemed a bit easier to be white. He was three years old."

"Yeah, but he grew out of that, and both our boys have always been very aware," Dexter picks up. "You have to start very, very young, nurturing that self-image, because the self-image isn't something that's easily come by at a late age. It's the positive stroking and reinforcement that you get early on that makes you comfortable by twenty-five. If you're still looking for it at twenty-five, then it's going to be pretty uphill. I'm not saying you won't make it, but it's gonna be pretty uphill."

Margaret turns to a picture of their two sons. "Yeah, you really have to keep stroking. You see them there; one is now, picking terms appropriately, the very darkest of persons. He really had a self-esteem problem. When he was younger, he said, 'Mom, why is John [his brother] yellow, you're light brown, Dad's dark brown, and I'm light black? Why am I light black?' And I explained to him that we are black people and we are a lot different colors and how you become the color that you are from your parents and grandparents, et cetera. I told him, 'If you were in Africa, you would be anointed king, because this is what kings look like; they're pure in color.' And then we had gold from Africa at Gold of Africa exhibit at the Detroit Institute of Art.

"The gold was so heavy [that] they had to hold [the wearer's] hands up. So, I would always show [him] this and the pictures of African kings and queens [who] are really dark people who wear this gold. You always have to reinforce that you are who you are because God made you who you are and you can't be anybody else. So when you start liking yourself others will start liking you, but you got to like yourself first.

"We just came from a family reunion in Alabama this morning. A young lady told him, 'Oh, you have such pretty eyes.' His eyes in the summer get a little hazel, and he's so dark; it's a stark contrast, and he told the lady, 'Oh, yeah, I've heard that a lot, especially from the girls.' He's thirteen."

Dexter speaks up. "Helping children understand the media and political control and the implications of that control—and if you have control over the media what happens—that's very important."

"Oh, yeah," Margaret continues. "One day, he asked why were there so many white people in this magazine. Just looking at a magazine, and he asked that. But we told him there are a lot of white people in that magazine because white people own that magazine. So, you know, economics is the issue, not that one is more attractive than the other or whatever; it's strictly economics. If you own the magazine, you would have your own in it, right?"

Margaret doesn't just talk ownership, she sets an example for her sons to follow. Margaret, in fact, owns a magazine. In 1993, she purchased *Corporate Detroit,* an ailing business magazine. "It was a unique opportunity. It was a business decision, and with my dollars I had wanted to develop it. When I was appointed to the school board in '91 to fill a vacancy, and when I ran to keep the seat in '92, I realized then and became real fascinated with newspapers and editors and how powerful they are without even knowing it."

George N'Namdi gained power in the world of fine art by cultivating collectors like Dexter Fields and Margaret Betts. N'Namdi met the right people at the right time—in 1986, just as the couple was ready to graduate from prints to originals. That was also the year that N'Namdi's gallery turned five years old and N'Namdi gave up his full-time job as a professor at Wayne State to devote all of his professional energy to the gallery.

Black collecting was at the dawn of a boom, for which Bill Cosby shares some of the responsibility on account of his displaying works of Romare Bearden in *The Cosby Show*'s Huxtables' living room. N'Namdi capitalized on the initial buzz by inviting New York artists to Detroit for private brunches with potential collectors. Through such a meeting, Dexter and Margaret met Al Loving. "We liked him," remembers Margaret Betts. "He explained how he makes his own paper. Can you imagine? He explained the entire technique. We wanted to own as many as we could." They began buying, doing most of it through N'Namdi.

Ten years later, in the summer of 1996, N'Namdi would open another gallery, this one in Chicago. He continues to do joint shows with small New York galleries and has developed a stellar reputation and national clientele that includes luminaries like Morgan Freeman. Yet some in the business say that he's limited by the nature of his success: he's impressive and known largely for building a strong market in a city that is not considered a center for high art; his success is rooted in a place that is not Paris or New York.

N'Namdi nevertheless insists that a Detroit base, with the city's healthy black middle class, is an asset. Some of his collectors grew up with art, others grew as collectors with the gallery, and he continues to build a clientele among many who were once like him—unaware of the value of a Bearden at six hundred dollars. Sometimes they just stroll into the gallery with no intention of buying, but find that a piece captures their eyes. George says that he can read such a moment, thanks to his own personal experience as a novice art collector years ago: he sees the quick intensity of the potential buyer staring at a painting that may be higher than the rent or monthly mortgage payment, just as George and Carmen once stared before spending a thousand dollars for a piece. "It was very tough for me. It's like, 'Ooh, what do we do?' you know? We just bought something for a thousand dollars. But after that, it became easier to spend money on art. Until this day, I use that feeling. That gut—that feeling I got in my gut when I spent a thousand dollars. When I'm talking to a person, who I know hasn't spent any money on art, I know how to touch that feeling. I'll say, 'I know just what you're going through.' And they always smile. I'll say, 'I know, I know you are like, what the hell am I doing this for, that's five thousand dollars or ten thousand dollars for this. This is crazy. I know what you're talking about.'

"I'll go back over the story about when I spent one thousand dollars and I'll say, 'Now, one thousand dollars may not seem too much, but one thousand dollars in 1977 . . . twenty-one years ago, that's money, that's a lot of money.'"

George has never taken an art class beyond elementary school. While he was growing up as George Johnson Jr., art was not a priority in his household. "My parents would have art on the wall, but nothing significant. I mean, it's like, I recall fixing up the house and getting new furniture. My mother would be the one who would get a painting at the furniture store to have something on the wall. I remember in '68, my parents moved, so she got this new French Provincial furniture and then she gets a French painting—a Monet kind-of-looking painting with the ornate frame. So it was significant in that sense—to this day you find people who don't even have that, and they're of means. We didn't grow up poor, but we weren't money, either."

Growing up, George lived in a house that had been in the family for five generations. His great-grandmother had moved into it from Pomeroy, Ohio, five miles from Gallipolis. George doesn't know much about the family roots beyond Pomeroy, which, like Gallipolis, was rich with Underground Railroad routes.

It may be impossible to neatly trace his interest in art to its origins. But an outsider can easily discern the beginning of his work ethic and his relentless pursuit of independence through business ownership.

His mother was the businesswoman of the family, the one who desired independence, or, as George puts it, "to do her own thing." She gave up what was considered a safe government clerical job to open a beauty parlor. "They didn't use the term hairstylist at the time. She was a beautician, and she owned her own shop—eventually two of them. After the war, there were a lot of government jobs that came about in the fifties, women working for the government. You see some of these old films with these women sitting in a large room typing. My mother had one of those government jobs. She worked at this depot, some government facility."

It wasn't just "this depot" or just "some government facility" to many men and women in Columbus of his mother's generation, products of the depression. A government job at the "depot," as it was known, meant security, a safe future. "If you got on at the depot, you were set for life, okay? It's one of those jobs when you retired, you maybe get $50,000, you know.

"Well, my mother, she quits to open her own beauty shop. She wanted to do hair. It was a major move to leave a real secure job at the depot.

"I think it was her spirit. I don't think it was a dislike for the job, 'cause I don't even think people thought about disliking jobs in the fifties—it was like you had a job and you just did your job. You got to think about it: people were just happy to have a job. They grew up in a time when what you wanted was a job, that's all. They didn't question that."

George's father, a former Negro League baseball player and the bookkeeper of his Baptist church, had two paying jobs. "My father worked on the railroad. Then, when I was a teenager, he got on at the post office, and he did both jobs for about three or four years. That's probably why he's not here now; I mean, two full-time jobs like that. He was at the post office from five in the evening to two in the morning and at the railroad at seven in the morning to three in the afternoon. Can you imagine that kind of work? You get home about two thirty, quarter to three, and you're up at quarter to six to be there at seven, and then you come home at three, and then you got to leave to get to the post office at five."

At one time, George looked to the post office for a future. "I was good in algebra. But I'm sitting in the back there, with the ones that shouldn't even be in algebra—and they're troublemakers. And they're like, 'Okay, George, you help us pass the course.' Well, they were copying. I remember the teacher pulled me aside and said, 'George, what do you want to do with your life?' I said, 'I want to graduate from high school, get a job at the post office, and buy doubles.' That was two-family flats—I said I wanted to buy doubles. I didn't say real estate, I just called them doubles, two-family houses.

"In Columbus, you didn't have many apartment buildings at that time. I don't remember any. Everybody lived in houses, a single, two-family, or the four-family. You may have six families in a cut-up house, but it wasn't no thick apartment building like Chicago or New York. So doubles for me is like saying I want to own apartments. Today, you would know to say real estate.

"Anyway, I said, 'What do you want me to do?' He wanted me to be a teacher. I said, 'You want me to be a teacher? Hey man, I could make more money at the post office than being a teacher.' He couldn't even say anything to that. As an adult, I was upset that he couldn't respond, 'cause he felt I was putting him down—which I was, but wasn't.

"You remember, teachers used to make five, four or five thousand dollars a year, so it's like, that doesn't make sense. You're looking at a person [George] who's got maybe a couple hundred dollars in my pocket, legally. It's not like the kids today who are sellin' drugs or something like that, but legally."

From the time he was eight, George either had a business or a job or both. There was shopping for the elderly for a fee, paper routes, head cashier at the local supermarket, and, as a teenager, throwing dances and prom parties at the local hotel. "I had also set up a little janitorial business that I went and did things with, you know, cleaned up nursery schools and barber shops and beauty shops. I was twelve years old, and I remember I loaned my mother two hundred dollars. This was in '58 [and, then,] that's a lot of money."

Like many working-class black youths, George says that he spent a lot of his money on clothes. "That's where my money went. Clothes were a pre-occupation with me from the time I was ten years old."

Clothes provided a source of self-esteem, a way for some to distinguish themselves from others. "When I was kid, you didn't have welfare. We had what was called charity."

N'Namdi says that people "getting charity" received clothes that were not too different from those his own mother would buy him—jeans and plaid shirts. "If you were getting the charity clothes, you would get a plaid shirt and blue jeans. When your mother took you to the store, you'd get a plaid shirt and blue jeans. The only difference [between] the charity clothes and those you got from your mother was the color, maybe green-and-brown plaid for charity and if you go to the store, you got a light blue, you got red. But it's the same damn shirt.

"When I was ten, I swore never to wear a pair of blue jeans again. That was in 1956. My next pair was in 1981. At ten years old, I started buying my own clothes, khakis and pointed-toe shoes on my own from my paper routes. So, my parents didn't buy my clothes after that. I never wore jeans and those big boot type of shoes. It's a derogatory term; we used to call them hillbilly shoes—these black boots that had big taps on the toe, taps on the heel.

"In high school, I used to have my shoes shined. I was really into leather coats, too. I had long leather coats, suede coats. My nickname was Seven Rock—I had a diamond ring with seven diamonds in it, and another ring with five diamonds in it. I worked for those things.

"I never really felt poor, 'cause whatever we needed, we got. We didn't get extra though. Okay, if you wanted extras, you had to work for it. I don't ever recall having a dollar given to me, just to be given a dollar. You got a dollar for you to go to the movie, take the bus there, take the bus back, get a popcorn, get you a drink, and pay for your admission. No extras.

"I think the only time we thought about not having money was Christmas. My parents would come to us and say, 'Daddy gets paid after Christmas, so you all will get the bulk of your gifts after Christmas.' You got eight kids, you know—that's the only thing they could do. If they didn't say anything, we probably would have been fine anyway. That was it.

"My father went to college for two years. My grandfather graduated from college, but we never talked college. We never talked, like, 'What are you going to do?' We didn't have those kinds of conversations, okay? We didn't have that. It wasn't like an expectation. Finish high school, that was your expectation.

"I was a hell of a manipulator of the system. In eighth grade, I would cut school every other day for almost a year, every other day because they would never call your house unless you missed two days in a row. . . . Then they would say, 'Well, you're going to flunk this course if you don't get your work done.' So, you know, we had six-week grading periods. So the last two, I may get all As so I end up with a D average. I was like, 'Do I have a D yet? I can pass.'

"I was the kind of person who just used the institutions. But it was to my detriment now. I think of the skills that you miss—you know what I mean? So I had to do a lot of makeup."

The problems crystallized at the end of George's junior year in high school. He wanted to go to college, but had a low grade-point average and little money for tuition. Most of his money was in his wardrobe. "I'm working at A&P, my math teacher comes in. He said, 'Hey, I know this guy, he just received his Ph.D. from Ohio State. He's moving to Milwaukee, he and his family. He's looking for someone that he could help put through school, watch his kid, work with his kid, live with them.' It's like having a housekeeper—you get a student that you can help put through college and you're getting your needs met by having someone with your kid. And you're doing some housework, but he would pay your way to college and give you a little spending money. So, he met me, he's interviewing kids. He's a very formal guy, particularly at the time; I'm eighteen, he was ten years my senior, a big difference if you're formal. That's how he was, too. So, he interviewed me and he said, 'I like you.' Then he gave me a battery of tests, 'cause he was a psychologist, educational psychologist, so he gives me all these tests and he looked up my grades."

George's competition was the valedictorian of his class, yet despite her advantage in grades, George won the job. "I remember he told me that I had a greater chance of succeeding than she does, the girl who was the valedictorian. Now when I go back to the reunion, I [don't] have the highest degrees or the most degrees of anybody in my high school class, but damn near the lower ten percent of the class."

George started the summer after graduation, moving with the professor, his wife—a teacher—and their five-year-old child to Milwaukee. George was the child's baby-sitter, as well as the family's housekeeper, car washer, and errand runner. He performed whatever job was needed to help a young two-career couple manage a family and both of those careers. "I became part of the family. They went out on Saturday night, Friday night, which they always did. I would take care of the kid, so they had a baby-sitter. I used to take the kid to school and pick 'em up—I was the person who did that."

George was eager to start college, but the professor decided that George wasn't ready and spent the summer tutoring him. "He tutored me. I mean, I had classes—I went to school for one-on-one tutoring for like two hours a day, plus he assigned me books. I had never read a book in high school. The only thing I read in high school was *A Raisin in the Sun*. So, he started tutoring me that summer, before we went to Milwaukee. He started me on English grammar. I remember taking a seventh-grade program textbook for English, and we went through it all the way through high school. We started there, and we just went. I read more books. I remember that first year out of high school, I read sixty books—*Black Boy, The Silver Chalice, Native Son, Go Tell It on the Mountain*."

In the fall, he enrolled in night school and continued to take high school courses. He started community college in the spring. But George couldn't stand Milwaukee. "I was lonely, okay? Remember, you're talking about Seven Rock. In Milwaukee, you could have all the clothes you want, it's still cold. It's too cold out there to be dressed up and trying to get a bus. It's not like Michigan cold. It gets cold early. So I wasn't used to that.

"I couldn't live like that. In Columbus, I was a popular person. [But in Milwaukee,] you're looking at the best-dressed kind of guy in some environment where people don't dress, they don't know you. You're in another city. We were the first Africans ever to live in the suburb of Sherwood in Milwaukee, and the only way we got in there was because another professor went out of town on sabbatical and he leased his house that year. Everybody would come in and ask his wife, 'Is the lady of the house home?' and all that kind of stuff. And remember my Columbus background—at the most, it was twenty Europeans in my graduating class. Well, going there, it was just the opposite."

George returned to Columbus after a year of private tutoring, night high school, and community college. "I decided to go to West Virginia State. Ohio State had a program where you can come in as a transient student and just take classes. So that summer [after the year in Milwaukee,] I'm in Ohio State and working to save money to go to West Virginia State. My brother had a '57 Chevy, and I'm driving it and I'm speeding recklessly and wrecked it."

The money he saved for college paid for the repairs on his brother's car. With low tuition for state residents, Ohio State and living at home were the only options.

Before he left Milwaukee, George had vowed to the professor that he would go to college and continue the legacy by one day helping not one but two restless and smart teenagers with potential. Two decades later, N'Namdi would bring three young adults into his home. One of them, today a guidance counselor in Washington, D.C., is now mentoring two young teenagers himself.

"We grew up in this kind of regular neighborhood, working class," says George. "Everybody was a home owner. A couple of streets away, there may have been people who were renting. But most of the people owned their homes."

Dexter and Margaret are products of Paradise Valley and Black Bottom, two similar black, multiclass neighborhoods in a very different Detroit. Both grew up in working-class families that nurtured them to grow up and become members of the professional class. Margaret's father was a security guard who also refinished furniture. He referred to her as "Doctor" from the time she was eight. Dexter, whose father was a tool and die maker at an auto plant, says he never even thought that college and professional school might be elusive goals—even after his father died when Dexter was eleven and the family suffered economically. Before her husband's death, Dexter's mother was a homemaker and mother of eight children. After his death, she was forced to work as a domestic to support the family. Through it all, she encouraged her children to seek higher education at Detroit's well-regarded and affordable Wayne State.

When Margaret and Dexter were coming of age, black businesses thrived in Paradise Valley and Black Bottom, and social classes lived side by side and mingled. Professional people were more visible figures in the community. "We were able to see the doctors and lawyers and, you know, judges walk down our street, and we were able to baby-sit for them or deliver a newspaper to them," says Margaret. "We lived in communities together. In order for us to arrive, we had to."

Today, there is no Black Bottom or Paradise Valley, and Margaret says that many African-American teenagers see very few examples of professional success. This statement leads into a familiar argument: black middle-class flight from the formerly segregated communities robbed the black community of its Talented Tenth, causing a brain drain and economic drain. The Tenth's departure left no more upwardly mobile role models for poor blacks and deprived black businesses of an automatic market. This argument has become as customary as a shouting amen in a Baptist church, and it is one that would win a nod, maybe even a reflexive cheer, in countless other households. It usually crops up in conversations about the cause of social problems plaguing America—national problems that often wear a black face in the American mind.

This argument relies on a romanticization of those good old segregated black communities where people of all classes lived near one another, did business with one another, and supposedly shared so much (including, perhaps, the fear of racial violence?), and it feeds into the angst of middle- and upper-middle-class African Americans about their diminishing contacts across class lines and how that negatively impacts the inner city. Even the many black professionals who decide to remain within the city limits often live in places like Palmer Woods or with other professionals, and take their dollars to the suburban malls to shop. Their contact with those who are less fortunate may not be as substantial as that of the lawyer in the Jacob Lawrence painting.

But where does that argument lead? Back to legalized segregation, segregation by choice, or forced choice or social engineering that automatically places people into close proximity? And if those old neighborhoods were such rich self-esteem boosters for all, why did Margaret want to look like the woman in the Mustang? In my mind, her old desire for blond hair and the preferences of the children in the Kenneth Clark study sobers the nostalgia for those old segregated communities.

At Ohio State, George met Carmen who began as a drama major but changed to education. The daughter of an entrepreneur who owned gas stations and stores, Carmen N'Namdi grew up an Episcopalian in a family that had been in Cincinnati for at least three generations. "It was a tight-knit community. Most of my friends' parents were friends with my parents and our grandparents were all good friends. I can remember things like our parents gathering us all, teenagers in the neighborhood, for dance classes with a college student. I would later learn the parents were worried about how this young woman was going to afford tuition at Fisk. One of the mothers had gone to Fisk and she got everyone to pitch in and pay her to teach us some kind of dances so she could get to college.

"I think it is easy to look back on those days, the fifties, as good times and forget about the things that were not so good. I mean people were not as enlightened about differences. Kids were expected to learn the same way, and different learning styles were not appreciated, not that they're appreciated as they should be today. It's like when people who were associated with Nataki in the early days say, 'Oh, remember the beginning days of Nataki; it was great.' And I think 'really.' It was, but it was also a struggle I wouldn't want to go through again. I mean George and I put everything into the school and were so broke."

In 1979, George N'Namdi was restless, looking beyond psychology and Nataki Talibah. "I always had a yearning to have something of my own. I guess that's my mother in me. I got these secure jobs, but I really wanted something of my own.

"The school was really Carmen. It's not me because, first of all, I'm not going to just sit in any classroom. I'm figuring out how can we get big. . . . If it was up to me, I would always look to do much more with it than she does. See, my whole thing always was to make a big institute. You know—you got a teacher training here, you got the school there, you got a consulting department here. . . . That's how I think, but she's like, 'No, no, no, let's do it this way. Let's get the school done.' She's more of the operational person. I'm more of the dreamer. . . .

"I've always had a love for the arts, and I was looking for something that I wanted to do. What bothered me most in psychology is, there's something missing with African-American people. I came up with this: it's the lack of a love and respect for our culture, not from a social and anthropological perspective, but from the arts. We think our music is second rate. Although we love the music, we don't give it the respect, admiration.

"For instance, let's say a lot of modern dance is really based upon African dance, and African people do those dances a lot. But as opposed to having our kids learn something with an African base to it, we think it's more important that they learn ballet, okay? If they learn music, although jazz is the original American art form, we still think it's more important that we learn European symphonic music. We think of that as the epitome. We're the only people who think of other people's culture as greater than theirs—not different, but greater. . . . We tend to always love what we have, but we don't put it on a pedestal, we don't give it that utmost respect. In fact, when you look at psychology, I feel that we are kind of unbalanced, in a way, as a people. I think we're unbalanced because we don't have an anchor. You know, the anchor for any people, for any civilization, is its culture, is its art, is its history. If you're not the protector of your culture, someone else other than yourself controls your culture, and they really control you. . . . They end up defining you. They end up defining your beauty standards. They end up defining your history. And, of course, if someone else defines you, they're going to define you in relation to themselves. They can't help but to do that. That's human nature.

"As a psychologist, I think that the conditions, some of the social problems of our community are there because we're not connected to our culture in a loving way. It's not just the poor. Our middle class is off balance. So I felt that we need this cultural connection. If you have a cultural connection, it gives you stability. . . . Culture creates a boundary for you, and when you know your boundaries, you become freer because you become boundless. You don't have as many limitations by knowing your limitations.

"When our young people go to the museums to see the work that we have created, I'd like for them to see that we have given that work to the museum, that we have loaned that work. If everybody else [collectors] gets showcased for a Rockefeller collection of African art, it's, again, someone else controlling your culture and someone else dictating to you what you are."

So N'Namdi seeks control by building a base of upper-income black collectors to support African-American artists and thereby help to define excellence in ways that the traditional art world may not always embrace as it does black folk artists or someone like the acclaimed Kara Walker, whom wealthy white collectors, museums, and even some African Americans have praised for her work depicting blacks in the slave era in ways that many African-American art critics find demeaning.

N'Namdi learned through experience that it isn't easy building a base in the world of high art—especially as a neophyte player. At first, his love of theater drew him to the stage, and he tried to make deals to bring theater companies to Detroit. Months of traveling to New York and negotiating with companies produced expensive travel bills—but no shows or deals. Simultaneously, he continued to develop his expensive art habit, without even considering that art could be his platform. After the thousand-dollar piece, art slowly moved from a pastime to a passion. Eventually, N'Namdi dropped drama and made his trips to New York for another purpose. "A friend of mine introduced me to some of the artists, like Al Loving. I didn't know these artists, so I took off, just going back and forth. I went to New York every month, meeting these artists, and it just opened my eyes. I would ask them, 'Why did you put that blue dot there?' I asked all these questions that sound stupid, that most people didn't ask, but I asked them. They told me. They loved it. These guys, particularly Al Loving and Ed Clark, they talk and you ask questions. I did. I asked them, and they told me. . . . Now people consider me having a very good eye for art."

The trips to New York carried N'Namdi beyond commercial art, reproductions, and litho prints and into the originals. Money from this second job started moving into a savings account, building toward opening a gallery. In 1981, having been a serious collector for two years, GR N'Namdi opened his gallery in downtown Detroit. Its first show featured mostly abstracts and all New York artists. The *Detroit News* called it "the best group show of the season."

Nanette Carter's work was exhibited in George's first show, and she traveled to Detroit for the first time. She grew up in Montclair, New Jersey, where her father was mayor. She says she was shocked to find neighborhoods in Detroit that reminded her of her hometown.

"I thought I was going to see projects. You know, I thought I was going to see large apartment complexes. On the wavelength of Cabrini Green in Chicago, I guess that's what; there are not a lot of projects. I didn't see any projects. And George drove me around to some of the neighborhoods and I visited the collectors. I thought I was at home. It was so much like what I grew up around.

Carter says N'Namdi created a much-needed commercial and cultural space for African Americans whose work focuses on abstraction. She says black abstractionists sometimes have difficulty finding acceptance in the world of art because abstraction is perceived to be one of the more intellectual forms of fine art. "I hate to say this but this country—I don't think that folks are ready for that, you know," says Nanette Carter. "They really still don't see us as a thinking people. They see us as people who emote. Hopefully, you know, we'll change that. All this stuff takes time. . . .We don't only emote. We can do that too and there's nothing wrong with that. But there's another side to us . . . when you hear a Duke Ellington or see a Romare Bearden or Hale Woodruff or Norman Lewis. I mean this man was amazing. . . .

"I think that George has a wonderful process, and that is that he really makes sure that the artists come out and we all would give talks at the gallery. He really goes into the sort of educational mode.

"When people, black or white, confront abstraction, many of them tense up in general. George tries to get people through that process with education.

"There's a younger group of African Americans. I think actually some of them are doing very well and they're being collected by whites and blacks. But their work is about identity, you know. And when you see it, you certainly can see this was probably done by an African-American person. I'm not saying that's wrong. I think that identity was really certainly the movement of the nineties if one looks back at certain works that have been exhibited in our big museums.

"But when we [African Americans] take on universal themes and our images are not being projected in a way that you can say it's probably done by a black person 'cause there's a black child in the painting, it gets difficult in the larger community for people to accept it."

N'Namdi's strong debut, however, did not ensure success in the competitive gallery business. He's made it only with collectors willing to spend at least four figures—and preferably five and six figures—on art. "The tricky thing about art is that you'll be dealing with an artist whose price is about a thousand dollars," he explains, and that price is also the "definition of your gallery. Then when the artist's prices increase, the artist would be forced to leave. I've been with some of the artists when they were one [thousand] to five [thousand dollars], and some of them are now selling at ten to fifty. A lot of people can't do that because the more the prices go up," the more the people you are selling to changes. "But my commitment was more to the artist, so as their prices and stature went up, I just went up with them."

George traveled up with his artists by popularizing collecting among Detroit's upper-middle class. He befriended those with the incomes to become serious first-generation collectors. And, eventually, those with a history of collecting came his way. Now his calendar was marked with Links, the symphony and Jack and Jill balls. In fact, Margaret Betts is president of the Detroit Chapter of Jack and Jill. "You know, I have to go to those kinds of things so I can be seen," he says. "So I have to go around with that group a lot. And then, socially, I become a model for them. If they come to my home, they say wow, and that gets them thinking that they should have some art. You get me. But if I'm not hanging with them, they dismiss me and say I'm kind of bohemian and avant-garde—uh, no: that is another lifestyle, and they won't live like that. It is a whole lot of psychology."

N'Namdi suspects that many black galleries and arts organizations fail because the owners or leaders are not social insiders in the black mainstream and may be too isolated from potential patrons, who are dismissed as "bourgy."

"I have a lifestyle that is somewhat compatible with [his patrons']. I have to hang with the people who could buy my things, right? For me, the social events are what I do. I really have to pump that."

N'Namdi says that his business took off with collectors like Lascel les Pinnock, an otolaryngologist and Nataki parent who built a home in a Detroit suburb and purchased a large collection of pieces of art from N'Namdi in one swoop.

Initially, some African Americans were resistant to N'Namdi's gallery because of the dominance of abstract pieces. They expected to find black faces painted in the frames—not colorful shapes and symbols uniquely wrapped together with messages for the beholder to find and interpret. "We started off like that, and people came in all insulted—'I thought you had a black gallery.' It is, I told them. It's African.

"Then they would start coming back in three months. 'I was confused. This stuff really grows on you.' That's what they would say. This gallery is very rare in terms of showcasing abstract work like this. Most of them don't have this ratio between figurative and abstract. . . . Most galleries have a larger proportion of the figurative work."

N'Namdi looks around. "There's only a few artists that are in the figurative category that I deal with." One of them is Fenton Smith; a work of his hangs nearby.

"Why?" I ask.

"Partly because it's my taste, and that's what I have. . . . That kind of figurative [painting] and that realism is not the African-American strength. Not figurative, but realism, where it looks almost like a picture—that's not our strength, and I really haven't found too many African Americans who can do that and do it very, very well, you know, just do it real good.

"African Americans are really going into major abstract work. The African Americans who do folk art get so much play, but it takes you away from the real issue. African Americans are kicking out some major abstraction that can have an impact on art history, but if we don't give them that attention, it may pass, or it may get noted in a footnote, or it may be way after their time that we give importance to it. . . . Did you ever see that piece on *60 Minutes* where they interviewed the folk artists? Those people get a lot of attention because they get controlled. Someone buys up the works and so now [that person] controls the works."

Folk artists, N'Namdi argues, have an easy forum because they validate many stereotypes regarding African-American culture. They underscore the idea that African-American talent is "raw" and "natural"—never skilled, learned, and refined. N'Namdi says that well-educated artists like Carter, Loving, Clark, Driscoll, and others who are versed in art history should not be divorced from the culture of people of African descent or seen as anomalies with identity crises. They are not Europeans in African face, but an integral part of African-American culture, just as folk artists are. "It's our whole esthetic; our whole esthetic is very abstract and reflected in their art. It's like jazz, even. You look at how we dress."

With that, my attention turns to N'Namdi's red glasses and porkpie hat. "It's very abstract. Red glasses with a red wire, reading glasses around a neck—now you tell me, have you ever seen that? One example I use: I was a therapist at a federal prison here, and I was one of these independent consultants there.

"Every inmate had the same pants, the same shirts, shoes, and scarf. Beige pants, white shirt, and a red scarf . . . one would have his pants creased to the lines. So, it's like, wow, look at the crease in those pants. Someone else has real wrinkles. You think it's linen—that's how wrinkled their clothes are; just the color will look different because the wrinkles will give you certain saddles. Someone else may have his scarf tied one way.

"So they have abstracted what they wear to the point that everybody wears the same thing, but no person is alike, to the point where you don't even see them wearing the same thing. When you see those wrinkled pants, you mostly think of them as a different color than the ones that have the real starch crease. The guy who has the handkerchief hanging out the back pocket, it seems different than the guy who has one around his neck—you see what I'm saying? So everybody has taken these other things and given them their own twists. Somebody's rolling up their pants so they're showing some of the white sock. So, now, if you look at it as a picture, it's abstract in the way that it becomes very different."

One can argue that the prevalence of abstraction, in George's view, imposes another cultural restriction on the face of black identity. Speaking of contradictions, what about the Johnson/N'Namdi move to Birmingham in 1987? And then N'Namdi decided to leave downtown Detroit, following the path that most white business charted a generation ago. N'Namdi counters that his move wasn't in the tradition of white flight; he was only following the money. That may not trigger a second thought if the mover was not someone who created a philosophy and way of life called "the norm." But placing a business outside of the heart of that norm, the African-American community looks like a huge contradiction. "Life is full of contradictions," N'Namdi says. "Part of my consistency, by the way, is contradiction. That's how you grow, through contradiction. That's part of my background. I studied dialectical psychology, and growth is all dealing with contradiction. That's how you get to the next level. But you come on, come with your point—what . . . contradictions?"

We've been talking in the gallery for more than an hour, and N'Namdi's temperament has been even, comfortable, accommodating, and confident without any arrogance. But in a mild snap he becomes slightly defensive when confronted with questions about leaving Detroit, which only underscores the sensitivity of the issue. "This is a tricky answer I have to give, but it's not really tricky. Is it better for me to have a hundred-thousand-dollar business in Detroit or a million-dollar one in the suburbs and bringing money into Detroit? You understand what I'm saying? So, in a way, the city ends up with more money, because I make more money, you see. Just having a gallery there is more symbol than substance. Sometimes you want to be in the market so that you're the main game. . . .

"It is more profitable to be in Birmingham selling art than in Detroit. That's a fact. It is more prestigious to be in Birmingham than in Detroit selling art. That's also an opinion that people almost take now as a fact."

Profitable, yes. But using his philosophy of the norm as a guide, one would assume that prestige is determined by its proximity to the people who set the norm. That drives my questions. "How can you call the art business in Birmingham more prestigious, if you take your philosophy of the norm to heart?" I ask.

"The art business in Birmingham is more prestigious, okay? We're not talking about the quality . . . we're not dealing with race or anything else. It's the art business that's more prestigious. That's all I'm saying. If we just stayed in Detroit, [we're] not in the real gallery world.

"I think it boils down to your understanding of the norm. It's the way you approach things that makes it the norm. It's not just your numbers. It's not that you're in a predominantly African-American environment, 'cause you could be in a predominantly African-American environment and stuck on a European frame of reference. So it's not that. It's your perspective. And that's the important thing—it's your perspective.

"The norm means you share, you're more sharing with the norm than without it, 'cause it's like, I got something I want to share with you 'cause I got some bad stuff, you see what I'm saying? You want to come with your stuff, see. When you don't have it, it's like maybe you're always trying to deal with whether my stuff is as good as yours. When the norm is strong enough, you can share. And that's the beauty of the norm—you're coming out there with your stuff. . . . I have a gallery. The gallery is the norm. That's the whole norm. . . . 'Cause when I sit at the table they got to deal with me. But, if I'm in Detroit, forget it, you know, it's like, 'Oh, this black guy down there in Detroit,' believe me. But now it's like, 'What do you think, George?'

"The norm doesn't mean separation. You can't do these things in isolation. And so it's almost like this: you start a magazine, and there's a place called magazine row. And you did a magazine for, let's say, an African subject matter. You want to make sure I got the best product. But I'm still in the magazine industry, and they've got a place where all the publishers are, all the advertisers are. So, it's better for you as a successful magazine publisher to be in that environment, so when the deals get made you're in the environment where they get made. Then you have a successful magazine. You can say, 'Well, I want to have mine in the Bronx.' So is the bigger picture here in the Bronx with your magazine or you getting the work out, you getting a quality magazine out? It's like, for me, is it more important to be where the museums come when people come from out of town? When people come from out of town, they will visit the galleries of Birmingham. I'm in the industry—I don't want to be a second thought. So, I feel like it's best to be in the gallery district if you're going to be in the business. If I was doing theater, you think I'd rather have a theater on Broadway or in Harlem or off Broadway? Very few businesses make it, out of the loop of other businesses. To me, to be strong in the gallery business is to be in the gallery district."

N'Namdi says that for many blacks, the move to Birmingham legitimized him as an art dealer. Many African Americans in Detroit and elsewhere are accustomed to leaving their communities to shop anyway, and they associate quality with goods found outside their communities. The majority of N'Namdi's customers still live in the city of Detroit. Are such patterns not a violation of the very ideas that drive N'Namdi's success in the Detroit region—a certain independence of the standards that determine quality based on distance from African-American culture? Who should need Paris or New York when you have the norm in Detroit? Who needs Broadway if you have the norm in Harlem? The answers to those questions are not easy when one holds the reality of economics and the conflictual and complicated attitudes of African Americans up to what George may call "their norm."

"This Birmingham here is about the fourth or fifth richest community in the country and it has about forty galleries in the area. I felt that if I didn't move out here eventually, someone else would and would be selling, say, some African artist, and the artists would leave me because it's hard, because it's a greater market than, say, Detroit.

"You don't want to shortchange your artist because of your conviction to redevelop a neighborhood. You see what I'm saying? You always got to think of the artist and the art. I mean, the art, these objects, getting them out is the most important thing. My job is to promote the culture, to promote the arts. My job is not neighborhood development. I'm not trying to redevelop this neighborhood, all right? My job is to get our art out there and collected to support the artists. I just want to do art. I don't want Al Loving the black artist. I want Al Loving the artist. I know critics are going to call him that anyway. But I don't put it out there like that."

Dexter Fields and Margaret Betts debated about George N'Namdi's move. "It was a business decision," says Dexter. "I understood it. You know, he was not doing as well [here] as he felt he could do out there, and I think he's doing a lot better."

"I did not like it, and I shared with him that I did not like it," is Margaret's take. "Of course, we're close enough that we can share our feelings, you know—my kids call him Uncle George. He mentioned to us about the financial advantage. . . . If you live in this country, [this] capitalistic society, you got to at least play their game to win."

"It was a business decision, a sound one," Dexter reiterates. "To view it otherwise is a reflection of how we get along with each other or really don't get along with each other. It's someone else defining what's so-called black enough. I think that's another part of it: if you're really a brother, you're going to do so and so, you're not gonna do this, that, and the other thing. It's the really very critical light that we hold each other in. One is not allowed to make one's individual decisions for whatever reason about whatever topic or subject."

"You see, we differ," says Margaret. "There's a philosophical difference. When you see the migration of people in communities, people, they migrate together. You'll see Chinatown, Greektown; the Arabs, you know, live in the same community. But the African Americans don't have that same connection. I think that has created a problem for us. All of the money, all the tax, all the political power is disbursed as well."

"We don't disagree," says Dexter. "We both know how and why it's going on, but I think the difference is the emotion that we have about it. I think you're much more emotional about it in terms of why can't people do this and that. I accept that they are individuals and they're gonna do what they want to do."

"Oh, I accept it," says Margaret.

"You can lecture and tell them the history and all of that, but they're still going to make their own individual decisions."

"I agree with you. I'm just sharing with this gentleman some of the nuts and bolts of why people leave."

"But, again you have as many reasons as you have individuals who leave. I feel torn," admits Dexter. "What's going to happen? My hope is that we as blacks are going to come together more. We're going to better educate our children. We're going to keep more of our children here. They're going to see that this is a place that they can have a future rather than just having a beginning here and then leaving. I think it's also going to mean that whites are going to get to the point that they realize that we're going to have to work together or we're all going to go under together. That it's not city versus suburbs, and it's not blacks versus whites. It will be the living or the dead."

Dexter and Margaret are looking at their walls again. The focus is now on Herb Gentry's *Second Kiss*. "Love," says Margaret, pointing to the piece. Two faces, in profile, are superimposed on one another so that they are joined by a single pair of lips. A bright red, yellow, and blue are the dominant colors. "Very exciting emotion. The first kiss, the first one is like every kiss. Every day—the first one every night or the first one every morning. It's just a very open, friendly sort of emotional piece."

"When I saw that, it seemed more like a memory, more like a memory of a kiss than a current kiss."

"Yeah, I see that too. Remember that first one and try to go after it again."

A smaller Al Loving collage is on the same wall. "They are bright, liberating colors." Margaret observes. "They are intense colors, intense colors. The orange, yellows, and reds. I mean, your spirit is free. Your spirit can fly on those. It opens up, it's like light—light you always move toward. And then the arrow pointing to this select sky and stars, the universe."

Like George, Dexter says that his interest in art parallels his profession as a psychiatrist. "Some of us feel the need to look deeper into things, to consider deeper possibilities and answers to what's going on, and I think I'm one of those people."

It has been more than two decades since Dexter became a psychiatrist. He's seen a massive increase in the number of blacks seeking treatment, particularly black males. "I haven't seen anything that's uniquely African American, you know. I don't think we have any more depression than anybody else. I don't think we're more hyperactive, and I definitely don't think there are more of us who are psychotic. I think a lot of our behavior is incorrectly diagnosed as being psychotic, but that's because the vast majority of clinicians are non–African American.

"We're becoming more savvy about treatment and are also becoming more savvy in terms of who we want to do the treatment, you know. There are many African Americans now; when they call they want to know are you black or not. And if you aren't, they don't want to talk to you."

"Same here," says Margaret, "because my name is not Fields. I kept my name—it's not a common name. So they'll call and say, 'Is Dr. Betts black?' My secretary will say, 'She's definitely black. Come and see her office and you'll realize.' I guess it has to do with the self-image; it has to do with keeping the money in the community, you know, all of those things that I see as positive."

"It isn't that all whites can't treat blacks; it's that some whites can't treat blacks. Finding someone who understands you: that's what the process is about."

Dexter, in fact, has had two analysts—both of them white. "I am rubbing shoulders with most of the blacks in this field and am friends with many of them. I did not want to see someone I am rubbing shoulders with."

Dexter says that some blacks seeking black psychiatrists can't see beyond race and thus can't get the help they need. "I've seen black people who say they want to see a black therapist, but they really want to use my color as a means to talk about the world and race, not to talk about themselves and their own problems. Human problems, not black problems. They want me to validate them and their blackness in some respects.

"Racism is not the issue. Certainly, there are unique experiences we all have as a result of it. But I've found when people come into treatment and race is the focus of it, it's usually because there are other issues they are not dealing with and are not facing. We are a lot more complicated people than the color of our skin and how it's valued or devalued.

"We have problems with relationships, like everyone else, that need to be examined, but we can't do that when we are hiding behind race and racism.

"I've seen an increasing number of black men, black professional men. Some would like to make the problems of the greater society their problems. But they have their own individual problems: some will talk about how the system is doing them wrong and doing this, that, and the other to them. Yet you're able to get to this position, you've been fighting it all along, so why do you not want to fight now? Many professionals come to me talking about the racism they've encountered. They wouldn't be a professional had they not gone through the racism, and that's part of the process, you know, part of being here in this country. And if they were a true victim of the racism, they wouldn't have achieved that status. So we have to understand racism has always been an issue. And as long as we're here, racism will be an issue. What else is new? Essentially, that's what I try to say, because racism is part of the American experience. It's often a matter of supporting the patient's strengths that they obviously have or they wouldn't be where they are."

By now, Dexter's analysis sounds very familiar, especially in Detroit.

Like George, Dexter says his therapists are also on the wall. "Art helps me to relax. It helps me in terms of looking for other perspectives and looking deeper into things, looking for other angles, other possibilities, but it doesn't happen on a conscious level, though. That has to happen unconsciously.

"Art is very therapeutic. Sometimes just rearranging the pictures, having them in different places just gives me a different perspective."

Four

SOUL AND COLD COUNTRY

Highway Preacher

PASTOR Elease Gray wears the color of her enemy and then dances before a crowd.

Her body moves in a cinder block building that was once an amateur boxing club. She fights—not with her hands, but with her feet. And while tennis shoes or ballet slippers seem more suited for her at this moment, she makes the heels of her red pumps look as if they were made for jumping jacks. "We take all the devil's dances and give them back to the Lord," Gray says, during a break. "The devil stole all the dances. Because when the children of Israel crossed the Red Sea, Miriam taught women how to dance.

"MC Hammer didn't invent anything. Neither did Ike and Tina Turner. They just doing what the Christians should be doing."

Gray gives my feet a look. "Have you ever danced before a church? You ever did the do-si-do? When you dance for the Lord, all the shudders go away."

The church service is over but the dancing continues until Gray and the worshipers are out of breath, or, as they would say, until the spirit stops them.

Gray's body, in a red cotton dress, marries the sounds of religious music coming out of a tape player's speaker; the music is probably a better companion than the two abusive husbands she's outlived. The bodies of others in the congregation also embrace the music: some stand and clap; others even jump along with Gray; a few just sit with their feet tapping like drum sticks—everyone moves in some way. "Some of us were brought up in a real strict background. We need to loosen up," says Valerie, a dancing woman in the congregation. "My other church was a dead church. This is a live one. Now I just can't sit still. If I sit still, I think I'd lose something."

"King David danced," Gray says. "King David danced all night long, and he danced so long until his clothes fell off."

"Well, we don't do that," says Valerie.

"We don't do that," Gray concedes, "but do you notice, we don't have perspiration dripping off? We are not sweating, but if you go to a dance hall and were doing that kind of dance, everybody would be sweating. The men would be taking off their coats. The women got the shoes off, the whole nine yards. It's the power of the Holy Ghost. Yes—it keeps us cool and just right. We don't sweat in here."

Drops of sweat are not an unusual sight on the face of an energetic preacher, but Gray's honey-colored and flawless face is indeed dry as she moves. Gray isn't sweating while she jumps, and it is early August 1993. Of course, the air conditioner in the cinder block building could explain how such an active spirit could remain so dry. So could the fact that this church doesn't have packed pews and isn't a crowded storefront or an elbow-room-only nightclub. Moreover, heavy perspiration isn't something one associates with Portsmouth, New Hampshire, anyway. In this coastal city, the nose easily absorbs the salt of the sea the closer you come to the water. Summers here are short. Winters are long and demanding. The cold season usually claims many days of spring and fall.

Gray's nondenominational ministry survives all four seasons. She only closes during her periods of seclusion, which run for thirty days, a couple of times a year. During those days, she fasts and lives in a walk-in closet with only a Bible and juice in reach. A quick trip to the bathroom is the only thing that brings her out of the closet.

Gray's ministry was born in her beauty parlor a decade ago after she left a Baptist church because it denied her the job of head pastor because of her gender, she says. Today, fifty people celebrate its tenth anniversary. Her presence in the city is a spectacle, but not at all because she is among the miniscule 2 percent of Portsmouth's population that is African Americans. Gray's wide visibility in the city owes to her presence each dawn at City Hall, where she has begun each day of the last few months marching with a sign proclaiming JESUS. Yet you don't have to come to City Hall at dawn or to her church to witness her ministry: if you drive down the busy Route 101 during the morning rush hour, you'll see Gray. That is her second stop after her "Jericho walk," which is what she calls her morning march at City Hall. On the highway, she wears a robe and a hat, carries the sign, and yells either "Jesus," or "Boom," or "Praise God" at anyone who blows a horn at her presence.

If you ask African Americans who know Gray about her, some will say "she's crazy" but provides a valuable service. As one woman said, "She saves you a trip to Boston. Her beauty parlor is the only place where you can get your hair done in Portsmouth."

Most whites in the Portsmouth area may not have known Gray before she turned to the highways to preach. Most black women here, however, have known her for years. They remember the old Elease Gray who danced to James Brown and twirled her head and shoulders to Count Basie, the Gray who was an active member of Kwanzaa, which is not only a holiday but also a New Hampshire civic organization founded by black women in 1981 to provide scholarships for black students and sponsor dances and banquets for black adults, which raise the money for the scholarships.

Gray's career as a hairdresser long predates her ministry and the moment she was "saved." She opened her first shop thirty-four years ago, when she was twenty-two years old. "I'm fifty-six years old," Gray says. "Do I look it? I had my first baby when I was twenty-nine and my last one when I was thirty-seven."

Gray proudly points out her three children, two of whom traveled a long way to celebrate the anniversary: her oldest, Robert, twenty-five, is an Air Force Academy graduate now stationed in Cheyenne, Wyoming; her daughter, Sonya, is a teacher outside of Atlanta; and her youngest son, Eric, is a nineteen-year-old student at the University of New Hampshire.

Gray's church is tucked away in a building in the center of a low-income housing development. The wood-frame apartments of the development resemble log cabins. Nearly all of the residents of the complex are white, but the worshipers who attend Gray's Sunday services are mostly black.

The church doesn't look traditional. It lacks a steeple, stained-glass windows, pews, an altar, and an an elegant carpet. "You don't really have to join the church. You just come. So, I figure about thirty or forty come. But you can come and go—many come and have left for bigger and better things. They get their lives squared away, and they can go. They move away from the area or go to other churches.

"We just take whatever money we have in the office. If anybody needs anything, we give it to them. We don't just try to have or build up no big treasure. We buy the clothes and we feed them and pay their rent, light bill, or whatever is needed. We just kind of like go on and do it.

"He was on drugs when he came to church because he was really lonely," Gray continues, pointing to a member. "And the Lord spoke to him when I was preaching on forgiveness. So he decided he better start forgiving people."

"This is my first time here," says Karen, a secretary. "She braided my hair, and I've been talking to her about the different churches that I don't like and how I felt better if I opened up the Bible and read to myself than going to somebody for an interpretation."

"I have to drive thirty miles to get to her, but she's worth it," says Rene, another church member.

"Like, the church of Shwerner was a small little church," says Gray. It was going through persecutions, afflictions, poverty, but that's where the riches are and the blessings are. You won't find it on Wall Street."

"I can't miss her," says Cindy, a biomedical technician. "My week won't go right if I do."

"Rich was like a mediocre Christian till he came to my church and God really turned his life around," Gray says of another of her flock. "When he came, he had his financial problems. He was living in New York because he's a freelance photographer and an artist. And his finances flourished when he got here."

Most of the worshipers are black, and most of the whites here are women. A sandy-haired white male stands out.

"This is Matthew," Gray introduces him. "He's a friend of mine that the Lord placed in my path. And Matthew has been with us for a few weeks now."

"Where are you from?" I ask.

Matthew offers a bewildered pause and stare and then he slowly speaks.

"Um, well, I came from another state."

"He doesn't talk that much," Gray says. "He's kind of shy. He lives with me."

Gray met Matthew during her "Jericho Walk" one morning. "He would ask me for money to help out. And then I would give him money. And then he asked me if he could come stay with me for a little while, and I said yes.

"If Matthew takes anything in my house, being a homeless person, I don't care. God will restore it back to me seven times. I feed him. I bought his clothes. I wash his clothes because he doesn't know how to use a washing machine. It's just a strange person that I'm treating nice because I could be entertaining Jesus or an angel.

"Homeless, drugs, alcohol, um, women with no husbands, and the Lord just sent them here. Some just left New York and came with no clothes or nothing. And now they're doing pretty good—not bad, huh?"

Gray is on a roll. "You know God sent you to write this book so we can make a movie right? I'm serious. I'm getting something done in New Hampshire through the blood of Jesus Christ . . . and Spike Lee will be making movies. Ain't he hip? I'm telling you. I say you don't have to make no movie off of Malcolm X—he's dead. I'm alive here, and I'm still doing stuff. Don't wait till I die to make no movie, okay? Come on now, baby. Who needs a movie when they dead? I need the money now to do something with it to help people."

But though anxious for fame Gray says that before gaining it she must pass a test, which she believes has come in the form of Matthew—the man. "God planned it to see if I can handle being around a male person in my house and not to be overcome by a lustful spirit and try to pursue Matthew to come and have sex with me. And I've got to be able to stand those kinds of tests if I'm going to do the will of the Lord. God's not going to send somebody out there ever again to embarrass him like these other big-time preachers, like even Martin Luther King. God's not going to have to do that anymore. No, no, no. So you will pass that test before He'll put you out there to do anything for Him.

"It's only two tests you really have to pass. There really is—lust of the flesh and the lust of your eyes. Once you pass that, you're home free with God."

It is the day after the anniversary. Traffic is as it always is on Route 101 at seven o'clock on a Monday morning—bumper to bumper. Gray has finished the Jericho Walk and prepares for the highway. "The last time I was out here, it was pouring-down rain. I was drenched. 'Let it rain, I said. I don't care.' I stand up here. It doesn't matter if it rains or not. I take the rain as an anointment from God."

Her van is parked in a parking lot on a street off of the busy 101. Gray slides the side door open and from the back pulls out a hat that she throws on her neatly permed hair. She says she wants the hat to cap the signs of vanity and take attention off of her hair and force the motorists to focus on the JESUS sign. Gray says some minds imagine other things. "When I hide my hair, they think I'm a baldhead freaky person.

"When the police came once, they said, 'What kind of hat is that?' They don't even recognize the cap." It is the hat her son tossed in the air when he graduated from the Air Force Academy. "Well, this graduation hat represents my son's graduation from the United States Air Force Academy. It's one of the finest academies in the entire world. You have to be a real good student to get in there. And a lot of people are screwing their children up. You can hardly get them into the United States Air Force Academy."

Gray pulls a black graduation robe from the van and begins to pull it on over her dress. "Now, this robe represents my daughter graduating from a Jewish college in Massachusetts. So I see the Lord, the Holy Spirit, said, 'Well, you put that robe on because I'm the God of the Jews," she says, touching the robe to demonstrate. "And Gentiles," she adds, while taping the brim of the hat.

Draped in her cap and gown, Gray is ready. "I was defensive at first. If people laughed at me, I would get angry. Or I would say, 'Do you laugh at the pope? So don't laugh at me. If I look funny, the pope looks funny.' I would tell them, 'I'm not going to graduation'—they would ask me that. I would say, 'Did you ask the pope that?' I would lash out, but now I've gotten a lot better. I don't say anything now. It doesn't bother me when they laugh."

Gray grips her signs and walks to the shoulder of Route 101. Her zealousness reminds me of antiabortion protesters who spend their time in front of clinics, but Gray says that there's a huge difference between her ministry and their cause. For one, Gray says that she isn't imposing her views on anyone. And two, she is prochoice. "I'll tell you, and I never uttered this before, but I believe that when women do those abortions they're making a really conscious decision. And when God chose the Israelites to kill the Amalekites, he said, 'Kill every one of them. Kill the men, the women. The kings have poisoned the throne.' You get what I'm saying?

"I had an abortion one time. I had to. I was bitter. I was angry. My marriage was going down the tube. It was just a whole lot of stuff. And I went to one of those clinics in New York City, the clothes hanger–type places. I was really depressed, hurt. I didn't care.

"I believe that when God says kill, he forgives. He forgave me. Look at me: He knew I had an abortion, but he picked me up and used me for his glory. Not one person in this city could do this but me.

"So sometimes when you don't want a child you already have, the child is already dead. You haven't killed him. Then, you should be able to go ahead and just get an abortion. God forgives. He knows what's happening here.

"If God wanted to intervene, he would [have]. So all these people that's marching with their abortion signs are no more wrong than the woman getting the abortion. Why don't they hold this up?" Gray asks with a nod toward the sign in her hand. "I'd rather for them to hold up Jesus. Go stand in front of the abortion clinics and hold up Jesus. Lift up Jesus. They can't do anything. Only God can do it. I wouldn't ever put an abortion sign in my hand—I wouldn't. No. Just Jesus. Just Jesus."

Gray steps on the highway's shoulder and immediately horns start blow-ing. "Boom," Gray yells. "When I say 'boom,' it means that the love of Jesus is just exploding inside."

"We almost had a revival on Route 1, one Tuesday. Boom! Praise Jesus.

"Everybody was screaming. A lot of times, they don't speak. They just wave. I don't really preach or talk that much. I'm just here holding up this sign. I'm like a little vessel. But they do acknowledge me. The children sometimes quote Bible verses to me.

"Boom!" she says, loudly this time, in response to dogs barking from the backseat of a station wagon. "Even the dogs praise the Lord. Hallelujah."

Today, Gray gives away many smiling 'booms.' A man in a suit driving a Volvo waves as though Gray is the security guard he passes in front of his office every day. Boom. Two baseball-capped men in a pickup truck blow their horn, laugh, and scream. Boom. Members of her church and women whose hair has been in her hands give a blow and a friendly wave. Boom. A black man behind the wheel of a BMW stares at her until she looks back at him. When their eyes meet, he turns his head with a grimace. He doesn't blow his horn. "Black people are naïve. They just think that I'm stupid. . . . Black people see this sign and they think this is ridiculous and that I'm ridiculing them and that I look like a fool. So what? If I want to look like a fool for Christ, that's my prerogative. I don't say nothing about them when they dress up and do those dances for the devil. They don't know what this means. Maybe they're embarrassed or fearful."

Gray took her ministry to the highway a few months ago, after she was snubbed by the local newspaper. She had contacted the paper to seek its support in her campaign to bring prayer into the schools and push drugs out of the classroom. She was obviously unaware of the concept of journalistic objectivity and doesn't see the need for much separation between church and state. "I went to the newspapers, and I said, 'What are you going to do about this drug thing' and 'Can't you encourage the children to pray?' The story editors, they looked at me kind of strangely. First I went to an editor. I made an appointment to talk with him. And, uh, he was rude. Very rude. So after he was rude and kind of belittled me, I started really praising the Lord right outside their office. The Bible says when a matter of evil turns against you, you rejoice. I decided I was going to rejoice on the sidewalk. They threatened to call the police, and the police came; and they told the police I was crazy. And so that's when I started doing it—to draw attention to the Lord."

The next day, Gray was at City Hall. A few days later, she was on Route 101. Just last week, the police stopped her. "I was over there the other day," she says, indicating a nearby spot. "A cop said, 'You're obstructing traffic.' I said, 'Well, where can I stand so I won't do that? I want to obey the law.' He said, 'Well, just stand over there.' I said, 'No problem. I stand over there.' I don't care where I stand. I stand up for Jesus.

"Then the newspaper reporter came out here. I said, 'I don't need you. Don't put my name in your trash can.' They could have had a wonderful story, but they ridiculed me.

"I know I have to repent. I have to repent. And I really have to try to stop calling the papers a trash can."

A hoarseness reduces Gray's voice to a tenor, but she keeps 'booming' in between explaining her campaign to rid sin from the state known for its first presidential primary. Gray, who says she prays for President Clinton and America every day, says she is also taking her JESUS sign to pornography shops and bars. "I've been in all the bars. I went in one the other day. They treated me nice—they gave me some chips and soda. I walked through the door, and they were playing cards. They all looked at me, looked at each other, and kept playing. Somebody made a mistake in the game and said, 'Oh, Jesus.' And then they put their hands over their mouths and they laughed. They didn't know what was happening.

"I sent flowers and a religious message to the owner of the X-rated stores. There's still time to repent."

After her normal two-hour stretch on the highway, Gray is ready to go home and see her children off. The beauty parlor is closed on Mondays. She drives and talks about her life.

"When I was twelve, I received the baptism of the Holy Spirit. And it was there, but I didn't have the teachings. It was there all the time. It never leaves us."

Elease Gray was born in Twin City, Georgia, the baby of three girls. Her father was a sharecropper who hated the job. When Gray was still in diapers, he decided to find another way to live, and moved to Summit, Georgia, where he found a job at a meatpacking company. Eventually, he became a butcher. He also owned and operated a juke joint on weekends. "That's how he took care of his family. My mother didn't work," Gray remembers. "We were the only family around that had sugar and silk stockings. We had pork-chop sandwiches in our lunches and steak sandwiches."

At thirteen, Gray became an entrepreneur by developing a talent that would carry her through hard times as an adult. Today, she tells the story of how she unwittingly became a hairdresser with the drama and religious fervor that accompanies her description of most experiences. "One night, I heard this voice. It said, 'Get up and do your hair.' And I washed my hair and decided I wanted to straighten it."

Gray didn't have a straightening comb, so she decided to heat up a fork. "We had kerosene heaters, you know, those little crude oil burners."

Gray warmed the fork on the heater. When it became hot, she slowly pushed its teeth though her hair. It did the job of a straightening comb. Then Gray cut up a paper bag and layered its pieces onto her hair rollers. With a few strokes of a brush and comb the next day, she had a head of curls, firm yet loose enough to flow in place. Long bangs danced off her forehead. At school, all the girls had one question for her: Who did your hair?

The answer spread across the school, and by the end of the day, everyone wanted Elease's hands on their hair. "I started practicing on their hair. And when my mom found out I really wanted to do hair, she gave me the money."

Gray took the ten dollars from her mom and rode a bus to Savannah, Georgia, an hour's ride. "I went to this beauty-supply store . . . I got the supplies myself. All that I needed, the curling iron and stuff, the pressing comb, the pressing oil, shampoo, everything.

"I would do everybody's hair in the whole town. I would even do the teacher's hair. They would come [from] miles away, like fifty and sixty miles away, to get their hair done. I would do hair sometimes all night."

A driver's angry horn startles Gray and interrupts her remembrance. The honk is an impulsive response to Gray's attempt to change lanes—she mistakenly pulled in front of a Honda, forcing its driver to swerve to miss the back of the van. Gray smiles an apology into the rearview mirror and continues to talk about growing up in another region and another time. "I was just fast. I was a smart girl, too, don't get me wrong. But I was just fast. I was a pretty girl, beautiful, beautiful woman and very mature."

As she describes herself, Gray's cadence becomes ministerial. "I was flamboyant and I could meet people and I could dance and I had money. And I knew how to dress. I had charisma. I had character. I had integrity. And I had respectability. Yes."

Listening to Gray makes it easy to imagine her as a teenager exuding confidence. In a softer voice in the same conversation, though, she admits that the violent spells of her parents' relationship sometimes shattered her security. One fight in the juke joint became embarrassingly public. "He shot her. We just saw blood, and we were screaming out. I was fifteen years old. He didn't kill her. She stayed there even after the shooting. She's still living. He died last year. She's eighty years old and still drives around town in her car.

"He was jealous. They would fight on the weekend. My house was chaotic every weekend. It was never peaceful. . . . That's why I like Matthew—you understand what I'm saying? He's just here to say hello or how you doing or how was your day, anytime I come home."

"You were never greeted like that?" I ask.

"No," she replies.

After high school, Gray made another fast-girl move. She took what was considered the hip step for an eighteen-year-old in the South during the late fifties: she headed to New York City to live. "Everybody said that's the best place to go if you want to do anything. So I went. I worked at the Waldbaum's and the A&P."

Before Gray moved, she met a thirty-year-old military man at the juke joint. He courted her and proposed. She declined, but he pursued her with letters and a few visits to New York. Before she turned nineteen, she surrendered, and she married him just before he went on an overseas assignment. While he was overseas, she moved back to Georgia to receive more formal training as a beautician, at Luvennia's School of Cosmetology in Augusta. In less than a year, her husband was assigned to Pease Air Force Base just outside of Portsmouth, New Hampshire. He settled and sent for his wife.

Gray says that it was a long bus ride—too long. She can't remember exactly how many hours, but guesses it was at least thirty-six. She arrived in Portsmouth at six in the evening, just as downtown closed. "When I got off that bus downtown, there was no husband. A young woman, nineteen years old. It still hurts. I couldn't find him. But, anyhow, God planned it."

Gray searched a strange Yankee street for something familiar, but found nothing to bring the feeling of warmth and excitement that often comes with the first steps in a new home. For a Southern woman in New England for the very first time, the closest thing to hospitality she could find was two men in military attire, one black and one white, walking down the street. She told them of her situation. "And these officers got me to the base and put me up in a guest quarters on the base so I could stay the night. It was horrendous."

Gray spent the next day trying to find her husband, who returned to the base by evening. She later learned that he had spent the night in Boston with friends. "He said he didn't know I was coming in so soon. He knew. I said we'll just move on."

Her husband's four hundred fifty dollars a month wasn't enough to provide the lifestyle Gray wanted. So she immediately unpacked her beauty supplies. "You do what you have to do. I was a good hairdresser and I knew I was a good hairdresser. So I did this lady's hair for free. I wanted her to let people know that I was a really good hairdresser. She just passed, and I'm still doing her daughter's hair right now."

The word spread, though not quite as fast as it circulated through the school when Gray was a thirteen-year-old. It took time in New Hampshire. Still, in addition to the five "original" black families in the Portsmouth area at the time, Gray recalls that a community of black newcomers tied to the air force base was also building. Many of these people decided to stay when their days in the service were over.

They found a meeting place at Gray's. "Well, you could go in there and you'd never know how long you were going to be there, for one thing," says Vivian, a retired guidance counselor in Portsmouth who is a friend and loyal customer.

Gray got to know most of the black population in Portsmouth and surrounding towns in Maine and Massachusetts. "I mean I would sometimes do, maybe, fifteen to seventeen heads a day."

For Gray, the transition from an all-black community in Georgia to an overwhelmingly white community was made easy by her career. At times, blacks would seem like a majority in Portsmouth, because she spent many days seeing only black women. They would enter her living room, get their hair done, and remain for hours, engrossed in conversations about everything from gossip to the civil-rights movement. "It really didn't bother me that there were not many black people here. I was the one that ruled the roost. They came to me to get their hair done. So I saw a lot of black people all the time."

It didn't last. After one year in Portsmouth, her husband received assignments in Wichita Falls. She followed him with her straightening comb ready to ride through heads of hair. Then it was off to Colorado Springs, and back to Portsmouth. Gray was swinging combs through it all, and friendships grow when there is familiarity between the woman in the chair and the woman with hands moving above the chair. Gray's customers—friends—began to question her about the bruises on her face and the black eyes. "I'd say, 'Don't ask me any questions. I didn't ask you to come here . . . I'll do your hair. But if you don't want me to do your hair with a black eye, you can go. . . .'"

In 1965, Gray had saved enough money to buy a shop. She was bringing in a thousand dollars each month—more money than her husband, which she believes was at the core of their problems. According to Gray, his jealousy contributed to his infidelity and abusiveness. "I just couldn't be my own person because he was older. So I had the respect from the start. Some

women just have a submissiveness to their husbands. . . . I really didn't
shake it. . . .

"But after the baby [her abortion], I couldn't take the hitting and the jealousy. . . . He was bad. If some man comes in the shop and says hi, I would
be fearful I would be hit or slapped. I was growing older then and I was experiencing things on my own about my life . . . I didn't want to be controlled anymore.

"The manipulation was too much." His infidelity also troubled Gray.
"And I was a woman, and, you know, I said, 'Well, I'll just get me a
boyfriend too. I don't care.' I did."

Gray says she was raised to believe that divorce wasn't a viable option—
even if you don't have children and even if you have the economic means
to support yourself. "You keep the peace and hold the marriage together
and try to work things out the best you can, because you just can't jump up
and get a divorce every time your husband hits you, because you'll be
jumping up to get a divorce every time you look around."

When her husband received another assignment to Dover, Delaware,
Gray didn't go. She continued to build her business in Portsmouth. The
commuter marriage dissolved in eight months when her husband asked for
a divorce. "After the divorce was final, he cried. The first time I ever seen
him cry. I was very bitter toward everything. I said it takes a divorce to
soften somebody's heart and show somebody that you really care."

Within a year, Gray's boyfriend became her second husband. That man
would not only be the father of her three children but also, eventually, another wife batterer, according to Gray.

"They were both jealous," Gray says of her husbands. "When I got
dressed up, I was very pretty. And everybody liked me because I'm a giving, caring, and outgoing person. And they couldn't deal with it—it was too
much. It was too much.

"I wouldn't say everything was their fault, because I was a hairdresser
making my own money, manipulated by the system, the George, the
George Washington, the dollar. Not being able to say, 'Okay, I'm going to
take care of my husband. I'm not going to work three days a week and I'm
going to give the rest for my husband. Show him my attention. Give him my
love. But I couldn't do that because I had to work . . . I was the breadwin-
ner. And I really shouldn't have been."

"Why shouldn't you have worked?" I ask.

"Because it is according to the Bible . . . he's held accountable for his
whole household. So I really robbed both of the men of their manhood and
from taking care of their household."

"So you say you robbed them of their manhood. What did they rob you of?" I ask.

"Nothing. They made me stronger. I'm telling you—I was made tough. Very tough."

Done with the Monday-morning routine, Gray returns to her split-level brick house. As we pull into the driveway, I am digesting her ideas about marriage, abuse, and the importance of a breadwinning man to a family. Her belief in patriarchal supremacy would perhaps make her an ideological companion to Daniel Patrick Moynihan. Perhaps there are also traces of Sharizard Ali to be found in Gray's acceptance of physical abuse and her large need for a dose of feminist Michelle Wallace. I ask Gray about the three. "I don't read nothing but my Bible. That's all I need. I don't watch TV. I do read the trash can every now and then," she adds, referring to the local newspaper.

Gray isn't a fan of feminism. "I think it stinks," she says. "I think everybody has rights. You don't have to be a feminist or whatever if you make up your mind and believe it's the spirit of God who opens doors. You don't have to vote or anything. You don't have to march or anything. You don't have to do all that to get you a place."

"So do you think Martin Luther King's marching was needless?" I ask.

"Well, I think God planted Rosa Parks on that bus for a specific reason. I think he planted Martin Luther King there for a specific reason, to be an instrument for that to happen, to come about. He's not saying you just fall out of the sky with this stuff, either. I just talk about God. I'm not into Malcolm X. I'm not into Martin Luther King. I'm not into Mother Teresa. I am into Jesus.

"The son of Abraham, how are you," Gray yells to an African-American man across the street watering his lawn. He smiles and waves. "We have the same bloodstream that Abraham has," she explains. "And we are the descendants of Abraham."

Her next-door neighbor drives up and also says hello. "He's writing a book," Gray tells the middle-aged brunette, nodding toward me.

"She's an excellent neighbor, a great neighbor," says the woman, Mary. "And, you know, there's no stopping her, no stopping her. She's got a mind of her own. At least she's not radical about it, I guess. She just stands there with her sign and looks pretty. I see her out when I'm buzzing around in the summer."

• • •

Matthew is at the couch where he slept last night, folding the sheets. "This is Matthew's hotel room here," says Gray. "Hey, Matthew. You had some breakfast, Matthew?"

"No. I was going to get some doughnuts."

Gray hands him the car keys. "Okay, well, you just go and bring the car back in a few minutes."

"Okay."

On the mantel above the couch are pictures of three children. "My husband framed these pictures before he passed away. He kept everything. He framed them all and he put them on the wall. He was very proud of his kids. He was a great father."

Gray takes me downstairs to see even more pictures and dozens of athletic, academic, and cheerleading trophies on display. Her daughter, Sonya, enters, politely speaks, and quickly leaves, obviously in a hurry or preferring not to answer questions. "My children are getting a little jealous of Matthew, I think. . . . They're so protective and all. They've never seen me do something like this. But I can't please them anymore. I have to please God."

Gray's oldest son, Robert, also makes an entrance.

"Did you see me down there on the highway, Robert?" Gray asks.

"Nope."

"You were probably gone."

I ask Robert Gray about living in Wyoming. "It's like being here, for the most part. It's about the same size town; it's a little smaller.

"I think living in a nearly all-white area, [whites are] more likely in general to accept you as a black man. They'll accept you by yourself, because they're like, 'Well, you can be with us because you're not too bad. You're not like the rest,' stuff like that. But if you have to depend on them, when it comes down to it, I wouldn't trust them like I trust my own people.

"I date black women now. I used to date white girls when I was here, but then once I got away and got with people that weren't associated with this place or that grew up in different areas, my eyes kind of opened up; and I was like, man, I was a brainwashed kid, you know, living here, because I didn't get exposed to a lot of kinds of different things.

"I'm not going to say that I wouldn't do it again, but more than likely I don't think I ever will. I wouldn't marry a white woman."

Robert dates but refrains from sex. He says he's been a celibate for six years. "It's a matter of self-control. I'm not in any rush. I'm not missing anything."

His celibacy is just one example of how his values are influenced by his mother's ministry. "I don't drink and I don't smoke. I try not to curse. I try to be a good example. I try to lead by example."

Elease Gray says that she would discount the obvious suggestion that her tolerance and endurance of the abuse encountered is connected to her childhood and the tensions between her own parents. Her son predicts that when he gets married, he will have to make a conscious effort to avoid becoming a husband like his father. "I pray to God that I won't be like that," asserts Robert Gray, who describes himself as quiet and says that he's a fan of Terry McMillan, James Baldwin, Carter Woodson, and Malcolm X. "But you know, I don't think I will. I'm pretty sure that I won't be because I have peace with myself."

Robert Gray suspects his aversion to alcohol could be related to his father. "I thought it was pretty bad, the drinking and all that. I've seen what it does to people, and I don't want to.

"He was still a big man. He was the dad. You know this is his house. We were pretty old-fashioned, I think. Not like kids today."

Robert Gray was a star athlete and stellar student in Portsmouth. Two weeks before he graduated from high school, he found his father in his parents' bedroom, dead of a heart attack.

Robert Gray is a fundamentalist who, like his mother, believes in a strict interpretation of the Bible. "I believe in God. I go to church and study my Bible. But, to me, a church has to be a Bible-reading church—you know, they have to read the Bible. And then if they don't do that, they're not worth two cents."

Admittedly, though, he finds his mother's ministry too visible. "It's just, I think there's, you know, different ways of going about it. If it was me, I'd be more in tune to write stuff, write things to the paper, get my opinion out that way. And I'd try to foster some support from the people I associate with and get them to help me. And that's pretty much how I would do it. But nobody's ever said anything to me about the way she does it, and I don't think anybody would ever say anything to me."

Robert Gray was in the middle of his teenage years when his mother's transformation took place. Elease Gray was born again, and it happened when she was at her lowest point. "Sometimes I would have black eyes for days and I would cry for days. I even went to get the divorce three or four times, and because of my children, I just didn't want to. I remember one time I said, 'I'm not going to do this anymore. If he kills me, fine. I don't care.'

"The Lord really plucked me out because I just cried out. One day I was being abused by my husband. I said I can't take it anymore. And the Lord just really said, 'You don't have to, after today no more.' I did have to take some more—but now I don't have to take anything, because he's gone."

Gray recalls something much simpler and much smaller than the pain of physical abuse as the last and final piece of anguish that drove her to the Bible: the spark that ultimately led her to surrender her life to her religion was her husband's breaking a promise to escort her to a friend's twenty-fifth-anniversary celebration. "I just got tired of going alone all the time," she says. "He was drinking all the time.

"I was distraught. And then I decided that was it. That day, that was it. That was when I turned over everything to God."

The next day, Gray picked up the Bible, something she hadn't done in years. "My life changed so abruptly. I didn't talk to friends or anything for days. I started reading the Bible nonstop. God became real in my life. I knew that there was something better than what I had. A new energy, a new spirit took over. My spirit was different. My life was different.

"It upset him. It just blew his mind. He didn't understand, because we were two different people at that point."

And, at that point, Gray says that her husband's abuse didn't matter: she had God. "I wouldn't pay him any mind. He'd go one way and I'd go another. The more he would do his thing, the more spiritual I got.

"My children had to go to church every Sunday. He didn't go, but he made sure the children went. I'll give him that. And it shows, because my children are great children. And he did take care of the children. I won't take that away from him, because I was working. I didn't have time to do that."

Gray became an active member of the New Hope Baptist Church, one of the oldest and most established black institutions in New Hampshire. "A new minister had came to town and everybody thought I had flipped out over him. Lord, I done changed so abruptly, everybody thought I was flipped out over the minister. They thought I was having an affair with him.

"Everybody recognized I was a changed person," Gray reiterates. "I used to be an entertainer. My house was open. I could have the best parties ever. I could cook. I was a great hostess. I knew a lot of people. And I went to dances. I liked to dance and party. I did drink alcohol at one time. I even smoked pot one time. I stopped all of that."

Within a year, Gray would apprentice with the minister of the church, become licensed, and be named the assistant pastor.

Some might say that a Baptist church isn't true to its birthright without a big congregational fight over its minister somewhere in its past or present. The drama of those battles rivals the intensity of congressional feuds over balanced budgets. But the fights visibly illustrate how Baptist churches have long been successful laboratories of democratic principles in African-American communities. Where there is democracy, there is sure to be feuds that test the politician in those who would claim to be everything but. As assistant pastor, Gray would find herself embroiled in the fight over the minister who befriended her and brought her into the ministry. Some might say that she became the equivalent of his Judas.

There was a move to overthrow him by a faction in the church, and Gray initially supported him—until she saw him put the fourth estate before God: "He has just bought a van. And he left the communion on the table to go out and take a picture for a newspaper reporter. And that won't work for me. And that's the only reason."

With Gray's blessing, the minister was eventually ousted, and Gray was the interim pastor for five years, hoping to become minister. Instead, she was passed over twice and was eventually asked to leave. "So after I got there and was preaching and ministering, the people were coming back and putting money in the collection, and the church was building up. Then they decide they were ready to call another pastor. So I said fine. That really hurt—the worst hurt I ever had in my life, I'm telling you. I couldn't talk for three days. I couldn't talk to my husband. I couldn't talk to my kids, I couldn't talk period. Couldn't say one word. If I did, I would cry. It was worse than anything I ever felt in my life.

"And then the Lord just said, 'Okay, it's time.' And when God says it's time, it's time. So I started the church in my beauty parlor."

Gray insists that she was rejected because she was a woman. Though she rejects feminism, she sees equality in the pulpit as a major issue.

Within days of launching her ministry, Gray saw a church building and tried to raise the sixty-five thousand dollars required for a down payment. In a week, she raised thirty thousand from family, friends, and supporters. Still, it wasn't enough to buy the building, so she gave the money back to the donors. She kept ten thousand dollars, from the diehard supporters, however, and bought a church van and a piano. Eventually, she spotted the boxing club and met the owner, who told her that she could use the building if she would fix it. It wasn't a desirable building: the ceiling had collapsed; gaping holes in the walls let in debris from outside. "It was a wreck," Gray says. "The no ceiling; the walls were painted red and gray. There was no covering on the floor. We put in air-conditioning, did the floor, brought curtains, painted, fixed the roof. We did it all. And it's been a blessing to me ever since.

"I was hurt in the beginning," Gray says, remembering the day that her church's board told her that she would not become pastor and was no longer needed as the associate pastor. "I needed to stand back and take another look. I would have never had a church if I would have just stayed there. I wouldn't have been able to find out what I could really do. I would have been a different person."

Chapter 17

Dreams of Georgia

I often say Jesus was never compelled to pastor a black church in the inner city, and certainly that would be a challenge, even for Jesus," says Arthur Hilson, the second pastor of the New Hope Baptist Church since Elease Gray left to start her own ministry.

New Hope is hardly in the inner city. But in the minds of many African Americans as well as whites, "inner city" sometimes applies to all blacks—even those who are suburban, rural, or from old-line families in northern New England. In reality, the New Hope Baptist Church sits on a quiet two-lane highway among homes with sturdy New England porches that are separated by wide yards. The white one-story building has a basement cafeteria for church members to congregate for meals after the service.

The church may be a distance from the inner city, but it remains a challenge to any pastor, considering that Hilson is the church's seventh minister in twenty-five years. "Some have left under less-than-desirable conditions," he says, with his full bass giving depth to each word. "They've been driven out. I understand a few people were prepared to physically assault pastors. We've had pastors in this church who had their tires slashed, and people would throw pennies and toll tokens in the plate and say, 'We want you out.' So this is a challenge."

Challenge is an understatement when it comes to selecting a minister. Democracy and religion bring out idiosyncrasies and differences that easily erupt in feuds that can consume a Baptist congregation when it is time to search for a new minister. "Baptist churches are usually autonomous and not governed by another body," Hilson explains. "And each church will decide who will come to lead it and how long the leadership will exist and when and how they will out the leadership. So there have been known to be struggles. I know of cases where churches locked doors and changed locks on pastors' studies and sanctuaries."

It doesn't happen everywhere. Hilson hopes to shift the compass of New Hope in the direction of churches with dynamic Baptist spiritual leaders who remain popular and in the same pulpit for years—sometimes even decades. He may be on his way to achieving that for New Hope: his first sermon was Easter Sunday 1991, and it is now August 1993, and many members of the congregation still adore him.

When Hilson arrived, church membership had dwindled to thirty-five. It now exceeds 125. What exactly does Hilson have that his predecessors lacked? Hilson answers that question in the tradition and rhetoric of Christian modesty. "What I hear from a number of our members is that things have moved toward a sense of community and togetherness, if you will. I certainly take no credit for that. I'm but a vessel. I think it all goes to the positive spirit of God."

Arthur Hilson sits in the pastor's study between the front of the church and the back of the chapel. Behind him is a bookshelf lined with literature on religion and the civil-rights movement along with the works by Toni Morrison and Langston Hughes, among other writers. "The church, through the years, has been an equal-opportunity employer for black folks, for men and women who were at the lower echelon of the economic ladder. They worked as janitors and whatever during the week, but came to church and were suddenly empowered because they held, if you will, front seats as deacons and trustees and head of the mission board and all of that. They sat alongside other members of the community, professionals, as equals."

New Hope does not display the broad economic diversity that one might find in many Baptist churches in many cities and suburbs with larger black populations. In Portsmouth, the black community, and thus the church, is overwhelmingly middle class. There are the five old black families that have been in northern New England for generations. There are also some professionals who arrived with corporations based in the area. But the majority of the African Americans in the city came via Pease Air Force Base, just outside of Portsmouth. As a result, says Hilson, "You don't have a community of black folk who come out of the ghetto and who are welfare survivors—you don't have that. People are all able to stand on their own. Now, there may be one or two around who drink a bit, but even the one that I know that has a problem with that is also retired from the military. Most of them are retired military. They found a place where there was not a lot of problems, a nice scenic area, and so when they got out, they found a place where they came and bought a home, and they live here. And that's it."

Their passions stir over the church because New Hope is the strongest anchor for African-American culture in the state. It is one of the only area institutions that bonds a community by race in a society where race is a cultural obsession. Although there are two other local organizations—Kwanzaa, an organization of black women that raises money for scholarships for area African-American children, and the Sea Coast Men's Club, a social organization of black men—the church is more than an organization with meetings that rotate among favorite restaurants or the homes of members. New Hope owns land and a building and is long established: it was founded as People's Baptist Church in 1823, according to Valerie Cunningham, a local historian who focuses on the black community. Even as its numbers once declined to the loyal thirty-five, the building and the parsonage stood sturdy. "We assemble here in this place and then we leave and go to the four winds, geographically," says Hilson. "There isn't a black neighborhood here. I don't know of any neighborhood where on any street more than one or two of us may live . . . the only black community in Portsmouth, New Hampshire, is the church. And this church, I think, represents the epitome of the black community."

Hilson acknowledges that gender bias could be one reason why Elease Gray couldn't make it as pastor of the church. But he also says that her perspective on Christianity did not take race enough into account for the oldest living black institution in the state. "I don't believe she has a focus on the black community. And so I think it's like night and day from my focus. Elease Gray . . . is committed to the cause of Christ and would espouse that . . . we're all somebody and the same in God's sight, and I think that's wonderful. And I certainly say that. I say to the white man that I am your equal and you are my brother. But I don't think that she will stress the uniqueness of us as a people as I do."

It's a fine line, because even as Hilson says this, New Hope's history tells of one minister thrown out for seeing black uniqueness in a sixties-style way. He literally wore his black nationalism in the pulpit, and it was too Afrocentric for the New England congregation. "He wore an Afro and carried a big fist with a cross on it."

Often the person who leads New Hope is like Hilson, a newcomer to the community who must find a comfortable place as a leader to strangers. Hilson grew up in Cincinnati and never imagined living in Portsmouth, New Hampshire. As a boy, he envisioned himself one day wearing a tuxedo and waving a baton before an orchestra playing Beethoven's Fifth or Dvořák's

New World Symphony. He played that role on Sunday mornings before the television set.

He maintained his love of classical music through his teenage years but expanded his taste in music, too. "Then I got into jazz. I could not tolerate blues or anything like that. There was no funk then. For me, it was all classical, jazz."

After high school and a stint in the navy, Hilson turned away from pursuing a future in music and looked toward a career in education. He attended the University of Massachusetts at Amherst, majoring in education. He remained there several years, eventually receiving a doctorate in counseling and administration. Having worked his way up the administrative ladder, he ultimately became dean of student services. And then came the "calling." Hilson describes it as a powerful and mysterious voice that turned him in yet another direction—back to school, for a master's degree in theology. In school, he worked part time as an associate minister at a Baptist church in Holyoke, Massachusetts, while still a full-time administrator at UMass Amherst. After completing his master's, he accepted the offer at New Hope. It is his first position as head pastor.

Becoming the first family of New Hope required a huge financial sacrifice from the Hilson family. Hilson's income dove from ninety-five thousand dollars per year to a base salary of nine thousand dollars annually. Officially, the church considers the job of minister to be part time. Hilson insists it's a full-time commitment on a part-time salary. In any case, his salary rises at the mercy of the congregation. Now, two years after he was hired, he's up to thirteen thousand a year.

It's not as dire as it might sound. Through consulting contracts at universities and his navy pension, Hilson has managed to bring his salary up to fifty-five thousand dollars a year. And the pastor's job also comes with tax advantages and a parsonage for the family. Still, none of that could hide the fact that Hilson's oldest daughter, Gabrielle, fifteen, was two years away from college when the family, which also includes Hilson's wife, Florine, a seamstress, and their two other children, David, seven, and Antoinette, nine, moved to Portsmouth in the spring of 1991.

In the summer of 1993, Gabrielle Hilson sits on the front porch of the parsonage, a white wood-frame, two-story house next door to the church. Cars race down the road. From the pastor's study to the porch, the minister and the preacher's daughter anticipate the new life for Gabrielle Hilson. In two weeks she turns eighteen, and in three weeks, she's leaving home.

In June, Arthur Hilson was consulting at the University of New Hampshire, leading a workshop for parents of prospective freshmen. He wondered why he wasn't in the audience. "Every night, I'd go and I'd think I've got to deal with this, too. That's my baby. What happens on the twenty-fourth when we leave her on the campus of Spelman? Like any other father who sees his daughter go away, I will probably think in some sense about . . ."

Hilson pauses, and then says it. "Sex. Sex and all those things I've done workshops on, and yet I'm guilty in some ways because the way I'll probably feel when my son goes away may be different, you know. I saw a talk show not long ago where parents came on with their daughters who were sexually active. And that evening, my wife and I, we talked about it. She [Gabrielle] knows obviously all about sex at this point. She has not been active sexually.

"Her mother is talking to her. She brought her down and had her physical and all that. In the physical, the doctor came out and said, 'You know, she's nonactive sexually.'"

"So you are opposed to premarital sex?" I ask.

"Yes."

"Do you believe that's realistic for someone of college age in this day and age?"

"I think if you give them what you believe in, then they make their own choices."

"Did you practice that?"

"No, no, but that doesn't make it right. I can't say I support premarital sex. I don't."

"Are you going to tell your son the same thing?"

"Absolutely, absolutely. Absolutely . . . I think sex is a beautiful thing. A healthy thing. I think it's when you're with someone that you treasure and you love."

Hilson tries to keep his children's routine as pure as possible—a lot like Henry McKoy. That means no MTV for the two younger children and none for Gabrielle if she's in their presence. The father and daughter concede that the rules are strict when compared to those that Gabrielle's peers live under. I wonder if the Hilsons' puritanical edge is sharpened by conservative social values designed, perhaps, in part, to protect them from the stereotypes of African Americans as sexually promiscuous. "We must be able to define who and what we are," declares the pastor. "We must be able to define our values. And the only thing I can teach my children are my values. At a point that they begin to develop their own values, I would hope that what I instilled in them will be the core of theirs, but they have every right to begin to redefine for themselves their values. I will never love them any less. And my son may turn out to be the biggest whoremonger in town. I wouldn't love him any less, but I would be concerned about his behavior, because there may well be a price that he must pay for that, you see. Not only in the life after, but in this life."

The Hilsons struggle with raising African-American children in a state where black is beautiful to many only because it is so rare. It is not a new struggle for the family. Before moving to Portsmouth, Gabrielle was a student at Smith Academy in Hatfield, Massachusetts. There were never more than two black students at the school while she was there, and the Hilsons were the only black family living in Hatfield for most of those years. In that respect, Gabrielle's teenage years differ enormously from her father's.

Hatfield was far from the conservative black working-class community in Cincinnati that shaped Arthur Hilson. He describes growing up in a black neighborhood in West Cincinnati in the 1940s and '50s much like Butch Gaines describes growing up in Lawnside—the Hilsons too were "poor and didn't know it." His was a neighborhood of renters a couple of streets away from the Ohio River; it sounds much like an urban midwestern version of the rural community that shaped Henry McKoy. The rod was appreciated as the sure way to punish as well as instill discipline, good habits, the value of resilience that would persevere through racism and social injustice. In Arthur Hilson's memory, West Cincinnati is another example of the old-fashioned black community celebrated today in nostalgic reveries by many who lived through it, and criticized as suffocating by many black liberals. "It was a neighborhood of working folk trying to make ends meet, and since we didn't have anything to compare it with, we all felt we were doing well," says Hilson. "We didn't see our community as being the ghetto—we knew it was the West End. We were all down there.

"Our elementary school was Harriet Beecher Stowe, behind our street. You began in the kindergarten, and so a number of us would start together in the kindergarten and head all the way through, and went to high school. We all sort of grew up together on the same street, stayed, went to the same school. It was a kind of growing together, knowing each other well. Everybody—well, your whole class—lived within a matter of blocks in the West End.

"Everyone was black," Hilson says, "except for one kid who was white. He lived in the neighborhood."

Cincinnati was above the Mason-Dixon line, but segregation still ruled. Blacks, Hilson says, were not permitted in some movie theaters. "We didn't know that, 'cause it was never an issue. There was one, two, three, four . . . we had five, six movie theaters. So we didn't worry about going to a white theater uptown."

Hilson says it was difficult to grow up in his old neighborhood and have just one set of parents: even now, he stays in touch with the three women whom his mother called her best friends and whom he still calls on Mother's Day—three years after his mother's death. "Well, I met them through my mother, [they were] friends of my mother, and they were in church. . . . Just about everybody's parent was your mother and your parents' friends were a lot like your parents. And so there was this respect for elders, and you didn't question it if you were told to do something—you just did it. I think it was good, because they always had your best interest at heart. I mean, they wouldn't tell you anything that was wrong. If you were doing something that was wrong—you usually knew you were wrong—you know.

"I think that the big thing for me growing up was for a couple of us to get a bottle of blackberry wine . . . and we'd go to the movies and drink some of that and smoke a cigarette. That was it. We didn't have the kind of pressures there are today, because there was nothing about drugs. And there's a lot that happens with the white kids at the academy. There's some vicious drinking and drugs down there."

Gabrielle Hilson, a popular cheerleader and class president at Smith, resisted the peer pressure and never became an active drinker or drug user. But even if she had, either way, she would have fulfilled someone's expectations of a girl in her situation, she says: "Most people would probably think that I'm supposed to be this little angel. There is also a stereotype that the preacher's kids are the worst kids, but I think I've always been the quietest. As far as when I was younger, I was always the well-behaved person. So it's just the way I grew up."

Like many black families, the Hilsons number among their friends white liberals, who may have a more open attitude on race. Yet the Hilsons themselves live by a mixture of liberal and conservative values. The conservative streak, via Cincinnati, collides with the perspective of many liberal whites who embrace Gabrielle and the family as friends. The Hilsons have taken refuge from the conflict in the black church, which they view as a place to reinforce the conservative values of the old village for children growing up in a world so vastly different from that of their parents. Still, however, the church provides only an incomplete shield: parents in Holyoke and Portsmouth alike find that congregations can't help but feel the effects of the world—no matter who's the pastor. Nowhere is that more evident than at the Holyoke church, where four of Gabrielle Hilson's best friends, all black teenage girls, are either pregnant or young mothers. The girls are devoutly Christian, antiabortion, and not joining the welfare rolls. Yet their middle-income parents are helping raise a generation of children conceived outside of the bond of marriage that they and their church value so highly.

It is clearly a different time for Arthur Hilson. When he was growing up in the late forties and early fifties, the number of out-of-wedlock births was only a fraction of what they are today—even as the numbers have declined significantly among black women, dropping from 90.7 per 1,000 unmarried black women in 1989 to 78.4 per 1,000 in 1996.

Despite these statistics and all of the changes in the culture, the household that raised Arthur Hilson and the one he has constructed to raise Gabrielle share a signficant trait: the ability, born of necessity, to create and nurture strong family bonds beyond bloodlines. Arthur Hilson had little contact with his biological father, and he was raised by and had close ties with a stepfather. Likewise, Gabrielle Hilson is not Arthur Hilson's biological daughter, yet he has raised her and they have a close relationship.

When Gabrielle Hilson's father discovered that her mother was pregnant, he deserted her, according to Gabrielle. Her mother fell in love with Arthur Hilson later, marrying him when Gabrielle was six years old.

Every family has its secrets and crippling moments that test the strength of its bond. Strong families keep such matters internal and project comfort and force. The horrors of the past are unimaginable to the outsider who only momentarily gazes inside. The Hilsons are no exception: they don't display their problems. However, they also don't hide any of the delicate struggles in their past. They don't dwell on them, but the struggles are there and acknowledged by everyone. It is the bond of family that sustains them through horror and keeps the past from polluting the present.

Arthur Hilson shares a story that illustrates this: his wife's birth was the result of her mother being raped at age thirteen.

Two years ago, Gabrielle was thrilled to move to New Hampshire, of all places, on account of her impression that her new school would have a large population of African-American students. At a school of nine hundred, there were twenty-five black students. "And she got here and she was saying 'Wow, all these black students.' For her it was a whole new world," says her father.

As a black girl, she became a unique member of the self-described

"Homey Crew" at Portsmouth High School. Most of the girls were white. All of the boys were black, many trying to project an image of inner-city manhood. Gabrielle says that most—not all—of the guys rejected academic success because it violated their idea of cool. The girls placed sleeping with the boys above schoolwork and the objections of their parents. Gabrielle was the smart and trouble-free member of the group. Her ears were the cup for all the girls' secrets.

She had few close white or black friends who shared her academic interests. In Portsmouth, her white classmates in calculus and honors courses were polite but distant. "I never made friends with people who were on my track," she says. "I guess I never had white friends who were on my same track because they were not used to interacting with blacks."

In Portsmouth, Gabrielle grew into a black female angel with all the righteous answers for the fun-loving, exciting, and sinful white girls and black boys. She played the role of a shadow saint, with no major problems of her own beyond listening and helping others with more imposing and pressing collections of social needs and desires.

Arthur Hilson sees black college life as his daughter's escape from the role of armchair–peer shrink and emissary for white girls interested in black boys. He also hopes that she's establishing a new tradition in the family and model for her younger brother and sister to follow, similar to that which binds branches of the McKoy family to Hampton and North Carolina A&T: Gabrielle is the first in a second-generation-college family to attend a black school. Her choice, in fact, has become a popular one for an increasing number of black middle-class students. Since the mid-eighties, enrollment at many black colleges has risen, reversing a decline that occurred when integration widened the doors of predominantly white schools. Spelman received six applications for every single space in 1993's freshman class of five hundred. Like Gabrielle, many of the students entering Spelman this fall are graduates of predominantly white schools. "I just felt it important that she had this kind of experience, better than what she's into now," explains Arthur Hilson. "They've got good students there. And a lot of them come out of backgrounds similar to the one that she's come out of.

"Her guidance counselor had advised her to go to Oberlin, where she [the guidance counselor] went," Hilson continues. "The guidance counselor is black. A black woman steered my daughter away from black schools. She told me, 'Your daughter will be accepted wherever she applies.'"

"She didn't think I could make it at a black school," says Gabrielle of the counselor. "Now if I don't make it, at least I tried. She thought because I'd been in a white environment, I should stick with that. When I asked about black colleges, she handed me maybe one book on Spelman, and that was it. She was pushing me to go to Oberlin. She said they were hospitable to blacks and they were the first to admit blacks and I should really go there. She didn't help too much. I can't say she helped me as much as she helped a lot of the white kids. I don't think counselors encourage black colleges.

"My dad used to always tell me about Spelman, you know. Spelman was a great school. Either Spelman or Smith."

Safety was and is a big issue for Gabrielle, especially considering that she's still haunted by recurring nightmares about attending a black school. They began when she first began applying to college. "I would have dreams that someone would come up to fight me because they thought I said something about them. I just had this fear."

Usually in the dreams Gabrielle is in an enclosed area, surrounded by a group of African Americans, whose faces are anonymous. Sometimes it is a group of black girls who approach Gabrielle in a bathroom and stand ready to attack her.

The dreams illustrate the power of negative images of African Americans—so powerful they fester even in the minds of those who are raised to defy those very images. Gabrielle has never come into personal and direct contact with black-on-black violence and crime, yet she can't stop dreaming of violence at Spelman, a school with a long tradition and reputation of gentility and middle-class values. "And when I was thinking of going to Howard, I was having dreams that I might get shot going down the road or something, 'cause my aunt lives down there and they were talking about black people getting killed and people just driving off and stuff like that. So I had dreams I was going to die."

I ask a question: "If you had these dreams, what made you still want to go to a black college?"

"I've been around white colleges. At the University of Massachusetts, kids were having racial problems. Things were going on. I did want to go to UMass for a while, because I thought that it might be cheaper. But I've been there ever since I was a kid. I saw the University of New Hampshire, and I couldn't deal with it. I'd been in a white school so long, and I don't want to go. Plus, I'm going to be a social worker. I'd like to work in the inner city, the black community. So I felt it would be better if I went to a black school. There are problems in the white community, but it's just that I'm thinking about working with my own and helping my own. Like I said, the media and everybody portrayed black people as having such a hard time. I want to help. And if I find out they don't have such a hard time, then maybe I'll do something else. But right now I'd like to help my own people."

"What are the roots of those fears and dreams? Have you seen a lot of violence and black kids fighting?" I prod her.

"I think it's the media. You see these black people going to jail all the time."

"In New Hampshire?" I ask.

"On other news—national news. There was a fight between some black and white kids at a movie theater here. You don't always see violence happen in white neighborhoods. You don't see the bad sides of the white communities. And then you see the movies that portray what happens in the black community. They never show the good half of what happens. You don't see that on TV. You don't see that in movies half the time. All you see is the bad stuff most of the time."

I take a look at her T-shirt, which coincidentally says something appropriate to the discussion. "What does your shirt say?"

"FEAR OF A BLACK COLLEGE," she says, laughing. "I got that at UMass."

It is not unusual for Arthur Hilson to have a long list of calls from church members requesting that he counsel them or relatives in the midst of personal problems and moral dilemmas. "I had a call last night, someone who said that her sister is pregnant again by her boyfriend, and she wants to get rid of the baby. I'm going to call her and talk with her and hear her concerns, and just let her know that there is a way and she can survive."

"Are you pro-choice?" I ask.

"I respect the woman's right to decide for herself. I'm not part of what you'd call the fundamentalist movement of the church. My theology would be defined as a liberal theology. But do I support abortion? The answer is no. I do not support the taking of a life, but I respect the woman who decides for herself that she must do that. I would never condemn or judge her. The Bible says we are to judge not lest we be judged. And so I respect the right of any person to make a choice for themselves.

"I've talked about sometimes how little Adolf's mother had to love him. He was her baby, then little Adolf grew up. . . . I'm sure his mother loved him, but if she had known that little Adolf was going to be what he became, maybe she would have aborted him. If you have a child that you know is going to be one of the world's worst murderers from birth, you'd lock him up. But you don't know."

I ask another question. "I know this is unlikely, but if by chance your daughter did become pregnant, would you support her right for an abortion?"

"If my daughter came and said, 'Dad, I'm pregnant and I want an abortion,' I would do anything I could to talk her out of that. I would agree to take the child myself. But it's her body. She has a right to make her choice. I'd give my best advice."

It is the first Saturday of November 1995. Kwanzaa chose the first weekend of the month for its annual fundraising ball. In this room of two hundred people, you could easily forget the African-American population of New Hampshire is less than 1 percent of the state's total. Nearly everyone in the room is black. New Hampshire is hardly Harlem, yet the ballroom of the restaurant is decorated as the legendary Cotton Club. Such is the theme of the party: Kwanzaa's Cotton Club. Most of the attendees are from Portsmouth, but some come from Maine and Vermont for the event. Women in sequins and ruffles dance with men in tuxedos or dark suits. A giant cardboard pink Cadillac is parked in a corner of the room and used as the backdrop for photos.

The ball helps Kwanzaa provide scholarships to promising students like Gabrielle Hilson, who received one this year. She is still in school, but she didn't return to Spelman for her junior year. She is now at the University of New Hampshire.

On Sunday, the day after the ball, she sings in the choir at New Hope. She stands next to her mother and sometimes holds her mother's hand as she sings Baptist hymns.

New Hope choir members don't wear robes. They are in dresses and suits. Gabrielle wears a green maternity dress. She is seven months pregnant.

Chapter 18

The Girls of the Homey Crew

O N her porch in August 1993, Gabrielle Hilson looked as if motherhood was so far in the future that it was not even a thought. It
would come one day, but not before a Spelman graduation, the
start of a career, and a wedding in a white dress at New Hope Baptist Church. With high school only just finished, she exerts maternal
instincts on Eric (not his real name), the six-month-old son of her good
friend Danielle, seventeen, who is white.

Today Gabrielle plans to spend quality time with Danielle and another
friend, Jessica, whom she's also leaving behind for Atlanta. Jessica, a Puerto
Rican, and Danielle only date black boys.

Gabrielle drives her parents' green Impala to Danielle's house in a small
town in New Hampshire. Danielle's parents are divorced, and she and her
son live with her mother. Danielle comes out of the house as Gabrielle
parks. She is short, blond, and looks weighed down as she walks to the car
with a baby, car seat, and diaper bag. After parking, Gabrielle jumps out and
grabs the baby as Danielle hooks in the car seat. Gabrielle elevates her
voice to a baby-language soprano to communicate with Eric.

Once they are settled in the car, Gabrielle turns up the radio.

"I like this song," she says, snapping the fingers of one hand while keeping the other on the wheel. The dial is tuned to a Boston station that pumps
out hip-hop and contemporary R&B. Some of the music probably wouldn't
be permissible in her father's presence. This includes songs like "I Got a
Man."

It is a twenty-minute ride from Danielle's to Jessica's. Danielle, who will
enter her senior year of high school in September, gives Gabrielle the latest

on Jerry (not his real name), eighteen, the father of her child. An African American who grew up in Portsmouth, he's moving to Arizona with his family. She says the family is now en route—driving across the country. They stopped in Harlem yesterday.

"They were on One Hundred Twenty-fifth Street, he said, and somebody got shot or something," Danielle recounts. "They saw a lot of cop cars coming."

"Things like that," says Gabrielle, "when you hear it, that's the kind of thing you think about. I remember at my church in Holyoke a while ago: We were coming out of Bible study, and this little kid was running up and down the street going, 'Everybody hurry up and go home, there's going to be a shootout.' This was a black and Puerto Rican area. So those kinds of things bring fears to me. But I deal with them, you know. They talk about when it's your time to go, you go, it's your time. So I figure if it's my time to go in the street, somebody's going to take me down in the street, that's when it's my time to go . . ."

"They're in Ohio now," says Danielle.

"Now, is he still in high school also?" I ask.

"No, he just graduated."

"Okay, what is he planning on doing?"

"He wants to go to college. He doesn't really want to live in Arizona. His father's job transferred him there. He [Jerry] plans to come back here in a year anyway. He doesn't want to be here in the winter."

Gabrielle turns in to a condominium complex of log-brown contemporary wooden two- and three-story units.

"Okay, where do I park?" she says, looking at all of the full spaces. We pass the clubhouse and see the diving board of a swimming pool.

"Jessica has a pool—she's so stupid she doesn't use it," muses Danielle.

Gabrielle laughs.

"She's so lazy," Danielle says. "She stays in her house all day and watches TV."

"Yeah," affirms Gabrielle. "You can never get her to go anywhere."

Gabrielle sees a car pulling out of a space not far from Jessica's place. Jessica has recently moved into the complex with her mother, Nora. Jessica sees our car from her window and runs outside. She is tall—about five-feet-eight—and has long, dark-brown hair.

Her arms reach for Eric. "You're so cute."

She carries him inside, where Nora's arms extend in Eric's direction. Nora is a short, roundly shaped woman. Her Puerto Rican accent is a contrast to her daughter's speech. Jessica talks with the speed of a Valley girl—so fast that she drives the New England accent out of her speech.

"I haven't seen you in a while," Nora says as she cradles Eric. "You've grown. Oh, he's so cute. He's so cute."

"He's got blue eyes," says Jessica.

"He's cute," Nora repeats.

"Isn't he? Oh, he's precious," coos Jessica.

"He's strong," Nora comments.

"Yeah, he's twenty-one inches," says Danielle.

"Did we come too late? I'm really sorry," Gabrielle says to Nora.

"No problem at all," Nora replies. She then goes to the kitchen and brings out sodas. When she returns, Danielle is briefing her friends on her difficulties getting along with Jerry's family.

"She's scary. Oh, my God," Danielle tells them, referring to Jerry's mother, her son's grandmother. "I told you how she yelled at me: I went over there with Dawn last year. Knock on the door she goes, 'Go get the newspaper!' She just screamed at me and she, like, doesn't know me then, and she was like, 'Go get it!' The lady's mean. She's mean. She's scary. She hates me."

"Why?" asks Nora.

"I don't know," answers Danielle. "I never did anything to her."

"How does she feel now that you have the baby?" Nora asks.

"She's mean to me," says Danielle. "She's always mean to me."

"Why do you think that?" asks Nora.

"'Cause I'm white," she says.

"They hate Daniel's (not his real name) girlfriend because she's white," adds Jessica.

"Who's Daniel?" I ask.

"Jerry's brother," Gabrielle tells me, then turns back to her friends. "Yeah, they're really strict, though."

"Yeah," agrees Jessica. "How old is Daniel? He's, like, twenty-one, and he was not allowed to go stay at his girlfriend's house. Hello! He sneaks around."

In teenage terms and manner, the conversation moves on to the discussion of racist black people, including a black girl at the school who does not like Danielle.

"She's so black, and everyone else, they're just white honkies and all this," says Danielle. "She sat there and one day she looked at me and she was like, 'I hate you black-white relationships.' She was like, 'Mulatto people don't understand who they are. They don't know who they are.'"

"Just not making any sense whatsoever!" says Jessica.

"She said something about how blacks should stay with blacks," Danielle adds.

"Yeah—and wasn't she dating an Oriental guy?" Jessica asks.

"'Cause it's true," says Gabrielle. "She's real racist."

"She complains about how everyone else is racist," Danielle continues. "'Oh, this place is so racist.'"

"And she calls Malcolm a sellout all the time because Malcolm studies," Gabrielle observes, referring to a black classmate who's going to Boston University next year. "Malcolm hung out, but he didn't hang out with her."

She remembers something. "I forgot to tell you all about this. I had a class called Another View; it's a class where you study about history from a minority point of view—not just blacks, but Asian and so on. And we were talking about the sixties and stuff, and we were doing a scenario about a roller-skating rink in the white part of town. So the couple [that owned the rink] wanted to make money, so should they let the black people in or not? Well, I said, 'Blacks and whites got along.' I said, 'My mother gets along with white people and got along with them in the sixties.' She raised her hand and said, 'Well your mother was just a good little nigger, wasn't she?' And everybody including the teacher just waited for me to get up and knock her out."

"Yeah, you should have," says Nora.

"You should have knocked her out," agrees Jessica.

"You all know me," says Gabrielle. "Like, if somebody had laid a hand on me, okay, I'll fight you. I was upset. But, I mean, there were so many threats going to that girl after that—not from me, but from other people. Everybody threatened to kick her butt if she said anything about my mother again. I mean everybody. For a while, she stayed away from me."

Jessica says she missed that dispute. By then, she had dropped out of school—her third time doing so. "We moved and I quit," she told me.

"You quit in your senior year?" I ask.

"My sophomore and my junior too," she says.

"Why did you quit?" I ask.

"I was bored," she explains. "I don't know. I'm lazy. I just never get motivated."

"She never went to school," says her mother, Nora.

"If I did night school too I could probably catch up and still graduate next year."

"Which is not bad," says Gabrielle.

"I don't want you to do it for me," says Nora. "I want you to do it for yourself. Once you're finished your high school, you can decide you want to go on to college a lot easier. If you quit and you never finish high school, it's going be a lot harder. I'm always getting on her case, and she gets upset because she thinks I'm picking on her. She's very stubborn."

Jessica exhales a sigh of impatience and speaks. "You are always on my case."

"I don't do it because I want to get on her case; I just want her to realize that it's for her own benefit."

"People think we're ditzes but we're not," Danielle states.

"Yeah, we're really deep! We are!" says Gabrielle sarcastically.

They all laugh, and the conversation moves back to boys. In some ways, the conversations illustrate Arthur Hilson's rationale for encouraging Gabrielle to leave New Hampshire, since he believes she does not have much in common with Danielle and Jessica. He hopes college will bring her in contact with young women who share her values.

"Did I tell you what Kareem did?" asks Jessica. "He went up to Lena and Sandra in the park and said, 'You wanna kick it with me?'"

"Kareem?" asks Danielle.

"Yeah. They said no, and he said, 'Not even a little bit?'"

They laugh and Jesssica says, "I was like, what is he, desperate or what?"

"He's a loser," says Danielle.

"He came over the other day," Jessica continues. "Like, when he came upstairs, he didn't want to talk to anybody, and he came in. He didn't even want to talk to any of us. He was like, 'Kathy [not her real name], come on, let's go.' Kathy's coming over to me. She's, like, eating some of my corn on the cob. She's, like, taking bites off it and hanging out."

"Kathy's going to get braces," Danielle says.

"Kathy?" asks Jessica.

"Does she want them?" asks Gabrielle.

"Well, she should," Nora asserts.

"She needs them," says Jessica.

Danielle looks at the baby's bottom and then pulls out a diaper. "These are multicultural diapers," she says.

They are white with colored elephants.

"Ooo! They're so cool!" Jessica enthuses.

"They're so cute," Gabrielle concurs.

"They've come a long way from when I used to have to do that," Nora points out.

"They have so many different kinds," Danielle says. "The elephants turn pink."

"Do they seriously?" asks Jessica.

"It's white with elephants on it," answers Danielle. "When he goes to the bathroom, the elephants will turn pink."

"Those cost more money, I bet," Nora comments.

"When the baby goes to the bathroom, the bottom of his diaper turns to, like, jelly. There's a layer, so you can feel it, and it changes the color of the elephants."

"Oooh, gross," says Jessica. "I know they stink! Oh, God!"

Danielle changes Eric's diaper as the subject turns back to boys. "Oh, that guy David," says Danielle. "He went to Somalia."

"He's not in the army, is he?" Jessica asks.

"I think I might go to the army next year," jokes Gabrielle.

"No, he's in the marines," says Danielle.

"No," says Gabrielle. "He said he wasn't in the army."

"Marines," Danielle repeats.

"The marines don't fight," says Jessica. "They stay out in the ocean."

"No!" Gabrielle disagrees.

"The navy, marines, it is the same thing," says Jessica.

"It is not," Gabrielle corrects her.

"The army's the one that fights on the ground," says Danielle.

"All I know is that my dad's in the air force," Jessica states.

"My father's in the marines," says Danielle. "He wasn't in the ocean the whole time."

Later, after two hours, it is time for hugs, well wishes, and good-byes.

"Gabrielle, you know you're one of a kind," says Jessica. "An Oreo cookie."

"Remember you used to get called an Oreo cookie?" asks Danielle. "She's considered the smart one. Jessica's brother considers her the smart one because—"

"All of us are stupid," Jessica cuts in. "And Gabrielle's the smart one. Date a nice guy in Atlanta!"

"Keep doing what you're doing," Nora advises. "She got pretty far. She's gotten far. I know that much. She's worked hard. She's worked real hard."

Jessica picks up the baby for one last hug. "I like nice babies here. I told her [Danielle] that when he gets older, he's going to come to my house. He should have karate lessons. Go beat up people."

"No. Tae kwon do," says Gabrielle.

"No, you're going to be a sumo wrestler," says Jessica to Eric. "And he looks like the Michelin tire man!"

"Okay, give me my kid, he's mine!" says Danielle finally.

"I don't want to let him go."

"All right, Jessica, I want to go home," says Danielle.

"Oh—give me the address so I can write you," Gabrielle remembers.

• • •

"We don't swear as much anymore," Gabrielle observes as we are driving away from Jessica's. "We made a pact once the baby was born. We don't do that any more."

Eric is asleep in his car seat.

"You definitely wanted to have the baby?" I ask Danielle.

"Yeah."

"Her mother didn't want it at all," says Gabrielle.

"No, and now she absolutely adores him and touches him every chance she gets."

"When she and her mother came to me, they were like, 'We want your opinion,' and the only thing I could tell her was, 'Don't have it if you can't handle it,'" says Gabrielle. "Having a baby is such a serious thing. If you don't have support, money, you can't really have a baby. It was her decision . . .'"

"My mom didn't exactly like Jerry," adds Danielle.

"I think your mom was kind of naïve about the kinds of things that you used to do," says Gabrielle. "I mean, she kind of knew."

"She knew."

"She didn't really, you know. She didn't really know the people you were hanging around with. Who did your mom know? She knew, like, me and Jessica pretty well, but other than that?"

"She knew Dawn . . ."

"But she didn't really know a lot of the people that you hung out with, and I think that came as a shock to her when you were pregnant."

"Did you consider other options?" I ask.

"Yeah, I considered other stuff. Before I was pregnant, my mom would be like, 'You're getting fat. Are you pregnant?' I was like, 'No.'"

Gabrielle picks up. "Then they [Danielle and her mother] came in to school, and they had to tell me something. Danielle was pregnant, and I didn't know whether to laugh or cry 'cause we had been joking about it. Then we sat there with really serious faces."

Of course, their lives are serious—more so than the two-hour farewell conversation at Jessica's would suggest. In addition to Danielle's pregnancy, they faced grim issues surrounding their friendships. Among their peer group, three teenage boys now face charges connected with an alleged gang rape.

"Is Mike [not his real name] out of jail?" Gabrielle asks Danielle.

"Yeah," Danielle replies.

"How can Mike always get out? I don't understand that. I mean, everything they do, they get out."

"Yeah, while those black people that beat up the other guy? They're facing, like, life or something.

"Mike was a big black guy," Danielle explains. "At first I used to think he was really cool, you know, 'cause he was so black. I just had this fascination with Mike, and then after a while it was like, wait, Mike is scary, you know?"

"They were part of the Homey Crew," Gabrielle says of the boys involved in the alleged rape.

"The girl involved was, like, fifteen years old, and there was supposedly more than, like, two guys, and I don't know," Danielle says of the incident. "She had a real bad reputation. So I don't know. If they did it, I certainly don't think it was right."

"So, was she black or white?" I ask.

"I think she was white. I don't know," says Danielle.

"Just knowing them," says Gabrielle. "They would do something like that, but, see, I don't know the whole thing."

"But there were other people involved."

"They're still on the street, and they've done so much."

"They are friends with Jerry. Jerry's not bad. He doesn't steal and he doesn't rob."

"There are pretty much levels where everyone pretty much knows each other," says Gabrielle. "You can choose to do what you want to do, you know? Some are doing drugs or selling drugs, but nobody stops talking to them. When my friends did drugs, I didn't stop being their friends, but they would never invite me to do that because they know I don't do that. But I was still a part of the Homey Crew."

"And the Homey Crew is?" I ask.

"It's basically the black population," Danielle explains. "The black kids around the area, we all hang around each other no matter how bad someone gets."

"It's just the Homey Crew," says Gabrielle. "I can say we all stick by each other. If we ever had a problem—like, somebody bothered me, Danielle, and Jessica—we can tell one of the guys in the Homey Crew and they would be after them in a minute."

Gabrielle turns into Danielle's driveway. Eric is still asleep.

"You coming back for Christmas?" Danielle asks Gabrielle.

"Yeah," Gabrielle replies. "I'll be back. I can't remember—it's about the fourteenth of December that I get out, and I go back in January."

"It's a strange thing . . . people who have gotten pregnant," says Gabrielle as she drives home. "It kind of seemed like a fad lately. The girls are just getting pregnant and not thinking about each other's futures. They're just doing it to keep their boyfriends. They were doing it because someone else had a baby. I know for myself, I can't handle a child right now. My parents wouldn't throw me out, but having a child would be a big responsibility right now, and I wouldn't want to be in my parents' house. When I have a child, I would want to support that child for myself. I would want an education. I want them to know that I can go through high school and get through everything and be a responsible adult . . . I want to grow up first, and I don't think I've grown up yet. It's been really strange—a lot of people have teased me lately about me being the next to get pregnant, because all my friends in Massachusetts, my black friends, each one has gotten pregnant and had a child. They all had babies. [And] Danielle just got pregnant."

I later learn that Danielle's mother came to Florine Hilson seeking advice when she discovered that Danielle was pregnant. "What would you do if Gabrielle was pregnant by a white boy?" the white mother asked the black mother. "Would you be happy? What would you do?"

On the ride home, Gabrielle says that many of her white friends in Portsmouth are subject to a term she considers offensive: they are called "whiggers"—white niggers. "That is used a lot around here. I know a lot of kids use it at school. It's just another offensive term."

"A lot of black kids or white kids use it?" I ask.

"Both. Everybody. It's just a term, you know, but if somebody says it in my presence, I will quickly inform them, 'please don't say that around me because I don't like that term,' you know. It offends me and it's kind of cruel."

Gabrielle says that she saw her legacy at Smith Academy when she visited her old school in Hatfield last February. As a student there years ago, she pushed for multicultural and black-history displays. When she returned, there were no current students pushing for such, but white teachers and students were eager to show off the black-history bulletin boards done without the heavy presence or influence of African Americans. Progress? I guess. "They said, 'Oh, Gabrielle, come look at our Black History Month [display]. Look what we did this year.' I just felt really great. And I was so happy that they actually did that. At first, they were really ignorant, in a sense—they just had so much to say about black people [but] didn't know them. I went to [a Smith] basketball game at an inner-city school, and my friends were afraid because they had never been to a black school to play. And they said, 'Gabrielle, we're really afraid. Talk black to them.' And I said, 'Is there some language?' and they said, 'You know how to talk to them.' I thought it was just ignorance. But I was afraid that since I was the only black person, something might be said to me or people would hate me because I was the only black person on the cheering team."

Perhaps Gabrielle's tolerance level for "ignorance" must be high in order for her to sanely survive as such a minority and maintain a healthy social life and relationship with peers. Why should she respond to ignorance in an angry and hostile way? Wouldn't such anger and hostility corrupt her own possibilities to experience humanity beyond the borders of race? Yet even without anger, she still obviously assumes responsibility for enlightening those who would ask her to "talk black" to her people. If she becomes consumed with correcting other people's racial naïveté, where is there room for her own humanity to dwell and thrive beyond the color of her skin? Her father finds the answer to that question in Spelman College. But I wonder how she will make the transition from minority to majority, how it will reshape her view of the world, if at all. "How do you think Spelman will change the way you look at things?" I ask her.

"I don't think anything will change the way I look at my friends. We all just have this love relationship. We all just love each other to death. With my friends before in Hatfield, it was the same. We'll walk around and say, 'I love you, I love you,' and we can say that to each other. They're my best friends, no matter what they do."

Chapter 19

The Ebony Towers

THERE'S a Burger King at a crest on Lee Street in southwest Atlanta. The walk or drive down it is a panoramic journey to the ebony towers. College students swagger up and down the hill, many of them with knapsacks bouncing on their backs and Walkman headsets plugged in to their ears. Nearly every possible style of dress—from rugged to casual chic—is represented. Then there are the drivers. You don't hear them or the motors of their cars: both are inundated by the music roaring from their car-stereo speakers. It drowns the hope of hearing any other sound as they pass.

The backdrop of it all is a stereotypical urban stagnation—sparse greenery, cracked sidewalks, a housing project, and old wood-frame houses. There are also the mundane-looking apartment units and the raggedy-looking liquor store that is almost indistinguishable from them at the foot of a concrete hill known as "the Bottom" by generations of college students.

What sits still in places such as the Bottom is inert and defines a community for those who know it only through an urban-planning report. Bloodless pieces of data, however, scream for the context provided by the community's life: those who walk and drive as if they own every piece of this space and make it breathe.

The Burger King and the liquor store are spaces where students and permanent residents of the community are likely to come into shoulder-to-shoulder contact. Many of the residents live in housing projects or old and in some cases neglected houses nestled behind and beyond the six campuses of the Atlanta University Center—Morehouse, Spelman, Clark Atlanta, Morris Brown, Interdenominational Theological Center, and the Morehouse School of Medicine.

From the bottom of the hill, the view ahead away from Burger King is level and looks more like a strip of a college town than does the hill. Academic buildings and dormitories are everywhere I look. The Atlanta University Center Bookstore is two corners away. From the stoplight on that corner, the tranquil campus green of Morehouse College is just across the street. Through tree branches, I see students in lab coats walking from science buildings. Closer to me, a cleanshaven man wearing a bow tie sells *The Final Call,* the newspaper of the Nation of Islam. In 1994, over the objections of many students, the Morehouse administration attempted to bar Minister Louis Farrakhan from speaking on campus.

The trees are majestic for stabilizing the view of tradition. Their branches extend over the preppy, the avant-garde, the hip-hop, the urban chic, the Afrocentric, the junior buppie, the bourgie, and the junior corporate. All of those styles respire into one another and sometimes blow from the same body. Those airs don't carry the sturdiness of trees. But they breathe an excitement that almost turns the memory of two old men into a smoky cloud—and I saw them just a minute ago, before I reached the stoplight on the bookstore corner, as they were walking away from the liquor store. One wore a green plaid shirt that didn't fit him well; the other had on an acrylic sweater despite the Georgia summer being less than a month away. Their skin looked weak and wrinkled—possibly owing to the contents of the brown bags that they carried from the store.

I don't know when the Bottom first earned its name among Atlanta University Center college students. I suspect that it was born in the seventies, in the wake of black middle-class flight from the community. It was not a new term when I entered Morehouse College as a freshman in the fall of 1977; by then it was uttered with the casual comfort that comes with a well-worn phrase.

The faces of people like the two men I saw leaving the liquor store—residents of the community who were not college students—are lost in my memories of Morehouse, the all-men's school across the street from its all-female sister college, Spelman. These people were barely perceptible and nearly invisible from my everyday life as a student. I sped by and around the community when I left and returned to the Morehouse campus. A sense of the neighborhood beyond was shut out of our routines by the rigors and inherently closed nature of campus life. Perhaps this distancing isn't unusual for a campus located close to an economically deprived neighborhood (and so many are). Maybe I notice it now because I teach at New

York University, an urban institution that is almost synonymous with its Greenwich Village neighborhood.

The distance between the schools and the community—even the larger metro area—mirrors many patterns in residential segregation. The Atlanta University Center campuses may be seen as ebony towers situated in a low-income neighborhood. It is easy to find jewels tucked away in an economically deprived neighborhood, but in African-American communities such jewels generally are residences rather than schools—upscale pockets that are separate yet not even blocks away from the other sections that may typify the entire neighborhood in census portraits and outsider perceptions. Many people never think of Hamilton Heights or Striver's Row, for example, when they think of Harlem. And who thinks of Palmer Woods when considering Detroit? Where there's a low-income black community, there's often that pocket of affluence with a world of its own, somehow holding itself aloof from the larger community's despair. And where there is an affluent white community, there's sometimes a small black residential enclave secluded from the larger community, as in the cases of black communities like Sag Harbor in the Hamptons on Long Island or Lake Ivanhoe in Kenosha County, Wisconsin. This pattern stretches from the days of segregation and continues via steering, choice, and tradition. Inevitably, some students of Morehouse and Spelman will graduate into this residential pattern of life.

In looking back on my own days at Morehouse, I remember all of those conversations and discussions in sociology classes, a popular black psychology class, and late-night dormitory bull sessions, in which the problems of the poor were framed in a generic sense, and solutions were tossed around as if we had real answers to the problems of people who lived so close to us. Yet we, or at least I, never stepped into the house of an area resident. Some of us volunteered in tutoring clubs for neighborhood children; some classmates coached Little League teams, but a large number of us didn't know anyone (except fellow students) who lived smack in the community. The world of the Bottom, was one that school protected you from ever having to enter. Still, at the same time, the neighborhood surrounding the campuses was a reminder, false or otherwise, of where a black man or woman without a degree could land. The bachelors of whatever degrees would become another layer to help shield us from ever falling into that place so close yet so far. The message was subtle yet clear: failure as a student could send one tumbling toward life in some bottom—A Different World from the secluded life of a student at the Atlanta University Center and the one that awaited us upon graduation.

The neighborhood wasn't even a major part of our conception of the Atlanta beyond the campus. Who thought of the Bottom when considering the city that earned a national reputation as America's "black Mecca"? Even today, when I read or hear certain Atlanta statistics—crime and poverty rates, for example—I have a hard time measuring them against the Atlanta I knew and know. Students there in the late-seventies saw the city as a golden place where black power seemed so possible and real that the phrase itself wasn't even a part of our common thought or vocabulary. In my first semester in Atlanta, I voted for the first time and volunteered in the campaign that reelected Maynard Jackson, the city's first black mayor, to a second term. Jackson was also an alumnus of Morehouse, and there was little celebrity attached to his presence on campus, because it wasn't abnormal for him and other noted politicians, civil-rights leaders, entrepreneurs, and corporate professionals to lecture in required assemblies or even in some classes. Their presence merely reinforced the idea that we, as ambitious college students, were not pioneers or rare breeds of a race. These men validated our goals and the idea that ambitions for African Americans were not ephemeral dreams that required some kind of magic to realize in the world beyond the natural order of a tree grown on campus.

And if you were leaving campus for Atlanta back then, the Bottom probably wasn't your destination unless you were a pothead or harder drug user popping in and out of a neighborhood location for a buy—which you would bring back to the dormitory to smoke or snort in the comfort of rebellion among friends anyway. If you were leaving campus for Atlanta, you were often going to the Omni, the Lenox Mall, Mr. V's Disco, Ebenezer Baptist Church, or the downtown hotel ballrooms for the many fraternity-, sorority-, and student organization–sponsored parties with themes that trigger chuckles at reunions today: the Cold Climax, the Fly Affair, the Black and Gold, and so forth.

We had not come to college with the kind of mission that claimed the attention of students who were here a decade before us. Their idealism drove them to the civil-rights and black-power movements, through which they endeavored to change the world. In contrast, we were idealistic about the world that had been changed—how much was always debatable—for us.

There was no real movement for us to join. Some of us studied students of the past in a political-science class entitled Black Protest, but we saw our education largely as preparation to enter worlds that the subjects of that class knocked open. Atlanta reflected the hope of that openness, and not just for us. It was the dawn of the era when black professionals scrambled to get to Atlanta, and their presence helped suburban De Kalb County grow into one of the wealthiest black zip codes in the country.

A black professional class is not new to Atlanta, however, because traditionally, many graduates of the schools now in the Atlanta University Center
nurtured and grew the city's professional class by settling there upon graduation. The community existed during segregation before the civil-rights
movement, with entrepreneurs, teachers, physicians, and attorneys just like
today, only not just in Dekalb. Then, the neighborhood around the Atlanta
University Center was home to some of the city's professional elite. But
with integration, they fled the area, many not moving to integrated neighborhoods but to newly established black subdivisions in the suburbs.

What was relatively new in 1977, and not just for Atlanta, was the developing black corporate class, which swelled as business became the most
popular major at Morehouse. Looking back, though, we were not totally
me-generation children obnoxiously dreaming of a "buppie" (black urban
professional) heaven invented *for us*. We were grounded by our knowledge that racism doesn't die with a degree, career, or business: in assemblies, lectures, and classes, there were always reminders that the struggle for
racial justice was ongoing. You could even see the truth of that lesson if you
traveled into some predominantly white parts of the metro area.

In my senior year, the city was torn by the serial murders of young black
boys in the city, and I remember a student protest on the steps of City Hall
calling for more attention to the killings. There was also a legendary veteran
of the black-power movement roaming the campus. Actually, he was more
of a legend to us, and not for his accomplishments so much as his wander-
ing about the campuses screaming "Pan-Africanism" and offering handouts.
We generally nodded politely, smiled at him with respect, and often
laughed the minute we left his eyesight. He didn't always command respect. I do remember a student, who today is a minister of a large inner-city
church, punching the activist for pointing with joy to the "African" roots apparent in the would-be minister's facial features.

That confrontation and the kind of conflicts highlighted in Morehouse
alumnus Spike Lee's movie *School Daze* are anomalies in my memories of
Morehouse, and they fade, like the faces of the two men I saw exiting the
liquor store in the Bottom. They fail to diminish the reverie that materializes
yet still surprises me every time I return to Atlanta. Just as I am passing the
campus green, I begin to remember the fresh excitement of youth in the
first years of adulthood. I even come as close as I probably can to feeling
the vigor of that period in my life. Most or any discomforts of that time escape my memory, and though I am generally a realist, I become a romantic
when I see the campus and memories of that time play through my mind.

I can't remember when I first learned that a Morehouse or Spelman existed. I do remember my mother mentioning the schools during my sophomore year in high school, telling me that Martin Luther King Jr. was a Morehouse graduate. A year later, I was studying in the cafeteria of my predominantly white high school when the idea of Morehouse really hit me. Another student, Greg Griffin, now a Democrat-turned-Republican lawyer and party operative in Montgomery, Alabama, told me that he was going to the school that educated Martin Luther King. Greg, who was a year ahead of me, was the closest thing to a radical that my high school had to offer. In one of those ten-years-from-now columns in the student newspaper, the editors predicted that Greg would be cleaning the ashes left by the cross burned on his front yard the previous night. On one trip home to Raleigh a few years ago, I picked up *The Carolinian,* the black newspaper in which I first read about Henry McKoy's candidacy. This time, there was an article on Greg's challenge of the racially exclusionary rules of an Alabama country club.

Greg was smart and boisterous, a rebel who introduced controversy into the status quo wherever he went. He challenged whites at Garner Senior High School and blacks at Morehouse. When he ran for student offices at each, most students voted for or against Greg—not on other candidates' merits. I have to struggle to remember his opponents. At Morehouse one year, he initially lost a race for student-body president, but a few days after the election, discovered an irregularity in the voting and forced a second election. He won an upset victory that angered his opposition, which speculated that he helped create the irregularity in the first place.

In the cafeteria at my high school that day, Greg handed me a Morehouse brochure. I glanced at the description of the school and was immediately impressed when I saw the graduates listed—Julian Bond, Maynard Jackson, Lerone Bennett—along with a host of other convincing statistics about the representation of graduates in various professions. I found out more, and the school became my first choice.

The some five hundred men in my freshman class chose Morehouse nearly a decade before Bill Cosby wore a Morehouse T-shirt or made casual references to "the Morehouse man" on *The Cosby Show.* We chose the school before *Cosby* spinoff *A Different World* popularized the black college life of the post–civil-rights era. The twelve hundred women across the street at Spelman chose the school a decade before Bill Cosby's $20 million gift to the school drew national attention. We all chose the schools before media coverage lifted the image of black colleges above survival and struggle into an attractive possibility. At the time, in fact, black colleges were not widely regarded as places where young adults could learn and grow beyond the boundaries of race. In a sense, we lived in the secluded world that became the popular and attractive option among families like the Hilsons and the N'Namdis.

We also chose Morehouse before the Berkeley affirmative-action scare, the *Bakke* case that challenged race-based admission policies at University of California at Davis Medical School. *Bakke* didn't strike until my junior year. Opportunities at predominantly white schools were abundant when we were college applicants. Thus, we were an eclectic collection of black men and women. Some could have gone anywhere but chose Morehouse and Spelman despite being courted by schools considered to be the best. There were among us, of course, those who were just barely above-average students but still had collections of invitations to apply to liberal arts colleges, second-tier private schools, and leading state universities. There were also average students—the kind of underachievers that the black college experience is famous for lifting beyond mediocrity. Those underachievers probably couldn't get accepted at Morehouse today because of admission standards raised by massive increases in applications over the past decade. Nevertheless, in the seventies, even underachievers too had other choices: there were many state and community colleges after them, and even some more-selective, super affirmative action–driven schools offering money and remedial programs.

So why did we choose this different world at a time when most predominantly white schools were at their most inviting moment in history? The answers are as diverse as our class. There were many children of black college life among us, upper-middle-class students that Morehouse and Spelman were notorious for attracting. Some grew up hearing Morehouse and Spelman in the way that Marcia McKoy heard A&T. Others, myself included, could look at the branches of their family trees and see products of historically black schools that no longer carried the cachet they once possessed; Morehouse and Spelman were among the few academically viable options where one could carry on the tradition of black college life. Some were first-generation college students, children of the working-middle-class families that raised a large share of today's black corporate class. For many students, particularly if they were northerners who did not have a family connection to black colleges, there was a black guidance counselor, teacher, or mentor who steered them into this world. If they were from the South, they were immune to the negative images held elsewhere of black colleges, because the schools historically have played a dynamic role in Southern black communities. In a sense, these Southern students' perceptions of the black college were independent of the mainstream view in the same way that Detroit carries different meanings in black and white middle-class minds.

Tradition aside, I do not remember being drawn to Morehouse solely because it was a historically black college. I do not recall choosing the school as an escape from my educational experiences in predominantly white institutions for all but two years—kindergarten and first grade, when I attended PS 134 in Hollis, Queens. I am sure that played a part, perhaps subconsciously, in my choice. But I do not remember myself or my college classmates speaking of this place as merely a refuge from a mean world of whiteness. In conversations with classmates years later, we all acknowledge the richness of our experience owed in large measure to our being free to learn and grow socially without the burdens of race. But such a notion wasn't a large, conscious part of my thinking when I chose Morehouse.

Today, many students choosing black colleges are trying to escape the complications of race or to capture a family tradition, as in the case of Marcia McKoy or that of sons of Morehouse fathers, who are known to hear a warning: "You can go to college anywhere you want, but my money goes to Morehouse." Aside from legacies like that, Morehouse and Spelman, by the mid-eighties, grew into the black middle-class solution to tensions instigated by integration. I discovered this in 1989 when I wrote a piece on enrollment increases at select black colleges and heard student after student not only proclaim the virtue of this kind of experience but speak of how they chose this environment specifically so that they could have a time to swim in their own river. "I think it's very difficult to be in America and not have some level of discomfort around the issue of race, particularly being a male," says George N'Namdi, whose son, Jumaane, is a Morehouse freshman at the time of this visit in 1994. "I think you always have that level. I think what I am seeing now is that people in my age group, the first group of baby boomers, were somewhat radical. Then, my age group, they came into some of your biggest corporate jobs, which most people started interpreting as 'I made it, now I am going to make sure my kids make it. So therefore, for them to make it, I'm going to put them in a primarily European environment. That's where you make it.' Well, they can be in a European environment with a different attitude, too. But what's happening [is that] now my age group is saying, 'We got to get these kids to Morehouse and Spelman, now those schools like Morehouse have eight hundred slots and they get four thousand applicants,' it's like, wow, because they see something missing. They worry that the kids will see themselves as 'the other,' and everything they [parents] have worked to give them will be meaningless."

N'Namdi says if their children see themselves as "the other," they are more likley to shortchange their goals and attitude. In some ways, parents and students who gravitate toward black colleges are rebelling against one-way integration, in which blending in is the black man's burden. They are rejecting a manner of thinking that deems the sting of desegregation's thorns to be worth enduring for the prize of a party—integration—that promises a hangover. The choices presented almost seem too safe to be American (and black). They are clearly too surreal for a black fatalist or racial pessimist, who sees black failure as the only possibility in America, or who sees racism as eternal in defining the black experience, save everything but a revolution. This is a world that promotes the immortality of the race without having to win a race war. It is never stated directly but nevertheless comes through clearly in the habit, or the way of life developed over four years. Those who digest this unique experience expect to acquire the American comforts and to face challenges that are equal to their intelligence, which isn't uncommon among black college students anywhere. But to take that expectation as a given is itself rare and foreign to many Americans' (and even black Americans') thought.

There's a reverence for tradition that runs strongly through the African-American middle-class and upper-middle-class cultures. The threats of racism, real and imagined, make many American blacks live cautiously: sometimes the risks required for (certain) potential successes are just too great to take. As a result, tradition, or anything tried and true, becomes almost sacred. Of course, this aversion to risk isn't universal in black culture and, one hopes, will die in time. Many black heroes achieved their renown at least in part because they rejected steering the safe course. Even among the less well known, risk has its values: Carmen N'Namdi is an example of the risk taker. Still, most black private elementary and secondary schools, Nataki excluded, appeal to largely working-class and lower-middle-class families whose only educational options are troubled inner-city schools or overly pricey traditional private schools. In fact, Carmen N'Namdi, whose school attracted a healthy number of upper-middle-class families, says that it was still difficult attracting many black professional parents because those families tended to prefer more established, elite schools in the Detroit area. And some of those parents who bypassed Nataki now have children at Morehouse and Spelman, due to the same attraction to tradition and the tried and true that drew them to established, predominantly white elementary and secondary schools.

The traditions do not always originate in one's own experiences. For example, the Hilsons and the N'Namdis are not the only Morehouse and Spelman parents who attended predominantly white colleges.

I do not discount the value that students here place on finding a world where they don't have to be on a mission to upset stereotypes or prove their literacy, where a mistake can be a mistake—not evidence of a substandard culture. This environment does help one learn to live and exist independent of baggage imposed by stereotypes or racism. But when race isn't there to produce discord, something else—class, politics, even personality—will. Conflict is human and inevitable.

Many African Americans I hear complaining of racism are not as critical of classism, and I wonder if this stems from their belief that they have earned their way into the middle or upper-middle class through education and hard work, while those who didn't allowed racism to determine their fate. As I reflect on the families I've encountered on this journey across the country, a common trait among them is a fundamental belief in the values of American meritocracy. Even if they conclude that those values are undermined by racism, they believe in playing by the rules of middle-class life. From Sarah Johnson Sow and Henry McKoy to Carmen N'Namdi, the Hilsons, and Stephen Smith this was consistent. Yet to varying degrees, they also resent the system for allowing whites to cheat with racism. Still, despite that, like Detroit's Dexter Fields, many blacks are as tired as whites are of hearing blacks complain about racism. The difference is that blacks, like Fields, Joshua, and Flora Young, who are tired of race whiners, do not discount the impact of racism, as many whites do—they merely see a preoccupation with it as crippling and dehumanizing.

At the same time, many African Americans admire whites, like Bill Clinton, whose hands, like theirs, may be marked by bootstraps. They place whites who remain on lower socioeconomic levels in a category well below low-income African Americans because whites of that strata didn't have to deal with the baggage of racism yet still are failures. In the black mind, these must be truly inferior people.

I pull into a parking space in the lot in the back of Spelman's campus. There are only two legal entrances to the school, and I walk around to the front gate. As I do, I begin to remember how people found creative ways to get on this campus after midnight, when men are supposed to vanish. Some jumped over a high brick wall, and with the help of their girlfriends, were smuggled into the dormitories. I recall a night when I lay covered by a blanket in the backseat of a car as my girlfriend and a friend who played lookout drove on campus at midnight.

At Spelman, rules are strict when compared to many other campuses. Curfews for first-semester freshmen are still in place—12:00 midnight on weeknights and 2:00 A.M. on weekends. Men (and probably suspicious-looking women) must show identification to security guards before being allowed on campus. At some hours, non-Spelman students must leave their IDs at the gate with the guard and pick them up on their way out. Men are barred from Spelman dormitory rooms unless they are signed in during "calling hours," which run from six in the evening to midnight. The ghosts of old-fashioned courtship still haunt the campus, too; the word *caller* is a common part of the vocabulary. When one visits a student—a "lady"—one must stop at her dorm's front desk. From there, the work-study student on duty contacts the resident through the intercom: "Deborah, you have a caller." If the lady does not sign you up to her room, the two of you sit in a dormitory lounge. Most of the lounges, with large couches and the occasional piano, resemble large parlor rooms.

The customs impose a Victorian veneer on relationships, but it is too superficial to prevent eighteen- to twenty-three-year-olds from engaging in that word that Arthur Hilson had such trouble saying: *sex.* The school clearly must recognize this, because Spelman's health services freely issues condoms to students. (Spelman is perhaps more realistic in this regard than some of its alumnae, who in 1994 protested the condom distribution, according to Dr. Glenda Price, provost of the college at the time of my visit, who is now president of Marygrove College.)

It fits tradition that Spelman—the only all-women's school of the Atlanta University Center—is the only closed campus. The same strict rules did not apply at Morehouse, at least during my student days. Women were free to spend the night in all but one dormitory, where the director, whose sexuality was the source of speculation and gossip, would sometimes chase women out.

I leave my ID with the guard. Just past the gate, construction is under way on a new building to be named for Camille Cosby. I am scheduled to meet Gabrielle Hilson at the student center in the middle of campus. On one side of the center is a circular, tree-shaded driveway winding between an island of grass and a collection of academic buildings and dormitories. The other side, with newer buildings, is more concrete than green and more sunny on a good day.

I wait in the student center's snack bar. Couples sit together; loners huddle over their books. Then there is the other daytime fixture of this all-women's college: a cluster of young men laughing and watching women. Some traditions don't die with generations. I begin to see faces that look too familiar for this to be a sane moment.

I almost do not recognize Gabrielle Hilson as she approaches me. She has new wire-rim glasses and braided hair extensions that trail down her back. "I didn't do this for politics or anything," she says, referring to her braids. "I just saw this hairstyle and liked it and got someone here who does it to do it for me."

There are signs in the student center advertising a community meeting to discuss Atlanta in the wake of Freaknik, the annual gathering in the city of tens of thousands of black college students and young adults from across the country. City officials have tried to discourage the event, and many Atlanta residents consider it a nuisance. (One year after my visit, Freaknik grabbed national headlines when youths vandalized stores in response to an inhospitable Atlanta resisting their presence.) The sign in the student center says that the community meeting will focus on alleged misogyny and mistreatment of women at Freaknik.

"Some crazy stuff happened at Freaknik," says Gabrielle, going on to explain that many of the attendees from out of town see the event as a chance to rebel and run amok, since they are away from home or their college campuses. "Basically, I just walked around. I had enough clothes on so that nobody would try anything—I knew girls that were stripping, guys were stripping, having sex in the back of cars. You know, everything was out in the open. And I was there. I went to a show Friday night, and I hung out at West End. I have never seen that many black people in my life. It was really heaven."

Obviously, Gabrielle's nightmares are gone. "People were very friendly during Freaknik. I didn't understand when they had all the news hype about it before and they said Freaknik is bad and it's not good that black people do this, or black people do that. People were not bad. They were so friendly, they were like, 'Well, it's Freaknik, come over here and give me a hug.' The girls that were a little more revealing, they got harassed. They got humiliated. It was not a big, smoking, drinking fest. And the black people would just chill, you know. I think a lot depended on how you were dressed. Most guys were like, 'Give me a hug, can I have a picture with you,' and it wasn't anybody, like, grabbing my butt or anything.

"Jessica really wanted to come down and visit . . . she wanted to be here for Freaknik and see what was going on. But Jessica is the kind of person that I would have to keep an eye on, because she would probably be over at Morehouse, more than I would. She would know just as many people, if not more. You know, she's a wild one. But she would love it down here. She would be the kind that would fit in.

"They [Jessica and Danielle] loved my braids at Christmas. Both of them love black people. Anything that has to do with black people, they love it. I really don't have to put up a face for them. If I'm talking some sort of slang, they want to pick it up. They say, 'You learned that in school.'

"When I went home for Christmas, it felt so different to be around them. Their lives are so much more serious than mine. Here, my friends, we sit around and watch cartoons and dress up and pretend to be Diana Ross and the Supremes in the hallway and play. We don't have the kinds of responsibilities that Danielle has with a baby. When I saw them at Christmas, I saw I wasn't as grown up as they were anymore. It sounds kind of weird. When I got home, they were like, well, 'Let's go out with the guys, we're going out drinking,' and I was like no, let's sit down, relax, and watch some Bugs Bunny cartoons or something. I was real laxed about a lot of things. I was all about having fun when I got home, and they were all about getting older.

"Jerry is now living in Danielle's house. I really don't know a lot about their relationship. I try not to ask too much, but he's living in the house with Danielle's mom and her. Danielle's mom has gotten around to where she accepts it. She loves the baby. She doesn't really like Jerry, but Jerry drives her car. His parents are in Arizona. They want him to take the baby. I don't think they've really accepted it yet. But, you know, I think they are doing a little bit for him and the child. I think Danielle is supposed to go there over the summer.

"Danielle is doing well in school. I am really proud of her, because I know when we first met her, she didn't care, and now she's doing so much better. She's making honor roll. I think she's graduating with honors. She's pulled herself right up. I think that's wonderful. I think she's only going to UNH next year."

Gabrielle herself expects to make the dean's list. She earned a 3.7 grade-point average last semester and expects to do just as well this time. There's one course giving her trouble—Introduction to Sociology. Understandably, she no longer wants to major in sociology and become a social worker. She's considering majoring in economics and pursuing a career in hotel management. This followed a visit to a Hyatt in Atlanta where a relative worked. "I'm real excited about hotels," she enthuses. "I love the hotels now. When I went to the Hyatt, I thought this would be a really nice thing to do. It's nice. There's a lot of stuff you can do in hotel management. It's busy all the time."

From the window of the student center, we begin to see large numbers of women walking toward the tree-shaded side of campus that houses most of the academic buildings. Gabrielle knows it's close to eleven o'clock. She grabs her knapsack, and I follow her to sociology class.

Gabrielle is dressed casually, in jeans, like one would expect of a college student. At the same time, I look at the other women walking to class and remember another aspect of this life—fashion consciousness. I see young women in stylish tops, neat makeup, and well-coiffed hair. Some are even dressed as if they are going to an office on Wall Street.

Gabrielle takes a seat in the back of the class, next to a friend from Milwaukee. The classroom is full of young women when the professor, Dr. Bruce Wade, a shaven-headed man wearing a blue blazer, enters with a formality that ends the small talk and chitchat. He distributes graded exams. Gabrielle frowns and shows me the paper, which becomes yet another reason why she wants to change her major. She received a 79.

The topic of the class today is social stratification, and the lecture and discussion focus on readings and *Roger and Me,* a documentary on life in Flint, Michigan, in the wake of a local General Motors plant shutdown. "The examples of gender stratification in the film were subtle," says Wade to the class. "They were there. One of the more open examples had to do with the position of women in the management structure. . . . Roger Smith and most of the elite members of that hierarchy or that management structure were white males. Most of the females were in subordinate positions or in middle management. And that is very much related to the concept of stratification.

"We also saw examples of gender stratification in terms of what was happening to some of the families that were affected by the mass layoffs of General Motors. We've talked earlier about the feminization of poverty. The fastest-growing group of people faced with poverty would be women and their children. This would be a function of divorce, but also some other factors. In the film, we saw the harsh impact of the layoffs and how the single parents were impacted very harshly by those layoffs."

Wade, who speaks in a deep, distinctive baritone, centers most of the discussion around the large sociological issues in the case study. It has very limited direct connections to African Americans, but at the end of the discussion, he shifts the focus and asks students if there are any ideas from the film and readings regarding stratification that apply specifically to African Americans.

The hands of students shoot to the ceiling. They cite examples of social stratification among African Americans—according to skin tone, money, family background. The divide between the Spelman campus and its neighborhood doesn't find its way into the examples. Gabrielle and her friend are both quiet throughout. When the class ends, a number of students flock to Wade to discuss their papers and the readings. Gabrielle and her friend leave the class.

"So, what did you all think of the class?" I ask.

"I was sleepy," says her friend.

"Yeah, I don't know," says Gabrielle. "It might be his voice. It's just so relaxing. Sometimes I get tired of sitting there and just thinking of why society does things. I can do that on my own. I want to get into more career-oriented classes."

The "just do it" credo of contemporary American youth breeds an impatience with intellectual critiques of society, which may seem irrelevant to

more pressing "career-oriented" pursuits. I initially discard Gabrielle's glib
dismissal of sociology class as a reflection of her stage in life. Years from
now, she'll see such discussions as a long-gone luxury and regard her failure to appreciate them as an eighteen-year-old as a moment wasted by the
impulses of youth. But a few minutes later, I find that she isn't entirely
squandering this opportunity: when I ask about her new life at Spelman,
she refers immediately to a quote from one of her sociology class's tests, Du
Bois's *The Souls of Black Folk:*

> [T]his double-consciousness, this sense of always looking at one's self
> through the eyes of others, of measuring one's soul by the tape of a world
> that looks on in amused contempt and pity. One ever feels his twoness,
> an American, a Negro; two souls, two thoughts, two un-reconciled striv-
> ings; two warring ideas in one dark body, whose dogged strength alone
> keeps it from being torn asunder.

She doesn't repeat the quote, but she's given it much thought. "When I
read that, I was like, 'It's true, you do have to put on another face for white
America, but you don't want to lose your Afrocentric views,'" she says. "We
have a double consciousness. I mean, as of right now, black people right now
can't all be Afrocentric. They've had people from businesses and corporations
come in. Some of them went to Spelman. They tell us how to make it up the
corporate ladder, and you can't have braids—or they would have to be really
small. Don't wear African clothing. These are African-American people who
come in to tell us how to make it in the corporate world.

"I don't think Spelman knows exactly what it wants us to learn. Spelman
wants us to learn our black heritage, but still we have to fit into white America. It's not a thin line.

"It seems they say you can't make it anywhere without being Eurocentric, and I don't like that fact. I'm starting to think that African Americans
should try and build their own nation. I mean, don't go back to Africa—
we've been raised in a Eurocentric society, [and] we've kind of assimilated
to it, but we need to learn that we need to take care of our brothers and sisters. You can't totally live by Eurocentrism. I really get tired of hearing the
European man's way of thinking. Whatever we do is wrong. The black
woman being in a family by herself, that's wrong. . . . I see it as we really
have to start working for ourselves. Actually put our money back into the
black community. Work for ourselves. We talk about that sometimes, but a
lot of women here don't really see it that way."

I now struggle to reconcile the two Gabrielles—the one on the porch in
New Hampshire and the one with braids. Gabrielle appears to have difficulty

reconciling what I would call her emerging nationalism, which is perhaps a stage, with her eighteen years of relative comfort. She is also unsettled by some class readings that highlight harrowing statistics of black life. When she looks up from the books, she sees herself and her classmates, and their lives do not resemble the texts. "I didn't realize that if you look closely, we, as African-American people, haven't made that much progress as a whole, if you look at a lot of statistics. There are still forces oppressing us, and sometimes it's hard for me to believe, looking at the way I grew up and looking at the way a lot of my friends here grew up. Look at them. . . . But you look at . . . even me and other people here, my friends at Morehouse, [and] you really don't know or see some of the problems that you see in statistics."

Gabrielle's experience demonstrates that one cannot escape the uneasy questions of race and class in America even in ebony towers like Morehouse and Spelman. To do so, in fact, would undermine the very purpose of a liberal arts education. And in following Gabrielle for three hours today, I see that she has come much closer to facing unsettling questions about her own experiences and how they diverge from others'. I wonder if she's in a safer yet more stimulating place to consider those questions than would be offered in New Hampshire or at Oberlin, where her black guidance counselor suggested she attend. I think she is, but, as a product of this environment, my answer carries a clear bias.

The more she talks, the more impressed I become with how clearly she is seeing conflicts and contradictions, and the more I see the sociology class influencing her thought and ideas. As a professor, I've seen that it is often the quietest students in a class who are the most reflective and, as papers indicate, in many cases absorb more of the reading and lectures.

Gabrielle now easily filters seemingly race-neutral ideas through the prism of the black experience. She recalls a study that the sociology class read, comparing the attitudes of college women in the 1940s and the 1990s. The study, as expected, found that college women of the nineties were less likely to "play dumb" to please men, an idea Gabrielle finds irrelevant to her own experience. "As far as black women go, you can't play dumb. You can't be a dumb blonde because you have to be good at what you do. White women know they can act silly and get away with it, because society is there to protect them. They have nothing to lose by playing dumb. We, as African-American women, have something to lose."

"What do you have to lose?" I ask.

"If I tried to act like a dumb blonde, I'd get called out faster than a white woman. People would say, 'She's a stupid black person; they're expected to act dumb.'"

A Spelman Sophomore

GABRIELLE Hilson rarely drinks. Still, she creates what she calls a "wet bar" on the walls of her sophomore-year room: She collects Bacardi rum advertisements and displays them. She also plasters the walls with perfume advertisements and pictures of Nantucket and Zimbabwe that she's cut from a travel magazine.

She's moved off campus because she missed a deadline for on-campus housing applications. Now she lives in a boarding house near campus. It is an old, comfortable wood-frame house with spacious rooms and hardwood floors. She has her own room there; the other residents are a collection of students—many of them fellow Spelman women. They are free of the campus rules. Men are now men—not callers.

"My first year, I was a little excited because I met a whole bunch of different people and I was off on my own," says Gabrielle. "But I was skeptical to do anything and still had the parents over me. And then in my second year, I was like, 'Okay, I'm gone. I can get out and do what I want to,' and I was basically excited about everything about being out there the first week. I had lost some weight. I was cute. I was more attractive to everyone. So, it was like, 'This is fun, you know?'"

She's changed her major to economics and doesn't want to just manage a hotel: she now wants to own one and is looking to a career in investment banking as a step toward that goal. "Sociology never really coincided with what I always wanted to do," she tells me during a brief visit that semester. "And what I wanted to do is own a business. And I've talked to people about building the hotel. Some students that I know want to be architects. I mean, I'm in the business aspect, but I do know students who can be my accountants or whatever, you know. I mean, it's kind of a dream, but hopefully I can make it."

She also makes a new set of friends this year; two of the three come from more-affluent, upper-middle-class families. The four shop together, go to parties, frown over exams and paper deadlines. On the surface, it looks like the ideal and balanced life for a nineteen-year-old with ambitions, dreams, and goals—good school, good friends, and good parties. But when we talk about it a year later, Gabrielle says it didn't feel right. Looking back at the period, her experiences don't feel as if they belong to her: "I can't even think of a major bad part about it," she tells me in this later talk, "but it just wasn't what I was . . . what I was used to. It probably was that I was homesick. Like, I just wanted to be home . . . be able to just kind of call on my parents whenever I need to and all that kind of stuff. So maybe it was the fact that I wasn't exactly ready, or something like that. I really felt out of place. . . . It was just a feeling that I had that it wasn't the place for me."

She finds herself going to more and more parties but feeling more and more like going home. "You do what everybody else does. You went out and partied and all that kind of stuff. And I've never actually been one to go out and party, you know? I haven't been a big social person all my life. So it was a lot different for me, I think. You know, it was something new to me, 'cause I hadn't done it often, and then I was starting to do it and . . . you realize that even though you never did it before, it's not necessarily something that you want to do."

She says that her friends were not snobs, but they assume that she can shop like they do—anytime. "You had to have money when you go out with them. I didn't always have money. Their parents were giving them money to go out and everything. They didn't seem to have any problem as far as affording Spelman. It was like, 'Okay, we're going to Spelman and we can go home whenever we want to and we can call long distance every night to talk to California,' or, you know, wherever they lived, and it's no big deal, and, you know, 'Let's go shopping today, Mom sent me the credit card.' And I would say, 'I spent all my money. Sorry.'"

In addition to Gabrielle, a second girl among the four didn't come from a background as affluent as the other two either, but her circumstances were unique. "She had a rough year too. Her father was murdered while she was in the house last summer. Her brother was a musician, so they had a benefit concert, and her mother would send her money. All the money from the benefit concert went to her. She had all that in her bank account, so she was set for the whole year. So, financially, she was okay. But there were days where she, of course, was going to have it hard. She was at home when her father and brother were murdered. But [during the summer] all her mother would do is say, 'Well, why don't you go out shopping?' So she went out shopping. She would say, 'Come on, Gabrielle, let's go out shopping.' I'd be like, 'Okay. I have no money, but I'll pretend like I do. You're having a bad day, let's go out shopping.'

"They were my good friends and they could do that. At that time, it probably made me feel a little bad that I couldn't do it."

During sophomore year she also begins to face another issue that she realizes she was unprepared to confront: sex. While Arthur Hilson thought that he was sending a virgin to Spelman, Gabrielle had actually had one sexual experience before college, in her sophomore year in high school at Smith Academy. It was with a white classmate, and started with kissing and petting, and she thought that she wanted to go further. But as they progressed, she said, "Stop." The boy, however, didn't. "I wasn't probably as afraid as I was probably curious, and then very regretful afterward. You hear so much about that kind of experience, and you think that it's supposed to be wonderful and joyous and then it's a letdown."

Then, during her freshman year at Spelman, she found herself reliving that experience three times. It begins with kissing. When it progresses, she says stop—but her partner refuses. "You don't really want to. You don't know how to get out of the situation, so you just kind of let things happen, thinking that maybe it's supposed to. So I remember there were times where I thought, 'I don't want to be here, but I already got myself here.'"

During the spring semester of her sophomore year, she has a crush on a Morehouse student. Later she overhears him telling another guy that he's not at all interested in her. "He was interested in someone else. And so I found that out and was like, 'Okay, that's it for you. Forget him, I'll find somebody else.' The first person I found happened to be the father of my child."

The father to be, also a sophomore, invites her to his apartment in midtown Atlanta on a Saturday night. She takes buses and trains to get there. At first, he fixes her a drink, which she doesn't want. "He tried to get me drunk. Orange juice and some kind of liquor. Probably gin. I don't know.

"I sipped it, but not enough of it, you know? I barely drank it, and he kept trying to get me to. But I don't like alcohol that much."

He turns on the TV. "Something was wrong with the cable. It was broken."

He turns off the TV and kisses her. "First, it was kind of mutual, because it was real innocent, like the whole situation. It wasn't a big deal. And I started getting in over my head, and I was like, 'Hold on, stop,' and all this kind of stuff.

"I remember his face being really angry and mad when I was saying stop. It's not like he didn't hear me or anything. I didn't know what to do."

She gives in. "Afterward, the buses weren't running anymore. . . . I wasn't going to walk home, so I . . . went to sleep. In the morning, I got up to catch the first bus. And he asked me if I wanted to stay. I told him no and went and got on the bus and went home. I never saw him again."

Before she realizes she's pregnant, she decides to transfer to the University of New Hampshire. She doesn't know how she will inform her parents that she wants to leave the school they are so proud to see her attend. But when she returns home, she discovers that there is something far more serious to tell them.

Home

URHAM, New Hampshire, is a college town, a mixture of academic buildings, small stores, fast-food establishments, copy shops, dormitories, and tree-shaded houses.

Gabrielle, seven months pregnant, is walking on campus, carrying three heavy books—one from a hotel-management class. She politely refuses my offer to help her carry them.

"Even though I am having a child, I haven't stopped going to school," she says. "I haven't stopped having goals.

"At first, I thought people would come down harder on me than anybody else, but that's really not the case. Everybody has been more than supportive. They've already started to bring things over. They said, 'Whatever you need, give us a call.' I think people would probably be harder on me if I was constantly doing bad things, but like I said, this was a shock for everyone because this is not something that they're used to me doing. I was not the kind of person that would be wild and stuff like that. So it's kind of like they view this as a mistake that happened. It's not that the child that's coming is a mistake. That's actually a blessing."

But Gabrielle does admit that Jessica and Danielle had difficulty accepting the news. "It was rough. I waited and told Danielle and Jessica just Friday night. I had seen them only a few times before since I've been back. They couldn't tell I was pregnant then. I just told them and the first thing out of their mouths was, 'You're the preacher's daughter. You're Gabrielle. You don't do this kind of stuff. This is for us to do.'"

Gabrielle has not had a conversation with the father of her child since their encounter. "There's not really a way for me to get in touch with him. I did try and call him. By the time I had gotten a number, though, he had moved. The person on the phone didn't know where he was and thought either somewhere else in Georgia or he moved back to Chicago.

"I do think that it's unfair that he has a child and does not know. Once I tell him, I'm not going to tell him that I have his child and he needs to do this and that. I'm telling him, 'This is your child and you need to know this and whether or not you choose to do something about it or not, that's up to you.'

"It was something that we both did, and I think everyone needs to know whether or not they have a child on this earth. If I can get in touch with him, if I can find him, I will definitely tell him. So if I can find him, or when I do find him, he will know. But I'm not expecting anything from him: I'm not going to find him to tell him that he is solely responsible and he needs to give me money and do this and that, no."

Gabrielle says that a recent lecture at Dartmouth College (Gabrielle traveled there with a group of fellow students) by feminist scholar bell hooks reinforced her inclination not to devote too much energy to pursuing a commitment from the father of her child. "She said the child does not need, per se, a biological father in the home. They need a loving male figure in the home. People are always putting this emphasis on [the absence of the father]. But there's a lot of children out there who have uncles and grandfathers and all that, people who are there for that child who are good influences on that child; that's what the child needs. They don't need anybody who's negative in their life."

Gabrielle didn't really need hooks to help her understand those ideas: Gabrielle lived them in her own family life. She doesn't call Arthur Hilson her stepfather—she knows him as her father, just as his stepfather was the father he knew. "My father and I are almost exactly alike," she says. "People notice it. The way we talk to people. I mean, it's just to the point [that] people, even my friends, will say they don't see how a parent and child can be so similar and not to have a biological bond."

"I had heard her at Spelman," Gabrielle says, referring to hooks. "I thought she'd be just as good at Dartmouth. But she wasn't as intense as she was at Spelman. She wasn't as dynamic. It was a totally different audience, I think. At Spelman, she could pretty much speak freely. Here she was talking about feminism and racism and how they intertwined, and when you're talking to a bunch of white people, it's a different tide.

"I mean, she was so soft-spoken. She was firm in what she was saying, but [it was] the way she said it—it didn't sound like she was really driving at the points. She didn't really speak as controversially as she did at Spelman. At Spelman, she just broke everything down. She had everybody in an uproar about black movies and sexism and all kinds of stuff. People were just so excited. I guess whenever she goes to Spelman, she puts on this really great show."

Gabrielle discovered that she was pregnant when she returned home from Spelman last May. A few days later, her parents returned from a vacation in the Poconos. "I didn't know how to tell them. We were watching a movie. As a matter of fact, the young girl on the TV, she was pregnant and she had run away. I couldn't even watch the end of the movie in front of them. So I went upstairs . . . I don't remember the title of it, but I went upstairs and watched the rest in my room and went to sleep. My mom came in the next morning and I couldn't stop crying, and I told her. She sent me to work, and when I came home that night, she sat down with me and told me that we couldn't really keep this from my father. She said it wasn't something that she needed to tell him—she said it was something that I needed to tell him. So we brought him in and I told him that night.

"My dad, sometimes he'll yell. If you get on his nerves, he'll yell. But this was a sensitive situation, so I couldn't see him yelling. I had no idea what his reaction would be, but I knew somehow that he wouldn't yell at me. I knew my mom wouldn't yell at me. It would just be something that would be hard to take. I mean, it's just as hard for them to take as it was for me, maybe even harder because I wasn't used to being in this situation. I was used to just being in a situation where I was perfect—not to say that I never did anything wrong, but in a lot of people's eyes, I really didn't do too much wrong. I did those little silly things wrong. I never did anything major. They couldn't see me doing anything major . . . and this is not a little thing.

"It was, of course, a shock to them. I knew they'd take it hard. I didn't see anything harsh coming at me, though. I knew I wasn't going to get kicked out. I knew that they wouldn't say they weren't going to support me."

"I suppose I've shed a tear or two," says Arthur Hilson as he sits in the pastor's study.

Two Sundays after his daughter told him she was pregnant, Reverend Hilson was in the pulpit delivering the toughest pastoral remarks of his life: he announced his daughter's pregnancy to the congregation. "I informed the church that my daughter was awaiting birth. I told them although it was nothing I approved of, I certainly love my daughter and support her, and I wanted them to know that that's what it was. I felt the important thing to do was to be up front before they see her suddenly put on weight. I put it up front from day one, as soon as I discovered."

"Did you worry about the reaction from the congregation?" I ask.

"Well, there is certainly some concern, since I've taken such a strong stance about morality. But, again, I wanted them to hear it from me, so they would know that I knew and I was supporting my daughter. They came by after church and told me that I'll get through it. Some of them have been through it, and said they were praying for me and that was it. They were supportive. In fact, the church threw her a tremendous shower."

With religion as his guide, Hilson stands firm in his belief that preaching abstinence can be an effective weapon against out-of-wedlock births and sexually transmitted diseases. I am not advocating promiscuity and I respect Arthur Hilson, but I wonder if Hilson's values—spoken values championed from the pulpits of many churches—are locked in the past and oblivious to the reality of hormones, mating, and a sexual revolution that is older than Gabrielle Hilson. I also think the morality advocated by Hilson and others can sometimes stand in the way of open and realistic discussions on sexual responsibility, leaving young adults unprepared to act with clear judgment in regard to their sexuality. Hilson disagrees. "I think what we've done is encourage premarital sex by issuing condoms in public schools and by preaching in our communities about the importance of safe sex. When you say 'safe sex,' you are simply endorsing sexual activity. There's not enough being done around the issue of abstinence, because people want to believe that people are just going to respond to that animal urge."

Hilson says that the family never considered abortion. "Never," he states emphatically. "Never given it a thought.

"Admirably, Gabrielle is back in school," he goes on. "Her situation, you have to admit, is not like the stereotypical situation. She's in school, and she does have a very supportive family. So do you think its impact on her life is not going to be as costly as it would be for other young people? I don't think it will be as costly. My own concern as a father is that it is certainly going to create for her another stress in life that we would like to have avoided. But the bottom line is that Gab is certainly committed. She's carrying a full load. She's continuing on.

"Personally, I would have preferred her to have still stayed at Spelman; but she is now at UNH, and she'll do well."

"My dad, I think he's kind of stuck on the name—you know, Spelman. It's a good school. When I said, 'I'm not going back to Spelman,' he kept saying, 'Go back to Spelman, don't worry about everything, go back to Spelman.'

"He said, 'You'll be more respected if you go to Spelman, and we'll do what we can to help you go back.' I think he was just still caught up in the name.

"Going to school here or Spelman . . . they're two unique experiences, and I don't know if one's any better than the other. I know I never applied to any white schools; I simply did not want to go. That's what I've always been in, and I wanted the experience [of being] with other black people and only black people. And to tell you the truth, there's not a whole lot of difference with somebody's skin color, because they can treat me the same way here as they can at Spelman or Morehouse. It's just different skin color. That's it. I don't know if it's worse here, because when I was at Spelman last year, all I wanted to do was come home.

"The students here aren't so bad. I can't say I know a lot of the white students here. I haven't made an effort to be very friendly. I don't even make an effort to be that friendly with the black people.

"At Spelman, one part of the school, they would tell you about your heritage and 'you're a beautiful black woman and you're this and you're that and be proud of yourself.' But the next minute, if you're going to career services or training, they make sure that your makeup was just as right as possible, make sure you're done up like this and that. That's a very Eurocentric way of looking at it.

"I felt they tried to teach you how to be a white woman, and I already knew that."

This is the third time I've heard Gabrielle criticize Spelman for exposing students to the conservative ways of corporate culture. She calls it teaching students to be white, but what would one say to a white male with a long ponytail who wants to work on Wall Street? Or to the white woman with long and untrimmed stringy hair? I suspect that the advice wouldn't be taken as being advised not to look too white. For the most part, graduates of any college who have risen up the *Fortune* 500 ladder maintain the conservative appearance that is de rigueur in that culture. People who choose careers in academia, the arts, or running their own businesses are not confined by those standards, but by others perhaps just as exacting. Should a career counselor at any school ignore the reality that some professions have developed standardized codes of dress and grooming? Is it teaching a student to be white to make him or her aware of that? Moreover, isn't it anyone's personal choice to follow or reject that standard and accept the consequences?

Gabrielle began the spring semester with a full load of courses, but after one week of classes—on January 22, 1996—Nia Imani, a baby girl, was born. A week after the birth, Gabrielle was back in school. During the first six weeks of Nia's life, Gabrielle carried her to classes: the two were inseparable. The new parent was determined not to rely too heavily on her own parents, who were both working. After six weeks, though, she found a retired woman from the church to watch Nia while she was in class and at work. She found a job as a bank teller to help support her new child.

Initially, the pressure of motherhood was too consuming to juggle with work and a full load of courses, so Gabrielle eventually dropped two courses. Then, during the summer, she decided to drop the hotel-management major. "It was going to take me longer to graduate," she explains. "I walked along campus one day and took a big long look at stuff that I wanted to do. I do like to write, and I do a lot of critical analysis. That's what most of my professors will tell you. One thing I'll do in a minute is read a book and give you every little detail that I think is wrong with the book, you know? Or things that don't fit."

She changed her major to English and in her first writing class confronted the experience of her daughter's conception. "I guess you can say I repressed it or I don't know. In my mind, I had gone there—I had been in this place where I shouldn't have been. When I took my first English course, one of the first things I started doing was writing about the situation, and I wrote about that evening and a lot of the stuff I remember. One of the assignments was to hand the paper to three people, and they were supposed to read it and send some notes on it. And people were amazed."

Some of the readers considered it date rape, but Gabrielle has trouble calling the experience rape. "I wouldn't say that. Or I'm not sure."

"Are you fifty percent sure or are you about ninety percent sure? Eighty-five percent? Ninety-five?" I ask.

"Probably about ninety [sure]. Like, my only problem with the whole situation is that I went there. I was in the apartment. I let it begin. My issue is, hey, you know I was there. Wasn't like I stopped you in the beginning. I did say stop eventually."

But doesn't no mean no at any point in a sexual encounter?

By fall 1996, Gabrielle had charted a new life at the University of New Hampshire. She joined the Black Students Union and a diversity coalition—something she didn't have to do at Spelman. She also developed what she considered her healthiest male-female relationship ever with Lamont, the director of the Gospel choir, which she also joined. In May 1998, Gabrielle graduated and accepted a job as director of multicultural events and services at Kenyon College, a predominantly white school in Mount Vernon, Ohio.

Chapter 2 2

The Graduate: The Mom

T HE hymns on the Sunday before Christmas are predictable: "Joy to
the World," "Hark! the Herald Angels Sing," "Away in a Manger."
Gabrielle Hilson is at home with those songs, and that is probably
a good thing, because this is the first Christmas season in her
twenty-three years of life that she will spend away from her parents. "Last night Nia and I watched *It's a Wonderful Life*. It's a tradition
every year for my mom and me to watch it together. We watched it for a
few minutes over the phone together."

On the Sunday before Christmas 1998, Gabrielle Hilson sits with Nia,
now three, on her lap in her new church: Trident Baptist in Columbus,
Ohio, an hour's drive from Mount Vernon. It was an early morning for the
family: Gabrielle just joined this church a month ago, so she had a new-
members class at 8:30 and service at 11:00.

Finding a church was Gabrielle's first priority after settling into an apartment. She says that she chose Trident because the minister here discusses
the Scriptures and doesn't just scream at the congregation. She visited six
churches, including predominantly white congregations in Mount Vernon,
but the services didn't feel right. In fact, she says, she felt out of place—she
experienced feelings similar to those that followed her at Spelman. "It
wasn't the place for me," she says, referring to those churches. "None of the
churches that I went to at first are what I'm used to, and I think that was my
biggest problem. I am looking for New Hope Baptist Church in Ohio. The
first one I went to, I'd say, was like Billy Graham on TV—the people were
falling out; they were filled with the Holy Spirit. Not that that doesn't happen . . . but I was not able to concentrate. Then, I remember, in that service,

they also had this young man. I don't know if it was his first time there, [but] he was just really happy. But every five minutes, he started to cry. And so all of these distractions in the service were just getting to me. And I just figure if I can't concentrate on the service, I don't need to be in the service, you know?

"One that I went to, the minister was like Ferris Bueller's teacher. And then the other one, it was just flat-out boring, you know? Everybody was nice, and the pastor, he did teach some from the Scriptures, but it was boring. And there has to be some kind of passion for the Lord.

"If you think about things, there is no way you can sit and not be excited. Like, if I know right now, if I have no money in my pocket, I know that I don't have to worry about anything, you know? She [Nia] may need braces or something. [But] I don't have to worry about it; I know I'm taken care of. I need to be excited about that.

"That's why you need to be excited. It's not only that you know that you're going to receive from this relationship with God but you know that he's done already everything that he said he was going to do. . . . It's hard to take this into consideration, but somebody sent their child here and let that child die for me. I'm not sending my child anywhere to die for anybody. That's a hard thing, if you think about it—sending your child somewhere to be picked on, ridiculed, and all that and then killed.

"You have to be excited about the Lord, but I don't want the minister to just shout at me. That's what happened at some of the black churches I visited. I want to talk about the Scriptures. That's why I chose this church, eventually: he preaches from the Scriptures."

He also seems to do a lot of shouting, actually, and so does the congregation. When the minister reaches the climax of his sermon, churchmembers feel free to stand and wave their hands. After the sermons, they are invited up to testify to the glory of God. "I was not doing well in school," says one woman who appears to be Gabrielle's age. "But I kept praying and God got me through the semester. I did well in my classes." She wins enormous applause from the audience. There are amens and claps at all of the stories.

The service ends at 1:00. Gabrielle has three hours to spare for me: she and Nia have to be back at church this evening for the Christmas play. We go to lunch at Applebee's, a mall-type bar-and-grill restaurant. There we find a well-integrated crowd, but there is a consistent difference between the whites and blacks: Every black person here—every one—is in Sunday attire—suits and ties, and dresses. This is clearly after-church brunch for them. Every white person here, on the other hand, is dressed casually; some are even gathered around the bar area for drinks. It strongly reinforces the idea that 11:00 A.M. on Sunday is America's most segregated time of the week.

Gabrielle orders a children's meal—hot dogs and fries—for Nia, and a steak for herself. Gabrielle always has goals. She says that she likes student services, but sees it as a step. She plans to eventually work at a school offering a graduate program in English and tuition remission for staff, because she now wants to be an English professor. Beyond that, she looks toward branching off into real estate and, someday, owning a bed-and-breakfast. In addition, Gabrielle says, she must also balance her goals with her relationship with Lamont, who also graduated last year and is teaching school in Maryland. In some ways, she is following the career path of her father, who built a career in university administration while going to school.

Another factor has come into the mix, too. In recent months, her biological father has entered her life. "He showed up at my college graduation," she says. "And he was trying, I guess, trying to make amends. His mother called me last year, and, as a matter of fact, she left a message on my machine saying, 'This is your grandmother calling. I think I'll call you back later.' I listened to it a couple of times and my immediate reaction was this was not Mary McClarey [her maternal grandmother], [it's] just some old lady with the wrong number. . . . This is not my grandmother. 'Cause that was the first time I ever heard from her, like, ever, in my whole life. And they wanted me to come down this summer for a family reunion. I mean, they are all very apologetic, but it's kind of hard to say I'm in his family. I'm afraid of how my parents would react. Like, I don't want to do anything that would upset them in this situation . . . I think that's one thing that scares me about trying to create a relationship with my biological father—that I'd be hurting my parents . . . I have this father who was there. . . . He was there. And to try to go back and say, 'Well, now, this is my father, I am going to have a relationship with him.' I don't know."

She's more concerned about what she will tell Nia about a father, because that man doesn't even know that he has a daughter. "I don't know how to deal with the whole father issue," she admits. "Who knows? I don't know. You know what? I have nothing but love in my heart for that guy."

"You have nothing but love in your heart?"

"Yeah. I mean, I got Nia. I didn't get anything else but Nia, and she's special; so I can't hate him for that, and I have no reason to take revenge on him.

"I just hope what happened to me doesn't happen to her," Gabrielle says as she looks at Nia eating a french fry. "There's almost kind of a history. My grandmother was, you know? Like I said, I hope it doesn't happen to her, but it's happened down the line."

"Do you think things may have happened differently for you if you had had more open conversations with your parents?" I ask her.

"I think things might have been a little different if I had more open conversations. My parents are not that open. We talk about a lot of things. We talk around a lot of things. And a lot of times we don't get to what we need to be talking about—you know what I mean? Like, at this point, I'm pretty sure my parents probably know that Lamont and I have had a physical relationship. They probably know that. But to the point of us talking about it? We wouldn't talk about it, or we would talk about it but not talk about it. We just kind of talk around the situation. You know, if I come home and I say, 'You know what? I feel nausea and sick,' they're concerned. They're like, 'Okay . . . so you got anything on the way? You and Lamont?' You know, it's kind of like I just feel sick, maybe I ate something. . . . So it's kind of like those situations where they don't say for sure, but still make those little side comments. And I just think that's how we grew up. That's how I grew up."

"So how will you deal with those issues with Nia?"

"That's real hard. I mean, I have no idea. I have no idea what I'll say to her."

Five

LEISURE

American Beach

QUINTON Jones begins Sunday mornings in the summer with hot dogs, potato chips, and sodas. He's not eating, though—Jones probably won't taste a hot dog until the sun is long on its way to another part of the world. During the week, he's a supervisor of juvenile counselors for the Florida Department of Correction. Jones, a stocky, brown-skinned man with a resonant voice, has a small vending business. It doesn't produce that much supplemental income, but money is not what drives him to set up his hot dog cart at American Beach, an unincorporated resort town of 125 homes located on Amelia Island, Florida, thirty miles north of Jacksonville. "One of my thrills of having my hot dog cart open is to just listen to older blacks . . . walk and talk to their kids about what used to be," says Jones, who is president of the American Beach Merchants' Association. "I like to see them look at the buildings, and pointing and saying, 'When we were little, or when I used to come down here and we used to do that, and oh, that place closed,' and talking to their children about what used to be. The kids can't really see it. To them, it's a bunch of junk now. But that history is here, and those people have lived it and they still come down here. We don't have the facilities for them, but they still come down here—and they'll always come to see this ocean.

"I was born in '59—I'll be thirty-five this month. So, you know, I'm young, and I got thirty years of history on American Beach."

Jones's memories of American Beach begin with the days when he was awakened early on Sunday mornings by the roars of bus engines. "As a kid, I used to run out and count all the buses—you know, thirty, forty, fifty buses parked down here. And we were able to accommodate people, busloads of people coming down here. That was a thrill . . . it would be nice for some of that to come back, you know, so we can keep it and preserve it."

The tone of Jones's voice is nostalgic; his accent is different, but the tenor is the same as that of a Gallia County resident mourning the "old-style" Emancipation; of James and Ellen Benson looking back at Lawnside before the newcomers and new times "changed" the fabric of the town; and of Dexter Fields and Margaret Betts recalling the "cohesion" of Detroit's Black Bottom.

There are no buses to be heard or seen from Jones's house on this Sunday morning in 1995. In fact, it is quiet enough to hear the seagulls on the beach more than a mile away even without a window open.

You can't see the beach from Jones's house, a cottage in a wooded, rural area of American Beach. You can, however, see one of the area's most scenic attractions, a fifty-four-foot sand dune sitting prominently a few yards away from the ocean.

By 10:00 on Sundays, Jones is moving his cart toward the beach. The cart stirs up dust on the unpaved roads, and when Jones reaches the pavement, he must stop to wipe off the bags of potato chips before he continues pushing and walking.

Once past the dune and closer to the water, the view drastically changes. The huge trees and wooded lands surrounding Jones and his neighbors disappear and there's no respite from the sun. Sunglasses seem almost essential. Jones, without them, squints when his eyes catch the open sun of the oceanfront area.

A wooden boardwalk leads to the public beach. Off of the beach, the several abandoned and boarded-up properties stand in sharp contrast to the view to the north and south of the two-hundred-acre American Beach community: American Beach's southern neighbor is the Amelia Island Plantation, a well-manicured golf-course community of homes and condominiums starting at three hundred thousand dollars. To the north is a brand-new Ritz-Carlton hotel and a number of other golf communities. American Beach is the only underdeveloped section of Amelia Island.

Most of the streets on American Beach are named for founders of the Afro Life Insurance Company. Founded in 1901 by Abraham Lincoln Lewis and six other men who all contributed one hundred dollars, Afro Life was the first life-insurance company, black or white, in the state of Florida. As the name indicates, however, the company was established to serve blacks, many of whom at the time could not purchase insurance or afford burials. "The Afro," as it was called, was a good investment for Lewis and his part-

ners: it became a power in the segregation era and made Lewis not only a
millionaire but one of Florida's wealthiest men too. (In 1987, Atlanta Life,
another African-American–owned company, purchased Afro Life.)

In 1935, Lewis and other Afro owners decided to establish a retreat for
their employees and purchased two hundred acres on the south end of
Amelia Island. They sold lots to employees and, eventually, others, and the
area grew to become American Beach. American Beach catered to crowds
that were forbidden by Jim Crow and segregation to go elsewhere. As more
people came and businesses opened, American Beach became the weekend playground for African Americans from throughout the Florida, Alabama, and Georgia area. And like many similar communities, American
Beach was home to two worlds that sometimes mixed and sometimes
clashed: there were the summer homeowners for whom the beach was a
second residence, and then there were the hundreds of tourists who
danced at the clubs and cheered at bathing-suit contests on the beach.

Black romantics who long for one of those segregation-style "classless"
communities should come to American Beach, where they would find
judges and retired janitors living on the same block among retired teachers
and mill workers. Here, there are refurbished homes with modern architec-
tural designs and decorated with African-American art sitting next to common bungalows. "That's healthy," Quinton Jones reasons. "I wouldn't want
to be in a community where everybody makes one hundred thousand dollars or more. That's boring—there is no diversity. There is nothing unique.
There's nothing to cherish, to see where you have been and where you can
go if you work hard."

American Beach has been described as a unique vacation community in
some newspapers and even by a couple of residents who told me that "this
is the only black beach in the country" or "the only place where black folks
still own oceanfront property." Such statements are far from true: There are
at least eight traditionally black vacation communities across the country,
including well-known spots like Oak Bluffs on Martha's Vineyard as well as
more remote places like Maryland's Eagle Harbor and Highland Beach.
There is an African-American enclave on North Carolina's Topsoil and in
New York's Sag Harbor. There's Indiana's Fox Lake, Michigan's Idlewild,
Wisconsin's Lake Ivanhoe, and South Carolina's Atlantic Beach. And these
are only the best known. All are different and suit the styles and tastes of
their residents—some modest, some snobbish, some open, some down-
home, and some seedy.

Beyond its existence as a surviving black vacation community, American
Beach's story mirrors that of many other black institutions, colleges, and or-

ganizations. American Beach too struggles to forge a new role and place for itself in the postintegration era, and that has created tensions in the community. Some want a quiet residential community, while entrepreneurs want swinging crowds that can sustain businesses.

American Beach, like many other black spaces, thrived during the era of segregation, hit a low point, and now may be on the road to recovery. With integration, the middle class fled. A loyal few stayed on, living on nostalgia, memories of the glory days, but it wasn't enough. American Beach became marginal and troubled, as most of the thriving businesses that once made it a vibrant, hopeful community died, leaving behind the boarded-up properties. Then, however, came the late 1980s, when the crowds gradually returned. Several black professionals invested in property; today I see a few houses under renovation.

The coming of new residents should be good news for the community, but it is in fact a mixed blessing, because it does not ensure the survival of the American Beach that many residents would like to see. American Beach is situated smack in between some of the most highly valued real estate in northeast Florida and the appetites—and money—of its neighbors and outsiders threatens to swallow it. The Amelia Island Plantation began developing the area south of American Beach in the eighties, ironically, right at the same time that American Beach and the Afro ran into hard times. In 1987, the Afro sold eighty acres including the sand dune near Quinton Jones's house, to Tony Leggio, a white attorney in nearby Fernandina Beach.

Now the Plantation wants to expand, and Leggio is willing to sell it. The Plantation has an option on his property and plans to build a golf course and condominiums for senior citizens there. Many American Beach residents fear a spike in property values, and hence taxes, would force older residents to sell—further eroding the black community. A spokesman for the Amelia Island Plantation promises that that won't happen and says that the Plantation will "protect the beauty of the sand dune," but that doesn't quell Jones's fears. "The future of American Beach is questionable," says Jones. "We're surrounded by multimillion-dollar resorts, and the Plantation is in the process of trying to buy another major chunk of what was the original two hundred acres. Then they want to put a buffer between them and us."

By 10:30, Jones is ready to sell, having parked his cart on a lot just off the boardwalk. The building next to him once housed El Patio, a teenage club and restaurant that thrived throughout his youth but finally closed five years ago after years of dwindling crowds.

El Patio was a family business, owned and operated by Jones's father. That meant that Quinton Jones was one of the chief employees. "I would sell souvenirs to people in the club; I'd serve breakfast, lunch, and dinner. I was ten years old and was an assistant cook. I learned how to cook in my father's club and restaurant."

Jones is renovating the place, and the sounds of drills and hammers may sometimes be heard during the week. He hopes to capitalize on American Beach's increasing Sunday tourism; he hopes that the tourist numbers of 1994—the highest since the decline of the seventies—will continue to rise. Even through the slow periods of the late seventies and eighties, the crowds would hit one hundred on Sundays, but this year, the crowds have reached record highs—up to five hundred. "It's been a historical thing for some reason," says Jones, as he squirts mustard on a hot dog bun. "Sundays have always been the biggest day on this beach throughout history from the beginning. I don't know what it is about Sunday as opposed to Saturday. It's not only Sunday, it's late Sunday! So the crowd really doesn't come until four o'clock on Sunday.

"The sun may have something to do with it too, you know—it's hot earlier in the daytime, and we don't have a lot of shade, so maybe they're running from the sun. And for whites, it's just the opposite. They're out at nine o'clock in the morning. The other beaches are packed with white folks. And while they're home resting up for Monday morning, we're just coming out. But we can't get the same crowd on a Saturday. Sunday is the only day I open the hot-dog cart."

Today's crowd has grown to at least five hundred, according to police estimates. There are women in shorts and big hoop earrings, men from the nearby naval base, parents and children in vans with picnic lunches, men in Mercedes and BMWs—some presumed to be bought with drug money—twenty-something men and women toting cellular phones as casually as a reporter carries a pen. Yet while the crowds have grown in recent years, businesses catering to the beach's tourists are not abundant. Aside from vendors like Jones, the only open business is an oceanfront juke joint, selling beer and soda. People wander in and out, many congregating in an open field on the inland side of the oceanfront properties, where a deejay blasts music and games of horseshoes are being played. American flags hang on a wooden post on the field. Few people are actually on the beach, and fewer are in swimsuits. Those on the beach are just walking on the sand.

The field where the crowd gathers is owned by Frank Morgan, thirty-four, a Jacksonville real estate agent. Like Quinton Jones's family, Frank Morgan's parents owned property on the beach and spent summers here. Now, on Sundays, his company, Oceanfront Enterprises, opens this field to the public, hires a deejay, and cordons off a section of the one-acre lot for parking, charging three dollars a car. He's promoted these Sunday events this year through WROD-FM, a popular black radio station in Jacksonville. "We're trying to hold on to our heritage, but change seems certain," Morgan says.

"Now we're down to just this little Sunday thing," says Jones of American Beach events. "Hanging out on the lot on Sundays with the deejay. The horseshoes, that's something new this year.

"We've had a few nice homes purchased in recent years," he continues, "but there's been absolutely no new commercial development. There's been no remodeling of our commercial district up front. The property owners have died off. Some have gotten older. The real problem is that some of the family members didn't have anybody younger in their family to reinvest in the property. [Also,] we've got people all over the country that own property here on American Beach, as far away as California, [but] we've had no commercial investment from the current family members.

"A friend of mine, whose father owned another club, he had a chance to do something here. His father, right before he sold the place ten years ago called him up in New Jersey and asked him was he interested in coming back home and running the place. And [the son], for whatever reasons, was not interested in coming back home. He went to college in Jersey, he had started a career up in Jersey, and at the time he was like, 'Nah, I ain't got time to fool with that mess down there. Do what you want to do.' And his father sold it. And the boy eventually returned home, kicking himself today. In the seventies and early eighties, people didn't really want this: they wanted to see the world and do their thing. Now they want to come home. But look at home now—it's gone for some people.

"My father passed at fifty-three years old. He taught me early on that the only way to be financially independent is to go into business for yourself. You get money one of three ways: inheritance, you marry into it, or you go into business for yourself. I wanted to go into business for myself. My father told me that [when I was] nine years old, so I'm trying to live that out."

Jones's father worked full time on an assembly line at a box-making company in Jacksonville and ran his businesses on American Beach for a second forty hours a week from April to December. The main business was El Patio, the restaurant and club for teenagers. "He ended up being disabled, diabetes. And from diabetes, he had both his legs amputated and left the boxing company, but was still running a business.

"My father was in a wheelchair, but he had wooden legs made for him. If he didn't want to wear his legs . . . [he'd use the] wheelchair. Other times, [he'd] walk, which was a trip. People would do a double take.

"He built him a nice home in Jacksonville. My mother and father, they both separated and remarried, and they both had property down here. We grew up with the big house in town, pool in the backyard, boat, and all that kind of stuff. And cottages here. You know, my father had an eighth-grade education. But my mother, she has her master's degree, and my stepmother has her doctorate—Dr. Jones.

"My father, he had a lot of common sense and basic business sense. He started us out with collecting bottles—he taught us how to do that, aluminum cans—and to do a little carpentry work. But the real business was real estate. He had got in contact with this real estate lady. She was the main black real estate agent in Jacksonville at the time, and whenever [her company] needed yards clean to show people, they would call us in to do the yard. And this was back in the early seventies. I would say that we were doing fifty-, sixty-, seventy-dollar yards. She would call my father. We had these push mowers, but business got so good that we asked our dad to buy us a riding lawn mower. We got tired of pushing. It was too much. The yards were too big."

Jones left Florida for Wilberforce University in Wilberforce, Ohio, in 1977, and after graduating returned to Jacksonville. He eventually settled in one of his family's houses on the beach. Today, he rents the other three that they own. "It was always my intentions and my plan just to come back home and be part of this community," he explains. "Because most blacks from this area, whether it's Jacksonville or north Florida period, if they go off to college, they don't return, [and] the community is losing. So I'm going to have to come back and be part of the community that produced me and try to offer it something.

"This is a big country, and we [blacks] tried to spread out too far and go too far. And now we're realizing that we were better as having that sense of community, by pooling our resources and probably by targeting certain locations in certain areas. That's how we ended up with black mayors and black congressmen and state senators. It's not coming from us being spread out, it's coming from us being together in one particular area. People need to come back home to American Beach. I just remember what we had. . . . If you look at segregation in terms of how many black businesses that we had, the sense of community that we had . . . we had more businesses, black-owned and -operated businesses during segregation. That's how Afro American Life Insurance got started; white folks didn't want to insure us— yeah, because the white folks didn't want our money, didn't want to insure us. So [Afro American] did, and they were able to flourish and thrive, and that's how American Beach was born. There would never have been an American Beach if it wasn't for segregation."

"What's wrong with an integrated beach community?" I ask. "Why do you think you can't do that with white people around?"

"We can do that with white people around, but just like every other ethnic group in the country; they all have their sense of community and their sense of identity, whether it's the Cubans or the Haitians, or the Vietnamese, or the Chinese. Every other ethnic group had that sense of where they came from and the history and an identity, whether it's Little Havana, or Little Haiti, or Chinatown, and that's good, that's okay. And we should have that too. But we have white property owners down here, too—we're not saying they can't come and be a part of it. We're just saying that, hey, this is an African-American community, and preferably it should stay that way. If we don't, then we'll lose it, and it'll lose its identity and it'll lose its history. And it'll be lost forever."

"Would you not be offended if enough black people wanted to go to a place and had the money to go to that resort and white people said, 'Well, no, we want to keep a majority here to preserve white culture,' how would you react to that?"

"I don't have any problem with that. They can recognize and preserve their history, and be just as passionate about, just as I can be about preserving my history. I don't have any problem with that. Just like whether it's the Jewish community, or an Indian community, or a Chinese community, I wouldn't want to move in and take over. They need to have and preserve their culture, and we need to be able to preserve our culture. Just like the Mormons or whatever. Whatever group, it needs to be respected and allowed to be preserved and take care of their own, so to speak."

"How do you do that?" I press him. "Do you develop a quota system, saying okay, only one in five blacks moves into this community, no more than five whites—how do you regulate or preserve that?"

"Well," he replies, "it's different when you're talking about individuals moving into a community, which is what we have down here. In my apartments, the tenant that I have that's been there the longest is white, okay? I don't have a problem with that, about individuals moving into the area and appreciating your area. But when you're talking about a multimillion-dollar developer that wants to come in and literally rape the land and force your people out on a wholesale basis, that's totally different—and that's the case that we're dealing with right here on American Beach. We're surrounded by a multimillion-dollar developer, that's smelling, like, millions of dollars. So that changed the ball game all together."

But why should anyone expect otherwise? Why would a developer without a historic tie to the community act in the interest of preserving cultural traditions that do not benefit him financially? Perhaps the community's efforts to save and preserve itself and control its future are a little too late to win the battle against a multimillion-dollar developer. Until now, residents' interests in developing the community themselves have yielded limited results, leaving the community in a state of commercial decay for nearly two decades. And some residents, as I would discoverer, are not opposed to the coming development.

Jones insists he does not advocate a racially separate beach. Yet at the same time, he admits that he prefers a majority-black American Beach. His ambivalence is an expression of the complexity of black attitudes toward secluded black spaces. "It's been separate. We still got a beach in the city [outside American Beach proper] we call the main beach [where African Americans tended not to go]. As recently as a few years ago, if blacks went down in that area, some of the rednecks would say, 'Y'all looking for American Beach, ain't you?' Even today, this is still known as a black area, and main beach is known as the white area. Race relations in this area are poor.

"I mean, look at it: it's American Beach. The name is so appropriate—for me it sends a message saying that this beach is for everybody, and it had to be what Abraham Lincoln Lewis thought about when he dreamed up this place. Of course, he thought about his people, but it was never this exclusion thing, and we have never been that kind of people. We want our own, but we were not so selfish as to say, in my way of thinking, that just because you're a certain race or color you can't come here. I mean, we still have to fight that today so we wouldn't be any better than the slave owners or the rednecks and trying to keep people out, so the name is so appropriate and is fitting. It says that this is *American* Beach, so everybody is kind of welcome."

7

MaVynee

ENRY Adams, appointed U.S. district court judge by President Clinton in 1993, is not tuned in to the Sunday noise at the beach. He is in his two-story beach house two blocks from the American Beach oceanfront, smoking a Kool and watching a football game. His block of well-kept summer homes hardly looks like it would be in the same community as the strip of boarded-up properties fronting the water.

Adams says that he'll be an American Beach resident for years, but he expects new neighbors. "I think there's a good possibility that the black folks, the individual black folks who own property down here, will eventually lose this property by virtue of taxes. I think the taxes are going to become eventually prohibitive. That's one thing. But then I think about it and I see a lot of new people around here who can more or less afford the increase in taxes, so that goes well. There may be some hope, but I think a lot of folks are going to lose their properties to this.

"I don't think that the [Amelia Island] Plantation is going to take over this beach; that's very difficult to do because you got so many individual owners around here and it's probably cost prohibitive to go around and offer all of these individuals enough money to make them go. But if the taxes get too high, they have to sell, because most of these people are using it as a second place, a second home. You've got to pay taxes at home."

Adams grew up in Jacksonville, where his father was an assembly-line worker, and his mother did domestic work. As a youngster, Adams always dreamed of owning a place in American Beach. "Well, it's the beach that I've known all of my life. When I was growing up, I couldn't go to any other beach but this beach. I couldn't go to Jacksonville Beach integrated; I was just uncomfortable going down there. It's just my own personal quirk."

Adams purchased his house in 1985, a few years before the wave of newcomers started buying property. He says he was drawn to American Beach as an adult because of its history and his desire to be part of an African-American vacation community. I asked him why he and other black professionals have come back to this community, seeing as American Beach's future as a black resort community is uncertain. He prefers to see the area rebounding: "You're talking about people who probably could afford the increase [in taxes to come], so that's the positive side of it. You see a lot of people, especially the new people who are coming in here can afford the increases so that looks good for us. That supports the survival of this as a black beach."

Adams also admits that some are interested in the community for reasons other than a desire to rebuild this black resort and reestablish a connection with African-American heritage. With Amelia Island development certain, some see this as the time to buy: Predictions are that properly values will only keep rising.

On Monday morning, the beach is quiet, the streets clear. A few people sit out on porches. I have an appointment with Annette Myers, the president of the American Beach Home Owners' Association. I can't find her house and finally stop at a cottage to get better directions.

"Do you know how to get to Ervin Street—five-forty?" I ask.

"Annette Myers's house," the middle-aged woman replies, and gives me directions. A few minutes and a couple turns take me to the end of Ervin, actually a dirt road. Myers comes outside to greet me.

"You got lost," she says politely.

"Yes, how did you know?"

"Someone called me and told me you stopped at her house for directions. Won't you come in?"

I enter a three-story gray stone house. Inside, there are hardwood floors, oak paneling, and a dog that barks loudly locked away in another room.

This house was once a popular place for honeymooners. In fact, Annette Myers, today a sixty-four-year-old retired schoolteacher, and her husband, a computer programmer who was killed seven years ago in an automobile accident, were introduced to it on their honeymoon. A few weeks after that, the aging owner decided to move. Myers and her husband were eager to buy. "I always loved this house," she says. "I've done a lot to it. I want more of our residents to take great care with their property."

Myers grew up in this county and came to American Beach on Sundays as a child. It was a different Sunday crowd then: "There was drinking, but no people walking up and down the street with beer cans and liquor bottles and that sort of thing."

Today, that happens, but she is glad that it might be changing. "Last year the commission passed a law; no drinking in public, [no] open container. I believe that has calmed it down a bit [from] when you had the walking back and forth, just like a big boardwalk down there, walking in the streets drinking, and loud music and that sort of thing.

"I would like to see businesses, thriving businesses that are wholesome . . . I would love to go down to the beach to a nice seafood restaurant . . . fine dining . . . a clean atmosphere—wholesome, you know? Somewhere you can dress up and go out."

For Myers, it all comes back to one word—*wholesome*. "I would say the kinds of entertainment and activity that's wholesome [would be] okay, whereas some of the activities have gotten out of hand. Now we've got to deal with the loud music. I can hear it over here, you know. To me, that's out of hand. . . . That rapping and promoting crime, and that sort of thing, that's not good music to me. But if it's good music and more low key, to me that would be fine. I would have no objections to it."

Myers has been one of the most critical voices of the Sunday crowd; she advocates more of a police presence. Some residents, however, question her motives, and she has been criticized for her cozy relationship with the developers of Amelia Island Plantation. Some say they fear Myers will sell them out. In response, she claims that she is eager to see how developers can help American Beach.

She must know that I will raise the issue, so it is perhaps not a surprise when one of her most shamelessly loyal supporters shows up during the interview and never misses the chance to praise the Homeowners Association president—even when without prompting. "Now, I don't know how you managed to know the right person to come to, but this is the soul of the community," Marsha Williams says. "Annette didn't get the way she is just now—I think she was just kind of like born that way. She is a driver, she is a doer, and anybody around her will do also. That's just a part of her fiber. And when she became our president three years ago . . . she worked for the whole of the organization. She doesn't do personal kinds of things: she works for the whole. We talk about projects and we want different things to happen, and Annette goes after them. And it's not 'me first' with her—it's the community first.

"A sidewalk was something that we wanted, and when she got to be president, a sidewalk was something that we had. We wanted roads paved, and we're going to have the roads paved."

"This year," Annette interjects.

"Now, there are some stiff challenges and those challenges are keeping up with the twenty-first century. I don't know if we'll be able to make it, as much as we love the place."

Can the Plantation help American Beach meet those challenges? Myers and Williams say that they don't see the two in opposition to each other, with Myers adding that some residents of American Beach may be living in the past and need to look beyond the glory days of segregation. "I do see it more or less moving to maybe a new American Beach," says Myers.

I am walking on the inland side of the beachfront houses. Those establishments are closed. I hear workmen buzzing around El Patio.

Up ahead, I see a woman with something big in her arms standing in front of a house. It could be a baby . . . but no, it's not. I come closer and see that it is fuzzy and dark gray, almost black. Is it an old cat comfortably curled in a fetal position? No—she walks toward me, and I see that it can't be a live cat. It *couldn't* be, because it has buttons of all sorts pinned to it. I see one of them reads SAVE THE WHALES.

She stares at me as we approach each other. I can't help but stare back not only because of the thing in her arms. Now I'm also trying to figure out what she is doing with the plastic bags hanging from her hands. There are long, skinny things in them. Despite her bizarre appearance, she carries herself with elegantly erect posture and a distinguished grace. The weight of whatever she's carrying doesn't affect her; I see no swooped shoulders or sloppy walk.

She stops me. I jump instinctively: it looks like a dead animal attached to her hair. She must be carrying a dead animal. "Who are you looking for?" she demands. "Are you looking for someone? Can I help you?"

Before I answer, I figure it out: it is her hair. I can't take my eyes off of it. Still, I pull myself together to explain that I'm writing a book. Now it's her turn to jump like I did, only hers is with pleasure and excitement. She ushers me into a small three-room cottage with a spanking-clean tile floor.

I have met MaVynee, the unofficial mayor of American Beach. She wants to talk about the beach, its past and its renaissance, but we can get to that later. First, I want to talk about her hair and about those long things in the plastic bags, which turn out to be her fourteen-inch fingernails. She's six feet, and her hair must be at least that tall. It's all natural—no extensions.

"All of it's hair," she says. "All of it's hair from back to front. I became a veg-etarian in '75. That's when the dreads started. This is almost a twenty-year growth—and don't forget that it's matted. If this was combed out and straightened, I'd probably need a shopping cart. One of these days, perhaps I'm going to write the *Guinness Book of Records* and find out what they have for a woman's hair and dreadlocks. I may have it. I may have the record, I don't know. I've never even taken time to look. But I use my hair for all my buttons, my causes."

She says that her hair is shaped in the form of the River Niger. It may be a stretch, but her big mat of hair loosely resembles the African continent. As it sits on her lap, she shows where different places would be. "My sister's an anthropologist, and she could do this much better," she apologizes as she pulls out a map and goes from the map to her hair. "Look at the river, look at the map. . . . Here's the River Niger. It goes up in a curve, like."

She now turns back to her hair. "This would be, like, Sierra Leone. This would be Nigeria, here in the back. And see, it's the African curve—like seven. If you notice, Africa looks like a seven, looks like a fat seven. And Florida does too. That would be Pensacola here, or Miami would be the end of the seven, right here."

Fifty buttons cover her continent or river of hair, including one that says CRUSH RUSH, referring to Rush Limbaugh, "This one says Columbus wasn't first," she says, pointing out another. "Did you know that Africa came to Florida, came south instead of going north? That's another reason I have the seven shape, because I love the connection between Africa and Florida."

There's a Spelman College bulletin on a coffee table. "Are you affiliated with Spelman?" I ask.

"No, I got that from my sister. She's the president of Spelman."

I immediately see the resemblance. MaVynee is tall and poised, with sharp and distinctive features, just like her sister Johnnetta B. Cole. "Here I am living a simple lifestyle in nature. My sister's a big president of Spelman. She handles millions of dollars. I love the contrast."

Each born in 1935, MaVynee and American Beach are today inseparable. MaVynee is known by at least three nicknames that are all tributes to her connection to the resort: she's the "Spirit of the Beach," the "Unofficial Mayor of American Beach," or just the "Beach Lady."

Judge Adams, sixty, and MaVynee, fifty-nine, are contemporaries. Both grew up in Jacksonville, but in different worlds. Whereas he came from a working-class family, she was a privileged child via her mother's side—her mother was the granddaughter of Abraham Lincoln Lewis. Meanwhile, her father, an architect, came from a more modest family in North Carolina. Mayvene says that he was brilliant but perhaps insecure. He worked harder than anyone in the family, trying to prove himself to his elite in-laws. He sometimes held four jobs. "Oh, Daddy, oh my God—unreal. The man just . . ."

MaVynee can't find a word to finish the sentence, but thoughts of her father trigger her memories of times gone by. "Well, he practically made the Afro what it was. When he married my mother, he had been an agent at Atlanta Life, and he came to Jacksonville. I guess they met there, anyway. After they got married, he became the agency director for the Afro Life Insurance Company. I mean, that company . . . let's face it, man, there were only three. The three big ones here in the South were in Jacksonville, Atlanta Life in Atlanta, and North Carolina Mutual in Durham, North Carolina.

"No one has told about how black people did their own thing. Man, we lived! And it wasn't a question of this exclusive elite up here. I mean, black people shared. Our house was like Grand Central Station, believe me. There was always someone there from the Afro sleeping overnight; every day at dinner there were ten or twelve people eating with us. We took care of our own. The Afro financed the health insurance for the children; there were free clinics for the children. The Afro built the churches. When I say built, I mean financed the money to build churches and schools. It was like a world in a world—that was the better side of segregation. Otherwise, the social, the humiliating part of what whites did to us was still a horror. But, as if to say, 'the hell with you, we'll do our own thing here,' black people picked up their own game and went from there. We had our own hotels here, and this is the sorry part of integration: that enough of that black base was not saved, because here we are now, consumers merely in this white-dominated structure here in America. We had our own thing."

Her parents met in an era when men of modest backgrounds but with drive, ambition, and intelligence would marry women of culture and status, and, conversely, college-educated women from humble backgrounds often married working-class men. She saw it all at American Beach growing up.

Her father was educated as an architect, and her mother was a teacher. "He did everything," MaVynee says of her father. "He would do people's income taxes. My father had about five or six jobs. You know, he was marrying into money, and I guess, poor little dumpling, he had to work so people wouldn't say anything. He proved that he was the main supporter. Oh, yeah, he did it all. He was the director of all the Afro. . . . One time he moved all the way out to Texas. He had branches out to Texas. At the height it was fabulous."

MaVynee pauses. "Oh, yes. He designed the houses. You should've seen what he did with my great-grandfather's house. Oh, man, I could cry every time I think about it."

The house was in Jacksonville's Sugar Hill neighborhood, an upper-class black community that died with integration. "Oh, man, it was fabulous! We lived right across from a park. Of course, with blacks, the doctor, the undertaker, the insurance man, and the preacher had all the Cadillacs. Well, of course we not only had one, we had two, but that isn't the point. The point is that [he rebuilt] this gorgeous house. The twenty-two rooms, we had the music room. Oh, God, it was fabulous. The ceiling, oh. . . . When the man got ready to put in the air-conditioning, he couldn't believe this was black built, black designed. This wasn't some white man's house that we moved into. Yet when we moved out into this white neighborhood—we were only moving 'cause we . . . couldn't save the house in the neighborhood—my mother brought her heavy drapery and the doggone stuff [in the new house] wouldn't even hold the drapes. Sheetrock and all this other cheap building material—you know the way they build them. It looks good on the outside, as all white neighborhoods always look good, with those manicured lawns. . . . We're supposedly movin' up in the world, ha ha.

"Black people had gorgeous homes and well built. But we couldn't keep [them]. It was one of those things; they wanted to put a hospital complex, which is now there. There is one man if you go by all these medical buildings, the guy refused to sell. So every time I pass by, I raise my fist. Yeah, man, we lived."

The young MarVynee's—that was her name then—favorite place in the house was the music room, because she had been drawn to music from an early age. She started piano lessons at four, and classical music would consume her youth. "My mother was the organist at the Mount Olive AME Church, which is a very famous church is Jacksonville . . . she gave me my first lessons, and from then I went to other piano teachers. So music has been a part of our lives. There was also the little male quartet my mother formed, and, of course, they were there at the house. I heard music all my life. I have a brother who is a jazz musician who now lives in Paris. Although he is ten years younger, there was always a sound of a drum, especially the bongos—whenever he got mad at us, he'd go into his room and start beating on them. I guess this was a way to get at us. At least it kept him from fighting us. Anyway, music has been part of my life. Piano was my first love and then I became interested in voice once I went to Oberlin."

She graduated from high school at sixteen. "I went to school at age four. Don't forget, back in those days, if you could read, you were in school. My mother, of course, was herself a teacher, and she read to us early on. So at four years old, I was already in the first grade. In fact, Johnetta didn't graduate from high school; she went from eleventh grade directly to Fisk, having also started at four years old in the first grade.

"It was the school they had there at Edward Waters College, which is one of the oldest black colleges in the state of Florida. There was a school right near there. I think some of the teachers, those who were getting their degree in education, were there as helpers, as I remember."

In 1951, she left the black world of the South for Oberlin. Founded in 1833, the school has a history of open and fair admissions and was active in the Underground Railroad. During the Civil War, one-third of the student body was black, and, according to the university, three African-American students participated in John Brown's raid at Harpers Ferry.

"I loved it. It was fun because of the music. I was singing in the choir; I was the soloist. I was traveling all over the United States during the spring break. I was a star . . . I loved it."

When MarVynee graduated, the civil-rights movement was in its infancy. But she missed that era in American life regardless: she was off to Europe. Where else was an aspiring black opera star to go in the late fifties? Europe, with its traditional fascination with black entertainers, was the place. "There was a student from Oberlin who was there—he was studying French. I knew that's where I wanted to go, and I already had a connection. My voice teacher had already studied with somebody in Paris, and so when I went there, he was able to get me a place to stay. [It] was really something: I stayed with a French doctor and his family. I was studying with this teacher who had studied with my teacher at Oberlin. And from there I went to Germany and auditioned, and they just accepted me. I started out with the most difficult opera there is: *Salome*. Usually, you start out with small roles, especially if you're unknown, but, don't forget now, this is 1958 or '59, [and] there are no blacks at all in northern Germany. I was like Queen Tut. Literally, I was the only black in the town. I mean, I would walk off the street and into a store in America and be the last one waited on, but there I would be the first. People would stop to talk to me, ask me what I wanted. My wish was their command. It was a life you would not believe.

"I started out with *Salome* by Richard Strauss. Strauss is . . . oh, my God, you would have a hundred forty members in the orchestra—so big was the orchestra. It was a very, very difficult role. You have to sing and dance. I danced the dance of the seven veils. You know in the Bible where it says she asked for the head of John, and the King says no, and he says, 'If you dance for me I'll give you the head'? The story is taken from that part of the Bible and was made into an opera. That's where I started. I started at the top rather than working my way up. I did *Madama Butterfly*. I did Carmen and other roles."

After five years in Germany, MarVynee moved to London. It was Great Britain that made her long for American Beach. "Well, after Paris and Germany, the British. . . . Well, ah, first of all the weather was awful. There were a lot of good students there, and there was a lot of good music. That was the main thing. Oh, God, the music there was unreal. Any big city in Europe, just like here, same thing. Music is a wonderful thing to have, if that's your thing. I couldn't tolerate a big city now unless I was into music. Anything else in the city is just barbaric. I can't deal with it. It was a wonderful time because of the music. . . .

"And the jazz at that time was . . . oh, my goodness! I met many jazz musicians who were terrible; but they were having a heyday in Europe because they were jazz musicians and Europeans thought that anybody that played jazz had to be good—which isn't true, as you know. But many jazz musicians had gone over there merely because of the fact that they were so worshipped and yet practically so damned here in America and treated like second-class citizens. It was a fascinating time, the fifties and sixties."

But back in London, MarVynee found the smog was overwhelming. "London, that place, the pollution, you can't imagine, in quote 'civilized' London. And when I came home I was breathing like this." She demonstrates deep asthmatic breaths.

MarVynee also returned to a different America in 1966. Many say that Sugar Hill was in decline by then, but MarVynee doesn't remember it like that. "It was not in decline—whites took it over. It's now a medical complex, and not even a historical marker is there. In fact, Jacksonville is embarrassing. There's not even a marker for James Weldon Johnson. The James Weldon Johnson who wrote the Negro national anthem! Born and lived in Jacksonville. There's not a marker for A. Philip Randolph?! Lived in Jacksonville. That man literally made the March on Washington—though Martin Luther King took it a bit further; it was his speech. But A. Philip Randolph, that man did it for black people, especially the labor movement. And Sugar Hill, it's gone."

Regardless of whether it was taken or in decline, by the mid-sixties, when MarVynee returned from Europe, the neighborhood wasn't what it had been. The Afro, too, had begun to suffer. MarVynee's father had died of cancer when she was in college, and now her grandfather's health was declining, so a cousin of her generation took over the Afro. However, he

lacked the business acumen to carry the institution into the new era that began with integration, according to MarVynee. They made a go of it, though,
as MarVynee helped her mother and the cousin manage the Afro. The problems only grew, and by 1974 others arose. That year, her mother's health
was failing, and MarVynee would lose both her mother and grandfather to
cancer in 1975. Then she too was diagnosed with colon cancer. However,
unlike her mother and grandfather, MarVynee shunned doctors, instead dramatically altering her lifestyle in an attempt to fight the cancer with nature:
She became a strict vegetarian and moved to the beach so that she could
bathe in the ocean. Salt baths in the ocean became a daily thing. She also let
her hair and fingernails grow.

Twenty years later, she still hasn't been to a doctor. "I heal myself. This
is . . . a healing place. I want it to be a health resort. You see that big sand
dune, all that land back there? It's now for sale. In fact, the Plantation—don't
you love that word—Amelia Island Plantation has an option to buy it. I'm
very sad, because they want it to be a golf course. I would love for it to be a
health resort. I heal here."

At the same time that she adopted her new lifestyle, MarVynee had also
become an active environmentalist at American Beach. Her environmental-
ism, or, more specifically, her outrage at Ronald Reagan for his neglect of
the environment, led her to officially drop the *R* from her name in 1980. The
letter that began his first and last names in her own name was too much of
an affront. So MarVynee became MaVynee. Even today, her passion runs
high. "Oh, yes. What he did to the environment—man, I mean, just—our
poor earth is just—well, black people are waking up now because it's hitting us in the cities and other areas. Do you know the largest toxic-waste
dump in the U.S. is in a black community? We're dying daily from all this
pollution. It's true. It's called environmental racism. . . . Consider what's going to happen here if they cut down all those trees back there. See, black
people, we need air, that's why we have wide nostrils."

What? Environmental racism may be a reality, but MaVynee's nostril theory? That's a new one. "We don't have it, the air, in the cities. Trees give us
cover—we lived just four hundred years ago in an area, in Africa, where the
cover was more in proportion to the people. So we're used to all this air, the
greenery and outdoors. So if they cut those trees down, that's just more pollution, because the cars can park on the beach here—they can't park at the
resort. So we get all the fumes. This is why black children can't concentrate
in school: they're hyper from breathing in all that polluted air from cars and
no trees. Look in the ghetto, what's the first thing you notice? No trees. You
ever notice that?"

Despite such concern, some of MaVynee's greatest fans are not black people in the inner city but, often, white environmentalists—an endangered white whale is named after her; a book on butterflies has been dedicated to her. Mayvene's prestige among environmentalists is understandable, as she's demonstrated her commitment to the movement in ways beyond dropping an *R* from her name and wearing buttons in her hair. After her mother and grandfather died, she donated her entire inheritance, nearly $1 million, to her favorite causes: animal rights, fighting environmental racism, saving the whales. "And help the jungles in Brazil [and] Africa. In five years' time, oh, my God, it was unreal. I mean, I supported biodiversity conferences in South America and Brazil. I did it all. And now the Pygmies. I'm really trying to save Pygmies."

Five years after the money was gone, she lost her grandfather's house to inheritance taxes. She began sleeping in a lawn chair on a friend's deck. Her sister was worried and gave MaVynee a mobile home. And what did she do with it? She turned it, she says, into an African-American history museum.

MaVynee dreams of the day when she can move these valuables from the trailer to a huge multimillion-dollar building. For now, though, she settles for the trailer. In addition to being adorned with a few more of MaVynee's ubiquitous buttons, the trailer-museum also houses documents, relics, Afro Life Insurance's founding papers, and other collectibles regarding American Beach history, African-American history in Florida, and material on Abraham Lincoln Lewis. "He was the most peaceful person I could imagine," she says of her great-grandfather. "He conceived the idea of a place where the average black person could just come and have a beach. Where can you find this? Where my great-grandfather, a millionaire, and others of means live with average folk. You see, in this country, we talk democracy—no one really lives it. Rich people live in one area, poor people in another, right? Not on American Beach. This is unique. We have every walk of life right here. Look at this cottage where I live: fifty dollars a month. I can take you down to Mr. Watson's house, worth three hundred thousand dollars—all in the same area. You see what I'm saying? This was his [Abraham Lincoln Lewis's] dream, that people of all walks of life could live and be together. And so the spirit is very alive, and very healing in that sense."

While MaVynee tends to her causes, her sister supports her with a check every month. "I hear from her every month. Of course, she takes care of me now. She's been back here a couple of times. Johnnetta never loved this place like I did. She sends me money to live on, which is very little. Which I like. I mean, this is my whole point, that life can be beautiful on a very simple lifestyle, and I live on a hundred seventy-five dollars a month she sends me."

Since the trailer is a museum, MaVynee usually sleeps in the house of a Miami family that doesn't spend much time on the beach. She lives in that house during the week and rents it out for them on weekends, when she'll either stay in the trailer or in a lawn chair on the beach.

MaVynee's days are often spent advocating causes concerning the beach, digging up history, finding ways to fight the Plantation, and supporting environmental causes. She says that her fight against the Plantation puts her in opposition with people like Annette Myers. "Here we go again. The friend deceiving you or [when you] think you can trust your own. Black people turning against their own. They did it in slavery—there was always what they called the house nigger or whatever, who would go out there and spy on the plantation, the slaves, and go back and tell master. What's the difference now? You just change the name, you don't call them the overseer, or whatever you called them. I got a word for them, but anyhow."

Told of MaVynee's comments Myers denies that she is "deceiving her own," and she says that she "has the true interest of her community at heart."

MaVynee glances at a spot on the floor and tells the time. "Oh it's two. I've got an appointment at three."

I ask her how she can tell the time by spotting the sun's marks on the tile. "At two, the sun is at this spot."

She walks a few steps. "At five, it's right here."

"What happens if it rains?" I ask.

"Oh, I don't worry then. What a life. What a beautiful life. I don't have to worry about time when it rains."

Chapter 25

Tuxedo Time

HE Cotillion Room of the Sheraton Washington hotel sparkles with the light thrown from overhead chandeliers. Deep-red carpet trails from the balcony to the stairway and down to the main floor. This is the room where many young women debut to society and waltz in white dresses with tuxedoed fathers and escorts.

Tonight, December 30, 1994, all the men in the room wear tuxedos or formal military attire for those in the service, but the gowns are not all white: many women wear black; a few are in red. A couple glitter with gold. They have all emerged from a cocktail party in an adjoining room. A band from Richmond is on the stage, but they've taken a break and a deejay plays Nat "King" Cole.

Two hundred people are seated at round tables, linen in lap and the proper forks clinking against china. This isn't a cotillion, though many of the mothers here were probably presented at just such an event back during the days of segregation. And even if this were a cotillion, the balls today aren't what they used to be, anyway, according to one mother here. "Today, they're made up of all kinds of people that shouldn't be coming out because they have been out since they were seven," says Carol (not her real name). "And to give you a good example, [there was in the past] a very good cotillion sponsored by a women's group, the Links. Unfortunately, [at the Links' events] a whole bunch of people used to come in the back door, and [a few years ago] some girl came to the cotillion who was pregnant. She wasn't in the cotillion—she came as a guest, and had a baby [which she left] in the trash and went back in. They found an abandoned baby that lived. Then they had to find out whose baby it was. Most people from our group don't participate in those [kinds of events]. The blacks who used to sponsor them couldn't sift through and sort out the kids the way they would have to [to stage the cotillion properly]."

Tonight is something else. An annual gathering first held in 1986—the year in which the tuxedo was celebrating its centennial, and for that reason, the three founding mothers decided to name the event the Tuxedo Ball. Yet although the suit gave the event its name, the founders consider this ball more valuable, because it celebrates something more important than a suit. The ball's "mission" is stated on a program neatly placed alongside the silverware:

> The Tuxedo Ball is a celebration of the tradition of Black achievement in America. This event brings together the children and grandchildren of successful Black Americans in order to give them the same sense of group pride that existed in their parents' and grandparents' generations. Its purpose is to reaffirm and pass on values of excellence in achievement, pride in family accomplishment, elegance, as well as a sense of obligation to contribute to racial betterment. In other words, to extol the characteristics of their part of the Black culture as it has existed for over one hundred years.
>
> For any Black person to achieve success in America much must be overcome; and yet, many Tuxedo Ball families can date their success to before The Civil War. We admire their perseverance and determination against the odds, and we are proud of our heritage of achievement.

In addition to this mission statement, the program contains the guest list: college students and recent graduates with their schools listed: Harvard, Yale, University of Virginia, Morehouse, Spelman, Stanford, Howard, Columbia, and the like. Carlotta Miles—or, feminists beware, Mrs. Theodore Miles—appears as chairman of the ball. Then the members of the ball committees are listed. All are women, but, like Miles, use their husbands' names. First, there's the Washington Committee. They are largely responsible for the event and have the ultimate say over who is invited. Next is the General Committee, women from across the country who come to Washington once a year for the ball. They often suggest potential invitees from their cities. Finally, the program carries the names of the ball committee. They are primarily college students of both genders. They are, of course, honored with Miss or Mr., as appropriate.

Even before reading these lists of committee members and invitees, one gets a sense of the attendees' pedigree at the entrance to the ballroom, where displays tell of attendees' ancestors, famous and obscure. There's a display that tells the story of Sally Hemings. Her descendants are on the guest list, along with descendants of the Syphax family, who are purportedly the black progeny of George Washington. There are also portraits of grandparents and great-grandparents of ball attendees on display. Past years' displays have included portraits of freemen and -women of the antebellum era and photos from the first meetings of Jack and Jill, the black social and civic organization founded in Philadelphia in 1938.

"What we have is a solid set of values that was passed on to us," says Miles, a psychiatrist. "And I can trace those [values] back to my great-grandparents."

At a recent year's ball, there was a display on one of Miles's maternal great-grandfathers. "Grandpa Henry Robinson was a freeman before the Civil War," she tells me. "He was a horse breeder in the state of Florida, sold matched sets of horses to people, black and white, and he amassed an enormous amount of property for a man of color—or, I guess, for any man. [He] had twelve children, and he gave each child on their wedding, a homestead. Now, the stories in the family are that Grandpa Henry was a very controlling man, and that he gave these gifts not out of total generosity, but because he wanted his children living where he could see them. . . . He called on his children every day, and my grandfather and my grandmother used to tell me about how every day he used to ride up to their bedroom window at their house—I guess what you call today a master bedroom, with big windows—and my great-grandfather used to ride up on his horse every morning at about six-thirty and tap on my grandparents' window with his riding crop and tell my grandfather to come out and talk to him. . . . My grandmother used to get extremely irritated by this because she thought it was intrusive. But he wanted to talk to my grandfather about his day. [My grandfather was] a married man . . . at the time with two or three children, living in his own house, and his father-in-law would do that every single day, seven days a week."

Miles grew up in St. Augustine, Florida, where her parents met and settled, after her father completed training in oral surgery at Tufts University and her mother graduated from Boston University. "Oral surgery was a new specialty—there weren't that many, and there certainly weren't that many black ones. And so I can assume what he had to tolerate, listening to stories of other black people who were in Boston at the time. . . . My mother was told at BU by a professor that she should go home her freshman year because she would never be able to graduate . . . she said the pleasure of her life was walking up in the graduation procession. . . .

"Now, I had a father who had an integrated practice in the forties, in a segregated town [St. Augustine]. He was the only oral surgeon in the state of any color. . . . All the white doctors had segregated waiting rooms: blacks in one room, whites in another room. [But] if you came to see Daddy, you had to sit there together, and they did. The sheriff sat there next to the domestic, and nobody died. And so I grew up seeing that there could be exceptions to institutionalized rules."

Miles says that there is no set criteria for Tuxedo Ball attendance, nor is there a typical Tuxedo Ball attendee. However, there are a number of common threads connecting many of the people in this room. Many of the parents here attended what are considered exclusive New England boarding schools and then elite colleges before such institutions "opened up" in the sixties. Most of the families represented boast three or four generations of college graduates on one, if not both, sides of the family (if only on one side, it is generally the mother's) and third-generation professionals. "Some of our kids are third-generation Ivy League," says Miles, whose husband, Theodore, or Tony, is a lawyer and a graduate of Exeter and Harvard.

I ask her about the inclusion of wealthy African Americans whose names are more known to the public through the media, such as John H. Johnson of the Johnson Publishing Company and the late Reginald Lewis. "I would say John Johnson is very successful in every way. You know, he made a lot of money, educated his children; [it] seems that he has been able to pass along his business on to his next generation. I don't know what his personal values are . . . I don't know anything about him, I've never met him. So I can't really speak for that. . . . I think for us, in this particular group, probably the most outstanding thing about us is our value system. Because a lot of us have no money—definitely have no money in the John Johnson sense or in the president of BET [Robert Johnson] sense. . . . They have megabucks. There are many tracks to prosperity in America . . . but I have no idea what they actually believe in. I don't know what they say to their children; I don't know how they treat their wives.

"I think one of the differences, perhaps . . . has to do with the broadness of the consistency, that it isn't just one person who is successful. . . . It isn't that one person has a million dollars, but their brother is a mechanic and is struggling. And it isn't that one person, you know what I mean, is successful and nobody else in the family is successful."

Tony Miles, the son of two teachers, grew up in Washington, D.C. "We were in a part of the city called Far Northeast, which in those days was almost like a country village," he recalls. "I can remember when I was small, the people two doors from us had a goat and chickens. And there were people that came around in the summer with wagons selling vegetables, watermelon, and fish, ice, stuff like that, so it was almost like being in a small town. Washington was a segregated city. The black community was energetic and well established. There were theaters and restaurants. It was a comfortable life."

Many of Tony's peers went to the famed Dunbar High School, a black school known for rigor and academic excellence, but his parents chose another route for him: Exeter. "That was my first encounter with Republicans," says Tony with a laugh. "I had never met anybody that didn't think FDR was God!

"I think my parents felt Exeter was going to be the best," he continues. "From an academic point of view, it was the most competitive environment in the country. I learned new sports—I played lacrosse, I played squash, I got some coaching in tennis. It was just an incredible set of experiences. . . .

"In my senior year, we had to write a paper in my American history class, so I wrote about free Negroes before the Civil War. My own feeling [was] that in this group, slavery was not all there was to [their] identity. . . . The Brown decision came out in my senior year, and I had a good friend, a white boy from Florida, and he said to me the day it came down, 'The people from the South will never put up with this,' and I said, 'Which people are you talking about, the white people or the black people?' . . . That kind of stopped him in his tracks."

Despite the opportunities and advantages he has enjoyed, Tony Miles has still felt the burden of race, too. "There were times when I considered leaving the country," he says, "because in those days I could look around my Harvard class and there were people that I could academically run rings around, but they were going to have opportunities that I was not going to have. They had an uncle with this Wall Street brokerage firm or their daddy was a partner in that law firm or whatever the case might be. You know, people have forgotten how far we've come."

From Harvard, Miles returned to Washington and attended Howard University School of Law, right at the time when many of the landmark civil-rights cases were being argued before the Supreme Court. The atmosphere was charged, and the law students immersed themselves. "When Thurgood [Marshall] would argue at the Supreme Court," Tony remembers, "all of us would pile into cars and go down and listen to him argue. . . . Some of them involved people who were in the sit-ins."

He chose Howard, though, not to be in Washington so much as for the institution itself: "Just about everybody I had heard of in our community had gone there, and the teachers were very well trained, very demanding, they pushed us hard . . . I think that whole business about '[you've] got to be better' was part of our attitude."

Still, Miles says that there were some who told him going to Howard would be a mistake. "I had one friend who said, 'If you go to Howard you'll never pass the bar.' Don't ever tell me I can't do nothing. So we only graduated twenty-two; seven took the D.C. bar. Five passed it the first time. I passed it with the highest score in the whole city. . . ."

"This was 1963, but again, to show you how things have changed, I wanted to go to the SEC [Securities Exchange Commission] because I thought that was where the money was, [and] I wanted to find out about this money stuff, [so] I went down and took an exam. . . . The guy called me the next day and said I hadn't done well, and I was devastated. I said, 'I'd like to come in sometime and go over it and see where I have done wrong.' At that point, my wife was pregnant—Wendell was about to arrive on the scene—and I'm trying to get a job so I can take care of things."

Two weeks later, Miles called again and explained the situation to another SEC employee. "He said, 'What did you say your name was?' I gave him my name. . . . He came back to the phone, and he said, 'I don't know why you think you hadn't done well—you were rated outstanding by everyone on the panel.' That thing really turned me off . . . this is why when white people talk about reverse discrimination I want to hit 'em."

Carlotta Miles also attended segregated schools until high school, when she went to the Cushing School outside Boston, and then to Wheaton College. "Even though it was predominantly white," Miles says, recalling Cushing, "the culture of the school was very very similar to the culture of my family. Books, music, privilege, good value system. You know—the New Englanders are very Puritan and the Puritan ethic was what I was raised on. If it's hard, work harder. Don't give up—work harder. So I never saw it in terms of black and white. . . . They were all white, but they weren't any smarter than I was.

"You weren't there to cluster," Carlotta continues, contrasting her experience to that of many blacks at predominantly white boarding schools in the 1980s and '90s. "You'd had that enforced by the American government. . . . We didn't feel the need to cluster. We didn't feel that somehow if we didn't cluster we would lose something."

The Tuxedo Ball is the brainchild of Carlotta Miles, one of the event's three founders. "Everywhere that I went—to Martha's Vineyard, Atlanta, Jacksonville, California—everywhere I went, . . . there was a group of black friends, like this," she tells me. "People were saying the same thing: they were worried about their children. They felt their children didn't have a context, that they were not rewarded in any way for what they were or what they were doing—aside from the reward, of course, [of] getting into good colleges and doing the things that we've always done. But they didn't get any affirmation from the greater culture for how difficult that might be for them, and they didn't know each other.

"Well, we wanted our children to just know each other. We wanted them to not feel overshadowed, either by the white world or overshadowed by all of the attention that was given to disadvantaged black children, for being disadvantaged. It was as if you got more credit for being disadvantaged than you got for already making it and continuing to make it generation after generation. Why bother? If you are not ever going to be patted on the back, and if you were constantly going to be attacked by your own people. . . . They were under attack in colleges: there were children who were pretending that their parents weren't paying their tuition. One father told me that he was highly insulted that his daughter pretended to be on a scholarship, and here he was paying twenty-five thousand dollars a year tuition, himself. And yet she felt under fire at a New England Ivy League school. I've seen a number of kids go through horrible identity crises, because other black kids have told them they're not black or not black enough, as if they could define for them who they were supposed to be and there was only one way you could be black. I'm a psychiatrist, so we go someplace and parents would sit down and corner me—'What are we going to do?' Many were lost."

So they created the ball, which is just the main act, but not the only event. Earlier today, for example, Warren Robbins, founder and president of the Robbins Center for Cross-Cultural Communication and founder of the Museum of African Art at the Smithsonian Institution, gave a lecture and slide presentation entitled "Unmasking Picasso: The Influence of African Art on Modern Western Art." In addition, there were career seminars where a panel of parents and recent college graduates give advice to the college students on careers in medicine, law, and education.

Now, at the ball, all are gathered for dinner and dancing, and socializing. And while Carlotta Miles insists that this is not a mating party, one father, who spoke on the condition he not be identified, says that many mothers have hopes that their sons will meet the "right kind" of black woman at the ball so that they wouldn't bring home a white fiancée. And another attendee, who has made most of the balls, recalls a moment when she was told that this was more than just a cocktail party: "I was standing above the balcony," says Cynthia Hawkins, and "an older woman comes up to me, and we are looking at everyone. She says, 'This is to make sure you all marry right.'"

But whether it's about matchmaking or not, "There is definitely a value system here," comments Martha Holbart, thirty-seven, who sits at one of the few thirty-something tables among all of the parents and college-age children, as she looks out over the room. "Some people with different values would not feel comfortable at their age socializing with their parents in the same room. These kids have to be very, very comfortable with themselves, having their mothers at the next table. And sometimes, some of these well-to-do black mothers will [be] hovering over, protecting, doing everything for them. My mother, literally, she would do anything for me."

Holbart, a woman with a Halle Berry–esque beauty, wears a formal black silk cocktail dress. She attended the first Tuxedo Ball in 1986, when she was twenty-eight. "My brother and I were invited; we went for years. I thought it was wonderful, but I was always the oldest young person there. There was never one person back in those days that was my age. We kind of grew up, past it. And then they asked me to be chairman one year, and I was asked to come back and work and be on the other end." So Holbart helps with the preparations, taking part in everything from creating the seating plan to sending out invitations.

Holbart, today the executive director of the District of Columbia Democratic Party, has Texas roots. Her great-grandfather was a doctor in Fort Worth, Texas, and both her paternal grandparents were principals there. It was through her grandmother's machinations, in fact, that her parents met. She tells me that while her father was in his final year of law school at Texas Southern, his mother hired his wife-to-be. "My mother started teaching at an elementary school in Fort Worth, Texas, and the principal was her future mother-in-law. . . . I wouldn't say it was arranged, but I think my grandmother had thought my mother was the perfect candidate for her son, and so they only went on seven dates before they married. . . . [My mother] was what you would consider a Southern belle—she was the last of four children, and she was at home with her parents. It was unheard-of in that time for women to move out . . . so the only way to leave home was to get married, and so people didn't have long courtships in those days."

When Holbart was five, the family moved from Fort Worth to Washington, D.C. Their first house was in Northwest Washington, in the neighborhood known as the Gold Coast. When she reached the junior high school, the family moved a few miles north to Chevy Chase, Maryland.

"We were the first black family to move in our neighborhood," she recalls, "and one reason why they sold my father the house was that he was the director of fair housing, and they couldn't say no. But I do remember there were no other black students inside my junior high school the total years I was there. The only other black person in the whole school was the janitor.

"One thing I can say about my parents: I felt we were well grounded. We had black friends. We went back to Texas [to see family] all the time. We knew who we were. There are so many of my friends who grew up in white neighborhoods, who went to white private schools, who are lost, basically—you know, would rather be around white folks than black folks."

In addition to making sure that she knew who she was, Holbart's parents also took care to teach her the value of social graces and encouraged her to educate herself, in and out of school. "I had been taught and reared and trained to be pretty, to be sweet, to be classy, to be appropriate, to be well read. My father paid me five dollars a book [for every book I read], every single summer—that was my job. And that was how I was groomed."

That grooming isn't always highly esteemed in the gritty and rough world of local politics, though. As executive director of the D.C. Democratics, Holbart interacts with a diverse population and must answer to the party's leadership, members of which do not always appreciate her refinement. "There's this one woman who's part of the Democratic state committee; smells horrible, wears a wig . . . you know—poor, never went to a day of college, and I don't know how she got to be where she is. She harasses me nine to five. She has nothing going on in her life, and she wants me out of a job so bad. She thinks I'm this privileged little bourgy kid, and she thinks Steve [not his real name] who also works, is another bourgy kid because his father is a doctor and his family vacations in Martha's Vineyard. She doesn't want either one of us in the job. And they harass us."

Holbart says that such harassment was even stronger when she was the office manager for a Democratic congresswoman and the chief of staff berated her at every step for her looks and her boyfriend at the time. "She was a woman who was very, very tall and not that attractive, and I'm the antithesis of her. (I'm more petite.) She's big and men don't want her, and she has no love life. I can remember I took a cut in salary to go work for this congresswoman, and I went back [to the chief of staff] and said after six months, 'You were going to bring my salary up,' and she said, 'We're not giving you a dime more. Your boyfriend is a plastic surgeon.'"

Holbart says that the Tuxedo Ball provides a refuge from harassment. "You can come here and be yourself. See, we deal with lower-class blacks being hateful—not whites. I lived in a very, very affluent neighborhood, and the affluent white kids were trained very well. They were not rude. They would never call you a name or speak out of turn. . . .

"In the end, it becomes a class thing. It's not so much black/white as it is class. Class is the biggest issue, always, for me.

"So what the [Tuxedo Ball] parents try to do is counteract it, to protect their kids from that abuse. . . . They can hardly protect them at jobs, but what they can do is give them the best education. Most Tuxedo Ball people probably don't even work for low-income black folks. Most probably have nice private-sector jobs, or they're their own bosses because they're doctors and lawyers or something like that."

Holbart says one of her biggest challenges has been dating across class lines. She has been involved with a number of highly successful men from different backgrounds, but she says the relationships have failed because of class differences. "Most of them were raised very poorly, humble means," she says. "They were smart boys, not that they weren't smart, you know. I look back now on my twenties and thirties, dating these men, [and] it was always the background that was keeping us apart, keeping us from connecting, as recently as the man I was dating the last couple of months. . . .

"I hate to be elitist—if that's being elitist. I love some of these guys and may have married some of them. I dated a guy who came to Washington, met him just as he had taken the bar. He went to one of the biggest firms in D.C. He's a partner there now. He hated bourgeois blacks completely. He finally married a white woman who is not educated. She's, like, a secretary. But she was white, so he felt that he had everything those other white lawyers had. He hated all my friends. He thought they were bourgeois. He thought my standards were uppity, and yet he had very high standards for himself. He bought only Brooks Brothers suits. He had wonderful taste in clothing. He was very, very traditional.

"I went down there [to his hometown in the South] for a wedding and I took the rental car and said let me just go see where this man came from. It was a dirt road. It was very, very poor. So consequently he just grew up thinking that white was always right."

Holbart pauses and reflects. "You can go to college and you can get all kinds of degrees and you can . . . buy a Lexus and you can buy from Brooks Brothers, but if it's not inside you and you weren't raised with family background and class, that's it. No matter how much money he'll have, no matter how that firm can promote him to be the head partner, he would still never have that feeling inside. So bourgeois blacks are a reflection of something that he can never be.

"Once, the firm sent him to New York on an assignment for eighteen months. . . . I went up there; he was living in SoHo, and we went out with all white people for dinner—his friends from the law firm. I said to him, 'I find it so fascinating that you hate well-to-do blacks, but all these people you hang out with are well-to-do whites—what is the story?' And he hated that comment. But all those white people . . . some of their fathers owned yachts and houses on Long Island and a home in Vermont. They were not poor white kids. They all had gone to Duke and to Yale Law School and Harvard Law School. . . . I said, 'Well, why do you hate well-to-do blacks, . . . but you like well-to-do white people?' I'm sure it'll stick with him for the rest of his life . . . and my mother always gets on me about being too blunt with men."

In a sense, Holbart's perspective upsets the popular perception of a black elite as distant, aloof, and eager to run far from any kind of "African-American" experience. It is Holbart who doesn't date interracially, while her former boyfriend, from a low-income background, marries a white woman and has only white friends. Holbart isn't the only one who's noticed, either, she says. "His wife met a girlfriend of mine, and my girlfriend said to [her], 'Oh, I know your husband—one of my good girlfriends used to date him.' And his wife said, 'Oh, well, I don't know why my husband doesn't have any black friends.' She's white, and she said she never understood why her husband didn't have any black friends, and he was black."

Holbart says there are other hurdles facing single black professional women, regardless of socioeconomic differences between them and many of the men they meet. "Men here are all looking for a perfect woman. I call it the Claire Huxtable syndrome: they all believe there's a Claire Huxtable out there, that they're going to find her. She's going to be witty and funny and sexy and smart and bring home eighty thousand dollars, and she's gonna be five-six. And there's tons of wonderful men out there, you know, who keep thinking, 'I'm going to keep looking until I find this woman.' [But] she doesn't actually exist, and they're not Bill Cosby."

She looks back at another relationship. "I dated a plastic surgeon for four years, and he wanted me to be perfect. He wanted my hair longer; he wanted me to be skinny. He wanted me to have a powerful job. He wanted me to go to law school. He wanted me to do everything. He wanted me to work in his office. He wanted just so much from me. And that was impossible, because I came from a privileged, sheltered life—I had a maid in my house every day that I woke up, you know, and my parents didn't pay a million dollars for me to go to American University for me to come over and clean up your house. And the guys just don't understand that.

"He was from, I would say, not middle-class, but lower-middle-class, working-class people, even though his parents were educated. His mother was a counselor in an elementary school and his father was a college professor in the South. [But] he didn't have the refinement—he's basically uncouth; everything is about money with him."

Holbart says that many of her friends don't understand why she's not married. "People expected me in high school to get married. I would have been the most likely to be married. I was Donna Reed, June Cleaver. People hear about my jobs, and they're amazed: they say, 'What, you were a lobbyist? . . . You were an office manager for a member of Congress? . . . You are the executive director of the D.C. Democratic Party?' People just expected me to be a sweet little Martha all my life."

In fact, this life isn't quite what she expected, either, and despite her accomplishments, Holbart has some misgivings. "I would have thought I would have two, three kids by now, and have a nice house in the suburbs and a Taurus station wagon. I just think my life went in a completely different direction, and it was completely against what I ever wanted.

"My mother always says, 'Your day is coming'; she says, 'One day, you'll just be fighting them off, because men will come full circle and will say, "Oh, well, that was the girl I should have married, that was the one my mother liked, that was the one who was honest and pays her bills and is going to church, and she's the one that I should actually marry."' But, see, it takes maturity for a man to appreciate somebody like me."

At Martha's table and beyond, one can't help but notice that many could be mistaken for white. Ironically, Carlotta Miles, along with another founder, Carolyn Thornell, are among the few brown-skinned people in this room. There is one dark-skinned man noticeable for his dreadlocks.

"They've gotten darker," says Holbart, jokingly comparing this year's crowd to earlier years'. "In the beginning, you could not tell that many people here were black. It was like its own culture. I tell you, probably Doctor [Carlotta] Miles was the brownest person in there. It just seemed like everybody was very, very, fair skinned. And we always used to tease each other and say, 'Why do we call ourselves black?' Well, now 'cause we're no longer black: we're African Americans."

Dinner is over and the band plays the Electric Slide, which brings a large crowd to the dance floor. Crystal Wright, twenty-eight, the daughter of a Richmond dentist, sits it out. "I hate line dances," she later explains. "I think they are corny and dumb. It's like being on Lawrence Welk or something. What's the point of that?"

The Slide aside, Wright still considers this one of her favorite parties of the year. She's been to every Tuxedo Ball and vividly remembers the first one. "It just seems like a little fairy tale, kind of Cinderella ball. I felt like the princess. It just felt like a thing out of a storybook or something that I have never imagined could happen . . . I remember getting dressed at the hotel . . . I went downstairs, and my mind was boggled at how organized it was, just how nice and formal it was. The fact that everyone was so well be-haved and had the same kind of upbringing that we had—you know, man-ners. . . . It was like being in a candy store where you could actually have everything. You were [not] limited to one item—you could just taste what-ever you wanted and it was okay, whereas before, in school, you go to a party and it was always like, let's try to find the one chocolate chip in the crowd and is he cute?"

Joi Sheffield, twenty-six, a first-year law student at Howard University, makes her way around the room, greeting friends as she goes. The daugh-ter of a judge, she also grew up in Richmond and attended a nearly all-white Episcopal girls' school. She says that she's grown away from those childhood friends. "It was hard to remain friends, because . . . people had their debutante parties . . . [and] I was not included in that coming-out process. . . . You can go as a guest, and I was invited to the parties. . . . These are the kinds of parties where you are invited, and they determine who your escort is going to be. So I'm always paired up with the leftover nerd, or whatever. But they invited me because they felt, 'We can't leave her out.'

"There were girls that I went to school with that were genuinely my friends. They still call and say, 'Come to this person's party; we're all getting back together and we wanted to see how you're doing.' I would go, but just for the sake of going. I don't have fun any more. They are just not part of my world.

"A lot of these girls come from families that are just so wealthy that they don't have to go to school if they don't want to. They'll go to school and major in art history, and then come out and do something just for the sake of coming out and having a job. [Maybe] their mom has a store, so they can just do that. But I just can't come out and do that. My mom does not have a store. . . . These are girls who talk about the guy they're going to marry, how much money he has, and what kind of wedding she's gonna have.

"Most of my white friends' mothers play tennis all day and do charity stuff. You're not going to find that, you're not going to find a Tuxedo Ball mother who plays tennis all day . . . because they're out being doctors and lawyers and helping their kids. That's a huge difference in my mind. We don't have that luxury."

The pocket of Northwest Washington near Rock Creek Park known as the Gold Coast is a neighborhood of Washington's elite. Theodore and Carlotta Miles have been in the neighborhood for more than twenty years.

Months before the Tuxedo Ball, I met them at their home on a Saturday. Carlotta Miles invited two other mothers connected to the ball to join the discussion as well: Carolyn Thornell, a sociologist married to a Howard University law-school professor; Marilyn Thunderburk, a former personal assistant to Rosalynn Carter and owner of a public-relations firm whose husband is a Washington, D.C., surgeon. She also invited two women who've attended since college: Karyn Thomas, a Washington, D.C., native married to an attorney, and Joi Sheffield.

"We've known each other all our lives," says Carlotta Miles, "but our children might not have. When there was segregation, our parents were very close-knit friends. People visited each other [when traveling]. My home was the Florida stop, because hotels were segregated. There was that huge expanse—say, between Washington and Florida—where there were no hotels, and so the professional black people stayed with each other. They did not sleep in cars by the side of the road and they did not stay in run-down, roach-infested places. They stayed with each other.

"Because of what might be called [another] Underground Railroad, so to speak, there was a huge network of the upper middle class that received people. People referred you—you would get a letter from your cousin in New York or your best friend's sister in Philadelphia saying, 'Dr. and Mrs. So and So are motoring to Florida, and would you please receive them as your guests? They are wonderful people, et cetera, et cetera, and you would open your guest room to them and keep them for two days, and then you might send them on to [another family] in Miami. . . . You always stayed in someone's lovely home, whether you knew them or not—all you needed was a letter of introduction that went ahead, or a telephone call, and you always stayed with another doctor.

"That's what you would call it today: a network. I hate the word *networking*—I think the English language is being contaminated with words like *networking*—but it was a network of people, of like-minded people, like-minded value systems."

The world of the professionals' children was similarly tight, says Carolyn Thornell, who grew up in Bryn Mawr. "Many of us went to Northern colleges, so-called elite or select, and we knew or heard of each other, who were in these different places. I went to Vassar. I knew who was at Yale at that time and who was at Smith."

Miles picks up again. "Now, the other thing was—we have to include this—you could not bring anyone into your home unless your parents knew who that was. . . . They would ask you, 'Who is that person? Who are their parents? What is his father's name? What's his mother's name, again? Oh, yes, they can come.' You could not just go freely into anybody's home, and you definitely couldn't date anybody's child, anybody's daughter without getting past all that. 'Who are you? What makes you think you can walk into my house and date my daughter?'—that was the message: You have to go by me first."

"I think my father's greatest pleasure was being able to meet people at the door and say 'no,'" says Thunderburk.

"That goes back, for me, two generations, to my grandparents' friends," Miles resumes. "[Today] we are not quite as tight, but we're tight.

"Well," she continues, thinking about generational changes, "my father really forbade me to go to the Dartmouth winter carnival, in a letter. So, I think, [today] we try to be a little more enlightened when it comes right down to it. You do express your opinion about the person they may be going out with, and we've done that several times, with all of the children. And we make a point of meeting people's parents. We either go to their houses or have them come here. We're not talking about money—we want to know what kind of values this one may have, what kind of people they are. You don't play around with the people part. I think the entire black culture and what it stood for and the structure that held it up at all ends, fell apart, in the sixties. The upper end, we suddenly were under attack by blacks and whites for our value system for believing you should dress a certain way. You don't get on a plane wearing jeans and old shoes and an old T-shirt. You get on a plane with a blazer on, if not a tie, a nice shirt. It used to be suit, gloves, heels, the whole regalia."

"That's right," agrees Thornell.

"All of a sudden you see that there was a lot of iconoclasm, so the whole culture of America was coming apart—the Establishment, right? All those standards, people were burning their bras and burning their girdles and burning their stockings. For us, [though,] those were important structural standards because they protected us. If you got on an airplane or train in a suit and tie you were treated differently as a black person than you were if you got on in sweat clothes."

"All of a sudden there was a rift created in the black culture between those who still believed that that was necessary, the so-called Establishment, and those who no longer felt it was necessary," says Thornell.

"Because whites were saying relax that, we're relaxing it," says Miles. "They were saying you don't have to do what those people are saying to do, and the black teachers were, you see, some of the people who told kids this is what you must do to earn respect or demand respect—you can't get on a plane looking like that, looking like a bum and then say, 'Oh, you were treating me like a nigger.' The way blacks were treated was very capricious, and you had to control that which you could control, because you could not control the greater culture. So you maximize the opportunity that you were going to be treated well."

"And if it meant that you presented yourself in a way that enabled them to distinguish you from ordinary blacks," Thornell completes the thought, "you did it. That was a survival strategy that was much more generalized through black society than it is today."

"So that it would be unheard of, at that time and probably in some quarters through today, for a working-class black woman or man to go to something they value or something that was important looking shabby," says Miles. "They wouldn't do it. So, all of that got broken down to the extent that persons who were continuing to do it fit into somebody's definition of the black bourgeoisie. They became hit harder because they were generally under attack. And that you remember that E. Franklin Frazier's book [*The Black Bourgeoisie*] came out."

"That was before that, late fifties, because I did a fair amount of work on it in college and afterward."

"Here he was, a black professor, attacking."

"Well, he was describing, but he was analyzing," says Thornell. "And he was saying that there is a lot that is fake, phony, and basically a façade among these people who feel that they are elite. And if you felt that you really didn't live your life that way, then you felt that the analysis was invalid, which I think many parts of it were. I'm a sociologist, and that kind of analysis is the kind that I spent a lot of time doing."

"Do you agree with his analysis?" I ask.

"No, I didn't agree with his analysis, because I believe what he was doing was finding those members of the black upper class who deserved the contempt that he really felt for them. I think he—"

"Where was he based?" asks Miles, cutting Thornell off.

"He was at Howard," I respond. "He was at Fisk before his first study."

"I think what he was saying was that the black upper class was frivolous," says Thornell. "That they were concerned only with the frivolous side of life rather than the substantial side of life. And he was identifying doctors, lawyers, and college professors as persons who were living this frivolous life. My parents' friends were in Philadelphia, and they were doctors, lawyers, and college professors, and they were not leading a frivolous life. Granted, I did not have a full perspective of the world like I have now, nor was I living in the midst of Howard University culture, and so I'm sure he was looking at a bigger world, so he had more opportunity to look at some frivolous elements. I think what he did, for whatever reasons, was focus on the frivolous elements and ignore the rest, and, there-fore, he painted a picture that was basically lopsided. I have heard that Washington, being the kind of society it was—very closed, very color con-scious—my understanding is that he felt that he was excluded by this black bourgeoisie world, that he was not the right color or background for them, [so] he kind of set out to hold this group up to ridicule, since obvi-ously he was a very substantial person and they didn't want him. This is what I heard. It's a general folklore at this point . . . I think there is no question, there are some cities that have historically been much more color conscious within the black community. I think Washington is one of them."

"Washington and Charleston," says Miles.

"Philadelphia is not quite as bad, but it has its patterns as well," says Thornell.

"And, look, nobody rode in on just color; even in Washington, it was never just color," Miles points out. "Someone once said it was family, color, and money. And you had to have two out of the three."

"Family, color, and money; I think there was probably an element of what you did to earn the money. Sort of occupational background."

"As opposed to brand-new, hot money."

"What is it today?" I ask.

"I think there are old values, and they have to do with old families—old-family values. I would say that I found the New England value was com-pletely in sync with my family's values, and that was so comfortable. I think that my grandmother would have said that: You do not hit people in the face with what you have. You just don't do that. You don't do things for show. You are a substantive person, and you want to be substantive, and if you want to have money, that's fine."

"People now—I was in a wedding, and the whole talk at the reception was, 'How much money do you think they spent?'" says Joi Sheffield. "I mean, everybody was just floored. 'This makes no sense,' you could just hear it all buzzing around. 'It doesn't make sense they spent this much money on this wedding; what are they trying to prove?' blah, blah, blah, blah. It was amazing, now, the more people show what they have, the more people resent them for showing it. They were saying, 'She doesn't need to [do] this.' They didn't even get this person. 'They didn't need all those flow-ers.' It didn't make sense, but it was like they had to prove a point."

"What was the point?" asks Miles.

"'We're going to have the wedding of the year. The governor's [Douglas Wilder's] daughter got married, and now we're going to show that up. It was, 'We can do this. We can do this, we have the money to do it; we have the resources.'"

"I'm not saying it's better," says Thornell, comparing the values shared by the people in this room to those of other African-American professionals. "But it's just a different culture. . . . I have friends who have much money, black friends who have much more money than we have, who look at my husband and me with real scorn, that we spend our money to send our children to private schools. They say, 'No, indeed, I'm not going to spend my money on that.' They spend their money on status symbols—cars, now that's their choice. Their house looks better than mine does; their car definitely looks better than mine does. They do not understand a collection of values that would say yes, we want our kids to have the benefit of the education that we think is appropriate, and in this town at this time that's to be found really only in an independent school. It's not private for the sake of private."

I ask Thornell how the Tuxedo Ball differs from Jack and Jill, because she grew up in the latter organization. "My children were members for a while and they became very disinterested because the values and the interests of the children in Jack and Jill were not their values and interests," she begins. "There was a lot of focus on going to puppet shows and wax museums and theater engagements, to make the children proud of being black. . . . My children have grown up in a house full of African art, [around] people who have spent their lives writing about this and have a whole history associated with this; their father teaches at Howard law school. We are not living in a white world; we are living in a black world, but it's been part of their whole nurturing. It's not something that is imposed on top of everything else."

Karyn Thomas, a Howard University graduate, recalls awkward moments at both Howard and the private, predominantly white independent high school she attended. She remembers that when the issue of slavery was addressed in a textbook in high school, the teacher turned to her and apologized for having to go over it in class.

"That's been really hard for me, to figure out who I am," she says. "I'm probably just now coming to that. I'm just now figuring it out and realizing that it's okay that I am who I am . . . I always felt like I have to be this person for the group that I'm in."

"It's exhausting," concurs Joi Sheffield. "It exhausted me."

"I felt schizophrenic," Thomas adds.

At this, Thornell speaks up again. "Psychoanalysts have always said that black people are inherently unanalyzable," she says. "They are inherently schizophrenic because they have two roles that they are constantly playing. I used to be so highly insulted by that characterization of the black psyche. Yes, we have these two things to do [succeed and do so in a white world], but we are not schizophrenic. But the amount of extra pressure that it puts on you is over and above what any white person has to deal with—"

"And to achieve in spite of that," Miles adds.

"When we were growing up," continues Thornell, "We were trained to do that. When people say to me, 'How could you stand being one of six [black women] out of fourteen hundred women at Vassar? Was it terrible?' No, it wasn't, because I was taught . . . my parents taught me how to survive in that situation. A much harder thing to cope with was when I was finally around a lot of black people, in graduate school [in the sixties at Harvard], who kept looking at me and told me I wasn't black enough: 'What's the matter with you?'"

"One of the things that characterizes this group is conservatism . . . beyond racial boundaries," says Carlotta Miles.

It is now dinnertime on Saturday night. Theodore and Carlotta Miles's three children—Wendell, thirty, in his final year of medical school at Georgetown; Cecily, twenty-eight, a Columbia art history grad; and Lydia, twenty-four, a graduate of the University of Pennsylvania looking toward law school, are all out for the evening. Carolyn Thornell, Marilyn Thunderburk, Joi Sheffield, and Karyn Thomas have all gone home.

"But what makes a conservative a conservative and a liberal a liberal, I don't know," Miles continues. "Tony can answer that."

"Would you call yourself a conservative also?" I press, turning to her husband.

"Oh, no."

"He's the house liberal," Carlotta says. "I'm saying, as a group, this is a conservative group. You're not going to find us doing wild and crazy things. We're just not like that. We believe in the tried and true."

I want to revisit the issue of the sixties, which came up this afternoon. Carlotta Miles thinks that the African-American community suffered a cultural breakdown in that decade. She's strongly in favor of integration and a supporter of the civil-rights movement, but feels that those causes were undercut to a certain extent by divisions in the black community, the consequences of which are still evident today.

"Let's face it, the judicial system was bad, downright punitive, there was a lot of things about American culture that had been missed or accepted just as part of the black condition . . . that had to be changed," she states of the pre–civil-rights era. "There were so many good things going on in the six-ties. . . . Segregation was brought to an end; that was excellent. . . .

"But, like I was saying, I also thought what they did during the sixties was to turn classes of black people against each other. Before, everybody wanted the same direction . . . whether they were rich or poor; they ac-cepted the guidance of the teachers. When the sixties came along, they no longer accepted the guidance. . . . You got a kind of divisiveness in the six-ties, where the lower classes made fun of the old standards—not necessar-ily fun of the people that kept the standards, but of the standards themselves. . . . So people had Afros out to here. 'Black is beautiful' and that gave blacks a tremendous amount of self-esteem, especially blacks who hadn't had self-esteem, but it took away direction, it took away idealism. People no longer looked up to achievers. . . .

"That piece was taken away from our people: they were given permis-sion to be mediocre. Just be yourself, do whatever you like, have illegiti-mate children, get drunk, use drugs. Those are not new things, and those are not things that only black people have been doing; black people are just like everybody else—they've been doing everything that everybody else has been doing. Except that white culture took a hit from the sixties and then recovered. Our culture took a big hit and it blew us apart, and we have never gotten back together. . . . We all no longer share the same value system. A new value system has grown up and flourished at the lower end and threatens to overwhelm the upper end.

"My mother [says that] our generation was the first generation [of African Americans] that had complete access to the white world—all the schools, all the jobs, all the apartment houses, all the neighborhoods. So we went head-long into accepting the access, not looking hard to see if we wanted it in the first place. There are a lot of black people living in mansions out in the mid-dle of nowhere, you see, without wondering what their kids gonna do or who they're gonna play with, . . . or you send your kid to some [school] and they're the only [black kid] in their class. That's what happened with Joi [Sheffield]. . . . People didn't stop to wonder if that's gonna harm my kid: Is she gonna know who she really is? Is she really [gonna] know that her great-grandmother was a violinist? Is anybody going to teach her things that black children need to know and be proud of? No—in a white school with one black kid, they don't teach any black history. You heard what Karyn said: there was a paragraph about slavery, and then the teacher apologized to her for even mentioning it, as if it were something to be ashamed of.

"What I said in my lectures [to colleges, and prep and boarding schools on curricular and counseling issues] is you must now teach . . . history [so that] the slaveholders' descendants and the descendants of slaves both leave the classroom feeling proud of themselves and their ancestors. Now that's a big job."

"Why should the slaveholders' descendants feel proud?" asks Tony.

"Because school is not about making kids feel bad about themselves," his wife replies. "When we teach history, you got to teach it in such a way that the kids understand that a man has to find his integrity within the system. People owned slaves in those times. How you treated them—"

"Some people had the courage and the sense of justice not to do it, to get out of the system," Tony cuts her off. "Some people gave up their slaves."

"The point is that if they did that, if they bought into it, there was an inner reality to it that they had to deal with, and that was the point of my question. . . . But what I'm saying is that you don't get up there as a teacher and say all those filthy, nasty, horrible slaveholders were just nasty, immoral, unchristian, horrible people, and have that child sitting there thinking, 'I am the descendant of filthy, horrible people.'"

"I think part of that question is the question of age appropriateness," says Tony.

"I'm talking about little children. That is not constructive."

"I think by the time you get to high school and college, you have to start to really push."

"You can say the institution is bad. Because they're at a stage of forming their self-esteem, you cannot teach little children that their ancestors were horrible people any more than you can say all the slaves were stupid and all the slaves were singing in the fields, which is what one history book said—it said they were happy and they liked servitude. You have to find a way to teach it so that everybody comes out okay, so the children come out of the classroom feeling okay about themselves. I don't care how you do it—it's a hard task, a very hard task, but they used to teach it so all the black people came out feeling bad and all the white people came out feeling good, and some people taught it so all the black people came out feeling good and all the white people came out feeling bad."

"Shouldn't we be teaching history from the perspective of truth?" I ask.

Carlotta turns to me. "You have a daughter. When your daughter grows up and says, 'Daddy, did they have homeless people when I was a baby?' and you say yes, and she says, 'Did you do anything about it?' What are you going to say?"

"Mother Teresa just said, 'Love is not love unless it hurts,'" adds Tony.

"That's right. 'Daddy, why didn't you take some of those homeless people home with you? You and Mommy could've let them sleep in the living room in the sleeping bag.' What are you going to say? 'Well, we got kind of used to the homeless people, honey. They were around all the time. We gave them a dollar here and there.' 'But you didn't take anybody home with you, Daddy.'

"All I'm saying is that it is very difficult in your own time to [foresee how your actions will appear in hindsight]. It's easy when it's all over and you look back on it to criticize it, but [not] if it's actually happening to you. You know, history suffers from presentism: we tend to judge history in terms of our present condition, judge what they could have done and what they should have said, you see? How can one white man control five hundred slaves? There were five hundred of them and one of him? Why didn't they just revolt? Why didn't they burn the place down? What kind of sheep are these? Just one white man and an overseer controlling two hundred slaves or a hundred and fifty slaves. . . . That's presentism: You're not looking at all the various devices of intimidation. You're not looking at how slow life was, and if you ran away, where are you going? Are you going to run to the swamps of Mississippi and get eaten by an alligator? Are you going to run down a road? We had no road maps, couldn't read. Now, some people did get to the Underground Railroad at great risk, but not in huge numbers. I mean, the whole one hundred and fifty didn't leave, and how are you going to judge those people who found their integrity within the system by just being cooperative and staying out of trouble and trying to make the best of it? We judged them very hard. Most people would've said, 'Oh, they're just Uncle Toms.' [But] that's all they knew: they'd never been five miles from home. All they knew was bad behavior got whipped; behave and get fed.

"But, at the same time, on the slavery issue, the white community was divided," says Tony. "It wasn't something where there was total uniformity. . . . There was [a] basic contradiction there, and there were huge fights the whole first half of the nineteenth century, politically: Are we going to extend slavery every time America gobbled up some more land from the French or somebody? Is this going to [be] enslaved or is [it] going to be free?"

A clear sky on a warm Saturday evening in May easily brings crowds onto the streets of New York. Crystal Wright, in a cream-colored blazer and linen slacks, and I walk through Harlem, her new neighborhood, on the way to a restaurant called Copeland's, for an interview and dinner.

Crystal is tall, slender, and fair skinned, with shoulder-length hair. "God," she says as yet another man gives her a smile. Some of her admirers give me a look that says I am a lucky man. "I should write a book or an article on what it's like to be a light-skinned black woman. Black men, white men, Hispanic men. . . . You know, about the trials of going through this world as a light-skinned black woman in this day and age, in this particular time in history, you know? It's a pain, a thorn in my butt. I really feel like that. . . . Like, for instance, at the deli next door to where I live, I walk in the deli yesterday, the first day [at my new job], to get a cup of coffee, and the Hispanic men behind the counter, they're, like, eyeing me. Then [it happened again] near where I work, in this Madison Avenue place where they wouldn't do that to a white customer. I was very annoyed by it, you know, to the point where I almost went up to the owner to say, you know, 'I don't want to come in here and be eyeballed by your staff. I want the same respect you give these white women who come in here to shop.' And I think if it happens again, I'm going to say that. I deal with this all the time. On a daily basis. Just going, you know, into a 7-Eleven, trying to get a cup of coffee at home [in Richmond] and people saying, 'Hey, baby,'—you know. . . . But now the world is such as it is, you can't defend yourself because you don't know if somebody's going to pull out a gun and take out their own kind of vengeance upon you for saying . . . because what you want to say is, "Get the fuck out of my face," okay? But I can't say that as a woman. I mean, I'm not a fool."

At Copeland's, I ask Crystal how she thinks her upbringing differs from that of whites of a similar socioeconomic background. "I think the values that we [blacks] are raised with are distinctly different from white upper-middle-class children," she states. "We're not taught that it's okay to get drunk at an early age and conduct ourselves in a slovenly manner and a disrespectful manner, even when there are no adults. I went to a private school where it was a rite of passage for these kids to do this, and went off to college to do it more, then their parents didn't see it. But to me, that just wasn't a black kind of experience.

"In high school, everybody was sort of into drinking beer and getting drunk, so for the sake of getting drunk, and whenever I went to those parties, I just looked at it like it was ridiculous—it was the stupidest thing I could ever imagine, and I watched these high school kids get drunk, and I just didn't understand it. So I got bored with that; it just wasn't interesting at all. My mother used to always tell us, 'You're not like that, you shouldn't do that.' I think [that] fosters a different outlook and way to behave.

"My black friends, at the same time, were going to parties and dancing all night long until three o'clock in the morning. . . . That wasn't really my scene either. . . . A lot of times the different parties turn into a big hooch fest; everybody is trying to get a piece of booty before they go home. I mean, you know, come on."

Crystal is ready to change careers. She first came to New York in 1990, fresh out of Georgetown, seeking a career as an actress, and found a job at a restaurant. "I had spent junior year in Paris and enrolled in a studio class there. [I] got encouragement from my instructor there and decided to pursue [acting] after I graduated. I had some great highs and some great encouragement, but, you know, the reality of it is it's just very hard out there. Right now I'm struggling with the fact that I can't get an agent, largely because the market for black actors is, you know, it's slim. I interviewed at several places and . . . I'm finding that if I had—I feel as though if I had gone to Yale or Juilliard, I would be having a lot easier time of getting an agent." So far the highlight of her career has been a role in poet Derek Walcott's stage adaptation of *The Odyssey* at Washington, D.C.'s, Arena Stage.

This is actually Wright's second stint in New York, as she has just returned after two years spent earning an MFA in theater studies at Virginia Commonwealth University in Richmond. She's working in an antique furniture store and has decided that she wants to study journalism. In fact, she tells me, she tried magazine journalism a few years ago while she was going on auditions. At that time, she won an interview for an editorial-assistant position at a leading women's magazine. However, despite a resume that detailed her strengths, among them her fluency in French and extensive travel, it did not pan out. "I walked in her office and her face dropped. She obviously was not expecting a black woman. Maybe she had a bad day, but she could have still called back later. She gave five minutes. She stared blankly at me in the beginning. I mean, I find that hard to believe—you at least give somebody some kind of courtesy."

She looks back at the experience. "I'd walk through hall after hall, corridor after corridor, passing receptionist after receptionist, just seeing no black people—you know, you have a couple at the receptionist, [but . . .] it was really a rude awakening for me after coming out of the sheltered college atmosphere, thinking I could do whatever I wanted. The real world operates on a completely different level. It was really a wake-up call.

"Oh, I wrote them a letter saying that I thought [the interviewer's behavior] was racially motivated—I had to speak out. I got this letter back saying, 'We're sorry you got this impression, Ms. Wright, but the job market is keen, many people want to work here.'

"I mean, as far as trying to break into publishing or get a writing job or a magazine job, I feel as though if I were white with my kind of experiences, I would have gotten the job. I feel the rage of disenfranchisement that everybody feels. It's a vague feeling for me; I can't really say it's rage. It's just a sort of popularized word now; it's been bastardized in many ways."

Still, Wright admits that she has chosen to pursue two competitive professions. Part of the motivation, at least with regard to acting, may stem from a desire to live her mother's dream. Her mother wanted to be a ballerina, but chose to be a teacher for its safety.

"My mom told me that the reason that she didn't [pursue ballet was] because it wasn't practical back then for her to pursue something like that; she could be a schoolteacher and nurse. Most of her friends were teachers.

"When my parents were my age—twenty-eight—they had two children. . . . My father had finished dental school and was practicing. They took the practical route. I wonder if I should have done that."

Chapter 26

Colored Balls and White Pins

As a lone trumpeter blares "Hail to the Chief," practicing for tonight, the chief for the moment, Saundra Sweetwyne, can't seem to walk a step without encountering a question or request. There's Judge LeVan Gordon reminding her that he doesn't yet have his list of contestants with the essentials to read as they walk before the audience. Contestants also follow Sweetwyne, with questions about the evening's format. The questions just won't stop coming, even after Sweetwyne, a fiftyish woman with a brownish-red permed Afro, has warned most of the people in the room: "I'm in a bad mood. Don't take it personal if I snap."

They are in the ballroom of the Sahara Hotel, a name that glows at night. Names are known to show off their neon in Las Vegas, especially the names of hotels. There are some 20 people in this room and most of them not from this fast-growing city known for its casinos and neon lights. Gordon is a criminal-court judge in Philadelphia; Sweetwyne is an accountant from Ventura, California. Pauline Davis is an accountant for the federal government in Washington, D.C., and George Hull is a process technician for Chevron in Los Angeles. Others hail from St. Louis, Tampa, New York, and Nashville, as well as many more communities large and small. Still, they all have at least a few things in common, one of them being that they are sure to take a week's vacation at Memorial Day every year, when they travel to the city lucky enough to host the annual convention for one of their favorite pastimes—bowling. They are among the 30,000 members of The National Bowling Association (TNBA)—10,000 of whom are here for this year's fete in Las Vegas.

The annual meetings of various black professional and leisure organizations draw thousands of people and have become both a source of community for the conventioneers and a much-desired market for tourist departments in most major cities. There are more than three hundred such conventions a year, including those of the National Medical Association, Jack and Jill, and National Association of Black Journalists. There's even a National Association of Meeting Planners, a group of African-American convention organizers, which itself has an annual gathering of its own.

Many of these conventions attract somewhat homogeneous crowds, because they are organized around professions or social activities. Hence, there is little socioeconomic variety at the gatherings of, for example, the National Bar Association, the Links, the Organization of Black Data Processors, the Association of Black Secretaries, or even fraternities and sororities. But bowling—because of its low costs—often crosses class lines and is known for its popularity among blue-collar workers. Thus, the bowling convention attracts an eclectic mix of people. In fact, there are families of bowlers here—some retired blue-collar parents whose children are college graduates and professionals, who grew up participating in TNBA youth tournaments and scholarship programs. "Bowling crosses the whole spectrum," says Perry Daniels, president of TNBA. "You can be out there bowling with a doctor or a lawyer or a janitor or whoever and you wouldn't know that until you all start talking about it. But everybody treats everybody the same. Not like golf, where you're only going to have a certain class of people, or tennis, a certain class of people. But bowling, a little bit of everybody bowls.

"I don't think you're going to find any national organization that is as diverse as The National Bowling Association," he continues. "We have doctors, some college professors, people that own their own business. We have people that work in grocery stores, schoolteachers, and some who are probably unemployed or between jobs. You know—just the whole nine yards. From having college degrees to Ph.D. to not even a high school education."

Some convention goers didn't even bring a bowling ball. In fact, Sabrina Miller, twenty-six, a reporter for the St. Petersburg *Times* and Chicago native whose parents are active TNBA members, doesn't even own one. Instead, she came to meet her family and see old friends. "It's almost like when people talk about our community in the old days. Everybody always asked how I was doing in school: 'Are your getting good grades?' It's like an extended family. I grew up in this organization, bowling in junior leagues. It was a Saturday morning ritual from the time I was nine to about fifteen. Unfortunately, I was never good enough to get to the point where I got to tournaments and things like that. I didn't get scholarships for having a high-game series. For me, it wasn't a competitive activity. I think it was another small piece of cultural affirmation. It was an all-black league in a black-owned alley. It was really nice just seeing [black] people around you, who were in charge, who were in control. Everybody was black."

"We start with our young people," says George Hull, fifty, who lives in the Los Angeles suburb of Pomona. "We have our junior program—and I mean junior—starting at five-, six-, and seven-year-olds—some of the kids in here that are bowling now, they were juniors; I remember them in the junior program. And as they grow up, they just continue to bowl in The NBA, because this is where they got started and this is what they know. This is their family. We do everything we can to encourage them: we train them, we school them, and we bring them back as adults."

In 1963, LeVan Gordon, fresh out of Howard University School of Law, was working at a law firm in Philadelphia while awaiting word on whether he passed the bar. Bowling became his source of leisure. "When I was practicing law, I used to bowl one night a week," he says. "I didn't take any appointments on Tuesday nights. I have been in this one league, the Tribune League, for thirty-one years."

The National Bowling Association's history is like that of many black professional and leisure organizations. Its founders were excluded from participation in predominantly white mainstream groups, in this case the American Bowling Congress and the Women's International Bowling Congress, so, in 1939, they formed their own. There was still another hurdle for black bowlers: They were barred from entering the alleys in many midwestern cities where bowling was big in the late 1930s and early '40s. So African Americans opened their own alleys. Boxing great Joe Louis opened one in Detroit in 1942; Negro Leagues baseball player Ted Page opened one in Pittsburgh in the same year.

By 1950, when the American Bowling Congress eliminated the exclusionary clause in its constitution and opened membership to blacks, the TNBA was already eleven years old and establishing its own traditions and a life of its own, which members didn't necessarily want to forsake just because the mainstream finally offered admission. To many members, the organization's history reflects the resilience of African-American culture, its ability to create thriving cultural spaces in the face of adversity. Even today, some members become offended when they're asked why they continue to maintain the organization when other larger, more mainstream groups are open. "Why do I have to justify a need for it?" asks LeVan Gordon. "It's there. It's ours. I don't have to justify it. They started in 1939 because we didn't have any place to go. Now because you said, 'Okay, we can go over here,' we shouldn't have it anymore? I've been a member over thirty years; I'm going to continue to be a member. . . . Never when I wake up in the morning do I say, why do I need NBA?"

Nevertheless, the organization's leadership recognizes that its membership lives in a multiracial world. The National Bowling Association is open to whites—though they make up less than 1 percent of the membership. And TNBA league participants are also required to be members of the Women's Interest National Bowling Congress or the American Bowling Congress, a role that encourages members to participate in the mainstream.

Some TNBA bowlers have gone professional, but producing expert bowlers isn't the organization's only focus—or a focus at all, for some members. Like many other African-American organizations, many see TNBA as social outlet. "The camaraderie is what draws us," says Wayde Brosend, a member of Atlanta's True Colors League. "A bowling league, that's an extended family. Every week you go and meet people, and you get to know those people over the years. So a bowler is never lonely."

And like other organizations, the group has a social-uplift component. Every year, the national organization awards more than $6,000 in scholarships, and its local chapters, or senates, give out thousands more.

It's the scholarship program that brings a collection of TNBA members into the ballroom on this Friday morning. While most other conventioneers are engaging in their sport or in the casinos, six women and two men are practicing their walks and waves for tonight. Just hours from now, they will stand on the stage, hoping that LeVan Gordon calls their name in the climactic moment when he reveals the identity of the man and woman who raised the most money for TNBA's scholarship fund this year and thus be crowned king and queen.

Black bowlers have been crowning royalty in their organization since 1961. The event called the Joe Thomas coronation, named for an active TNBA member. Going in, the contestants know only that they are the leading fund-raisers; no one, in fact, knows exactly how much money has been raised for the year, nor who the winners are. The candidates' final envelopes will remain sealed until the last moment. "Right before the coronation, I will meet with the coronation director and we'll open the last envelopes and add that to the totals," Perry Daniels explains. "No one else will know until it is announced at the coronation.

"We try to keep the suspense going to make a big deal out of it."

Saundra Sweetwyne says that the coronation mimics the showmanship and suspense of pageantry for good reason: "I was in the Miss Barnes beauty pageant in 1965, a beauty contest for Afro-Americans," says Sweetwyne, who was also one of the founders of the Women's Bowling Club in Ventura, California. "I think in the beauty pageant–type format, the recognition is greater. If we have an awards banquet and get up there and say, 'John Doe, we recognize you for your service,' afterward, you go sit down and you're forgotten. Who is going to come back four days later and say, 'Hey John, you were really great up there,' or 'Weren't you in the king-and-queen program?' Everyone likes to be seen. Everyone wants other people to know they have done this, this, and this."

Tall and muscular in a feminine way, Sweetwyne comes from a family of athletes. "Four girls, but we know how to play football, baseball, and basketball," she tells me, adding that one of her sisters was a professional skater with the Ice Capades. She has been bowling since she was a teenager.

"When I was fourteen years old," she recalls, "my cousin was in a bowling tournament and won a bowling ball and bag and he said, 'I'm gonna teach you how to bowl.'" He did, and from the beginning, she loved the sport, even when those early balls tripped into the gutter. She would eventually meet other blacks at the alleys, discover TNBA, become an active member, and wear the TNBA crown at 1985's convention, held in Louisville. (Along the way, she also helped found the Women's Bowling Club in Ventura, as well as became a mother of four and grandmother of three.) Two years ago, she was tapped by the organization's leadership to run the coronation. Since then, Sweetwyne has spent nearly all of her vacation time supervising the competition and traveling from her home to the convention sites to make preparations for this event. "I'm on overload, okay?" she frets. "I have a son that's graduating from high school, my youngest son. He's in the junior league. He's a natural. He's just a natural. He carries a two-oh-seven average. He bowls with his left and right hand and carries the same average with both. He will be attending the University of Las Vegas. So this is a dual trip for me. While I was here I came to visit the university, but it was very hard scheduling. He's also an athlete. So I had to share my time between his schedule, my work schedule, and NBA."

The event itself is much more than a contest between the fund-raisers; hometown pride is at stake. The TNBA is organized into senates representing the various cities with affiliate chapters, and senate members have sold raffle tickets or dinners to beef up the totals of their candidates. As incentive, the senate gets a percentage of their candidate's earnings for operational expenses, and bragging rights if their homeboy or homegirl takes the crown.

Gordon, the master of ceremonies, has his script and is now presiding at the podium. The contestants have lined up at the entrance of the ballroom, and the royal court of past kings and queens enter as Gordon narrates and the full band plays "Hail to the Chief." Then comes the reigning court: king, queen, prince, and princess. After that, the melody changes to smooth jazz and Judge Gordon calls this year's contestants one by one.

Saundra Sweetwyne stands to the side with a commanding stare on each contestant's move. It would take a powerful bomb to distract her gaze. Her eyes are fixed on the candidates as if each were a ball that she just rolled down the lane, a ball that better knock those ten white pins off their feet or else a scream from Sweetwyne will follow. Once you relinquish a ball, the rules of bowling prohibit one from stepping onto the lane to halt a ball from traveling into the gutter, but Sweetwyne can mend the strut of a contestant in an instant.

"Wave," she tells them. "You must wave to the crowd."

One contestant jokingly twirls her hands in a hip-hop wave as she walks down the aisle. "We'll have none of that," Sweetwyne snaps.

"It has been my goal to make it very elegant looking," Sweetwyne states, "not to rush it, but put it at a nice pace so people can enjoy it.

"We've had contestants who would just walk," she goes on. "They were afraid to express themselves. What I say to the contestants is, 'You, John Doe or Mary Jane, you have raised this money, so act like it.' That is what I want them to prevail to the audience: 'I worked for this money, I worked hard for it! This is for me! This is for me! I deserve the recognition.' When I was a contestant, my husband maybe saw me twice a week, because I was out to do fund-raising. I was out having raffles at bowling alleys. On the weekend, I was selling dinners. It's a nine-month commitment."

When the candidates reach the stage, they congregate around the throne, where the outgoing king and queen sit. They'd better bow or curtsey, depending on gender, or else they may face yet another interruption from Sweetwyne. "The bowing and the curtsey were never done before," Sweetwyne says. "I brought that into the program last year. That was a change I did. Once again, it is recognition: we are saying to our king and queen, 'For all of your hard work, we are your loyal subjects. We bow and curtsey to you in recognition of your hard work. He is chief. He is head honcho. So is she. You are top dog and you deserve all of the accolades and recognition that is possible, that I can possibly see that you have.' I mean, they have breakfast in bed, royal-carpet type of things, picked up in limousines. Royal treatment. Anything they want, we're at their beck and call. They raised this money. They've worked hard. They're supposed to have the recognition. So why not give it to them?"

Allen Shelton's attention focuses on the arch spanning the runway that tonight's participants will parade through. Sitting with his assistant at the helium machine, they inflate blue, gold, and white balloons. Shelton owns Dynamic Balloons, a special-events decorating company, and a nearby gift shop. He welcomes African-American conventions to Las Vegas, because they have become a major source of business for him. "Convention business has increased," he states. "And remember, this is already boomtown U.S.A."

Like most longtime residents, Shelton has watched Las Vegas change. It's one of the fastest-growing cities in the country. In fact, at the time of this visit in 1994, Las Vegas boasts 60,000 residents—a total that will mushroom to 120,000 by 1999. The growth is tied to the gaming and tourists industries, and the city is well known for its struggles to provide enough services to keep up with all of it.

When Shelton was growing up in the seventies, Las Vegas was just a few years beyond its notoriety as the Mississippi of the West. As far back as the 1930s and '40s, before the casinos, African-American workers waged civil-disobedience campaigns against the exclusion of blacks from plants. The city's resort hotels were known to appreciate black headliners like Lena Horne and Sammy Davis Jr. on their stages, but they were also known to refuse to give those entertainers rooms when the show was over. Segregation was rampant, and interracial marriages were illegal until 1959.

The city drew its first large wave of African Americans in the early 1900s, when in the first great black migration, many came from Mississippi, Louisiana, and Arkansas to work on the Hoover Dam project. Today there is still a Vicksburg Club for African Americans who came from Vicksburg, Mississippi, or whose parents are from that town, and a Fordyce Club for those from that Arkansas town, as well as several others tied to Mississippi, Louisiana, and Arkansas locales. Shelton knows those groups well, but notes that their memberships are aging: "My grandparents were active in those clubs, but today people are more likely to be in black Greek-letter organizations.

"Things have changed," he says, because today there are "a lot more professional African Americans who are moving here [to Las Vegas] from bigger cities [and] who have grown up appreciating the better things in life and won't stand for certain attitudes of Caucasians. Only one of four people that live here was born here. So it's a whole new scene."

He says that he didn't grow up in the segregated Las Vegas that his parents knew, though echoes of that era remained, especially when he began thinking of higher education. "Never was I led to believe that [anything] other than sports was the way up for me or for other blacks," he remembers. "A recruiter came to our school from Claremont McKinney College, which on the West Coast is considered to be like an Ivy League school. They selected me and some other students to meet with the recruiter, because of my GPA. So I thought it was great. And then my counselor told me, 'You don't want to go there. I don't think it would work out for you. Look at the tuition. For as much tuition as it would cost, you can get a car.'"

He gave up on Claremont, but would meet Bertha Johnson, the legendary NAACP leader, who encouraged Shelton to return to the region that many blacks had forsaken for Las Vegas just a generation earlier. Johnson guided him to Grambling State University in Louisiana, a school known for its football team, which produced such greats as Doug Williams. Shelton didn't play football. When he graduated and came home looking for a job, he couldn't find one. So he started his own business.

Shelton has placed ten balloons. He steps a few feet away from the runway to make sure they are well placed. He nods to himself and begins placing the others. "I see the issue now as economic and providing economic opportunities. We've had some strong African-American leadership in the community, people who stood up and are still standing up trying to get what's right and just, fair and equitable. But right now we're really moving into a whole new ball game. It's gone beyond human rights and racial rights to economic empowerment and development."

Shelton is finished with his arch. The balloons are in place. Now he's on to another hotel to decorate for a cotillion tonight.

The noise of a bowling alley is melodic. There's a bass when balls roll that blends into a soprano when they meet the pins. It becomes as constant as the sound of air on a windy day.

On this weekend, TNBA occupies thousands of lanes throughout Las Vegas, and it seems impossible to escape the music of the rolling balls and crashing pins. There are several tournaments going on,—some of them serious. Others, such as the "Battle of the Sexes," are purely for fun. Everywhere are stylish shirts—and even jackets, despite the sweltering weather—bearing eye-catching logos and proudly proclaiming their wearers' teams, leagues, or senates.

TNBA president Perry Daniels greets them all—sometimes by the name of a league or city. The politician isn't bowling much. He's been attending senate meetings and walking the alleys, mingling among his constituency.

John Mambey, of Asbury Park, New Jersey, stops Daniels when he realizes who Daniels is. Mambey is polite, but there's a skeptical look on his face.

"You are invited to the ABC," he begins, referring to a national meeting of the American Bowling Congress.

"Right," says Daniels.

"You couldn't make it, so you sent a substitute."

"Yeah."

"Did you hear anything about it?" Mambey pauses, but then speaks again before Daniels can respond. "Between you and me, don't ever send a substitute again, because, first of all, as little as I know about TNBA, I know more than he did. [And second,] you never go to a group and tell white people they're not invited, they can't join. Now, he was up on a platform making these statements."

"Well, that's the national vice president," Daniels says. "He's supposed to step in for me when I'm not available."

"I understand that," Mambey persists, "but he ain't supposed to say these things. You hear me, now: the TNBA is open to anybody. Am I right or wrong?"

"Yeah, baby. You sure that's what he said?" Daniels asks, taken aback.

"I'm positive that's what he said," Mambey continues.

Daniels, somewhat disbelieving but unwilling to directly challenge Mambey, sticks up for his colleague, "I guarantee you when I see him, he's going to contradict what you said," Daniels states. "This is the first time I ever heard that. And I talked to a lot of people that were [at the ABC], and this is the first time I heard somebody say that he told them that they could not join. There must have been some misunderstanding."

"He was answering questions from the audience." Mambey is insistent.

"What was the question that he was asked that would lead you to believe he said something?" Daniels asks pointedly, adding, "I will guarantee you he didn't say that."

"You'll guarantee he didn't say that?" Mambey looks angry now. Daniels, in effect, is calling him a liar.

"I will guarantee you he didn't say that our organization is not open to everybody," Daniels clarifies. "Tell me exactly what he said, without para-phrasing it."

Mambey draws himself up. "The question was put to him about who could join, and his reply was, to my best recollection, that it's open to all mi-nority bowlers. He didn't use the word black; he said 'minority bowlers.' The people that were putting the question to him were white."

"Okay, what was the follow-up question?"

"They wanted to know if they could join."

"What did he say?"

"And he says no, it's not open to you."

Daniels takes it in, still surprised. "I just find that hard to believe because we've had too many whites at many of our different events."

"Oh, I know this," Mambey replies.

"Matter of fact," Daniels continues, "where he's from in Milwaukee, where he was local president, they've had a large white population in that senate. You must have misunderstood something that he said."

"Yeah, I say it must have been something that was misinterpreted or he didn't understand the question," Daniels concludes.

"All right, well next time you see him, just bring it up," Mambey says, still not quite mollified.

"I absolutely will."

"And my name's John Mambey, and I'm from Jersey."

"Okay."

They shake hands, and Daniels continues to move through the alley. Daniels, with dark brown skin, looks as if he's thirty—not the forty-six-year-old that he is, with two kids in college and two graduates. He grew up in St. Louis and attended segregated schools there. He started bowling in his se-nior year in high school. "To be perfectly honest with you, there was a girl I was chasing, she bowled. So I said, 'Let me go out here and start bowling.' That's really how it got started. As much as I enjoyed football, I knew it wasn't too far I was going to go with football, but I played high school foot-ball. And as short as I was, I wasn't Spud Webb."

After graduating from high school in 1967, Daniels joined IBM as a clerk, and eventually worked his way up to operations manager. He says that he grew up in a close-knit community, but even despite that, his image of African Americans was largely influenced by the perceptions of mainstream society, which equated black life with violence and crime. He says he was in awe of the National Bowling Association because it defied those percep-tions.

"I was just so impressed at seeing so many black people in the room discussing things, debating things, and nobody's fussing and fighting and cursing and everything. And I was just impressed with the organization of it, of so many black folks being able to get along. People were disagreeing but not being disagreeable, you know. Black folks, back then—[it went against] the rep that we had."

Daniels pauses, then mocks the voice: "'You'd get a group of them together, you throw them a couple of knives in there, and you wouldn't have to worry about it, because they'd take care of each other.'

"That was the rep," he continues, now speaking normally again. "But to see folks just really sit there and debate and discuss, and sometimes have heated debates, and then just leave it there, and go out and party and socialize and do whatever it is that we do, I thought that was great."

We soon meet another TNBA member who says that he too was drawn to the organization because it defied his idea of how an African-American organization functions. "After I joined the local, they got to talking about going to the convention," says Edward Jones, a former senate president for Los Angeles. "And I just could not see going somewhere with that many black people. I'm going to be truthful with you: I just could not see them doing anything but going somewhere getting drunk and sitting down fighting and cussing and shooting. And they kept telling me it wasn't like that. Then, in 1965, they finally talked me into going, so we got in the car and drove to Cleveland. And I got there, and I saw how people transacted business, and I was amazed. And I've been hooked ever since. I've been going to conventions and tournaments since 1965."

It is two hours away from tuxedo time for George Hull. Still in his warm-ups and tennis shoes, he is sitting in Cafe Europa, a trendy bagel shop in the hotel. "I don't know if you know," he says, "but Los Angeles has crowned more kings, more queens than any other city or senate in The National Bowling Association. A couple of years running, we didn't do too good— we kind of fell way down. A couple of years ago, we ran a king and did real good, like twenty-five thousand dollars, which was a record. This year we started out kind of slow. Unfortunately, one of the guys who was the front runner, who we thought was going to be the king, had a heart attack."

So Hull stepped up to capture the senate throne. "'We have a tradition we want to keep. It's fun, but we have a tradition, our pride. But I don't know how we're going to do this time. We got a bad start. I think it's going to be the first, first time L.A. is going to be kind of shaky. We didn't go out one hundred percent like we normally do. We were pushing one guy and when he passed, we weren't doing anything for a month."

Still, Hull managed to raise enough money to place among the final six, picking up pledges from friends, dollars for each pin knocked over. Then there were raffles, bus trips to Las Vegas, and dinner sales—all for the cause of the crown and scholarships. Still, Hull, a former amateur race-car driver, is nervous. There is the threat of defeat looming—the possibility of embarrassing the City of Angels, stars, and Rodney King with a loss.

Then there is the possibility of another fall. The stocky Hull, a former high school football player with an athletic build that reflects rigorous body building, is worried that he may trip on stage. For now, he sits with his left hand extended across his stomach, holding the muscle of his right arm. The other hand massages his ankle, which rests on his knee. "It keeps my hands busy," he says by way of explanation. "If I don't, I'll start sweating. Yeah, it's nerves. I guess I can say I'm not as tight or tense as some people might be, because I played a lot of football. As a football player, I would always be nervous until I was hit the first time—it toughens you.

"I guess it's like a prize fighter," he goes on, looking for analogies, "until he gets hit the first time, he's tense. And after he's hit the first time, it doesn't seem to bother him as much, or like race-car driving. Sitting in a car, the car could do anything stupid. It could explode.

"It's kind of like if you're a bowler, throwing that twelfth strike in a perfect game," he continues, finding a comparison that hits close to home. "You're going to walk on that runway, like starting the approach on a bowling lane. You want to make sure you don't make a mistake. It's going to be on your mind. I want to walk right; I want to keep my head up. I don't want to make any dumb tripping mistakes—I don't want to make people laugh at me. I don't want to look bad. Until I make the first couple of steps, it's going be real tight. And then after I start walking, I'll feel a lot better. They give you this waving thing; that will take a bit of the pressure off because you're going to be doing something. There are some moves you're going to make. I think that's the thing I'm going to worry about, because early today in rehearsal, I tripped. I'm going to be conscious of tripping. It's like throwing that twelfth ball, a perfect game."

Hull goes to several tournaments a year, most of them integrated competitions where the majority of the bowlers are white. He says, those tournaments, lacking the dances, close friends, and coronation, can't match The National Bowling Association week. "Other tournaments are mostly a casual thing," he explains. "They're not going to have a gala event. We (TNBA) go to bowl and we have a good time. We climax our event with a gala affair. And to me and to a lot of African Americans, it says hey, we know how to go out, we know how to have a good time. We can have nice, formal affairs, whereas a lot of people don't think we can. So we prove to the world that we can go out and have a good time. We dress formal, our ladies dress formal. We show the world that we can do what anybody else can do—and that we will do it better."

The runway arch shines as lights beam through Allen Shelton's blue, gold, and clear balloons. Under the glow, hundreds of TNBA members dance, talk, and laugh. Soft-soled bowling shoes and garish team shirts have been left behind: women are in cocktail dresses and gowns, while men wear dark suits and tuxedos.

Saundra Sweetwyne surveys the room. "One thing about black folks," she says, "when we come out of town, we intend to party and have a good time, bowl and dance and attend all the activities. With the ball, you used to dance for an hour, you would have the crowning of the king and queen, then you had entertainment. We've had bands, skits, and things. We had a James Brown imitator one year. [But] all of the entertainment wasn't that great, okay? People came to party; they enjoyed the king-and-queen pageant, but they wanted to get up and move their feet and snap their fingers. But the whole program was entertainment—they didn't want that. That was one of the complaints: 'give us the pageant and let's party.' You know, dispense with that entertainment. We didn't come all the way from Timbuktu to sit around."

At 10:30, LeVan Gordon assumes the podium. "Welcome," he greets his audience. "Tonight, we will soon know who will be the 1994 king and queen of TNBA."

With this, many dancers stop, rush to their tables to sit and watch. Others grab for their cameras and seek out a standing spot offering a good angle, and a few ready video cameras. Some spectators flock to line the rope along the center aisle, down which the contestants will proceed on the way to the stage. None of this activity, particularly the moving camera-snappers, is a good sign for Sweetwyne as she peeks in on the scene from outside the ballroom entrance, where the candidates are lined up. "Accidents do happen," she worries. "I hope everyone will cooperate when you say please don't take any pictures until a certain point. I've seen people fall off the stage because of interference. Somebody's robe got caught, and the person tripped."

"That happened?" I asked.

"Yes, years ago, but yes," Sweetwyne affirms, closing her eyes and shaking her head.

Sweetwyne no longer has control and she is nervous. She has thrown the ball and if it rolls into the gutter, she can't retrieve it.

Onstage, Gordon calls the names of the candidates for queen, and the contestants file in, walking down the aisle smiling and waving to the cheering crowds as Gordon gives a little commentary for each.

Throughout, Sweetwyne peeks into the room with every "oooooh" and "aaaaah" from the audience. They are especially pronounced now, when Gordon announces that this year's eight contestants raised $67,000, almost double last year's $35,000.

As the noise quiets, Gordon continues. "Of course, if you are going to have a queen, you got to have a king," he proclaims. George Hull is the second of the two contenders to be announced, and he enters with a cool smile and a deliberate yet easy and slow wave. "Hey, it's the NBA wave," one spectator says, imitating him, slowly throwing her hand right to left.

With Hull completing the field onstage, the drum rolls and Gordon announces the princess, or runner-up to the queen. Then the prince. Hull is hoping that he won't hear his name at this point; there are, after all, only two candidates for king. He gets his wish: his St. Petersburg, Florida, opponent, Lee Smith, is the prince. At this, the Los Angeles bowlers erupt in a cheer that drowns out the Florida crew. "Some people call him the Hulk," intones Gordon. "Tonight we're going to call him the king: George Hull!"

The favorite son of Los Angeles steps forward with a cool wave and stares straight ahead as he is crowned and robed before the applauding crowd. "I wanted to scream and jump at that point," Hull says later. "But I remained calm and just stood and looked forward."

After Hull's moment, Gordon receives another envelope. "Now I'm going to let you know what I now know, and that is"—he pauses for drama—"who is . . . the queen . . . for 1994.

"The queen is . . . wait a minute, I lost my page."

The judge's joke brings laughs, but he starts right back up, yelling like a commentator describing the final blow of a fight: "Pauline Davis from Washington, D.C."

The band strikes up "Hail to the Chief" as the crowd celebrates. One woman in a black silk dress holds her ears and jumps up and down, while the beads of her friend's dress click together as she yells "What did I tell her last night? What'd I tell her last night? Didn't I tell her she was going to be the queen?"

The music segues into smooth, quiet jazz for a king-and-queen dance and more commentary from the emcee. "George Hull is known as the Hulk. He joined the Tropicana Bowling League in 1978. He's held many offices in that league. He's been an active member of TNBA since 1985. He held the office of vice president of the Los Angeles Bowling Senate for four years. In league play, he's shot two two-seventy-nine games back to back, sticking the seven pin in the seventh frame in both games. How's that for consistency? So far, the highlight of his bowling career came in 1985, winning the men's single event in the California men's tournament with a seven-ninety-seven series which included a three-hundred game. George is a father of five and is currently trying to develop his golfing skills while keeping a hulk's eye on five grandchildren. Ladies and gentlemen, the king of the NBA—George Hull."

After a short applause break, Gordon resumes. "Now, this young lady's name just rhymes with *queen*—Queen Pauline. She's a member of the Greater Washington Bowling Senate; she has been since 1980. She was born in Durham, North Carolina. She came to Washington at a very early age. She attended the University of the District of Columbia, majoring in business administration. She has worked for the federal government for twenty-eight years, holding various positions. She is the mother of two sons, ages twenty-four and twenty-eight. She doesn't look that old, now does she, folks? She's been a bowler for twenty-two years. High-game roll was two eighty, high series six ninety-eight. She has an average of one seventy-four. Currently she is the member of three leagues and the treasurer of one. Her hobbies, other than bowling, are fishing, crocheting, reading, sightseeing, and photography. She is a member of the New Bethany Baptist Church in Washington and a member of the number-two usher board. She is currently vice president of the Punk Dunk Ladies League. Ladies and gentlemen, Queen Pauline."

More applause, but Gordon isn't done yet. "Let me tell you this about our prince, princess, king, and queen. Our princess, Elice Johnson, raised sixteen thousand twenty dollars and eighty-four cents. Our prince, Lee Smith, raised two thousand one hundred dollars. Our king, George Hull, raised seven thousand eight hundred sixty-two dollars. And, ladies and gentlemen, Queen Pauliiiine raised twenty thousand dollars."

He steps aside and the cameras flash. Then the crowds close in on the royal court for hearty and healthy hugs.

Sabrina Miller wasn't in the running for queen, but she gets her share of hugs and good wishes from friends of her parents who haven't seen her in years. "I didn't get to come when my mother was crowned queen," she says. "I was in college and working that summer.

"This was special," she says of tonight. "We always find a way to honor and celebrate ourselves when the larger culture doesn't. Beneath all the pomp and circumstance, this was really just a way for the people of this organization to honor each other."

Eventually, the floor is cleared of the royalty and the dancing resumes. Now is Saundra Sweetwyne's moment; conventioneers congratulate her on a good show. "Everything I heard was positive," she says, beaming. "That pushed me up a little higher in the clouds. I was high after the pageant was over. I was on cloud ninety-nine."

Chapter 27

Alleys and Slopes

BOWLING is a Friday-night ritual for Cyril Miller. He rolls at Seattle's Skyway Park Bowl with the King and Queen's League. On this particular evening in October 1994, league bowlers occupy eighteen lanes.

Miller, fifty-seven, was born in the Bahamas, and at twelve, in 1949, he moved with his family to seek a better life in Fort Lauderdale, Florida. Initially, it did not seem better for young Cyril. "I had a difficult time because I came from an environment where ninety-five percent of the people were black, and you can go where you want to. I came here [to the U.S.] and segregation was rampant . . . they had colored signs—you know, 'colored only,' 'niggers and Mexicans don't eat here,' and all the other stuff, and I couldn't understand it."

Bowling offered Miller a refuge from segregation. He took up the game in 1952, two years after the American Bowling Congress began admitting blacks. He worked in an alley in Hollywood, Florida, setting pins, and joined a junior ABC league there. Miller excelled in the sport and went on to spend two years on the professional circuit in the sixties. Today, though, Miller regards his sport as just "a good form of relaxation and recreation all around. I compete now because I want to. There's a big difference between working because you have to and because you want to."

Miller also goes to Seattle Super Smoke every day at 4:30 in the morning, not only because the company has helped to make him a millionaire but because he wants to. "When you work because you love to, there's a certain amount of intensity that you put into it."

Anyone in Seattle who knows Cyril Miller knows that he's intense about

Super Smoke, his gourmet smoked-poultry business, which has been praised by *Bon Appétit* and *Food and Wine* and called the "best in the West" by *Sunset* magazine. He is a self-described workaholic, who also finds time to collect antique Rolls-Royces, read several newspapers a day, devour at least five magazines, cover-to-cover, a week, read one book a month, and, of course, bowl one night a week. "There's only twenty-four hours in a day," he says, "but I wish there was like thirty or forty hours."

One of his friends in the league tells me Miller is Seattle's only million-aire in overalls. You're likely to see him in the denim unless you catch him in a tuxedo at a benefit for the many charities he's involved in, including the Boy Scouts and the Leukemia Foundation.

He's the hands-on leader of a company of forty employees, a leader who sometimes has trouble resisting the urge to answer the phone rather than allow his secretary to take the call. His company sells thirty thousand turkeys between Thanksgiving week and Christmas, making that month or so its busiest season of the year. He began this Friday at one of his poultry-processing sites. The scent of smoked chicken and salmon filled the air as he supervised poultry production for his latest client and coup, Costco.

Miller is also the opinionated father of six adult children—three girls and three boys. His oldest son, now an attorney in Florida, many years ago re-jected his father's offer to work at Seattle Super Smoke. "We don't get along," says Miller matter-of-factly. "We don't hardly get along probably be-cause we're too much alike . . . I haven't heard from him now in four or five months; that's his choice. When I first started this company I went to him and I said, 'Hey, Dwayne, you've got an opportunity here—all you've got to do is come in. I'll give you twenty-five percent of the company, and if you come in and work hard, it will be worth something,' and he told me, 'Naw . . . I don't want to be bothered.' I could not accept that. I was disap-pointed because I felt that he didn't have the insight or the foresight to see what this could be."

Miller says there was a sign at the dinner table several years ago that his son desired to be ahead of his father's path. It was one of the usual family get-togethers in Fort Lauderdale, Florida, where they lived at the time, three generations gathered for Sunday dinner. "My son told me, 'Daddy, when I grow up, I'm going to be better than you.'"

That didn't anger Miller, actually. "That was the best thing he could say. It was great, I loved it: I wanted him to be better than me, you know? I felt really good. But the people around me said he's being disrespectful, and everybody was upset—my father was upset, my wife was upset. . . .

"I want him to be better than I am, and I want his son to be better than he is, and so forth and so on, you know? You set out to do that so that your children can be better than you are."

Miller takes a break from my tape recorder to roll the ball. The form of a good bowler resembles the precision of a ballet dancer, with the aim and slow move of the arm seconds before the ball is released and touches the wooden floor. With easy, fluid grace, he lets go what looks to be a strike in the making . . . but one pin is left standing. Miller frowns for a second. The ball is returned, he picks up the spare, and his teammates pat him on the back.

The league's membership is eclectic, much like that of the larger TNBA. Nearby, there's a nanny who works for a family that knows better than to tamper with her Friday nights; there's also a flight attendant, a union leader, teachers, a police officer, a social worker, a telephone operator, and several city employees. There are also Miller's two other sons, Maurice, thirty-two, and Elston, thirty, who work for Seattle Super Smoke.

Miller keeps one eye on the game as he listens to and answers my questions. He says that his oldest daughter is independent like him and didn't want a piece of the company, either. She owns seven nursing homes in Florida. Maurice couldn't escape his father's wrath when he joined the army nine years ago. "He decided to go to the military, and I said, 'Man, you don't have to do this . . . you're going to waste all this time. What you've got in there is a lot of losers—they can't make it any place else, so they go into the military. You don't want to be with a bunch of losers.' So he said, 'Well, Dad, you know, I think that's my decision. Am I right?' And he was right. He was right."

Miller says his son was also right a year ago, when he called after eight years in the army and said he wanted out. "He wanted to know if I had a place for him in the company. So I told him, 'I always have a place for you in the company. Soon as you get out.'

"The only reason I told him not to go into the military was because I had been in the military, and I know the mentality of the people in the military. I told him that . . . I knew it would be a waste of time for him to go in there, because he's not going to learn anything that's going to help him in a civilian life, way down the road. What I was trying to do was to give him the benefit of my experience so that he didn't have to waste any time going in and finding that out later. When he came back, I didn't say 'I told you so.' I said, 'Let's get on with your life, . . . let's do it. That's over.'"

Miller says that the toughest period for the family during his son's stint in the army was the Persian Gulf War, because Maurice, an armorer, was stationed in Kuwait. Miller didn't hide his anger when he was featured in a

Seattle Times article on the families of Gulf war soldiers. In the article, Miller said that he didn't want his son's life sacrificed in an unnecessary war. The next day, his phone began to ring, with callers angry over his position. Miller ignored the callers—and treated them like he deals with racial slights. He recounts a time when he was in the parking lot of one of his processing sites. Of course, he doesn't wait for a janitor if he spots trash. A potential job applicant passed him and entered the building.

"And so, he came in and asked Bernice [Miller's secretary] if he could speak to the owner because he wanted to see if he could get a job. So she came to me outside and says, 'He wants to talk with you.' So I walked in and I said, 'Can I help you?' He says, 'No, you can't help me.' So I said, 'Okay.' I went in the back and was working, and a few minutes later, Bernice came back and she said, 'That guy is still sitting there, waiting for you.' So I went back and I said, 'Can I help you?' He said, 'I told you once, you can't help me. I'm waiting for the owner.' I said, 'I am the owner.' He was looking for a job, and once he found out that I was the owner, he walked out."

"Some people would have been irate about that and immediately pushed him out the door . . ." I said.

"No, no, absolutely not. Why should I push him out? First of all, I'm number one. Why should I sink to that level? That's the issue. I don't want to do that, I don't have time for that. The one thing you cannot get back is time. You can lose your health, you can lose a fortune, you can lose everything, but if you don't use your time wisely, you will never get an opportunity to get that time back again. So I try not to waste my time."

Miller's refusal to whine about that incident echoes much of what I've heard on this journey. In particular, it was Detroit's George N'Namdi who distinguished between institutional racism (such as police misconduct) and everyday slights. The former deserves attention, N'Namdi says, while protesting loudly about the latter can turn slights into mountains that put the offender on top.

Such a perspective is not so naïve as to embrace the idea that racism is dead, but like many others I've met, Miller doesn't believe that racial injustice should deny him the American Dream. His impatience might stem from his childhood frustrations with his father, who ran a construction business. Miller worked alongside him, but became angry over his father's insecurities in dealing with whites. "My father was not an educated man, and so I think that bothered him a little bit. As I got older, I could go and tell him how much he should charge for a job, based on materials and all that stuff. Most of the people that he dealt with weren't used to having black people doing stuff like that."

And most of them refused to pay what the young Miller calculated to be a fair price. "My father would accept this and come back to me and say, 'Boy, you figured that plan wrong. The man told me it wasn't right.' And I would say, 'Well, you tell that man he doesn't know what he's talking about, because it is right.' I would challenge these guys, and then I became, you know, 'uppity.'

"I would say, 'Dad, you're just gonna have to stick to your guns. You can't let people screw you . . . if you're going to work this way, somebody's going to rob you.' And he told me I was causing a lot of problems. When I got to be eighteen, I said, 'Dad, I can't do this for you." That's when Cyril Miller joined the army.

While his father ran the construction business, his mother worked as a domestic. "My mother used to work in these houses of these wealthy people, and so she would come home and she would sit us down and show us how to use all the utensils in the proper way, and all the social graces. A lot of people don't realize how important the social graces are. Now families don't eat together anymore.

"I spent more time with my mother. My mother raised us. She had a certain depth for making sure that we do things right, and so she instilled that at an early age. That your name was more important than money. She was very strict. She was a disciplinarian. She did not play. She didn't fight, man—she whipped. She was tough. I mean, this woman was about five-six and weighed about two hundred pounds, and she was tough. She's been gone now for over twenty years, and I still miss her and I miss her influence. I miss her character."

One thing he doesn't miss is the toll that life in a new country took on both of his parents; each succumbed to alcoholism. "My mother died of cirrhosis of the liver when she was sixty. She died early. That's one of the reasons why I'm not into alcohol, because they both were drinkers. I took a look at them and said there's no way in hell that I'm going through this. I don't want my children to remember me like that.

"I miss her, but I didn't grieve over her death because I was glad that she died. I don't know why people insist on having people live when they suffer. I cried for my mom before she died, because I saw what she was going through and that bothered me. And so when she died, when I got the word that she had passed, I said, 'Well, I'm glad that she's finally gone.' My mom had been two hundred pounds. She was a very loving, jovial, cheery person. When she died, she weighed about sixty-five pounds. And how can you want to see somebody like that? This is what I told my sisters: 'I don't want anybody watching me suffer like this.' I said, 'What's the matter with you people? You're very selfish. You think only of yourselves. She's gone, she's out of her suffering, out of her misery. Why can't you understand that?' I was happy to see her go, and everybody got upset with me.

"One of the things that really, really got me—" Miller stops and sighs—"I went back to see my father one night because he lived alone after she died. I couldn't find him. He was in the house. The house was dark. And so I was just getting ready to leave when all of a sudden I saw this little glow. You know, when somebody pulls on a cigarette, the glow. I saw this glow of the cigarette in the dark.

"I said, 'You didn't even tell me, you didn't say here I am.' I turn the light on, and there he was, sitting up, and he was crying like a baby, tears all around his eyes. I didn't know what to do, because I have never put my hands on my father. I never hugged my father, never.

"And so I stood there for a little while . . . finally, I just said, 'Dad, are you okay?' And he said, 'No.'

"So I said, 'Tell me what the problem is.'

"He said, 'I really miss your mom. You don't know how much I miss her.'

"So I hugged him, and to have him hug me back, it was almost like a religious experience. And we just stood there in the dark, the two of us.

"And from then on, we got closer. I used to check on him all the time. I started involving him in some family things, Sunday dinner and all. The only thing that bothered me was he couldn't accept the fact that I didn't want the grandchildren to see him drunk. Instead of me saying, 'Okay, this is grandfather, he drinks,' I didn't want him around them. And that was my problem, because I should have explained things so they got to see all of life, not just the fortunate . . . I was trying to protect them at his expense, and so I took him away from them, from the grandchildren."

Miller scoffs at the idea that anguish over racism played a part in his parents' alcoholism. "A lot of people are alcoholics, black and white," he says. "It starts as a social thing. My mom drank because my dad drank. I know that for a fact; this was her way. A lot of alcoholism in the family happens that way. It's that one of the family members drank, so in order for the other family member to be close to that member, they drank too."

After his father retired, Miller took over the family construction company in Fort Lauderdale. By 1979, he had a payroll of fifty, but became "burned out." He took a consulting job in Seattle and fell in love with the Northwest.

The idea for the smokehouse—a "smoke boutique," as he calls it—came on a trip to visit his in-laws in Minnesota in the early 1980s. His father-in-law smoked chicken in the backyard, and Miller was so impressed with the results that he told him that he should sell it. His father-in-law wasn't interested, so "I told him to teach me how to smoke them, and I'd sell them."

That's exactly what Miller did, investing $50,000 of his own money in the operation in 1985 and reinvesting profits to help the company grow. Despite the growth, Miller contends that he's a long way from what he would call success. "I understand how rich people stay rich. I'm not rich. I'm struggling to get to a point where this whole family can be comfortable. When you get to a certain level, you don't even have to go out there and look for ideas. People come to you, and all you gotta do is have the feeling to make those ideas grow, which requires money.

"People come in my store and say, 'God, look at what you've done.' I don't feel that it's that great. If, several years down the road, I go to New York, there's a deli on this corner; I go to Boston, there's one over there; if I go to Philadelphia, there's one over there; if I go to Baltimore, there's one over there—that's what I think of as success. We're going to get to that level. I told my sons that, and they were all laughing. But I told them, before I leave here, we're going to have our own little jet."

The Royal Esquire Club sits next door to a tire store in the Columbia City area, just south of the central district of Seattle, where 60 percent of the city's African Americans live sprinkled throughout mostly multiracial communities. In the main room, decorated with portraits of Martin Luther King Jr. and Malcolm X and plaques bearing the names of deceased club members, there's a large dance floor and a bar. An adjacent room houses another bar along with a few steaming buffet trays of chicken wings and rice and macaroni, across from a photographer who takes $10 pictures of members and guests who want to document the night.

The Royal Room usually provides an area for "Gold" members and their guests to socialize more quietly. Founded in 1947, the club has been at the center of African-American life in Seattle for decades. When the Royal Esquire was established, the black population of Seattle was barely 1 percent. Blacks now comprise 10 percent of the population, and the club, too, has grown. Today, there are 162 "gold card" members, who pay a two-hundred-fifty-dollar-a-year membership fee for the privilege of free admission for themselves and guests on weekends. There are also a dozen honorary members, including a few superior court judges and Mayor Norm Rice, Seattle's first African-American mayor.

Neither the mayor nor the judges are here on this Saturday night. The dance floor is full of regulars, men and women ranging in age from twenty-one to sixty, dancing to the deejay's mix of seventies funk and nineties hip-hop. There's also a convention in town—the National Black Child Development Institute. Several of the convention goers found their way here tonight and paid five dollars to become associate members for the evening.

"On Saturday night, the whole facility is just jumping with very nice people, many of them very young; many of the young people out there are young professionals," says Bertram Williams, seventy-two, sounding like a proud father (which, actually, he is: "I have a daughter who's forty-six years old and I have a daughter who's going to be thirty-nine years old and a son who's thirty-seven. They're all college graduates and they all have advanced degrees and I feel I'm sort of lucky.")

"This facility is available to all regular members for their families," he says, as we sit in the club's office. "My son is getting married next Saturday, and the reception is here. This facility becomes mine then. Then there's a lot of baby showers, wedding showers, wedding receptions. The fraternities hold all their regular meetings here, the Alphas, Kappas, and Omegas. The NAACP will have some things here, the Urban League, too."

The club was founded by a group of young professional men and military buddies who settled in Seattle in the late forties. "There were five founders of the club, five young men," says Williams, who himself has held every office in the club, including president three times and chairman of the board. "They got together and they came up with the idea, got organized and started. There's two of the founders still living, the rest of them passed on.

"I am a charter member. The founding took place in December 1947. The club was formally chartered with the secretary of state in April 1948. I came into the club in March 1948.

"We've been putting names on the plaque out there for deceased members on an average of four a year. We just put the third name [this year] two weeks ago. I was joking with another member, asking who's going to be number four. I told him to be careful and make sure he doesn't rush out, and I'm going to be careful."

Williams, a stout man with tan skin and piercing brown eyes, was new to Seattle when he was asked to join the club. A Tulsa, Oklahoma, native, he had served in World War II with the 265th Infantry Regiment of the 92nd Infantry Division, the only all-black infantry committed to combat in the war. Staying in the service after the war, he was stationed here, where, incidentally, he also met his wife, Ernestine. ("She was one of the few black nurses that migrated here during the war.")

From the army, Williams joined the corporate world, retiring in 1985 as director of equal-opportunity programs at the Boeing Corporation in Seattle. Now he spends most of his time volunteering at the club, making sure that the bartender gets paid and ensuring that members follow the rules. "Anybody cannot belong, and when you get into this club you have to go through a process to become a regular member. You have to be recommended by the board of regular members, and you go before a membership committee that screens and evaluates you and brings you before the body with a recommendation. If the recommendation is favorable and the body accepts you, then you go on to a probationary period and you are assigned to a committee. There's an awful lot of volunteer work done around here and there are very few paid positions. . . .

"We have four policemen, some firemen—a fire captain and lieutenant— a half-dozen lawyers, three CPAs, so many engineers from Boeing. We make sure that that message gets out to the community: You don't have to have a college degree to get in here; you don't have to have a prestigious job someplace to get in here. Some of our most productive and hardworking officers have been construction workers, postal workers. We've got cooks, service workers, doctors, lawyers, teachers.

"Several events we have remain hallmark social events of the club and the Seattle area. We have an annual black-and-white formal ball. It's a grand affair, really grand. The community looks forward to it, and we look forward to it. We are more proud of our scholarship program. Last year we raised in excess of sixty thousand dollars and gave scholarships to very good children— very good—thirty-two of them. We honored them. It was a grand affair."

The club also has an auxiliary for spouses and significant others, which is full of wives and girlfriends. "Why is the club for men only?" I ask.

"Well, I have to be very truthful. We have had some female applicants that just didn't make it in. I think it's a question for the membership—I think you can answer that question as well as I can. . . It's a universal problem between female and male equality . . . I do not have the profound knowledge on that question. I think it's a question that will not be answered in my lifetime. . . . I've been around this corner so many times with my wife and daughters. Perhaps there are a lot of guys who would like to join a sorority, and there are a lot of girls that would like to join fraternities. I don't know how to answer that."

In fact, it appears easier for males of any race to join than it is black women, because Williams reveals that the club has three white men and two Asian men on the membership roll.

"When you come, you have to be on your best behavior. We've got a dress code, and we enforce it. We also adhere to our code of conduct, and every member is responsible for his guest. So if you come in here and act up, your sponsor has a problem. If you're a member and come here and act up, you go before a disciplinary review board."

"Has that ever happened? How many members have been before the board?" I inquire.

Williams pauses. "From time to time."

"What are some of the things that they go before the disciplinary board for?"

"Well, using vulgar language, and loud and boisterous behavior."

I can't help but chuckle and wonder if members would laugh at Williams's characterization as well. Though it is not a rowdy crowd, I can hear the loud and hearty laughs trail into the office with the music. This is, after all, a club on a Saturday night. It does not look allergic to profanity.

On the surface, it seems natural to conclude that the Royal Esquire reflects the black Seattle experience. Many, including the National Bowling Association member who suggested I come, wouldn't argue with that assumption. But Williams shuns the notion that the club, or any institution, could carry such universal cultural significance for a group as diverse as African Americans. "I really don't know what African-American culture is, do you?" he asks rhetorically. "We often forget that we so-called African Americans have various hues . . . and never stop to think about the number of people who 'disappeared' since the turn of the century, who decided to assimilate with the people they most resemble."

Such people, Williams explains, have left the black experience and passed for white, and have descendants who do not know of their African heritage. "Many white persons, so-called white persons, walking down the street with brown eyes and wavy hair may not know what their heritage is. I remember decades ago, there was such a thing as a United States Bureau of Vital Statistics on Negro Affairs, which said we were disappearing at a high rate. We know those people didn't get on boats. They migrated north and west and some of them remained in the South. Where are those people? Are they African American? What's your background? Are you one hundred percent African? Am I? Are most of us? You have to take all of these complications into consideration when you look at our heritage, our whole, and our being. I don't know what the answer is. For me, I guess black heritage is Martin Luther King, Booker T. Washington, Sojourner Truth, Joe Louis, you, me, Jackie Robinson."

Williams pauses, as if rethinking his statement. "I don't know anything about African-American heritage," he says. "I don't know what it is. I don't understand it."

Williams says that the Royal Esquire Club was founded at a time when it was a necessity for African Americans to create their own social spaces. Over the years, though, it has evolved, grown, and sustained itself through the strength of friendships, camaraderie, volunteerism, and organization—commitments that form human bonds regardless of race. Williams also says that he is sometimes troubled by people who are strongly motivated by racial concerns. "I do not have that strange sense of loyalty that some African Americans have. For example, there could be some brother in the neighborhood running amok, scaring everybody, and then the police come to find out information about the outlaw—and nobody knows him. That's the strange sense of loyalty that I'm talking about. I don't have it."

F. Glen Jones, forty, sips a screwdriver at the bar and watches the dance floor. He was just a year out of Brooklyn, New York's, Pratt Institute of Design, with a degree in art, when he came to Seattle eighteen years ago. "I was homesick like a motherfucker," says Jones as he sits at the bar, sipping a screwdriver and watching the Royal Esquire's photographer snap pictures of couples and singles. "I was young and dumb. There was a lady who I was dating at the time who was from Seattle, and she convinced me at the time that this was the only place in the world to live. I've since found out that's not true. I was a mere twenty-three. I was a young tyke.

"When I first came out here, I worked as a summer temp for United Airlines, and I was a skycap, which at the time was what they call a porter, basically. And then her father suggested I go get a real job. So I started working at the Boeing company. I worked in their graphics-design department as an illustrator. I worked on the maintenance manuals for aircraft—like, you know, do all the drawing and explore the views, lay out this and that. A real lot of technical, boring shit. And then they ended up laying me off. But then, from there, I did a series of different things. I installed telephones for a while. I worked at the *Seattle Times* as a news artist. Then I did some freelance, on my own. Then Reagan decided we were poor and unemployed and he needed to give us unemployment." Jones laughs.

"So I lived off a couple of unemployment extensions, and then I went back to United again as a skycap and got the free flights and all that—well, the 'reduced air travel,' as they put it. And I've been doing that ever since. Well, not anymore: Now I'm considered a customer-service agent."

The relationship that brought Jones to Seattle is long gone. But he's not alone in Seattle, his mother joined him here in 1989, moving from Mount Vernon, New York, two years after her husband died. "When my dad was dying, he told me to take care of my mother—he said that on his death bed.

I figured when somebody says something when they're dying, they must really mean it. So when he passed on, my brothers and sisters weren't really in shape to take care of her, and, of course, I didn't have any children, nor a wife; but I had a house, so I was the likely candidate."

"My mother is from Washington, D.C. My dad was born in New Rochelle, New York. He grew up there. Do you remember *The Dick Van Dyke Show*? With Rob and Laura Petrie? They lived in New Rochelle. They lived on the other side of town, though. We moved to Mount Vernon when I was four years old.

"My father's father was a chauffeur, and his wife didn't work because he made enough money as a chauffeur to support the family. His wife could have passed as white, but she chose not to. She married my grandfather, who was jet black. My mother's father was pretty much self-taught, [having had only a] third-grade education. He taught himself to be a tailor, and by the time he passed away, he owned three houses and had been to Africa. Very sharp.

"My father was a very dynamic man. He was about the greatest man that I knew personally. He was in the military. When he got out of the military, he worked for the federal government for a while, then for a dry cleaner. He was the first black fireman in the fire department in New Rochelle. He was the second black fireman in the state of New York."

Jones has dreams beyond the Esquire Club and the airport. When he isn't at one or the other, chances are he's onstage, as a comedian. He does two gigs a week and wants to make it big. It all started in 1983 with a dare at a comedy club—and after a few screwdrivers. "At a place called Swanee's Comedy Underground," he recounts, "they had what you call an open-mike night, and the people with me were saying, 'You're funnier than these people and blah blah blah.' So I had been drinking one drink too many, and I said if they'd buy me another drink, I'd go up there. They bought me a drink. I swigged it down, went up, and did five minutes.

"I told mostly old jokes, dirty jokes I knew, like, Why is a hunter a woman's best friend?" He pauses. "'Cause when a hunter hunts, he always goes deep into the bush, he usually shoots twice, and he always eats what he shoots.

"From there, I just started going to open mikes. I'm gigging a couple of times a week, and then a lot of open-mike stuff. Some gigs take me to Canada, Montana, Idaho."

Jones breaks off here to tell me that it's time for him to leave tonight. He's off to the suburbs, to the house of his ex-girlfriend, Jacqueline Jones, who is a member of the Seattle club of the National Brotherhood of Skiers, a predominantly black organization of fourteen thousand skiers who gather annually for the black ski summit. The chapter is throwing a picture party to share photographs from their Caribbean cruise over the summer, and he suggests that I tag along to see a different side of black Seattle.

Driving his Fiat on 406 east headed for the Newport Hills subdivision on the outskirts of Seattle, Jones relates that he is the product of a family with a long line of male breadwinners. For that reason, he says, it wasn't easy dating Jacqueline, whose earnings far outdistanced his. Until two months ago, when she retired at forty-six, Jacqueline worked as a director at Microsoft. "Well, at the beginning, I didn't think it was going to be an issue," he states. "I seriously tried not to make it an issue, but I think the differences did start to come up."

As he describes their problems, I begin to think that I'm listening to a Terry McMillan novel. "I think part of it was we had different lifestyles, schedules, and stuff. She's really type A, and she'd go to work weekends, working all the time. I'd do my little eight or six or whatever it was, and boom, I'm ready to get on a plane, you know? So I had a much more casual lifestyle than she did. She was chasing the carrot. That was one part of it, and I was preaching to her, 'you need to slow down,' and she was preaching to me, 'you ain't working hard enough.'

"And then, we socialized differently. She would rarely come to the Esquire Club. She and her friends were more into their private parties. Some of them will be there tonight, a lot of them were, you know, doctors, lawyers, a judge, business people: 'doing well Negroes,' as I used to call them.'"

Jones exits the highway and we are soon on a street of relatively new, colonial-style homes. Newport Hills, in fact, looks like many other communities recently built for upwardly mobile young adults. Jacqueline Jones's street is lined with cars of her guests—Saabs, BMWs, and a couple of Mercedes-Benzes.

Jacqueline answers the door and Glen introduces us. She has smooth brown skin and round brown eyes; her smile is curt yet warm. She seems to be a staid and introspective woman, and thus I have a hard time imagining her in a relationship with Glen. "I am not lighthearted," she later tells me. "I'm always serious. I'm very analytical and structured about the way I do things. I sometimes surround myself with people that are silly and naturally lighthearted. I don't consciously do this. But when I look around at the people that I have selected as my closest friends, they're pretty much very lighthearted. I'm the serious one in the group, all the time, and I just want to be like them in some ways—although I have one friend who keeps telling me, 'Learn to value what you have and who you are; maybe those lighthearted friends look to you because they need somebody to anchor them,' and that's the purpose I serve in their lives. I don't know . . . I have a hard time letting the child in me come out."

Jacqueline's house is a four-bedroom with an upstairs exercise room, where she has installed a treadmill, a weight machine, and aerobics equipment. There's also a Jacuzzi and a steam room. The decor in the family room, where tonight a large crowd gathers, is modern in black and white. Her bookshelves are lined with popular serious fiction—Tom Clancy, Octavia Butler, Toni Morrison, Alice Walker, Robert Ludlum, James Corvell—as well as several books on metaphysics and New Age psychology.

Jones spent eleven years at Microsoft. "I got in at Microsoft at a good time," she says. "I don't know if you know anything about their stock, but I've had stock options over the years. I'm fairly financially secure—I have enough money to not work for several years, at any rate, and still have my retirement investments in place for when I really reach retirement age."

Now Jones and two other members of the ski club have become primary investors in a shoe company. "It's not making any money yet. If I make enough money from that, I may not have to go back to work. We primarily market shoes, and we started out doing athletic-style shoes with college logos on them. Last year we licensed seventeen colleges. We have their logo embroidered on the shoes and sold them in the schools' local areas. So, around here, we do the University of Washington and Washington State. We do Oregon State and the University of Oregon. We do about three or four California schools, a couple of Florida schools, and [some other] fairly big schools. It generates some business."

Jacqueline Jones has approximately thirty guests. Some come with their pictures in packages straight from a photo shop. Others are arranged in dapper albums. Nearly all are members of the ski club. Many of the men wear blazers or sweaters that would look just right on Cliff Huxtable of *The Cosby Show,* and the women are in slacks and silk blouses. Glen is known here by Jacqueline's friends, and he is greeted with polite smiles in response to his hearty handshakes. They are lawyers, accountants, entrepreneurs, and a judge, nearly all of them baby boomers. Unlike a Tuxedo Ball party, for example, there isn't a test of lineage that anyone in this room must pass. They come from all kinds of backgrounds. What matters is where they are today.

In the family room, while everyone samples the pot-luck buffet, which offers teriyaki chicken, peach cobbler, baked ham, fried rice, sweet-potato pie, and a wide array of beverages, a crowd watches a home video of the cruise, passes around straight-from-the-shop envelopes and dapper albums of photos, and converses about everything from golf to gossip.

"The people there were anywhere from age twenty to eighty," Jones says of the cruise, which catered to black professionals. "Most of them in their thirties and early forties. It was a lot of fun. I went because, number one, I enjoy hot weather a lot, and I just knew a ship full of black people was going to be a big party and there was going to be a lot of fun, and I like to dress up. They give you a couple of formal nights, and I like to snorkel, and I like to shop, and so it was as if all the things I like to do were right there in this package. It was a big party.

"The deejays were great," she continues. "They played great music. The comedians were funny as could be. The shows were great: the Whispers, Chaka Khan, Keith Washington. Everybody was there to have a good time. It wasn't about discord—it was about harmony and fun and, you know, getting along with people."

Jones says it was her first black cruise and won't be her last, "because I exist in a white world—you know, from a business perspective. Let's face it, jobs are probably the primary focus in most people's lives. [And] I have always gone to white schools. . . . In all the jobs, I'm the only black person, or one of the few around, and so I interact with white people all day long, day after day after day. Though I don't resent them, they're different. We're just different. There are cultural differences, and people are always aware of the differences because of your skin color; and so you're just never quite one hundred percent relaxed in that environment." She corrects herself: "I'm not saying that I'm not relaxed, but I'm not necessarily at ease."

"What are those cultural differences?" I ask.

"Oh, it's so hard to describe. It's just the way people talk to each other. It's like, 'hey brother, hey sister'—you don't say that to white people. I have lots of white friends at work, outside of work. I don't socialize with all of them, yet I consider these people my friends. We get along just fine, but it's not who I choose to spend my free time with. I just don't naturally gravitate to white people. I don't know how you describe it—I naturally gravitate to black people, and so when I'm away from work, I want to be with black people. It's not really conscious, though; it just happens. That's who I am, and that's it. That's who I surround myself with.

"It's like mothers are always in control over the world until you're sixteen or so. And [among] black people, everybody always loved their mothers dearly and appreciates the pain and suffering they've had. Everybody has a story about their mother on one thing or another that happened to them when they were children and things that they tried to get away with and how their mother caught them at it and how she dealt with it. . . ." But is that so different from other racial and ethnic groups?

"I don't know if our (blacks') mothers raised us differently than their (whites') mothers did, but black people have stories about their mothers all the time. Maybe white people do too and I just never sat down and listened to them, but I don't know." As Jones talks, my mind drifts back to Cyril Miller's description of his mother.

"I just think it's more cultural. Again, I think black people who have achieved some economic status and who have the opportunity to do these kinds of things that are enjoyable have also gotten to the point that we can not only do those things [ski trips and cruises] but do them with each other. We don't have to do them with white people, and we don't want to.

"For me, I don't really think much about integration or segregation, 'cause I figure I can go anywhere I want to go anytime I choose to go; and I do that, and I deal with whatever environment I find myself in. I don't like being the only black person anywhere, but it happens."

Still, be that as it may, Jones admits that there can be an advantage to standing out. "So many times I run into so many white people who know who I am, and that can be helpful. Sometime I don't have a clue who they are, but it's because I've been in an environment where I've been one of the few [black people], so they notice me, but they're, like, everywhere, and I don't notice them." Nevertheless, "that can be just tiring."

Later, I mull Jones's statements in my mind. As I listen to the conversations in the room, I did not hear people saying "hey brother," or "hey sister." I heard more of that at the Esquire Club. I also wonder if Jones and her friends are merely creating a new box, a cocoon that excludes not only whites but African Americans of lower socioeconomic means. "No," she replies. "It's not that we don't want to do it with them [poor African Americans]. Poor black people can't do the things that we are doing—they don't have the money to do it. I think that that's totally different, and that's the only thing that's separating us from poor black people. They're poor, and we're not."

She has a point. As she and others have at least tacitly noted, are upper-middle-class whites expected to socialize with low-income whites? Why should upper-middle- and lower-class blacks be expected to mingle? Jones and her friends are yet another facet of the modern American black experience. Their circumstances are not unique or new; there are even some memoirs on the subject. Sam Fulwood III, for example, the product of a Southern upper-middle-class family and the Washington correspondent for the *Los Angeles Times,* writes in *Waking from the Dream* of his decision to concentrate his social life in a self-protected, black, upscale cocoon, isolated from whites and poor blacks. It is a lifestyle that resembles Jacqueline Jones's chosen way. By contrast, in *Our Kind of People,* a book on the black upper class, Lawrence Otis Graham, a native of White Plains, New York, writes about a black elite that mirrors the Tuxedo Ball and is intent on existing in both white and upscale black social worlds. Fulwood and Graham provide emerging models of the post–civil-rights, upper- and middle-class life. And there are many more.

While Jones's social world is largely black, she has dated men of other races, which isn't a surprise in Seattle, a city known for a high number of interracial marriages. "I have dated interracially once," she says. "One guy, for about a year. And now you're gonna ask why I left?"

She doesn't give me the chance to say yes before she answers the question. "I was never really comfortable with it. Well, this is a long time ago, about 1980. I met him at work when I had my very first job in a small computer-programming company. I hired him and taught him how to program. [But] we didn't date until a few years after that, actually. I really liked this guy as an individual. The two of us someplace by ourselves—we had a great time. But whenever we went out in public, people would stare. Black men in particular would make rude remarks, and, I don't know, it just didn't seem right, didn't feel right in some ways.

"My feelings about interracial marriages have evolved over time. I have always held the concept that one on one, any individual who meets someone and is attracted to them for whatever reason, it doesn't matter whether you're purple, green, yellow, whatever. I did have problems for a while with a large number of black men in this city who date only white women—I always thought that meant that there was something wrong with that man. Because to exclude your own race is self-denial, as far as I was concerned, and I guess I had some anger over that, over the years, watching that. But now, I've gotten to the point where I think that's a personal choice. For whatever reason, an individual decides that he or she doesn't want to associate with their own race in terms of a relationship, then, hey, more power to them. I hope they find somebody that meets their needs. I think the numbers of available black men is not that high in the Northwest, and so you certainly see more and more black women with white men around here. And I'm sure there's a few black women who would date only white men. Again, I say, to each his own. I just don't worry about it anymore. I have never had any problem finding a black man anyway, if I wanted to be with one."

Nevertheless, Jones says that there is a pattern in her relationships that concerns her: she often finds herself involved with men who are not on her socioeconomic level. The pattern stretches back to her five-year marriage, which ended in divorce. Living in a community-property state, she was forced to split everything with a husband who was out of work for much of the marriage. "I really only dated two other guys after my marriage," she says. "Sometimes I have to look at myself as well and say, 'why is it that the people you're attracted to are not in the same economic bracket?' Even with my ex-husband, we started living together after he had a serious accident and he couldn't dress himself, bathe himself, and whatnot. I moved in to help him out and never left. We continued to live together after he recovered; and there's a part of me, I think, that's looking to take care of people, and I'm trying to deal with that.

"Females innately have a more nurturing sense about them, black, white, yellow, purple, whoever. . . . But in the African-American community, black women have also had the responsibility of being the wage-earners. A lot of economic opportunities for black women have been in caregiver roles, too, child care, nursing care, social workers, and teachers. Those are the kinds of roles that have been open to us for a long time." Jones wonders if somewhere in the contemporary socialization of black women the need to nurture and care for others lingers—even in the lives of women who've risen on up the corporate ladder alongside men.

As we talk, I learn that Jones collects art by John Nelson, whose black-and-white pencil drawings match the modern decor of her family room. Nelson is too vividly literal, figurative, and, perhaps, popular, to be comfortable in the GR N'Namdi Gallery. Of course, just as every African American in Seattle doesn't have to like the Esquire Club, every piece of fine art doesn't have to meet the same taste or standard.

One piece is particularly striking. Depicting a black woman in a cotton field holding a book aimed at the sky, it holds special significance for Jones for what it, to her, illustrates: "She's not letting race and her situation limit her, and that's how I learned to live from my parents. I remember one of my brothers saying at my dad's funeral that the thing he learned from him was how to break out of the box. Never let anybody put a box around you to limit you."

Jones says that she saw her father practice that maxim when she was eight and the family moved to Cleveland from New Haven, Connecticut, in 1956. The elder Jones attempted to land a job as a car salesman. "Well, they didn't have any black salesmen before he got there, and they kept telling him, no, they wouldn't hire him, and he said, 'I'm not leaving until you do.' And, basically, [he] sat there. So, eventually, they said, 'Okay, we'll hire you to sell to Negroes,' and he said, 'I don't think so. If I'm going to sell cars, I'm going to sell them to anybody that walks in the door.'

"Our last names is Jones, so the first thing he did when he was hired was pull out the Cleveland phone book and call every Jones in there and said, 'You know, we have something in common. I'd like to meet you and sell you a car.' He became the top salesman there for twenty-five years. He was their number-one salesman.

"That is the African-American experience that I relate to: You know that there are people out there that are going to put you down; there are people out there that are going to try and limit your success, limit your ability to achieve whatever it is you want. You have to learn to not accept that and just take your own life in your own hands. I think that African Americans in general in this country have done that over the centuries—no matter what conditions white people have tried to impose on us, we've always managed to fight our way out of it and make something better out of our lives than what was available the generation before or whatever. And this follows true until the very recent history. I'm sure it's still happening in some segments of our culture, but, unfortunately, I don't think it's happening everywhere.

"My father used to always say to me, 'I know you're gonna be a great businesswoman one day. I think you can, and you will do well in the business world.' And it's funny, both of my brothers [and myself], we're all in the computer industry. I don't know where that came from, really. I just think that there's good logic genes or something in our family, because we all seem to have a good affinity for computers and logical thinking."

In fact, Jones saw the influence of her parents very clearly after she left Ohio in the early seventies and reinvented herself in Seattle. She was twenty-four years old and had survived a few rough years after graduating with a degree in business administration from Ohio University in Athens. Though she was a stellar student, she had another life in the counterculture: she was a drug user during her college days and the first few years after graduation, indulging in mushrooms, downers, even snorting heroin. "I have this whole set of values my parents instilled in me. I took a few years out. Then I thought, 'This isn't life. Let me get back to what I know.'"

During her journey to realign her life along her family's values, a college friend invited her out to Seattle. Within a few weeks of arriving, she decided to relocate here and began looking for a future. A smart place to find it in 1976 was the world of technology, so Jones took a few courses in computer programming at a technical college. With that experience, she landed a job as a systems analyst at a small company, where she did everything and helped it grow from two to eight employees. In her next job, she did sales training and wrote computer manuals for software companies. Then, on a whim, she answered a Microsoft job ad in 1983 and won a position as a systems analyst there. At the time, Microsoft employed only three hundred people—a small cry from the fifteen thousand of today. She rose through the ranks over the ensuing decade and retired as director of worldwide application support two months ago.

"I don't know if you know anything about Microsoft, but it's a very, very intense place to work," she says. "It's extremely stressful, more so than an average company, I think. They gave us lots of perks and luxuries and anything you can imagine, but at the same time they demanded such high volumes and quality of work that it was very, very stressful. You know, fifty hours a week is like absolute minimum time you put in. Sixty to seventy is more regular. [I did it] for eleven years."

She sighs. "The first seven years, I was on call twenty-four hours a day. I think for about a four-year period, I didn't get a single night's sleep all the way through without my phone ringing and someone [calling] me up . . . so I worked in this environment for almost eleven years. Very, very stressful. I was starting to get tired of it and [suffering] burnout. Then my father got cancer a couple of years ago, almost three years ago, and he died this past February. So I took some time off to be with my mom, who has had multiple sclerosis for thirty years and is a complete invalid. I was thinking, 'God, this job is so stressful, I'm so burned out—I don't know that I really want to go back to it.'"

And when she got back, she was startled by a piece of news that sent her looking for a new life. "A young woman who used to work for me when I was in purchasing—she's like thirty-one years old—was diagnosed with brain cancer, and we didn't know if she was going to live or what. She had a very bad headache. She went to the doctor—two days in a row. They did an MRI: nine brain tumors. They did surgery, and I'm thinking, 'Lord, I don't know if I'm going to be here tomorrow. I just don't need this anymore.' So I decided to leave; I just decided it was time to leave. I just needed to take time off and think about me and take care of me. I was trying to take care of my parents—financially, at any rate—for the past four or five years, and then when my dad died, the financial burden kind of went down. My mother, being an invalid, she doesn't get out. She doesn't spend a lot of money. I still have to help her because she lives alone.

"But I just decided to at least take a year off and just do nothing but relax, travel, have fun, read, hang out with my friends, whatever my heart desires. I'm just two months into that process now. Next summer, I'll sort of look around and figure out what it is I want to do next."

Six

HOME

The Ride Home

IN Lawnside, New Jersey, James and Ellen Benson say that they are always surprised when people look at their ordinary lives and see something unique. Mike Latting feels the same way, and he doesn't even live in Lawnside. He lives more than a thousand miles away, in St. Anne, Illinois.

Mike's weekdays are spent as principal of an elementary school. After school and on weekends, he's managing the family's hundred-acre ranch or getting the bulls ready to wrestle in one of the rodeos produced by the family business that fully involves three generations.

At both school and the rodeos, you are likely to find him with tobacco in his mouth. "I'm going to be me wherever I am," says Mike Latting. "I won't spit it on the ground at school, though."

The forty-three-year-old Latting is short, stocky, and could almost pass as his mother's twin. He and Harriet Latting are of the same height and have nearly identical short, broad faces, wide nostrils, brown eyes, and smooth, oak-colored and wrinkle-free skin.

When it's rodeo time, Harriet sits behind the time keepers and announcers on a stage, while her son is at the chutes at one end of the amphitheater. His attention is on the bucking broncos and a team of ten workers who either move bulls, horses, and goats to the right places or keep watch over the proceedings.

An outsider visiting one of the Lattings' rodeos can't help but notice something about this scene of bulls, horses, men, and women in big hats, jeans, and long-sleeved shirts: the audience is virtually all white. The few black faces stand out because there are so few. Of the hundreds of competing cowboys, all but a dozen are white. The people running the operation, however, are black. Specifically, they are the Latting family. "What tickles me, and I tell my kids about it now, when I went up in line in Wyoming to get my scholarship check," says Mike Latting, who attended Casper Junior College and the University of Southern Colorado, "I was in a rodeo scholarship line and a lot of the adults were saying, 'You need to be over in the basketball line.'"

Eventually, everyone on campus knew where Latting belonged. He was the Western Association Central Rocky regional champion in bareback-bronco and bull riding. "I think that my talent overruled what a lot of people thought and it opened up a lot of eyes."

Today, he's not entertaining or competing on a bull or bronco. He's running a big piece of the family operation, one that draws thousands of cowboys and cowgirls every year to compete. In doing so, he's following the path of his father, Thyrl Latting Sr., and keeping it clear for his two sons and daughter.

His father, Thyrl, competed and rode for years before starting the company and creating the profitable tradition of Latting rodeos in a region that is not rodeo rich. This is not Colorado, Wyoming, or Oklahoma, yet many still come from as far south as Oklahoma and as far west as Colorado and Wyoming to this Latting event at the county fair in Peaton, Illinois, thirty miles south of Chicago. On this Sunday night in August 1995, the family's third and final rodeo of the weekend is under way.

The Lattings have become the premiere rodeo production company in the Midwest and one of the best in the business, according to the Professional Rodeo Cowboys Association, which estimates that thirty thousand cowboys and cowgirls participate annually in rodeos nationwide. Latting rodeos have won several awards, too, including Best Rodeo of the Year for one produced far from their midwestern turf, at Madison Square Garden in New York.

Thyrl and Harriet don't live on the ranch in St. Anne, Illinois, where Mike and his family live. The elder Lattings and the rodeo company's office is in Robbins, Illinois. Actually, they could claim the more affluent town of Crestwood as their home and that of the company's headquarters, but Thyrl Latting prefers to call the company's base Robbins, a predominantly black and low-income South Chicago suburb where Thyrl grew up. "I live a half hour from where I was raised in Robbins. It's the town of Crestwood, but Robbins is my address, because I live right on the dividing line. A lot of people who live on my block, middle-class white and blacks, don't say Robbins."

"Why do you say Robbins?" I ask.

"Why not? I'm not the kind of guy that has to have a status thing. I feel like that's not necessary, [me] being who I am. You look on my card—Robbins, Illinois, that's where I am from. Well, some people look at me and they say, 'Robbins, Illinois?' I say 'Yes' as if, so what? I was raised there and there was no reason for me to leave.

"It's a special place. It was a poor place where most everybody there was poor, working class, and everybody there was black, but there was a good feeling about it. It's like this is our town. I didn't feel poor at all. I felt real good."

There is a rich tradition and history attached to African-American cowboys. Steer wrestling, of course, was created by the legendary black cowboy Bill Pickett. Thyrl Latting knew nothing of that tradition while growing up in Chicago: "My family didn't come from that side of the country."

He neither distances himself from the tradition in an effort to deny his race, nor celebrates that heritage as though it automatically belongs to him and is something that only he or an African American can appreciate.

Thyrl Latting grew up in Chicago in the thirties. When he was eleven, his family left the Windy City and moved to Robbins. His father was a machinist and self-taught carpenter, and his mother was a homemaker. Latting developed an interest in horses at a young age. "I had always been a horse lover. And I went to the movies and was kind of a cowboy guy—you know, a cowboy worshipper. So when I got to be about twelve years old, we moved out to the suburbs. That gave me an opportunity to buy a horse.

"They had truck gardens in Robbins, and the kids would work and crawl down the rows and weed onions and things like that. I worked for two years and saved the money and bought a horse. It cost sixty dollars. I was twelve years old. That was a long time ago."

By the time he was eighteen, Latting was riding with two other cowboys, both of whom were white. "I knew about rodeos because I was crazy about horses—you know, in the movies and books and all that. I would read about it and the kind of thing that a city kid does. But I had no experience about going or knowing anybody that knew anything about real horses or real rodeos. But I was a quick study. At seventeen, I first started riding bulls. It was no longer just laying around and liking horses. I was a cowboy from that point on."

It wasn't a popular time for a black man to love rodeos. The Great Migration north to the urban opportunities of the industrial age produced a black fondness for the city, and country life was associated with the spirit of Jim Crow and backward thinking. "When I was in my twenties, I would put my cowboy [clothes] on to go places or to a rodeo, and black people would ridicule me to the end. They thought that I was just country. I would put our hats in the trunk until we got out of town. They wouldn't allow me to be myself in our own neighborhoods. They would look at me like I'm some kind of fool. They would laugh. See you with a hat or some kind of boot on, they would think that I'm some kind of fool, okay, because I wasn't be-bopping. Well, since then, black people have turned around, and they have decided that being a cowboy is pretty good.

"But everybody discouraged me . . . even my dad."

And some of the encouragement from white crowds at rodeos was un-settling as well. "I've been at rodeos and some people in the audience would say, 'Come on ride him nigger!'"

Thryl Latting says race, more so than racism, did affect his company's be-ginning. The cowboys and rodeo sponsors were not the problem, he says—the competition was—rodeo production companies tried to use race as a means of turning the cowboys and potential sponsors against the company. "They thought I was going to get something that they had, which I did. So the first thing that goes through their heads was to say certain things. The thing about the women first, they brought that up, about white women, but I didn't do this because I wanted white women."

"What about white women?" I ask.

"Rumors that I was chasing white women and they were chasing me. Also, they would tell cowboys I was just a bunch of niggers, all up and rig it so they win your rodeo. Then it would only be a nigger rodeo. Well, I knew this: nothing is a secret if two people hear it. I have people all over the place. These are white people that I have ridden with all my life, and they were loyal cowboys. They came back and told me. They're not going to lis-ten to this stuff and not tell me. They are going to tell me what is going on, just like my brother would. I could see that this type of stuff was going on, and I felt that I must conduct myself above reproach to get around it. So that is my reputation. If you get a check of mine that has got lining on it, you might as well take it to the bank. Don't have to wait or whatever. And I have been in situations, long ago, where a customer would mess up and couldn't pay me, and then I would write the checks to my people. I would have to beat it to the bank and make sure that I could borrow from the bank to make sure that I could pay my own people. That happened. Doesn't happen now, but I have dealt with everything in order to keep my reputation a certain way. So that's the first thing: my reputation is above reproach. In fact, I go to conventions sometimes, and people go and try and find me. They don't even know my name, but they would say 'that black rodeo producer' and try to find me. That guy is the guy you want to get. So no longer is it a negative thing."

Through it all, Thyrl Latting persevered. Like so many other African Americans, success required that he refuse to allow others to define his destiny. Unlike Flora Young and Henry McKoy, he didn't have a supportive community of elders to guide him through that process. His experiences truly reinforce the idea that blacks "must be twice as good" at their endeavors. "I'm not down there on the edge trying to get to be better. I am better. And I know now if I wasn't better, it wouldn't have worked. We are determined to be better and we are going to have more to offer. An example: we talk about advertising and marketing. When I go to a new customer and we talk about the rodeo, what it costs and what it is like and all that kind of thing, that is only part of it. Then we get into some things that other rodeo producers can't do. We talk about how we are going to help you make money now, how are you going to make this thing pay? I help him lay out an advertising campaign and then we talk about how you go out and get sponsors. How do you do that. And I know all about that. Most of my new customers, I'll go out with them on the first day. Five or six meetings together in your own town with people who think you have money to spend and people that advertise. You look in the newspaper and listen to the radio for people who advertise—those are the people who we go see. Because we are going to show them a way."

Thyrl Latting is clearly popular in the rodeo world. Many of the 150 competing cowboys and cowgirls here in Peaton from across the country do not pass him without speaking. Still, there's an aspect to his popularity and his quest to build his company that is troubling: in some ways, it cheats African Americans out of the opportunity to be normal and ordinary. "I guess this is not good, as far as they [whites] either want you [as an African American] to be all good or all bad. For blacks, many whites want you to be their hero, and then will accept you as their heroes. That is a funny kind of thing. It is like the other side of the coin. And some say that you are a superman, but the rest of them aren't good."

In interviews with several sponsors and cowboys across the country, many affirm that Latting is indeed among the best. Perhaps his success is tied to the role of the rodeos in his family's life, where they are more of a passion than a business. Importantly, this family of teachers was never dependent on the income generated by the rodeos because they held other jobs and thus could reinvest all profits back into the company, which enables them to offer more services to clients like the county fairs. "My theory was that if we continue to put our money back into the business, we could support ourselves and we wouldn't have to worry about paying a lot of taxes. So, for years, we just bought more, bought more so we were just bigger, bigger without taking much. Now, for the past five years, I am not working anymore. I make a living with the rodeos, but we were able to make ourselves a heck of a base. We weren't like those old stereotypes and stories about ourselves, about the old black guy who got a filling station and started to be successful and the first thing he gets is a big car and a girlfriend, and pretty soon he is taking money out and he can't buy gas. So that kind of thing never happened to me. We just took our money and put it back and bought bucking horses, bought land, equipment.

"You know, that takes a lot of time and money to do those kinds of things. You start out with nothing. I think it was twenty-one years ago [that] Mike got out of college, and the last twenty-two years, Mike has been my partner. So when we do the rodeo, I produce the show, and all the people who work out in the area, like the announcers, the judges, they work for me. All the people who are back here getting the stock ready, they work for Mike. My daughter has a part in it. She is a bookkeeper, and she handles that."

Today, the Lattings produce two rodeos for the county fair. Like most others, the show begins with Mike's sister Tracy Latting, thirty-eight, riding Bubba into the pen in the amphitheater. Her left hand controls Bubba's reins, her right is in the air clutching a wooden pole bearing an American flag. Ray Charles sings "America the Beautiful" over the PA system. There are cheers, claps, and screams from the crowd of one thousand in the steel bleachers.

At this time, Mike's sons are ready to entertain. Only a few minutes ago, I saw them in T-shirts, but cowboys are always dressed when the rodeo begins. By the time Aunt Tracy and Bubba enter the pen, Chris, seventeen, and Kelley, thirteen, are on their horses, wearing red, white, and blue long-sleeved shirts with gold stars, jeans, and cowboy hats. They are ready for their trick-riding routine. Chris, a lanky, slender, six-footer, is the tallest in the family. Meanwhile, the brothers' sister Michelle, who isn't on a horse right now, stays with their mother, Nina, a part-time nurse. Michelle does not perform or compete—yet. The five-year-old has been training and riding for two years, because family tradition dictates that three-year-olds are ready to learn to ride. Today, though, Michelle walks with her mother along the side of the amphitheater where cowboys and cowgirls have parked their vans, cars, and trailers. Some will sleep here tonight before riding on to the next rodeo.

Nina Latting can relax a little now, as most of her rodeo work is on the front end: she schedules the events. She's a city girl, born and raised in Chicago, who married into the tradition. She met Mike Latting through his other sister, Joanna, who competed as a rodeo barrel racer before she died of sickle-cell anemia, in 1989, at age thirty-three.

The season will soon slow down because the school year started last week. Like many of the cowboys at their rodeos, this is the Lattings' primary passion, but not the total source of their livelihood. Mike Latting isn't the only educator in the family. In fact, education is as much of a tradition in this family as rodeos: Thyrl Latting is a retired vocational-education teacher in the Chicago public schools, while Tracy Latting, a former deejay, is studying elementary education in graduate school. "We all got into that, so we could rodeo in the summertime. We're different kinds of people than the average schoolteacher. I know there're a lot of good schoolteachers. I know a lot of good schoolteachers, but I know a lot of sorry ones, too. I know a lot of people who just can't make it, and so they end up being schoolteachers and ruining our kids."

Wild bulls rumble in the chutes. Then, suddenly, a bull shoots out, with a cowboy holding on and, perhaps, making a face that looks tougher and wilder than the bull. The bull-riding contestants determine their order arbitrarily, by a draw of lots. The selection of which bulls go first, last, and in between is everything but arbitrary, however. Mike Latting makes those decisions, because he knows that the selection is a piece of the production and helps create a winning rodeo for the crowd. "Everything that you just saw out there was choreographed, whether you realize it or not," Mike tells me after the bull-wrestling competition. "Now, I have no control over the way the animals buck, but I know how they buck by past practices and patterns, and therefore I set the stage so that I get the ultimate show from the horse and the rider."

It is all a matter of knowing your stock, being able to predict which of these wild animals will perform when the show is in need of a climactic moment. The bulls are a case in point: they are merely wild in the beginning, but build to a point where the man who gets the last number must beware. The final chute rattles long before that bull leaves the pen.

"Did you notice the first bull that went out?" Mike asks. "How everybody screamed and hollered? Did you notice the last bull that went out and everybody screamed and hollered? That was not by accident—that was on purpose. Because you want your ultimate good rides to either start or finish. But you want some meat in the middle, now, too, don't get me wrong. So we put a very active one in between, but my sensational ones I start and finish with.

"It's not like golf. It's not like tennis. It's kind of like hockey, as far as the contestants are concerned," he explains. "People want to go see hockey because they want to see near misses. If they cut fighting out of hockey, attendance drops. People want to see these guys come out here and these bulls jerk them around, and not kill them, but bang them around a little bit—or near misses, you know? And you can tell by the way the crowd oooohs and watches. We have to entertain."

Midway through the competition, the Latting sons perform their tricks. Chris Latting wears the hard and tough face of a cowboy but performs with the grace of a ballerina. His solo includes Roman riding, in which he rides two bareback horses, standing with one foot on each as he raises both hands to the crowd's applause. "There he is," says Mike. "Well, my older son Roman rides and I Roman rode. My younger son rides bulls and I rode bulls, but I rode bareback horses too. Kelley will be riding bareback horses when he gets a little bit older and gets more upper-body strength."

The Lattings' stock includes seventy-five horses and fifty bulls. Mike Latting knows all the horses by name, but not the bulls. "Well, I'm not really into big names on bulls. My horses are my pride. And, uh, like Angle face, Barbarosa, you know, Big-e-nuff, horses like that, I mean, they're famous. Yeah, I gave 'em to 'em names like my kids."

Danell Tipton arrives from Oklahoma just in time to wrestle in the last rodeo on Sunday. He wears an earring, a gold chain, and a baseball cap. "Those are my traveling clothes."

When it is time to ride, he's dressed like a cowboy. The twenty-two-year-old has been a finalist in the International Professional Rodeo Association finals for bull riding for the past six years. "I'm young. I been riding bulls probably, say, six years. My whole family rodeos. My great-grandfather Lloyd Tipton rode the range and stuff with Bill Pickett. And he's in the Cowboy Hall of Fame also. And it goes back, it's a tradition, I guess—I got to continue. I have a younger brother, he rides bulls too. He just finished high school, and he's in the college ranks now, and he's been riding really good. I just went straight to the pros right when I graduated out of high school. . . . Yes, it's in the blood. It's thrill-seeking. Man, rodeo is going to get nothing but get bigger. I mean, rodeo is the best thing that's going on right now. There's much money in it, and it ain't going to do nothing but get bigger. I'm just traveling the circuit. I got six rodeos to go to starting Thursday. I try to get to as many as I can. Most of the big ones."

Bull wrestling has been dubbed the "most dangerous sporting event in America" by the sportscasters of America. It requires the participant to ride a 2,000-pound bull for eight seconds, with only one hand on a short rope to hold on, while the bull kicks, twists, and spins and its loose hide rolls from side to side. Still, it is not the danger to cowboys and cowgirls that has triggered outrage: animal rights activists say that rodeo sports are acts of cruelty to animals. The Lattings, as one would expect, dispute the charges. "I'm allowing these animals to do what they really want to do," contends Mike Latting. "Take those bulls out there: I'm sure they'd much rather be working eight seconds a week, eating all the food they can eat, being able to frolic with the cows on occasion, than being at McDonald's with you sitting down, or any guy sitting down with his belly hanging over the table, eating on him.

"Now, I love meat, I love it," he quickly adds. "I'd be there too. But my belly wouldn't be hanging over the table. But I'd be there eating him too."

The Latting rodeos also include steer wrestling, bareback-bronco riding, saddle-bronco riding, barrel racing, and calf roping. To add to the entertainment, after the entrance of the flag, the Lattings present a stagecoach holdup. Of course, a good old cowboy comes to the rescue.

Mike Latting has three college students who work for him and live with his family. They are employees and aspiring cowboys. "There are people who I would still call my friends who maybe don't particularly care for colored people," says Phillip, twenty-four, who's from South Bend, Indiana. "But I really don't care, because that has no effect on me. I almost look to Mike as kind of a father figure. In fact, he has kind of taken me under his wing, like he takes a lot of guys. He sees in you that you really want to try and that you really want to go somewhere, he'll do anything he can to try and help you. So in that aspect, he has done a lot for me and I have come a long, long way just within the last two years. So I kind of look at him as more of a, maybe, father figure, a mentor.

"I think [for] a lot of my friends back home, it is not like I'm some big superstar, [but] they are impressed because they think it is neat what I am doing, because it is not something they see very often. I guess they just look at it as something that might be fun and I am enjoying it."

"The way I look at it," says Derrick, twenty-six, another worker, "my family and Mike's family, both families together, are more or less my family. At first when I came out here, there were some people that kind of looked at me like I was the minority in that town and around that area; I was the only white kid in town, so I was the one that was the minority. And there were a lot of people who would look at me. Chris and I would like drive down the road or something and they would say, 'Who's that white boy with Chris?' So [I] got sort of a taste of what it was like to be the minority."

This weekend's rodeo began early on Friday, and, as usual, Phillip and Derrick spent the morning getting the calves, bulls, and horses ready to load into their trailers, while Mike and Chris and Kelley were in school. By the time they came home, there wasn't much more to load besides the steel they use for the chutes and the pens.

All of the animals and equipment are at Mike Latting's house, a modest white ranch-style home on a dusty road. It looks small on its hundred-acre spread, with barns, hay, bulls, horses, pens, and goats all around.

The Lattings are producing three rodeos this weekend, which means that they're handling everything, from setting up the chutes to providing all of the animals. On Saturday, there is the annual Gay Rodeo. Then, on Sunday, they are producing the two rodeos for the Peaton county fair. Tonight, they will set up the steel chutes and pens for both and get the animals to their proper places.

I ride with Chris Latting and Derrick and Phillip. "I really want to be a serious cowboy," says Derrick. "There're weekend warriors and serious cowboys. A lot of guys ride on weekends—I'm talking about the kind of guys who want to get on and impress a girl, go back to the bar and tell stories, and are not serious about riding. I want to be serious."

"A serious cowboy is somebody who wins a lot and has the right attitude," adds Chris Latting, whose light and almost-soft voice is a stark contrast to his father's. "I don't know—some people, they win and all, and you can't stand to be around them."

"Yeah, they're like arrogant," says Phillip. "They are cowboys, but they're not, like, people cowboys."

"People cowboys?" I ask.

"Yeah, people cowboys are, like, somebody that you, like, talk to, and they're friends of yours," says Chris. "I think that's a real cowboy. Somebody you can back up what they say and that is approachable."

"People like us. Cockiness—we all have a sense of cockiness," says Derrick. "We've got it, or we wouldn't be in this business. Some guys take it a bit too far, I guess. We are all cocky . . . to the outside person who is not involved in the rodeo, they're going to look at us and think that we are pretty much all cocky. I think *cowboy* is more of a mental attitude, what you believe in your head and your heart, and there's kind of a certain attitude and a certain set of morals that go along with being a cowboy, and a lot of the guys that get on horses and bulls—you know, they're a cowboy, they do the cowboy thing, but they don't have the right attitude. Most of the guys you see around here, the real cowboys, are good, decent people, good to be around. Even if they didn't do what they did, you would still like them."

Chris Latting says he spends much of his time outside of school perfecting his trick-riding routines. He's also competed in several different events—steer wrestling, calf roping, bull riding, and his favorite, bareback riding. He plans to attend Caspar Junior College, as his father did, or the University of Montana. "I think it is a way of life," he says of the rodeo, because largely it's positive energy because it keeps you busy and you don't have to worry about being on the streets or anything, getting into trouble."

Representatives of the gay organization sponsoring Saturday's rodeo, along with several Latting employees, are already at the site when we arrive. Chris, Derrick, and Phillip immediately get the animals in place for feeding and watering, and then begin setting up the chutes.

Sarah, a white lesbian from Birmingham, Alabama, will be working closely with the Lattings as the chute coordinator. She says that the Lattings are the best company to produce this rodeo because of their professionalism, and she doesn't sense any homophobic vibes from the family. She says it is important that the producers are sensitive, because many of the participants are in the closet. For some, this is a weekend on which they sneak away from families and bosses who don't know of their lifestyle.

While Sarah praises the Lattings, she also says that like all heterosexual cowboys, they sometimes have a wary look hidden behind their polite smiles. She says that it takes jokes to bridge any gaps with the heterosexual cowboy men like Thyrl, Mike, and the others. She stands with them at the chutes. Chris Latting is putting the steel on the grounds, and workers are bringing in the animals. Before Mike talks, Sarah steals a laugh from the men. "What's the difference between sugar, Equal, and Sweet 'n Low?" she asks.

"What?" they ask.

"Sugar comes from your lip," she says and smacks a kiss at them.

"Equal is from your breast," she says as her hands cup her breast.

"And Sweet 'n Low is below the belt," she says as she places her hands below her own belt.

Everyone laughs.

This rodeo is like most others, featuring only a few unique events such as the "Drag Race," in which two teams of two gay men and one lesbian apiece race to rope a calf first. The catch is that one man on each team must be in drag.

"The thing with people in the business," says Thyrl, "their attitude about this kind of rodeo is different from ours. They really try to hurt these people. I don't believe in that, although I came to that feeling later in life. But I do feel that way now. . . . And they definitely don't have to worry about any of my guys being a problem to their guys."

I ask Latting if the company's attitude toward the rodeo has anything to do with the fact that gays and blacks have encountered discrimination. "I don't really think so, because many blacks have bad attitudes toward gay people," he states, and sees the connection in a different light. "We are also city people. We don't have quite the attitude those down-home boys have about gays. That is not a problem with us. In the rule book for this rodeo, it says that they wanted a high school–quality rodeo, like for little kids. So that is what we tried to provide them with. Again, most of the stock contractors are a lot different from us. Good old boys and their attitude about gay people is really tough. So they'll even ask them to do certain things. They'll bring some good ones [tough animals] because they would want to see one of them get hurt. And we are not about to do that."

The Lattings and a team of ten men and women spend the night setting up. Then it is up at seven the following morning for last-minute changes before the opening at ten. The call on Sunday is later, at one in the afternoon.

Tracy Latting remembers her years in radio and how much she missed the rodeo—even the smell of manure. "As long as it is not in the truck," she says. "But it is a fresh smell when it's mixed in the air."

Tracy says that radio was a sexist world, and she wasn't raised to be a second-class citizen. She worked at six radio stations in the Midwest. "Finally, I just had to give it up, even though I loved radio. I couldn't be treated like that."

So, now, she's following family tradition into an area that many would consider more sexist than radio. She does not agree. She will finish graduate school next year and teach, but also involve herself in the rodeo. Unlike her brother and the Bensons, she's not startled when people look at the family business and see something unique. "This is so unique, but I never really thought of it as unique because it is a way of life. There are people, I would say mostly outside people, who would probably be very amazed at the people who brought this rodeo in here. They're still enjoying it, you can tell—we had a packed house. They'd be very surprised to find the people running it are black. Now, whether or not it would affect them, you know, it's another thing. The main thing is that they're enjoying it, and we've found a way to live. So the thought or idea of second-class citizenship? I can't even think about that."

Epilogue

S
HE lives and works in a spacious Harlem apartment with a long hallway and wide walls to hold her work. It is June 30, 1999, and Nanette Carter is ending a very busy month. Carter, a prolific artist who creates seventy pieces of art a year, will soon begin to clear her apartment and studio of her works and send them to the galleries where she will be showing in the fall. She has a show at GR N'Namdi Gallery and one at the Sandy Webster Gallery in Philadelphia.

When I look at her walls, I begin to think of the last six years of my life, having set out to discover the many ways African Americans live in America. Many of Carter's pieces are part of her "Slightly off Keel" series and are works on mylar. In most of them, I find the image of a boat fixed among a complex web of other images. There's something red punctuating many of the pieces—sometimes a line, sometimes the outline of a boat.

"My main impetus is to give the sense of tension, slight tension," she says. "And so there are a lot of certain shapes, squares, and rectangles that are kind of diagonal. That helps to give you that tension. In the larger pieces, it actually looks like that diagonal square might be falling off the edge. So there's a sense of motion, too, which I enjoy. The red, I think, helps the tension just a bit—certainly one immediately thinks of blood and possibly even danger [to] you. I happen to love red. It's my mother's favorite color also. . . . I'm sure some of that comes into play. But certainly I think it's helping to tell the story in terms of this feeling of slight tension coming into the new millennium, realizing that we still have an awful lot to resolve in this country.

"Certainly a lot of stuff happened last year with Clinton and Lewinsky. . . . A whole lot of things I think have changed our whole look at the presidency and our country. It is an interesting picture and interesting tension. And certainly what I hear from a lot of people, especially those with children, is, 'What do I tell my children? How do I explain these things about our president going through this kind of lying to the nation and the world about his affairs. It's everywhere. It's in the papers. They're going to school and they're talking about it.' It's a whole lot of stuff.

"The sexual revolution is still going on, I guess, too. In many ways, certainly Viagra has changed things and . . . Viagra is going [now] under the whole thing where you can get your HMO to pay for your ten-dollar Viagra. Now people are saying, 'Well, what about the pill?' Okay. This one pill is going to help a man to make love, but why not help the woman who wants to not have children? Why can't we help her protect herself? So now that is being talked about going under the health plan, too. I mean, it should be covered if you're going to come right out and do Viagra.

"So all these things are still unsettled and need to be clarified and need to be discussed. . . . There is a slight tension that I think is going on, and I think there always is, but certainly I think it's sort of exacerbated with the millennium coming on."

Carter can also find something personal in the pieces. "There is this sense of water. I think there is a feeling of rippling and movement in terms of water. So it's accentuating that idea. . . . I happen to love wooden boats and . . . "Slightly off Keel" [is connected to sailing]. We're sailing and this is not a motorboat. If you're talking about something that is off keel in terms of the literal sense, you're talking about a sail boat with sails and a keel at the bottom. My brother-in-law is a serious wood-boat sailor, you know, and I dated a man for many years who still has his boat up here at Pelham Bay. . . . I can tell you I've been hanging out with black sailors for the last ten years of my life."

Yet racial identity is not the center of her work. It is there—in some of her artwork—but it is not overwhelming. It doesn't conquer the depth but laces it. That is a common thread of most of the people I've encountered on this journey into black America. They are not consumed with their racial identity, but they are not running from it either. It is contained in their lives much like the theme of race is present in Carter's work. Her pieces reflect thoughts that are clearly pertinent and unique to her existence and experiences as an African American, but her work is more largely embroidered with ideas that are significant to her citizenship in this country and in the world at large.

At the beginning of the twentieth century, Du Bois wrote, "One ever feels his twoness, an American, a Negro; two souls, two thoughts, two unreconciled strivings, two warring ideals in one dark body whose dogged strength alone keeps it from being torn asunder."

At the dawn of the new millennium, the twoness is there, yet it is no more reconciled than ever and is far from an automatic trail to a tragic life.

The two souls are not as warring. For many African Americans, they are as blended as the shapes of a Nanette Carter piece. There is also something still "off keel," especially as I contrast the way the people I saw live and the media images that so often hound the view of blacks in America. And there is also something still very unsettling as many African Americans find professional and economic success, only to turn on the news to hear about Amadou Diallo and Abner Louima and only to still face that simple struggle for a cab.

I live in Greenwich Village, which looks a lot more multiracial on the street than in census data since the community draws people of all hues as tourists but still remains overwhelmingly white. But as I learned on this journey, no matter where an African American lives today (Portsmouth, New Hampshire, or Birmingham, Michigan), one can find a secluded space of African-American culture. I saw this on a May night in 1999 when my wife and I left our apartment for a two-block trip to an art gallery in a trendy Soho building. We entered the June Kelly Gallery, named after and owned by the lone African-American member of the Art Dealer's Association of America. Nanette Carter will show here in the year 2000. Like George N'Namdi, Kelly focuses largely on the works of African-American abstractionists, but not totally as she has some non-black artists and collectors. In May 1999, the gallery sponsored an after-work lecture on the fine art of collecting with appraiser Michael Chisolm. Again, this was a cultural space where race didn't scream at you and whites were welcome. Yet there were 100 black professionals dressed as if they had just left Wall Street or Madison Avenue sitting between walls encased with installation art by Debra Priestly—her work made of jars and plates. It, too, was an example of identity forging a root, but the words black and African American were rarely uttered in the lecture and questions. It was almost as if the N'Namdis' idea of the norm had traveled to New York. After two hours there, my wife and I easily and comfortably returned home.

While many African Americans mourn the "good old days," who really wants to return to segregation? The challenge of African-American life in the post–civil-rights era was to find comfortable ways to live through integration, which so many African Americans have done, even those I found on this journey who look to the black past with nostalgia, who still may face discrimination but do not see it as crippling.

• • •

There are many comments I heard on this journey that can't escape my mind. I find myself sometimes agreeing and sometimes disagreeing with two of those remarks—one from Carlotta Miles and the other from Carmen N'Namdi.

Miles said, "I think one of the things that is denied to black people is the wish to be normal. I think it is a perfectly acceptable wish for anybody and everybody in the world to simply wish to live your life in as normal a way as possible. Somehow that wish has become interpreted as dysfunctional, as pathological; if you don't want to make race the centerpiece of your life, something is wrong with you. That's a very dysfunctional thought. All you are trying to do is be a painter, not a black painter, just a painter, and you don't want race to be the centerpiece of your life. And to the extent [that] you don't have race as the centerpiece of your life, you are hounded by it, simply because you can do it and somebody else can't."

N'Namdi remarked at some point, "I think many of us still see ourselves as either exceptions or victims. And I think that is because we don't see ourselves as normal.

Perhaps, but there are many routes to finding normalcy in the black experience in America, including a way preferred by George N'Namdi. "I don't believe in integration, I believe in cultural sharing. Well, I think I believe in true integration, which is cultural sharing. It's like I got my culture, you got your culture, let's share cultures. You follow what I mean. And I don't think . . . you can integrate if you don't bring anything to the table. What are you bringing to the pie? You're not integrating if you just come out and take a piece of the pie. If we say, 'Let's make a pie, but you say what are you bringing, I ain't bringing nothing, I just want your stuff,' we're not integrating, you're just trying to take my stuff. I believe in sharing, like with the gallery. I got my stuff, you got your stuff, let's see how we can share this. . . . Integration to me does not mean now I have the right to be the only African American out in the suburbs. That's not integration. That means I'm giving up my stuff."

But as I found, some African Americans find peace in the experience of being the only African-American family in a white neighborhood—with a Tuxedo Ball or a black ski summit to attend. Or maybe without one. Others may prefer a more integrated suburb with a strong black presence such as New Rochelle, New York, or South Orange, New Jersey. Still others may find affirmation in places like Mitchellville, an all-black community of upper-income African Americans or a more middle-class town such as Lawnside, New Jersey. Or they might want to join the black professionals moving to urban areas such as Harlem. With the civil-rights and black-power movements we won the opportunity to make those choices. However, it takes money to exercise preferences.

Black upper-middle- and middle-class African Americans still lag behind their white counterparts when it comes to the depth of their financial lives, according to a survey commissioned by Ariel Mutual Funds and Charles Schwab & Company, which compared the investing and spending habits of whites and African Americans with incomes of more than $50,000 a year. For example, the survey found that 71 percent of affluent whites have a mutual-fund or brokerage account compared to 56 percent of blacks. About half as many blacks as whites, 24 percent compared to 46 percent, grew up in a household in which stocks were traded, and more blacks listed traditional bank accounts, insurance companies, and real estate as the key places where their assets are kept or invested, while a larger percentage of whites listed brokerages.

All across the country, to refocus African-American collective energy on economics, there are movements by black churches, such as the redevelopment projects of Floyd Flake's Allen AME Church in Queens, New York, to the Winston-Salem–based National Coalition of Black Investors, which attracts large numbers of African Americans at conferences across the country with many participants from newly formed investment clubs. The Schwab-Ariel survey also showed signs of hope. Among noninvestors, 48 percent of blacks and 31 percent of whites said they were likely to start investing in 1999. African Americans surveyed were more likely than whites to have recently read books about saving and investing, attended an investing seminar, or joined an investment club. The spending power of blacks rose 73 percent from $308 billion in 1990 to $533 billion in 1999 as the number of affluent black households has grown three times as fast as the overall affluent market.

The number of African-American entrepreneurs continues to grow faster than the overall rate, from mutual funds such as Liberty Fund in New Orleans and Profit Fund in Silver Spring, Maryland, to Wall Street companies such as Blaylock and Partners, Doley Securities, and Williams Capital among many others. Perhaps the next revolution in the black experience in America is embroidered in economics and the growing wave of African-American entrepreneurs—the subject of my next book.

David J. Dent is an Associate Professor of Journalism at New York University and a writer whose work has appeared in the *New York Times Magazine, Playboy, The Washington Post, Newsday, Essence, Black Renaissance, BETWeekend, Black Enterprise, The Christian Science Monitor,* and *Vibe.* He is also a contributing correspondent to *Black Entertainment Television News.* He has worked as a television reporter for ABC affiliates in Greensboro, North Carolina, and Nashville, Tennessee. He is a graduate of Morehouse College and Columbia University Graduate School of Journalism. He lives in Greenwich Village with his wife, Valerie, and his two children, Lynnette and David Jr.